ANNUAL EDITIONS

Mass Media 09/10
Fifteenth Edition

EDITOR

Joan Gorham
West Virginia University

Joan Gorham completed her undergraduate work at the University of Wisconsin and received master's and doctoral degrees from Northern Illinois University. She is currently associate dean for academic affairs in the Eberly College of Arts and Sciences and a professor of communication studies at West Virginia University. Dr. Gorham is the author of *Commercial Media and Classroom Teaching* and has published numerous articles on communication in instruction. She has taught classes dealing with mass media and media literacy at the high school and college levels, as well as for teachers throughout the state of West Virginia.

McGraw-Hill **Higher Education**

Boston   Burr Ridge, IL   Dubuque, IA   New York   San Francisco   St. Louis
Bangkok   Bogotá   Caracas   Kuala Lumpur   Lisbon   London   Madrid   Mexico City
Milan   Montreal   New Delhi   Santiago   Seoul   Singapore   Sydney   Taipei   Toronto

The McGraw·Hill Companies

McGraw Hill Higher Education

ANNUAL EDITIONS: MASS MEDIA, FIFTEENTH EDITION

Published by McGraw-Hill, a business unit of The McGraw-Hill Companies, Inc., 1221 Avenue of the Americas, New York, NY 10020. Copyright © 2010 by The McGraw-Hill Companies, Inc. All rights reserved. Previous edition(s) 2005, 2007, 2008. No part of this publication may be reproduced or distributed in any form or by any means, or stored in a database or retrieval system, without the prior written consent of The McGraw-Hill Companies, Inc., including, but not limited to, in any network or other electronic storage or transmission, or broadcast for distance learning.

Some ancillaries, including electronic and print components, may not be available to customers outside the United States.

Annual Editions® is a registered trademark of The McGraw-Hill Companies, Inc.
Annual Editions is published by the **Contemporary Learning Series** group within the McGraw-Hill Higher Education division.

1 2 3 4 5 6 7 8 9 0 QPD/QPD 0 9

ISBN 978–0–07–812776–2
MHID 0–07–812776–9
ISSN 1092–0439

Managing Editor: *Larry Loeppke*
Senior Managing Editor: *Faye Schilling*
Developmental Editor: *Dave Welsh*
Editorial Coordinator: *Mary Foust*
Editorial Assistant: *Nancy Meissner*
Production Service Assistant: *Rita Hingtgen*
Permissions Coordinator: *DeAnna Dausener*
Senior Marketing Manager: *Julie Keck*
Marketing Communications Specialist: *Mary Klein*
Marketing Coordinator: *Alice Link*
Project Manager: *Sandy Wille*
Design Specialist: *Tara McDermott*
Senior Production Supervisor: *Laura Fuller*
Cover Graphics: *Kristine Jubeck*

Compositor: Laserwords Private Limited
Cover Image: The McGraw-Hill Companies, Inc./Lars A Niki (inset); © Corbis/RF (background)

Library in Congress Cataloging-in-Publication Data
Main entry under title: Annual Editions: Mass Media. 2009/2010.
 1. Mass Media—Periodicals. I. Gorham, Joan, *comp.* II. Title: Mass Media.
658'.05

www.mhhe.com

Editors/Advisory Board

Members of the Advisory Board are instrumental in the final selection of articles for each edition of ANNUAL EDITIONS. Their review of articles for content, level, currentness, and appropriateness provides critical direction to the editor and staff. We think that you will find their careful consideration well reflected in this volume.

EDITOR

Joan Gorham
West Virginia University

ADVISORY BOARD

Amy Aidman
University of Illinois

David Allen
Temple University

Edward T. Arke
Messiah College

Charles F. Aust
Kennesaw State University

Frank Aycock
Appalachian State University

Zoltan Bedy
Oswego State University of New York

Peggy J. Bowers
Clemson University

Xiaomei Cai
Georgetown University

Amy Callahan
Northern Essex Community College

Bonita Dattner-Garza
St. Mary's University

Maureen Dillon
Cincinnati State Technical & Community College

Kathleen M. Edelmayer
Madonna University

Anthony R. Fellow
California State University—Fullerton

Robert E. Fidoten
Slippery Rock University of PA

Edrene Frazier
Grambling State University

Craig M. Freeman
Louisiana State University

Katherine Fry
Brooklyn College

Allan Futrell
University of Louisville

Douglas J. Glick
Binghamton University

Therese Grisham
DePaul University

Petra Guerra
University of Texas Pan America

Paul Gullifor
Bradley University

Bruce Hammond
Saint Leo University

Janet J. Harszlak
University at Buffalo

John Allen Hendricks
Southeastern Oklahoma State University

Harry Hoffman
Minot State University

Ann Marie Jablonowski
Owens Community College

Edward Kanis
Butler University

Frank L. Kelley
Drexel University

Leslie Lamb
Dowling College

Mandi Lee
Cape Fear Community College

Nick Linardopolous
Drexel University

Debra L. Merskin
University of Oregon

Peyton Paxson
Middlesex Community College

Deborah Petersen-Perlman
University of Minnesota—Duluth

Mark Plenke
Normandale Community College

Joan Ramm
Delta College

Leslie Rasmussen
Iowa Central Community College

Jim Redmond
The University of Memphis

George Rodman
Brooklyn College of CUNY

Christine Roundtree
Rhode Island College

Michael Schmierbach
College of Charleston

Dick Shoemaker
Ball State University

Seema Shrikhande
Oglethrope University

Jacki Skole
Raritan Valley Community College

Reed W. Smith
Georgia Southern University

Darryl Smith
University of West Florida

William Sonnega
Saint Olaf College

Mark Thompson
University of Kansas

Theresa Villeneuve
Citrus College

Christine Von Der Haar
Indiana University—Bloomington

Nancy Wall
Idaho State University

Jeanne P. Williams
Defiance College

Ali R. Zohoori
Bradley University

Preface

In publishing ANNUAL EDITIONS we recognize the enormous role played by the magazines, newspapers, and journals of the public press in providing current, first-rate educational information in a broad spectrum of interest areas. Many of these articles are appropriate for students, researchers, and professionals seeking accurate, current material to help bridge the gap between principles and theories and the real world. These articles, however, become more useful for study when those of lasting value are carefully collected, organized, indexed, and reproduced in a low-cost format, which provides easy and permanent access when the material is needed. That is the role played by ANNUAL EDITIONS.

The mass media are a part of the fabric of American society. Learning how to evaluate media messages critically—asking who created this message? What is its intent? How objective is it? How does what I am seeing or hearing reflect and/or shape real-world realities?—is a part of being literate in today's world. The organization of articles in this collection reflects this media literacy perspective. Unit 1 offers commentary on mass media use and content, and its impact on individuals and society. Unit 2 explores media as sources of news and information. Unit 3 introduces perspectives on media access, ownership, regulation, and ethics. Unit 4 addresses relationships between the content and financial sides of media enterprises.

The articles selected for inclusion in this fifteenth edition of *Annual Editions: Mass Media* reflect the firm entrenchment of "new media" into the traditional media landscape. Issues of access, ownership, liberal versus conservative bias, changing interest in and definition of "news," and media effects on kids continue. However, where the "mass" in mass media has traditionally been about selected messages reaching large audiences through few channels—narrow on the head end, wide on the receiving end—it is increasingly about mass channels and messages.

The eminent media theorist Marshall McLuhan proposed four questions that help predict how new media invariably affect the form and content of old media: (1) What does a new medium enhance or amplify in the culture? (2) What does it make obsolete, or push out of a position of prominence? (3) What does it retrieve from the past? and (4) What does a medium "reverse into" or "flip into" when it reaches the limits of its potential? Network television, for example, added visual to auditory communication and pushed radio out of prominence by broadcasting serial dramas, comedies, and soap operas. Television retrieved those formats from the past, while radio flipped into talk and music programming. DVD players have flipped the way movies are made and marketed. Outtakes and special features such as alternative endings and camera angles became part of the filmmaking craft, enhancing depth and control of viewers' DVD experience, while movie theatres added stadium seating and enhanced sound systems, a return to the "grand cinema experience" of earlier years, with hopes of making movie-going a different experience than watching DVDs at home.

Technology is the conduit through which mass media messages move between senders and receivers. Its development is a scientific experiment, but its use is a social endeavor. Mass media shape the form and content of what is communicated, of who communicates with whom, with what intent and to what effect.

Most of the articles in this collection, even those that are primarily descriptive, include an editorial viewpoint, and draw conclusions or make recommendations with which you may disagree. These editorial viewpoints are more frequently critical than they are complimentary. They are not necessarily my opinions and should not necessarily become yours. I encourage you to debate these issues, drawing from the information and insights provided in the readings as well as from your own experiences as a media consumer. If you are an "average" American, you have spent a great deal of time with mass media. Your own observations have as much value as those of the writers whose work is included in these pages.

As always, those involved in producing this anthology are sincerely committed to including articles that are timely, informative, and interesting. We value your feedback and encourage you to complete and return the postage-paid *article rating form* on the last page of the book, to share your suggestions and let us know your opinions.

Joan Gorham
Editor

Contents

Preface iv
Correlation Guide x
Topic Guide xi
Internet References xiv

UNIT 1
Living with Media

Unit Overview xvi

1. **Almost Famous,** Jason Tanz, *Wired,* August 2008

   A profile of one young woman **becoming famous** for being famous, "armed only with an insatiable need for attention and a healthy helping of **Web** savvy." **Self-promotion, Twitter,** and **blog**-management feed aspirations for an **intentionally public** life. 3

2. **Discovering What Democracy Means,** Bill Moyers, *Tom.Paine.common sense,* February 12, 2007

   Bill Moyers extols the value of **highbrow media,** where philosophy and literature, and educated thought **cultivate conversation.** "The media's role was humble but serious, and that role was to take the public seriously." 8

3. **Off Course,** Michael Massing, *Columbia Journalism Review,* July/August 2005

   Michael Massing discusses **entertainment media,** public concerns related to **media effects on society,** and his analysis of The New York Times' reporting on **media and popular culture.** 12

4. **Reel to Real: Psychology Goes to the Movies,** Eric Jaffe, *Association for Psychological Science,* March 2007, Vol. 20, No. 3

   Researchers are reinvestigating the **behavioral impact** of films. Newer studies focus on the **neuroscience of viewer response** influencing both **cognitive and behavioral effects.** 18

5. **Are Newspapers Doomed?,** Joseph Epstein, *Commentary,* January 2006

   Joseph Epstein provides statistics on **newspaper readership** and a commentary on changing content, technology, and **"the national attention span."** 21

6. **Research on the Effects of Media Violence,** Media Awareness Network, *www.media-awareness.ca,* 2008

   This article is a sampling of major stands of research on effects of exposure to media violence, and the discussion of the three "grey areas" in **media violence studies** that contribute to **lack of consensus in interpreting data.** 26

7. **Japan, Ink,** Daniel H. Pink, *Wired,* November 2007

   This article about the Japanese **manga** industry is of interest on three levels to American readers. It describes a **mass media phenomenon** with broad and deep roots, from which movies, television series, and videogames have grown; it describes logistics of **media export;** and it illustrates cultural differences in the perception of "copying" and **copyright** within a **media business** model. 30

8. **Chica Lit: Multicultural Literature Blurs Borders,** Marie Loggia-Kee, *Multicultural Review,* Spring 2007

   Chica Lit is targeted to young, female readers. Marie Loggia-Kee expresses a writer's challenge to **reflect, affirm, and shape** the choices of **Latina-American** women through the **fictional characters** to whom they are introduced. 35

The concepts in bold italics are developed in the article. For further expansion, please refer to the Topic Guide.

9. **Cheap Thrills,** John Podhoretz, *The Weekly Standard,*
   September 3, 2007

   John Podhoretz suggests that the appeal of Disney's **High School Musical** and **High School Musical 2**—despite "horrible songs, lamentable choreography, and dreadful overacting from all concerned"—reflects how starved **pre-teen kids** are for "entertainments that don't require them to assume a false sophistication."   **38**

10. **The Diana/Whore Complex,** Lakshmi Chaudhry, *The Nation,*
    August 27/September 3, 2007

    Lakshmi Chaudhry writes about "***iconic blondes***" from Marilyn Monroe to Princess Diana to Paris Hilton, and how their larger-than-life media persona **reflect and shape cultural scripts** for femininity and love relationships.   **40**

11. **The Beauty of Simplicity,** Linda Tischler, *Fast Company,*
    November 2005

    How consumers use media is directly related to the **ease** with which they can use the products. This article looks at *Google,* the MIT Media Lab's Simplicity Consortium, and Royal Phillips Electronics as case examples of achieving "the right **balance between man and machine.**"   **43**

UNIT 2
Telling Stories

Unit Overview   **48**

12. **Whatever Happened to Iraq?: How the Media Lost Interest in a Long-running War with No End in Sight,** Sherry Ricchiardi,
    American Journalism Review, June/July 2008

    Coverage of **war in Iraq** has largely moved to the fringes of news reporting. **Gatekeepers** offer a variety of reasons including money, politics, focus on local issues and events, "war fatigue," and "**habituating.**" This article lends insight into media's **agenda setting** function.   **50**

13. **"You Don't Understand Our Audience": What I Learned about Network Television at Dateline NBC,** John Hockenberry,
    Technology Review, www.technologyreview.com, January/February 2008

    John Hockenberry captures the tension among the **editorial, technical, and business decisions in television news.** "The coveted **emotional center** was reliable, it was predictable, and its story lines could be duplicated over and over. It reassured the audience by telling them what they already knew rather than challenging them to learn."   **54**

14. **What the Mainstream Media Can Learn from Jon Stewart,**
    Rachel Smolkin, *American Journalism Review,* June/July 2007

    The Daily Show with Jon Stewart has achieved cult status reporting **faux news,** "unburdened by objectivity, journalistic integrity, or even accuracy." Rachel Smolkin analyzes *The Daily Show's* appeal, its relationship to "**straight news,**" and its **credibility** as a quality source of information.   **60**

15. **Other Voices,** Kiera Butler, *Columbia Journalism Review,* July/August 2006

    This article is about **personal narrative radio**. It focuses on StoryCorps, its low-tech focus on capturing **personalized stories of ordinary people,** and why mass media audiences are interested in them.   **66**

16. **Return of the Sob Sisters,** Stephanie Shapiro,
    American Journalism Review, June/July 2006

    This article analyzes the appeal of **sad stories** about fatal illnesses, agonizing moral decisions, accidents, and adversity. Such stories often run long and win awards. Differing views on their **intent and effects** are proposed.   **69**

The concepts in bold italics are developed in the article. For further expansion, please refer to the Topic Guide.

17. **Climate Change: Now What?,** Cristine Russell, *Columbia Journalism Review,* July/August 2008

    Media play a key role in **shaping public opinion** regarding **climate change.** The position in this article is that "whether" is no longer the story, and journalists now must turn to providing "a **guide to the policy,** not just the politics" that will instigate action. **73**

18. **Myth-Making in New Orleans,** Brian Thevenot, *American Journalism Review,* December 2005/January 2006

    Brian Thevenot reflects on reporting news following **hurricane Katrina** in New Orleans. **Gatekeeping** choices are framed in examples of second- and third-hand accounts, "official" information, race, and class. **78**

19. **Double Whammy,** Raquel Christie, *American Journalism Review,* February/March 2008

    This case study of national news media coverage of **racial tension** in Jena, Louisiana asks "What happened to **the race beat?**" Do media have an **agenda in setting** responsibility regarding race? Was the story initially ignored because mainstream media are too white? **84**

20. **Wonderful Weeklies,** Julia Cass, *American Journalism Review,* December 2005/January 2006

    Small-market media are frequently left out of the analyses of mass media sources and audiences. Their role as **local watchdogs** and **community voices** has, in rural areas, been little affected by larger media trends. **92**

21. **Beyond News,** Mitchell Stephens, *Columbia Journalism Review,* January/February 2007

    If news is a product, how do traditional news organizations achieve **product differentiation** "in a day when information pours out of digital spigots?" Mitchell Stephens suggests that mainstream journalists must shift resources from **"objective" collecting and reporting** of information to **news analysis** and interpretation. **99**

22. **Rocketboom!,** Paul Farhi, *American Journalism Review,* June/July 2006

    Rocketboom is a **videoblog, or vlog.** It exemplifies the state of media "in the hands of people, not just the pros." This article captures the **quirky creativity and expanding reach** of vlogs, and includes commentary on their **effect on traditional journalism.** **103**

23. **Epidemic,** Trudy Lieberman, *Columbia Journalism Review,* March/April 2007

    This article is about the **Cleveland Clinic News Service,** a representative of the growing partnerships between heath institutions and TV stations. **Health topics** are of interest to news audiences, and partnerships are seen as quid pro quo. However, critics warn that they breach the boundary between **editorial and commercial content.** **106**

UNIT 3
Players and Guides

Unit Overview **110**

24. **Break Up This Band!,** Ted Turner, *The Washington Monthly,* July/August 2004

    Ted Turner, founder of CNN and Chairman of Turner Enterprises, expresses his views on **Federal Communications Commission** (FCC) **ownership rules** and the **consolidation** of media companies. **113**

25. **Into the Great Wide Open,** Jesse Sunenblick, *Columbia Journalism Review,* March/April 2005

    This article focuses on the implications of **spread spectrum technology** on the **structures of media organizations** and on **FCC regulations** that are based on broadcast spectrum scarcity. Jesse Sunenblick explains the technology, and speculates on the future of **unlicensed radio.** **119**

The concepts in bold italics are developed in the article. For further expansion, please refer to the Topic Guide.

26. **Why Journalists Are Not Above the Law,** Gabriel Schoenfeld, *Commentary,* February 2007

Shield laws and *First Amendment rights* have been the basis for recent high-profile cases, testing the boundaries of *freedom of the press* against, and "the obligation of all citizens to give relevant testimony with respect to criminal conduct" in *Federal Court.* Gabriel Schoenfeld argues that protecting the dissemination of information is not always in the public's interest, and that a Federal shield law would compromise national security. **124**

27. **Copyright Jungle,** Siva Vaidhyanathan, *Columbia Jounalism Review,* September/October 2006

From Napster and *file-sharing,* to *Google*'s virtual library project, *copyright law* is under scrutiny. This article discusses the difference between content and container, and how the purpose of copyright play out in *digital media.* **129**

28. **Distorted Picture,** Sherry Ricchiardi, *American Journalism Review,* August/September 2007

Photoshop editing is easy, often motivated by aesthetics, and a hot topic at media ethics seminars. The *National Press Photographers Association* recommends a zero-tolerance standard. This article addresses the limits of acceptable practice. **134**

29. **What Would You Do?,** Daniel Weiss, *Columbia Journalism Review,* January/February 2008

Daniel Weiss ponders the *ethics* of *investigative "experimenters,"* who "step out of their customary role as *observers* and play with reality to see what will happen." The practice dates back a century, but has new prominence in *television newsmagazines.* **139**

30. **Naming Names: Credibility vs. Deportation,** Lucy Hood, *American Journalism Review,* April/May 2006

Anonymous sources are criticized for inviting fabrication and compromising credibility. However, reporting on *undocumented immigrants,* an issue of considerable importance in the United States, puts identified sources at risk of deportation. **143**

31. **The Lives of Others,** Julia Dahl, *Columbia Journalism Review,* July/August 2008

Julia Dahl relates her experience of writing "drama" pieces that *personalize victims* of tragedy. The essay discusses the options of *choosing and discarding* in the process of how stories are packaged for *reality shows* such as *America's Most Wanted.* **147**

32. **The Shame Game,** Douglas McCollam, *Columbia Journalism Review,* January/February 2007

Dateline NBC's "To Catch a Predator" series is an example of *reality TV sting operations,* set up in cooperation with the online watchdog group Perverted Justice. While the show draws solid *ratings,* it raises *ethical questions* of "delighting in another's disgrace," *paycheck journalism,* and *crossing the line between reporting news and creating news.* **151**

UNIT 4
A Word from Our Sponsor

Unit Overview **156**

33. **Generation MySpace Is Getting Fed Up,** Spencer E. Ante and Catherine Holahan, *BusinessWeek,* February 7, 2008

Social networking sites were developed with a promise of attracting advertising revenue by delivering *targeted consumers* at low cost. However, response rates are low, and social network users voice their views about *intrusive ad technology,* leaving advertisers wary of investment return. **158**

34. **The Massless Media,** William Powers, *The Atlantic Monthly,* January/February 2005

William Powers speculates on ramifications of a shift from "vast media spaces where [Americans] used to come together" to small, targeted outlets where "discourse happens only among like minds." He compares this "new" landscape to pre-television media, and concludes that *mass and niche media* can and will coexist in a symbiotic relationship. **160**

The concepts in bold italics are developed in the article. For further expansion, please refer to the Topic Guide.

35. **The Hollywood Treatment,** Frank Rose, *Wired,* August 2008

    This is an article about **Web video,** an "under construction" **media product** that is a commercialized, professionalized take-off from **YouTube.** A fly-on-the-wall insight here is the importance of Hollywood constructing a **traditional business model**—advertsing, distribution, financing, production—alongside a creative product. **164**

36. **Girl Power,** Chuck Salter, *Fast Company,* September 2007

    In contrast to "The Hollywood Treatment," "Girl Power" describes a **bottom-up media product,** created by a teenager, discovered by the **online marketing** company Value-Click Media, and morphed into an unconventional, **new-media business model.** **167**

37. **Online Salvation?,** Paul Farhi, *American Journalism Review,* December 2007/January 2008

    Projections estimate that **newspaper print advertising revenue** will decrease by half in the next ten years. Print **classified ads** may well disappear. Online ad revenue is projected to increase for some newspapers, not all. What should news organizations do? Cut costs? Phase out print news? Figure out how to attract web traffic that supports ad revenue there? Stop giving news away? Give more news away? **172**

38. **Home Free,** Lori Robertson, *American Journalism Review,* April/May 2007

    One response to the **volatile financial future of newspapers** is delivering free newspapers to affluent homes and giving up subscription and sales revenue in hopes of selling more ads. Lori Robertson examines the pros and cons of a **controlled circulation business model.** **176**

39. **A Fading Taboo,** Donna Shaw, *American Journalism Review,* June/July 2007

    Traditionalists shudder at **front page newspaper ads** as unprofessional and unseemly. Donna Shaw describes why these and other "new" **ad placements** (watermarks, cascading stairs, front page stickers, spadea) that **mix news space and ad space** evoke strong responses, and how newspapers come to terms with their subtext. **181**

40. **Nonprofit News,** Carol Guensburg, *American Journalism Review,* February/March 2008

    As news organizations trim their budgets and adjust their **business models,** new forms of **nonprofit, grant-funded news operations** are developing. "Done right, the journalism-funder relationship benefits both parties as well as the public they aim to serve . . . Done wrong, the association raises concerns about **editorial objectivity,** and whether it has been compromised by the funder's agenda." **184**

Test-Your-Knowledge Form **190**
Article Rating Form **191**

The concepts in bold italics are developed in the article. For further expansion, please refer to the Topic Guide.

Correlation Guide

The *Annual Editions* series provides students with convenient, inexpensive access to current, carefully selected articles from the public press. **Annual Editions: Mass Media 09/10** is an easy-to-use reader that presents articles on important topics such as *the coverage of war, advertising, the Internet,* and many more. For more information on *Annual Editions* and other *McGraw-Hill Contemporary Learning Series* titles visit www.mhcls.com.

This convenient guide matches the units in **Annual Editions: Mass Media 09/10** with corresponding chapters in three of our best-selling McGraw-Hill Mass Communications textbooks by Dominick, Rodman, and Baran.

Annual Editions: Mass Media 09/10	The Dynamics of Mass Communications: Media in the Digital Age, 10/e by Dominick	Mass Media in a Changing World, 2009 Updated Edition, 2/e by Rodman	Introduction to Mass Communication: Media Literacy and Culture, Updated 5/e by Baran
Unit 1: Living with Media	**Chapter 1:** Communication: Mass and Other Forms **Chapter 2:** Perspectives on Mass Communication **Chapter 3:** Historical and Cultural Context **Chapter 4:** Newspapers **Chapter 6:** Books **Chapter 9:** Motion Pictures **Chapter 10:** Broadcast Television **Chapter 19:** Social Effects of Mass Communication	**Chapter 1:** Introduction: Media in a Changing World **Chapter 2:** Media Impact: Mass Communication Research and Effects **Chapter 3:** Books: The Durable Medium **Chapter 4:** Newspapers: Where Journalism Begins **Chapter 6:** Movies: Magic from the Dream Factory	**Chapter 1:** Mass Communication, Culture, and Media Literacy **Chapter 3:** Books **Chapter 4:** Newspapers **Chapter 5:** Magazines **Chapter 6:** Film **Chapter 7:** Radio, Recording, and Popular Music **Chapter 8:** Television, Cable, and Mobile Video **Chapter 13:** Theories and Effects of Mass Communication
Unit 2: Telling Stories	**Chapter 4:** Newspapers **Chapter 10:** Broadcast Television **Chapter 13:** News Gathering and Reporting **Chapter 19:** Social Effects of Mass Communication	**Chapter 10:** The Internet: Convergence in a Networked World **Chapter 11:** Electronic News: Information as Entertainment	**Chapter 4:** Newspapers **Chapter 8:** Television, Cable, and Mobile Video **Chapter 15:** Global Media
Unit 3: Players and Guides	**Chapter 16:** Formal Controls: Laws, Rules, Regulations **Chapter 17:** Ethics and Other Informal Controls **Chapter 19:** Social Effects of Mass Communication	**Chapter 7:** Recordings and the Music Industry: Copyright Battles, Format Wars **Chapter 14:** Media Law: Understanding Freedom of Expression **Chapter 15:** Media Ethics: Understanding Media Morality	**Chapter 7:** Radio, Recording, and Popular Music **Chapter 14:** Media Freedom, Regulation, and Ethics
Unit 4: A Word from Our Sponsor	**Chapter 15:** Advertising	**Chapter 4:** Newspapers: Where Journalism Begins **Chapter 10:** The Internet: Convergence in a Networked World **Chapter 13:** Advertising: The Media Support Industry	**Chapter 4:** Newspapers **Chapter 5:** Magazines **Chapter 7:** Radio, Recording, and Popular Music **Chapter 8:** Television, Cable, and Mobile Video **Chapter 12:** Advertising

Topic Guide

This topic guide suggests how the selections in this book relate to the subjects covered in your course. You may want to use the topics listed on these pages to search the Web more easily.

On the following pages a number of Web sites have been gathered specifically for this book. They are arranged to reflect the units of this Annual Editions reader. You can link to these sites by going to http://www.mhcls.com.

All the articles that relate to each topic are listed below the bold-faced term.

Advertising
- 23. Epidemic
- 33. Generation MySpace Is Getting Fed Up
- 37. Online Salvation?
- 38. Home Free
- 39. A Fading Taboo

Agenda setting
- 12. Whatever Happened to Iraq?: How the Media Lost Interest in a Long-running War with No End in Sight
- 14. What the Mainstream Media Can Learn from Jon Stewart
- 17. Climate Change: Now What?
- 19. Double Whammy
- 20. Wonderful Weeklies

Bias
- 21. Beyond News

Blogs
- 1. Almost Famous
- 5. Are Newspapers Doomed?
- 19. Double Whammy
- 22. Rocketboom!

Books
- 8. Chica Lit: Multicultural Literature Blurs Borders
- 27. Copyright Jungle

Business model
- 7. Japan, Ink
- 13. "You Don't Understand Our Audience": What I Learned about Network Television at Dateline NBC
- 23. Epidemic
- 35. The Hollywood Treatment
- 36. Girl Power
- 38. Home Free

Celebrity
- 1. Almost Famous
- 10. The Diana/Whore Complex

Children and media
- 8. Chica Lit: Multicultural Literature Blurs Borders
- 9. Cheap Thrills

Copyright
- 7. Japan, Ink
- 27. Copyright Jungle

Credibility
- 14. What the Mainstream Media Can Learn from Jon Stewart
- 23. Epidemic
- 28. Distorted Picture
- 39. A Fading Taboo

Cultivation
- 2. Discovering What Democracy Means
- 4. Reel to Real: Psychology Goes to the Movies
- 8. Chica Lit: Multicultural Literature Blurs Borders
- 13. "You Don't Understand Our Audience": What I Learned about Network Television at Dateline NBC

Entertainment media
- 2. Discovering What Democracy Means
- 3. Off Course
- 4. Reel to Real: Psychology Goes to the Movies
- 9. Cheap Thrills

Ethics
- 23. Epidemic
- 28. Distorted Picture
- 29. What Would You Do?
- 31. The Lives of Others
- 32. The Shame Game
- 40. Nonprofit News

Fact-checking
- 14. What the Mainstream Media Can Learn from Jon Stewart

Federal Communications Commission (FCC)
- 24. Break Up This Band!
- 25. Into the Great Wide Open

Feedforward
- 17. Climate Change: Now What?
- 29. What Would You Do?
- 32. The Shame Game

First amendment
- 26. Why Journalists Are Not Above the Law

Gatekeeping
- 12. Whatever Happened to Iraq?: How the Media Lost Interest in a Long-running War with No End in Sight
- 13. "You Don't Understand Our Audience": What I Learned about Network Television at Dateline NBC
- 19. Double Whammy

Gender roles
- 8. Chica Lit: Multicultural Literature Blurs Borders
- 10. The Diana/Whore Complex

Global warming
- 14. What the Mainstream Media Can Learn from Jon Stewart
- 17. Climate Change: Now What?

xi

Google
11. The Beauty of Simplicity
27. Copyright Jungle

Government influence
25. Into the Great Wide Open

Highbrow media
2. Discovering What Democracy Means

Hurricane Katrina
14. What the Mainstream Media Can Learn from Jon Stewart
31. The Lives of Others

Internet
5. Are Newspapers Doomed?
11. The Beauty of Simplicity
21. Beyond News
22. Rocketboom!
25. Into the Great Wide Open
32. The Shame Game
36. Girl Power
37. Online Salvation?

Magazines
7. Japan, Ink
31. The Lives of Others

Manga
7. Japan, Ink

Media effects research
4. Reel to Real: Psychology Goes to the Movies
6. Research on the Effects of Media Violence

Media history
16. Return of the Sob Sisters
24. Break Up This Band!
25. Into the Great Wide Open

Media ownership
24. Break Up This Band!
25. Into the Great Wide Open
40. Nonprofit News

Movies
4. Reel to Real: Psychology Goes to the Movies

Music
27. Copyright Jungle

Narrative stories
16. Return of the Sob Sisters

Narrowcasting
22. Rocketboom!
38. Home Free

Newspaper business
5. Are Newspapers Doomed?
20. Wonderful Weeklies
21. Beyond News

37. Online Salvation?
39. A Fading Taboo
38. Home Free
40. Nonprofit News

News reporting
12. Whatever Happened to Iraq?: How the Media Lost Interest in a Long-running War with No End in Sight
13. "You Don't Understand Our Audience": What I Learned about Network Television at Dateline NBC
14. What the Mainstream Media Can Learn from Jon Stewart
16. Return of the Sob Sisters
17. Climate Change: Now What?
19. Double Whammy
20. Wonderful Weeklies
21. Beyond News
23. Epidemic
26. Why Journalists Are Not Above the Law

Objectivity
14. What the Mainstream Media Can Learn from Jon Stewart
17. Climate Change: Now What?
21. Beyond News

Photoshop
28. Distorted Picture

Politics
5. Are Newspapers Doomed?
20. Wonderful Weeklies

Product placement
35. The Hollywood Treatment

Radio
25. Into the Great Wide Open

Reality TV
13. "You Don't Understand Our Audience": What I Learned about Network Television at Dateline NBC
29. What Would You Do?
31. The Lives of Others
32. The Shame Game

Religion
3. Off Course

Sex
3. Off Course

Shield laws
26. Why Journalists Are Not Above the Law

Social learning theory
3. Off Course
4. Reel to Real: Psychology Goes to the Movies
6. Research on the Effects of Media Violence

Social networking
33. Generation MySpace Is Getting Fed Up

Target marketing
33. Generation MySpace Is Getting Fed Up
38. Home Free

Twitter
1. Almost Famous

Violence
4. Reel to Real: Psychology Goes to the Movies
6. Research on the Effects of Media Violence

War reporting
12. Whatever Happened to Iraq?: How the Media Lost Interest in a Long-running War with No End in Sight
13. "You Don't Understand Our Audience": What I Learned about Network Television at Dateline NBC

Web video
35. The Hollywood Treatment

Internet References

The following Internet sites have been selected to support the articles found in this reader. These sites were available at the time of publication. However, because Web sites often change their structure and content, the information listed may no longer be available. We invite you to visit http://www.mhcls.com for easy access to these sites.

Annual Editions: Mass Media 09/10

General Sources

Associated Press Managing Editors
http://www.apme.com/
Allows you to view all the front pages of newspapers across the nation.

The Center for Communication
http://www.cencom.org
The Center for Communication is an independent nonpartisan media forum that introduces issues, ethics, people and media business. The site provides archived seminars like the panel discussion on Marshall McLuhan entitled "Oracle of the Electronic Age." Students can tap into these seminars via video-streaming. This site also provides links to numerous other sites.

Current.org
http://www.current.org/
This is a newspaper about public broadcasting in the U.S. It is editorially independent and is an affiliate of the Educational Broadcasting Corporation.

Digital Forensics and Tampering
http://www.cs.dartmouth.edu/farid/research/tampering.html
Dartmouth scientist Hany Farid posts examples of photo editing, and illustrations of his work developing mathematical and computational algorithms to detect tampering in digital media. Links to articles including http://www.cs.dartmouth.edu/farid/publications/deception07.html "Digital Doctoring: can we trust photographs?" and http://www.cs.dartmouth.edu/farid/publications/significance06.pdf "Digital Doctoring: How to tell the real from the fake" (pdf files), well-illustrated with examples, historical and current.

Iowa Scholar's Desktop Resources
http://www.uiowa.edu/~commstud/resources/scholarsdesktop/
An encyclopedic resource related to a host of mass communication issues, this site is maintained by the University of Iowa's Department of Communication Studies. It provides excellent links covering advertising, cultural studies, digital media, film, gender issues, and media studies.

Media Awareness Network
http://www.media-awareness.ca/
Media Awareness Network provides resources and support for parents and teachers interested in media and information literacy for kids. Concise, vest-pocket summaries if issues including media stereotyping, media violence, online hate, information privacy. Includes educational games (e.g. Jo Cool or Jo Fool: Interactive Module and Quiz on Critical Thinking for the Internet). From Canada.

Netcomtalk/Boston University
http://web.bu.edu/COM/communication.html
The College of Communication at Boston University presents this multimedia publication site for daily perusal of a wide variety of news items and topics in media and communications. Click on "COMNews Today" for the latest happenings in mass media.

NewsPlace
http://www.niu.edu/newsplace/
This site of Professor Avi Bass from Northern Illinois University will lead you to a wealth of resources of interest in the study of mass media, such as international perspectives on censorship. Links to government, corporate, and other organizations are provided.

The Web Journal of Mass Communication
http://www.scripps.ohiou.edu/wjmcr/
This site can also be easily accessed from http://www.wjmcr.org The Web Journal of Mass Communication out of Ohio University focuses on articles that relate to how the web shapes mass communication.

Writers Guild of America
http://www.wga.org
The Writer's Guild of America is the union for media entertainment writers. The nonmember areas of this site offer useful information for aspiring writers. There is also an excellent links section.

UNIT 1: Living with Media

Children Now
http://www.childrennow.org
Children Now's site provides access to a variety of views on the impact of media on children. Public opinion surveys of young people, independent research on television and print media, industry conference proceedings, and more are available. An Internet resource list is included.

Freedom Forum
http://www.freedomforum.org
The Freedom Forum is a nonpartisan, international foundation dedicated to free press, free speech, and free spirit for all people. Its mission is to help the public and the news media understand one another better. The press watch area of this site is intriguing.

Geocities
http://www.geocities.com/Wellesley/1031/#media/
This site presents a negative perspective on how the media portray women. By clicking on its many links, you can find such varied resources as an archive on misogynistic quotes and a discussion of newspeak and doublethink.

UNIT 2: Telling Stories

Cable News Network
http://www.cnn.com
CNN's interactive site is considered to be an excellent online news site.

Fairness and Accuracy in Reporting
http://www.fair.org
FAIR, a U.S. media watch group, offers well-documented criticism of media bias and censorship. It advocates structural reform to break up the dominant media conglomerates.

Internet References

Organization of News Ombudsmen (ONO)
http://www.newsombudsmen.org

This ONO page provides links to journalism Web sites. ONO works to aid in the wider establishment of the position of news ombudsmen on newspapers and elsewhere in the media and to provide a forum for the interchange of experiences, information, and ideas among news ombudsmen.

Television News Archive
http://tvnews.vanderbilt.edu

By browsing through this Vanderbilt University site, you can review national U.S. television news broadcasts from 1968 onward. It will give you insight into how the broadcast news industry has changed over the years and what trends define the industry today.

UNIT 3: Players and Guides

The Electronic Journalist
http://spj.org

This site for The Electronic Journalist, an online service of the Society of Professional Journalists (SPJ), will lead you to a number of articles having to do with journalistic ethics, accuracy, and other topics.

Federal Communications Commission (FCC)
http://www.fcc.gov

The FCC is an independent U.S. government agency whose mission "is to encourage competition in all communications markets and to protect the public interest." Access to information about such topics as laws regulating the media is possible.

Index on Censorship
http://www.indexonline.org

This British site provides information and many international links to show "how free speech affects the political issues of the moment."

Internet Law Library
http://www.phillylawyer.com

Featuring abundant resources in communications law, this site includes the most recent developments on this subject.

Michigan Press Photographers Association (MPPA)
http://www.mppa.org

Ethical issues in photo journalism are featured at this site sponsored by the MPPA.

Poynter Online: Research Center
http://www.poynter.org

The Poynter Institute for Media Studies provides extensive links to information and resources on media ethics, media writing and editing, visual journalism, and much more. Many bibliographies and Web sites are included.

World Intellectual Property Organization (WIPO)
http://www.wipo.org

Click on the links at WIPO's home page to find general information on WIPO and intellectual property, publications and documents, international classifications, and more.

UNIT 4: A Word from Our Sponsor

Advertising Age
http://adage.com

Gain access to articles and features about media advertising, such as a history of television advertising, at this site.

Citizens Internet Empowerment Coalition (CIEC)
http://www.ciec.org

CIEC is a broad group of Internet users, library groups, publishers, online service providers, and civil liberties groups working to preserve the First Amendment and ensure the future of free expression. Find discussions of the Communications Decency Act and Internet-related topics here.

Educause
http://www.educause.edu

Open this site for an e-mailed summary of info-tech news from various major publications and for many other resources meant to facilitate the introduction, use, access to, and management of information resources in teaching, learning, scholarship, and research.

UNIT 1
Living with Media

Unit Selections

1. **Almost Famous,** Jason Tanz
2. **Discovering What Democracy Means,** Bill Moyers
3. **Off Course,** Michael Massing
4. **Reel to Real: Psychology Goes to the Movies,** Eric Jaffe
5. **Are Newspapers Doomed?,** Joseph Epstein
6. **Research on the Effects of Media Violence,** Media Awareness Network
7. **Japan, Ink,** Daniel H. Pink
8. **Chica Lit: Multicultural Literature Blurs Borders,** Marie Loggia-Kee
9. **Cheap Thrills,** John Podhoretz
10. **The Diana/Whore Complex,** Lakshmi Chaudhry
11. **The Beauty of Simplicity,** Linda Tischler

Key Points to Consider

- What purpose does media serve in your life? What are your priorities in selecting entertainment media? In what ways are you satisfied and dissatisfied with the media information you consume?
- Why is it so difficult for research to definitively resolve media effects questions?
- Do you think the Internet will make print media, such as books and newspapers, obsolete? Would you miss them if it did?
- Select a comparison sample of old and new media—for example, television sitcoms from about the time you were born (Nick at Night is a good source) and current television sitcoms, or women's magazines from the time your mother came of age and current women's magazines, or romantic movies from the time your grandparents were teenagers and current romantic movies. What changes do you see?
- Does media content primarily reflect social reality or does it significantly shape social reality? Should it do otherwise? Why or why not?

Student Web Site
www.mhcls.com

Internet References

Children Now
http://www.childrennow.org
Freedom Forum
http://www.freedomforum.org
Geocities
http://www.geocities.com/Wellesley/1031/#media/

© The McGraw-Hill Companies, Inc.

The media have been blamed for just about everything, from a decrease in attention span to an increase in street crime, to undoing our capacity to think. In *Amusing Ourselves to Death* (Penguin, 1986), social critic Neil Postman suggested that the cocktail party, the quiz show, and popular trivia games are reflections of society's trying to find a use for the abundance of superficial information given to us by the media. Peggy Noonan, a former network writer and White House speechwriter, has observed that experiences are no longer "real," unless they are ratified by television (which is why, she says, half the people in a stadium watch the game on monitors rather than the field). Marie Winn's memorable description of a child transfixed by television—slack-jawed, tongue resting on the front teeth, eyes glazed and vacant (*The Plug-In Drug,* Penguin, 1985, 2002)—has become an oft-quoted symbol of the passivity encouraged by television viewing. We, as a nation, have a distinct love-hate relationship with mass media.

Questions of whether or not, and to what extent, media influence our behaviors, values, expectations, and ways of thinking are difficult to answer. While one bibliographer has compiled a list of some 4,000 citations of English-language articles focusing just on children and television, the conclusions drawn in these articles vary. Isolating media as a causal agent in examining human behavior is a difficult task.

Media messages serve a variety of purposes: they inform, they influence public opinion, they sell, and they entertain—sometimes below the level of consumers' conscious awareness. Children watch "Sesame Street" to be entertained, but they also learn to count, to share, to accept physical differences among individuals, and (perhaps) to desire a Sesame Street lunch box. Adults watch crime dramas to be entertained, but they also learn that they have the right to remain silent when arrested, how (accurately or inaccurately) the criminal justice system works, and that the world is an unsafe place.

Nicholas Johnson, a former chairman of the Federal Communications Commission, has noted, "Every moment of television programming—commercials, entertainment, news—teaches us something." How such incidental learning occurs is most often explained by two theories. Social learning (or modeling) theory suggests that the behavior of media consumers, particularly children, is affected by their imitating role models presented via media. The degree to which modeling occurs depends upon the presence of *inhibitors,* lessons learned in real life that discourage imitation, and *disinhibitors,* experiences in real life that reinforce imitation.

Cultivation theory holds that media shape behavior by influencing attitudes. Media provide a "window to the world," exposing consumers to images of reality that may or may not jibe with personal experience. *Mainstreaming* effects occur when media introduce images of things with which the consumer has no personal experience. *Resonance* effects occur when media images echo personal experience. For example, recent research has found that knowing someone who is openly gay or lesbian is the single best predictor of tolerance of same-sex marriage, but seeing likable gay characters on shows such as *Will & Grace* also has significant effects on attitude. In one study, anti-gay perceptions in students with little personal experience of interacting with gay men decreased by 12% after viewing ten episodes of HBO's *Six Feet Under.* This is a mainstreaming effect. Heavy media consumers are more likely to be affected than light consumers, since they spend more time absorbing information from media. Television viewers who have had real-world experiences similar to those seen in a TV show may find that watching the show reinforces their beliefs (resonance). However, viewers who have had personal experiences that differ from the images portrayed on television, are not as likely to believe what they see on television over what they have observed in real life.

The readings in this unit examine media use, media content, and media effects. All of them acknowledge the increasingly complex interactions among media producers, technology, forms, formats, and consumers. They share concerns over media influence on daily living and on society. Some take a *feedforward* perspective, holding media accountable for shaping changes in public attitude and behavior. Others argue a *feedback* viewpoint, in which media simply reflect what consumers choose to make popular.

"Almost Famous" is about one woman's invention of a "celebrity self" using new media, perhaps modeling Paris Hilton. In contrast, "Discovering What Democracy Means" celebrates the place of traditional, highbrow media, such as PBS programming, that take their audiences seriously and nurture "a life of free and enriching communion." "Off Course" provides an overview of the public concerns about popular culture and themes of entertainment media, as well as media's coverage of itself.

"Real to Real: Psychology Goes to the Movies" and "Research on the Effects of Media Violence" summarize some key questions that have grounded research on media effects, with findings explained using both social learning and cultivation theories. "Are Newspapers Doomed?" addresses the process of change, noting "The time of transition we are currently going through, with the interest in traditional newspapers beginning to fade and news on the computer still a vast confusion, can be likened to a great city banishing horses from its streets before anyone has yet perfected the automobile."

"Japan, Ink" describes the evolution of Japanese comics called manga, providing a timely case study of international and intercultural media export: "What 20 years ago seemed too culturally specific for export has become another extension of Japan's soft power, what journalist Douglas McGray calls its 'gross national cool.'" "Chica Lit: Multicultural Literature Blurs Borders" is about a writer's challenge to reflect, affirm, and shape the choices of young Latina-American women through the fictional characters to whom they are introduced in books.

"Cheap Thrills" and "The Diana/Whore Complex" are about mediated stories, the former addressing popularity of the Disney entertainment product *High School Musical,* the latter soft news interest in "iconic blondes" from Marilyn Monroe to Princess Diana to Paris Hilton, and how their larger-than-life media persona reflect and shape cultural scripts for femininity and love relationships. The unit concludes with Linda Tischler's analysis of factors that influence adoption of new media technology.

Article 1

Almost Famous

Meet Julia Allison. She can't act. She can't sing. She's not rich. But thanks to a genius for self-promotion—plus Flickr, Twitter, and her blogs—she's become an Interest celebrity. How she did it—and how you can too.

JASON TANZ

I am five minutes late to catch Julia Allison's latest publicity stunt—literally *five minutes*—but I can see from two blocks away that she has already drawn a crowd. There she is, at the epicenter of Times Square. About a dozen tourists surround her, and more join every minute. All around them, theater marquees and building-sized billboards jostle for attention, but they are no match for Allison.

She has asked a few friends to join her this afternoon—former hedge-fund analyst Meghan Asha, handbag designer Mary Rambin, and Randi Zuckerberg, the sister of Facebook founder Mark Zuckerberg. They are all dressed in 1980s Jazzercise outfits; Allison wears purple spandex, leg warmers, and glittery eye shadow. Strains of Martha and the Vandellas' "Dancing in the Street" waft thinly from Rambin's iPod speakers. The four women bounce around, giggle, and shout encouragement at one another. Their audience is captivated. Allison has enlisted a couple of cameramen to document the event. Her new Web site, xojulia.com—like her previous sites, juliaallison.com, itsmejulia.com, and julia juliajulia.com—is dedicated to sharing almost every waking moment of Allison's life. Visitors to xojulia.com can follow her schedule of bachelorette parties and fancy dinners, see photos of her latest outfits, and read her dating advice. They can watch videos of Allison playing with her dog or horsing around with friends. If readers want an extra shot of Allisonana, her Twitter stream provides periodic updates like a postmodern news ticker.

After about 15 minutes, a police officer wanders by to bust up the party. Allison doesn't have the required performer's license, and her admirers are clogging up Times Square. No problem! The mob follows her a couple of blocks uptown, looking for another vacant patch of asphalt where she can make a scene. As we cross 44th Street, a passerby squints at us. "You guys are famous?" she asks. "What do you do?"

Good question. Allison may not be famous by the traditional definition; certainly nobody here seems to recognize her. But to a devoted niche of online fans—and an even more devoted niche of detractors—she is a bona fide celebrity. She says that more than 10,000 people read her blog daily, and gossip sites like Gawker, Radar Online, and Valleywag detail her every exploit. An anonymous blogger has set up a site, Reblogging Julia, dedicated to parsing Allison's posts. *The New York Times* has profiled her, and *New York* magazine has called Allison—a dating columnist for *Time Out New York* and former editor-at-large for *Star*—"the most famous young journalist in the city."

But with all due respect, Allison's renown has little to do with her day job. Indeed, it's hard to describe exactly what she's famous for. She's not an actress or a singer or a misbehaving heiress to a hotel fortune. She hasn't recorded any meme-ready videos like Tay "Chocolate Rain" Zonday or Tron Guy or the "Leave Britney Alone!" dude. She doesn't flaunt tech knowledge like bloggers Robert Scoble or Dave Winer. She is undeniably pretty—flowing black-coffee hair, sparkling eyes, gamine physique, broad smile—but beauty alone can't account for her celebrity.

Allison is the latest, and perhaps purest, iteration of the Warholian ideal: someone who is famous for being famous. Like graffiti writers who turned their signatures into wild-style gallery pieces, she has made the process of self-promotion into its own freaky art form. Traditionally, it takes an army of publicists, a well-connected family, or a big-budget ad campaign to make this kind of splash. But Allison has done it on her own and on the cheap, armed only with an insatiable need for attention and a healthy helping of Web savvy.

"She used this medium and became unstoppable," says Choire Sicha, former managing editor of Gawker. "She just made it happen in a way that seemed seamless and kind of magical."

It's easy to dismiss Allison as little more than a rank narcissist—and many of her vocal online critics are happy do just that. But come on, admit it: You've spent a good half hour trying to pick out the most flattering photo to upload to your MySpace page. You struggle to come up with the mot juste to describe your Facebook status. You keep a bank of self-portraits on Flickr or an online scrapbook on Tumblr or a running log of your daily musings on Blogger. You strategically court the gatekeepers at Stumble Upon or Digg. You compare the size of your Twitter-subscriber rolls to those of your friends. You set up Google Alerts to tell you whenever a blogger mentions your name. See? Self-promotion is no longer solely the domain of egotists and professional aspirants. Anyone can be a personal branding machine.

"People have been so paranoid about having any presence online for such a long time," says David Karp, founder of the Tumblr blogging service and a friend of Allison's. "A lot of them have gone through that transition of 'Well, shit, it's out there. I'm searchable on Flickr or Google.' The cat is out of the bag, and the only way to take back that control is to get out there and have a presence, have an identity that you feel represents you."

Like it or not, we are all public figures now—famous, as the new cliché goes, for 15 people. "By actively keeping a blog and using Twitter and maintaining my social network profiles, I am shaping my image," says Ian Schafer, CEO of Deep Focus, an Internet marketing firm in New York and LA. "Maybe not for the general public, who couldn't care less, but for the 500 or so people who care about me and are actively or passively paying attention."

And nobody gets people to pay attention quite like Julia Allison. In the week after her midtown dance party, reactions will pop up on blogs across the Internet. One typically tart comment refers to the tableaux as "suburban girls gone wild." Valleywag, Gawker's Silicon Valley sister site, publishes an entire gallery of photos.

Chalk up another win for the Julia Allison juggernaut. "This technology gives us direct power over our own brand," Allison says. "In the past, I would have had to go through a reporter or a PR rep. Now we are all our own publicists. And we all have to learn the tricks."

Step 1: Get Noticed

When she was a junior at Georgetown University in the fall of 2002, Allison decided she had a thing for medical students. They were smart and driven and a little older than she was, all big turn-ons. So she got a job at the medical school library, where she had the opportunity to meet the entire class—and date several of its members. Before long, she was getting invited to med student parties. She was given a nickname—the Medstitute—which she chose to interpret as affection-ate. At the end of the school year, during graduation ceremonies, her photo popped up in a slide show retrospective. It was all very flattering.

In late 2004, Allison moved to New York to break into the Manhattan media world and—as she wrote on a list of goals she brought with her at the time—"become a cult figure." It wouldn't take long, and she would accomplish it using the same strategy she employed to become the Medstitute: Discover a niche, position herself at its choke point, and stay there until people start to notice.

For Allison, that choke point was Gawker, Nick Denton's media-gossip site that pulls in millions of readers every month, many of them fellow journalists. It was the equivalent of the medical school library—the place where Allison would be seen by everyone in her target audience. She began writing a dating column for *AM New York,* a free commuter news paper, and

---

How to Become Student Body President

Last year, Sam Nelson beat out the most popular kid in class to become student body president of Shorewood High School near Seattle. We asked him to share his campaign tactics.

Move Fast
When the guy I was running against put his campaign video online, I knew I had only 24 hours to respond. Any longer and it would look like I was copying him. My brother, his friend, and I taped ourselves dancing to "This Is Why I'm Hot" by Mims and posted the clip that evening.

Become a Media Darling
If voters see that other people have watched your video, you look more popular. I took out a catchy URL, *hewouldbebomb.com,* that linked to my YouTube video, and put it up all over campus. That way people didn't have to search for the clip; they'd remember the name and go straight to it. Soon I had thousands of hits.

Rally Your Base
I was the underdog, so on election day I changed the theme song on my MySpace page to Frank Sinatra's "High Hopes," which is about overcoming long odds.

Reap the Spoils
I won 60–40. A month later, I got a blond-bombshell girlfriend. I couldn't walk down the hall without someone shouting, "Sam! Dude! Your girlfriend is so hot!"

---

peppered Gawker's tip line with links to her articles. Nothing. Then she started commenting on Gawker's stories; the site's editors banned her for "gratuitous self-promotion that makes even the gratuitous self-promoters at Gawker blush." It wasn't until she showed up at Nick Denton's 2006 Halloween party dressed as a "condom fairy," complete with a low-cut bustier festooned with Trojans, that Denton decided to act. The next morning, he met with managing editor Chris Mohney and demanded that he write an item about Allison.

Meatspace party-crashing may sound like a low tech way to meet the online cognoscenti, but Timothy Ferriss, whose skill at reaching bloggers helped turn his book, *The 4-Hour Workweek,* into a best seller, says it can be effective. "It's a matter of ensuring you have the channel with the least competition," he says. "Email is by far the most crowded channel, followed by phone. The least common is in-person."

Mohney's piece, "Field Guide: Julia Allison," was a vicious character assassination. In 800 words—a monster tome by Gawker standards—it charged Allison with exploiting a long-ago dalliance with then-congressman Harold Ford for its publicity value, published her given surname (Baugher, which she dropped when she arrived in New York), accused her of plagiarizing iVillage in one of her columns for the Georgetown paper, and said that "her habit of purring and flirting with taken or married men frequently brings the claws out from those menfolk's significant others." The piece garnered more than 17,000 pageviews and scads of vitriolic remarks from Gawker's notoriously harsh commenters. "I sure hope this is the LAST Gawker post we see about this useless ho-bag," one wrote. Allison says she cried for three days after reading the story. She begged Denton to take down the article (a fruitless effort that she would continue for more than a year). She considered sending a point-by-point rebuttal. Instead, she posted a photo on her blog of herself in her condom dress, displaying her shapely rump. "Dearest Gawker," she wrote. "Kiss my ass."

And so a complicated symbiosis was born. Allison befriended Gawker's writers, dropping by the office in Chelsea or sending instant messages with passive-aggressive story suggestions—an upcoming date she was looking forward to, or the fact that Fall Out Boy bassist Pete Wentz used to babysit her, or some faux humiliation. "She'd send these notes and say, 'Oh my God, I can't believe I posted this, it's so personal, please don't link to this,'" says Emily Gould, who wrote for Gawker at the time. "And I'd say, 'Are you sure? Because now I kind of want to.'" The writers, facing an unrelenting 12-posts-a-day workload, couldn't resist the easy productivity of a quick Allison item, although they usually took great pains to layer each story with a healthy coating of snark. Gawker's readers ran up the pageviews, even as they filled the comments section with requests to please, please stop covering Julia Allison. And Allison grew an ever-thicker skin, clinging to the *freude* and eschewing the *schaden*. After a few laps around this feedback loop, Allison could cross "become a cult figure" off her to-do list.

Step 2: Keep Them Hooked

A week before flying out to see Allison, I sign up to get her Twitter feed sent to my cell phone. I regret it almost instantly, as my inbox fills with mini-updates. *Bzzt.* "At sushi." *Bzzt.* "In the car on the way to the Hamptons." *Bzzt.* "In the Hamptons with the girls." I can see my wireless bill shooting up like a taxi meter on the Autobahn.

To be honest, Allison isn't exactly a power Twitterer. She has 1,300 followers and sends 10 or so updates a day—a paltry sum compared to entrepreneur Jason Calacanis (28,000 followers) or Robert Scoble (27,000 followers) or blogger Scott Beale (12,000 followers), all of whom average at least 20 daily updates. "For some people, it has replaced blogging," Beale says. "More people are going to see a link I post to Twitter than on my blog."

In the past, celebrities meted out photos and interviews to favored sources, carefully cultivating their public images by controlling the flow of information. Today, lifebloggers like Allison and Justine "iJustine" Ezarik deluge their fans with data. "I post 10 to 15 mobile photos to 10 different sites a day," Ezarik says. "I try to post one video a day. I usually collect all my posts on My Space and Facebook. I have a live show on Sunday and a Nokia phone that lets me stream live video throughout the day. It's kind of never-ending."

---

5 Ways to Be Like Julia

Want to be famous like Julia Allison? Here are the tactics she deployed to gain online notoriety. Use at your own risk.

It's Not Who You know, It's Who You're Next to
When you go to a party, be sure to get photographed with well-known guests—even if they have no idea who you are. By posting these pics on your blog, you can make yourself look like an established personality.

Dress against Type
Heading to a party filled with khakiclad geeks? Consider a flashy designer dress. Have a reputation for glamour? Stick with a simple T-shirt. Counterintuitive wardrobe choices keep your fans guessing.

Embrace Enigma
One day Allison announced that online haters were ruining her life and she'd never blog again. The next day she was back. Is she a train wreck or mastermind? Narcissist or self-satirist? No one knows—that's why they keep watching.

Let Your Minions Fight Your Battles
Sure, Allison has her critics—but all the discussion helps keep her in the spotlight. "Create two separate camps of supporters and attackers," says Timothy Ferriss, author of The 4-Hour Work-week. "Don't spend a lot of time defending yourself. If someone attacks you, let it sit there. If you respond, you don't give other people a chance to get engaged and defend you."

Be a Hot Woman with an Exhibitionist Streak
We're just saying.

Allison's greatest accomplishment isn't the volume of content she creates; it's that she gets anyone to care about it. Her trick, she says, is to think of herself as the subject of a magazine profile, with every post or update adding dimensions to her as a character. "I treat it like a fire," she says. "You have to add logs, or it'll be like one of those YouTube videos that flame out."

One way to add logs: blog about your active love life. Allison cemented her status as a Gawker target when she started dating *Men's Health* editor Dave Zinczenko in January 2007. Six months later, Allison began seeing Jakob Lodwick, a founder of CollegeHumor.com and Vimeo and another regular subject of Gawker gossip. They documented the courtship on their blogs, posting photos of themselves cuddling, videos of each other frolicking on the beach, and emails in which they debated the finer points of dating. One painful video, in which Lodwick accuses Allison of being too "demanding" and she fights back tears, was featured on Gawker, under the headline "Hey,

ANNUAL EDITIONS

> ## How to Twitter
>
> Used correctly, Twitter's 140-character blurbs provide a stream of haikus to your adoring public. But how to overshare without overwhelming? To find out, we asked Twitter's top talents what makes a great tweet. Here's what they had to say, in 140 characters or less.
>
> "If you want more people to follow you on twitter, give your real name on your account profile. Not everyone knows you by your username."
> — Scott Beale
>
> "Every single twitter post you write should be something that could get you laid, ruin a marriage, or bring a tear to a fat little kid's eye."
> — Joshua Allen
>
> "Don't answer, 'what are you doing?' be funny. be brief (duh). Leave your lunch unpublished. Ditto your late plane. Incomplete sentences."
> — Jason Kottke
>
> "Twitter is a community. It's not all about you. Engage your peers by asking them questions. You don't have to actually read the answers."
> — Micki Krimmel
>
> "Frequently linking to yourself from twitter is a terrific way to highlight your skills as an unlovable marketing knob. Go easy on the spam."
> — Merlin Mann
>
> "Don't try to impress—just be yourself. But go a little beyond your comfort zone; share something you're hesitant about sharing."
> — Evan Williams

Quit Paying Attention to Julia Allison and Jakob Lodwick!" In November, they started jakobandjulia.com to chronicle the "inner-workings of a *real* relationship, with all its flaws." Flaws, indeed; the couple broke up three weeks later—via blog post.

Soap opera aside, readers have been drawn in by the question of whether Allison is in control of her fame or victimized by it. Critics may pan her as a narcissist, but Allison regularly shows a savvy self-mockery. After Radar named her the third-most-hated person on the Internet—she placed just above the marine seen on YouTube tossing a puppy off a cliff—her knowing response won over even the most hardened Gawker commenter. ("I want to thank my agent, who has been with me since I was just mildly annoying," she wrote. "Of course I want to thank my self-promotional narcissism and my incessant desire for infamy at any costs. Thank you so, so much.")

But sometimes Allison's critics heave rotten fruit at her head with such force that even she can't make lemonade out of it. After she disclosed an ex-boyfriend's bipolar disorder in a Gawker Q&A, irascible vlogger Loren Feldman posted an anti-Julia rant, calling her a "vapid, vapid, cruel, mean monster" and "one of the saddest train wrecks in the history of the Internet." In January, Reblogging Julia launched to provide "a critical analysis of the public ramblings of the creature formerly known as Ms. Baugher, who provides a manic amount of content to parse." And after Valleywag ran photos of Allison canoodling with Digg cofounder Kevin Rose—publicity that Allison says killed their burgeoning relationship—she declared she had enough. "I can't do this anymore. It's ruining my life," she wrote on her blog. Gawker's Denton personally marked the occasion with a four-word item: "It's over. For now." The mini-post brought in 11,000 pageviews and 160 comments. Allison's site brought in more than 17,000 readers that day, a new record.

Don't worry. It wasn't over. The next day she followed up with a postscript: "I may have overreacted a bit." Three weeks later, she posted a video of herself lip-syncing 4 Non Blondes' "What's Up?" on a ski lift. And three months after that she officially resumed her regular blogging schedule.

Step 3: Extend Your Brand

"I thought that gawker post about you today was very nice," Allison tells Rambin over lunch salads at a Greenwich Village café. She speaks soothingly, like a mother comforting a child after a deflating T-ball game. Allison spends a lot of time encouraging Rambin, whom she befriended a year ago. She persuaded Rambin to take up blogging after signing her up for a Tumblr account last December. She linked regularly to Rambin's posts and uploaded pictures of the two of them together as a way of directing her site's visitors to Rambin's page. And when Allison went on hiatus, even more of her readers started following Rambin as a surrogate for their Allison fix.

And now, if Allison has her way, she will turn Rambin—and their friend Asha—into true Web celebrities, just like herself. In the same way that Denton used his platform to make Allison a proto-celebrity, she is now using her public profile to do the same for her friends. But this is not charity; it's her attempt to build the Allison brand. "Two C-list starlets can get together and make one B-list couple; this is very similar," she says. "Mary can meet with five people, and I can meet with five other people, and Meghan can meet with five other people, and all the press we get individually builds the team as a whole."

In July 2007, having conquered—and perhaps oversaturated—the Manhattan media market, Allison set her sights on a new target: the Silicon Valley startup world. In a flashback to her Gawker breakthrough, she flew to the Bay Area to attend the annual TechCrunch party thrown by influential blogger Michael Arrington. Dressed in a flattering Diane von Furstenberg dress, Allison made an immediate impression among the blueshirt-and-khaki-wearing attendees. The next day, Arrington posted a video on his site of Allison cooing for the camera, telling her audience that she had a thing for geeks, and urging them to call her. Soon Allison had become a Valleywag staple, befriended the likes of CNET's Caroline McCarthy and Sequoia Capital's Mark Kvamme, and—like Jack in the Box opening a new crosstown franchise—introduced her brand of ignore-me-if-you-dare provocation to the Web 2.0 startup world. When she left town at the end of the weekend, the Valley-based blogosphere reacted as if it had just survived a flash flood. "We are all in awe," one blogger wrote, "and quite honestly left scratching our heads over how someone, in such a short period of time, could make an incredibly controversial impact—with an entire community breathing a sigh of relief at her departure."

Newly reinvented as a tech-world ingenue, Allison began entertaining plans to launch her own business. Instead of using her outsize personality to drive pageviews to Gawker and Valleywag, she thought, why not capitalize on her reputation to launch her own Web portal? She signed up Rambin and Asha to act as cofounders of the site—nonsociety.com—and began developing content: lip-sync videos, a talk-show series modeled after *The View*, and the collected musings that the trio were already posting on their own blogs. They enlisted Shane Parrish, a marketer who had helped design Web strategies for Barneys New York and *Project Runway*, to serve as their creative director. In mid-June, Allison signed a deal with Bravo to follow the women's startup adventures and broadcast them as a reality show called *IT Girls*.

Can Allison really win an unironic fan base? Can someone who's famous for being hated convert that loathing into love? Allison insists she can—and readily forwards emails from fans who have been won over. But even if she can't, even if her new site is good for nothing more than providing continued fodder for the cannons that are pointed at her, that will be its own kind of success.

"There's no scandal that won't make her bigger," says Sicha, the former Gawker editor. "She could be dumped by whomever. She's crossed every line already. Nothing bad can happen to her."

Well, unless people stop paying attention. But that doesn't seem likely. One evening after trailing Allison for most of the day, I return to my hotel to see that she has sent me an email with a link to Gawker. It's the day's Gawker Stalker, a list of celebrity sightings emailed in by anonymous tipsters. Already, it looks like Allison's plan to celebrify her friends is paying off: "Union Square today around 2 pm. Saw julia allison and her 2 other friends mary and megan, noticed the other two first, dressed very well."

But it's the next sentence that makes my heart beat a little faster. "Julia Allison following them, talking to some guy." Hey! That's me! For a second, I confess, it's a thrill, to have my spectral presence broadcast to thousands of readers. But then I get annoyed. "Some guy"? That's it? No mention of my outfit, or my dulcet baritone, or even my height or weight? Not the slightest curiosity as to who I might be? Come on. What's a guy got to do to get noticed around here?

Senior editor **JASON TANZ** (jason_tanz@wired.com) wrote about Vice TV in issue 15.11.

How to Set up a Velvet Rope on Facebook

Facebook makes it easy to share your Vegas vacation snaps. But newly minted Webutantes, take heed: Some of those photos could be damaging should they fall into the wrong hands. Here's how to make sure that only your BFFs get the tawdry details.

Pick Your Friends
Faceslamming may sound violent, but it just means refusing to add wannabe buds to your Friends list—and it's totally acceptable, so don't be afraid to dis. For the people you do add, set up two lists: one for mere contacts and the other for actual pals. That way only your real friends get to see that you've updated your status to "itchy."

Protect Your Privates
To keep any schlub with a search engine from digging up your profile, change your privacy settings so only friends of friends can get to you. You can also keep strangers from finding photos tagged with your name. And does your boss really need to know every time you play a hand of Hold 'Em? Shut up blabbermouth applications by unchecking all boxes except "Know who I am and access my information" when you install them.

Cover Your Tracks
Consider setting up a second profile with an alias known only to your closest confidantes. Then dump all the good stuff there. (Sorry, "Philip McGroin" is already taken.)

Copyright © 2008 Condé Nast Publications. All Rights Reserved. Originally published in *Wired*. Reprinted by permission.

Article 2

Discovering What Democracy Means

BILL MOYERS

We are often asked whether our kind of journalism matters. People are curious about why we give so much time to novelists, playwrights, artists, historians, philosophers, composers, scholars, teachers—all of whom we consider public thinkers. The answer is simple: They are worth listening to.

Some years ago I was invited to testify before a House of Representatives committee on funding of the arts and humanities. Opponents were making their skepticism felt toward PBS, the National Endowment of the Arts, and the National Endowment for the Humanities. I had been present at the creation of all three during my time in the White House with Lyndon Johnson, and now all three were once again in the crosshairs of conservatives like Ronald Reagan who were asking: "Why should we subsidize intellectual curiosity?" Reading Shakespeare, it was said, does not erase the budget deficit. Plunging into the history of the 15th century does not ease traffic jams. Listening to Mozart or reading the ancient Greeks does not repair the ozone layer.

We had recently produced two series on poetry called "The Language of Life" and "The Power of the Word." Our series on "Joseph Campbell and the Power of Myth" was resonating far and wide, much to the displeasure of sectarian dogmatists. We had created a documentary special called "The Power of the Past," about how Florence valued art for public, and not merely private, consumption. Our series "A World of Ideas" offered conversations from a wide spectrum of voices: Chinua Achebe, Carlos Fuentes, Northrop Frye, Joseph Heller, Thomas Wolfe, Richard Rodriguez, Bharati Mukherjee, Jonas Salk, William L. Shirer, Tu Wei-ming, Toni Morrison, Joanne Ciulla, Ernesto Cortes, M.F.K. Fisher, Mary Ann Glendon, Leon Kass, and so many others who opened viewers to what my old friend and colleague Eric Sevareid once called "news of the mind."

Critics said these programs taught no one how to bake bread or build bridges. And they were right. Despite public television—not to mention symphony orchestras, municipal libraries, art museums, and public theaters—crime was still rampant, the divorce rate was soaring, corruption flourished, legislatures remained stubbornly profligate, corporations cooked their books, liberals were loose in the world doing the work of the devil, and you still couldn't get a good meal on the Metro to Washington. Why persist, some members of Congress wanted to know, when there are so many more urgent needs to be met and so many practical problems to be solved?

I did not have a tried-and-true answer for members of the committee. I could not hand them a ledger showing that ideas have consequences. I chose instead to tell them what they could have learned if they had been listening to the people who appeared in our broadcasts.

They would have heard the novelist Maxine Hong Kingston say: "All human beings have this burden in life to constantly figure out what's true, what's authentic, what's meaningful, what's dross, what's a hallucination, what's a figment, what's madness. We all need to figure out what is valuable, constantly. As a writer, all I am doing is posing the question in a way that people can see very clearly."

They would have heard Peter Sellars, the iconoclastic director of Shakespeare in a swimming pool and Mozart in the Bronx, explain that he wants "to put our society up next to these great masterpieces. Are we thinking big enough? Are we generous of spirit? What does our society look like, next to the greatest things a human being ever uttered?"

They would have heard Vartan Gregorian, then head of the New York Public Library, talk about how "in a big library, suddenly you feel humble. The whole of humanity is in front of you. It gives you a sense of cosmic relation, but at the same time a sense of isolation. You feel both pride and insignificance. Here it is, the human endeavor, human aspiration, human agony, human ecstasy, human bravura, human failures—all before you. And you look around and say, 'Oh, my God! I am not going to be able to know it all.'"

They would have heard the philosopher Martha Nussbaum confess that in one sense there is no message or moral in the ancient Greek dramatists—"simply the revelation of life as seen through the sufferer." But there is a value, she went on, in seeing "the complexity that's there, and seeing it honestly, without flinching, and without reducing it to some excessively simple theory." You begin then, she said, to realize that trying to wrest a good life from the world may lead to tragedy, but you still must try.

They would have heard the filmmaker David Puttnam tell how as a boy he sat through dozens of screenings of A Man for All Seasons, the story of Sir Thomas More's fatal defiance of Henry VIII: "It allowed me the enormous conceit of walking out of the cinema thinking, 'Yeah, I think I might have had my head cut off for the sake of a principle.' I know absolutely I wouldn't, and I probably never met anyone who would, but the cinema allowed me that conceit. It allowed me for one moment to feel that everything decent in me had come together."

And they would have heard Mike Rose talk about what it's like teaching disadvantaged older college students in California. He had recounted to me his battle with a street-wise grownup who was flogging her way through Macbeth. "What does Shakespeare have to do with me?" she would ask. But when she finally got through the play she said to Mike Rose: "You know, people always hold this stuff over you. They make you feel stupid. But now, I've read it. I can say, 'I, Olga, have read Shakespeare.' I won't tell you I like it, because I don't know if I do, or I don't. But I like knowing what it's about." And Mike Rose said: "The point is not that reading Shakespeare gave her overnight some new discriminating vision of good and evil. What she got was something more precious: a sense that she was not powerless and she was not dumb."

Some members of Congress got it. They realized that we were talking not only about how to improve our lives as individuals but how to nurture a flourishing democracy. Wouldn't we have been likely to deal more effectively and quickly with pollution if we had thought about where we fit in the long sweep of the Earth's story? Could we better tackle our spending priorities as a society if we were prepared to acknowledge and confront the pain of conflicting choices, which the ancient poets knew to be the incubus of agony and the crucible of wisdom? Might we better decide how to use our wealth and power if we have measured and tested ourselves against the greatest things a human being ever uttered? Are we not likely to be more wisely led by officials who have learned from history and literature that great nations die of too many lies?

Furthermore, if we nurtured the higher affections of our intuition—what has been called our "inner tutor"—might we be more resolute in sparing our children from the appalling accretion of violent entertainment that permeates American life—what Newsweek described as "the flood of mass-produced and mass-consumed violence that pours upon us, masquerading as amusement and threatening to erode the psychological and moral boundary between real life and make-believe?"

We know who the enemies of democracy are. In his Jefferson Lecture the late Cleanth Brooks of Yale identified them as the "bastard muses" propaganda, which pleads, sometimes unscrupulously, for a special cause or issue at the expense of the total truth; sentimentality, which works up emotional responses unwarranted by, and in excess of, the occasion; and pornography, which focuses upon one powerful human drive at the expense of the total human personality. To counter the "bastard muses," Brooks proposed cultivating the "true muses" of the moral imagination. Not only do these arm us to resist the little lies and fantasies of advertising, the official lies of power, and the ghoulish products of nightmarish minds, they open us to the lived experience of others—to the affirmations of a heightened consciousness—to empathy. So it is that when Lear cried out to Gloucester on the heath: "You see how this world goes. . . ." Gloucester, who was blind, answered: "I see it feelingly."

Many years ago we produced a series called "Six Great Ideas" with the didactic, irascible but compelling philosopher and educator, Mortimer Adler—one hour each on liberty, equality and justice, truth, beauty, and goodness. From the deluge of mail I kept two letters that summed up the response. One came from Utah.

"Dear Dr. Adler, I am writing in behalf of a group of construction workers (mostly, believe it or not, plumbers!) who have finally found a teacher worth listening to. While we cannot all agree whether or not we would hire you as an apprentice, we can all agree that we would love to listen to you during our lunch breaks. I am sure that it is just due to our well-known ignorance as tradesmen that not a single one of us had ever heard of you until one Sunday afternoon we were watching public television and Bill Moyers came on with Six Great Ideas. We listened intensely and soon became addicted and have been ever since. We never knew a world of ideas existed. The study of ideas has completely turned around our impression of education . . . We have grown to love the ideas behind our country's composition, and since reading and discussing numerous of your books we have all become devout Constitutionalists. We thank you and we applaud you. We are certain that the praise of a few plumbers could hardly compare with the notoriety that you deserve from distinguished colleagues, but we salute you just the same. We may be plumbers during the day, but at lunch time and at night and on weekend, we are Philosophers at Large. God bless you."

The second letter came from Marion, Ohio—from the federal prison there. The writer said he had been a faithful viewer of the series, and he described it as "a truly joyous opportunity . . . for an institutionalized intellectual. After several months in a cell, with nothing but a TV, it was salvation." Salvation. Deliverance. Redemption.

I had to think about this a while before I realized what he meant. He was, after all, a lifer. How is it a man condemned to an institution for the remainder of his years finds salvation in a television program? And then one day I came across something Leo Strauss had written. The Greek word for vulgarity, Strauss said, is apeirokalia, the lack of experience in things beautiful. Wherever you are and however it arrives, a liberal education can liberate you from the coarseness and crudity of circumstances beyond your control.

As I watch and listen to our public discourse today, it seems to me we are all "institutionalized" in one form or another, locked away in our separate realities, our parochial loyalties, our fixed ways of seeing ourselves and others. For democracy to prosper it requires us to escape those bonds and join what John Dewey called "a life of free and enriching communion"—to become "We, the People." The late James W. Carey, one of our noted scholars of communication, wrote that the very concept of "public" could once be defined as "a group of strangers who gather to discuss the news." In early America the printing press generated a body of popular knowledge. Towns were small, and taverns, inns, coffeehouses, street corners, and the public greens—the commons—were places where people gathered to discuss what they were reading. These places of public communication "provided the underlying social fabric of the town and, when the Revolution began, made it possible to quickly gather militia companies, to form effective committees of correspondence and of inspection, and to organize and to manage mass town meetings."

The public was no fiction, Carey said. The public had no life, no social relationships, without news. The news was what activated conversation between strangers, and strangers were assumed to be capable of conversing about the news. In fact, the whole point of the press was not so much to disseminate fact as to assemble people. The press furnished materials for argument—"information," in the narrow sense—"but the value of the press was predicated on the existence of the public, not the reverse." The media's role was humble but serious, and that role was to take the public seriously.

It would be hard to argue that we do so today, except in isolated examples. Our public conversation is mediated by politicians who have mastered "sound bites" sculpted from polling data, by "pundits" whose credibility increases with the frequency of exposure despite being consistently wrong, and "experts" whose authority depends not on reason, evidence or logic but on ideology and affiliation. The public, J.R. Priestly observed, "has been transformed into a vast crowd, a permanent audience, waiting to be amused."

What kind of "public intellectual" survives in such an environment? Turn on the television and you're likely to see them talking about the war in Iraq, for which they were cheerleaders, or the upcoming presidential race—still a year away. Notice where they sit—in a Times Square studio or a media stage in Washington, their messages beamed across the public airwaves courtesy of huge media conglomerates whose intent is not the informing of citizens but the maximizing of profit through the delivery to advertisers of mass audiences addicted to consumerism.

How forlorn a figure Socrates of Athens would be in this environment. Arguably the first public intellectual, proclaimed by the oracle of Delphi as the wisest of men, Socrates went about Athens on a divine mandate of self-reflection, some celestial spark glowing in his breast, some voice whispering in his head that only he could hear. Led by this voice he went to the wise men and great poets and master technicians of the city to cross-examine them, casting doubt on their knowledge by exposing their received opinions and unexamined assumptions, the deep-seated corruption of thought which leads to grave moral danger; or sometimes simply pointing to the common failing of so many experts: that of mistaking their expertise in one subject or practice for universal wisdom about the human condition.

Exposing the ignorance of the leaders was Socrates' way of helping the "cause of God," as he explained when he was put on trial. He reasoned thus from his interviews with them that the wisest of men—as the oracle, remember, described Socrates to be—is the one who is most conscious of his own ignorance, most aware of the limits of knowledge which are introduced by our limited methods of obtaining knowledge. Meletus, the main accuser featured in Socrates' Apology (as told by Plato), was a young religious fanatic who charged Socrates with believing in deities of his own invention rather than the gods recognized by the state. Scholars now believe that Meletus was simply a "front man" for political interests, put forward to stir the public against the philosopher—a forerunner of modern punditry, or maybe something quite like today's political fundamentalism.

I sadly think of [former Secretary of State] Colin Powell addressing the United Nations in February 2003, with his artist's renderings of those trailers that were supposed to be mobile biological warfare factories; and I think of all the rest of the cooked intelligence that sold so many of our public intellectuals on invading Iraq. It was too crude to even qualify as false wisdom on the Socratic model, really, but the resulting disaster—as great a blunder as Vietnam to which many of the same mistakes could be assigned—would result from relying on the knowledge of self-interested experts and deluded leaders. When they sentenced Socrates to death, he reminded them that they were proving how groundless knowledge made it impossible to escape from doing wrong. Succumbing to wishful thinking that leads to disastrous self-delusion, he pointed out, is the only real death. "When I leave this court," he said of his jurors, "I will go away condemned by you to death." But his accusers, he told them, "will go away convicted by truth herself. . . ."

The Hebrew prophet was another kind of public intellectual, one who was also condemned and persecuted by the political elites he addressed. A century before Socrates, one of those prophets—Jeremiah—came from a small village into Jerusalem to preach repentance to a faithless Israel, with its houses full of treachery, and its rich kings and princes who gave no justice to the poor widow and the fatherless child.

And of course, near the end of his life, Jesus of Nazareth also went to Jerusalem, to preach the same message in an even more dangerous public way, confronting the ruling elites before great crowds on the Temple grounds. When he predicted their imminent destruction in his parable about the wicked tenants who hoarded the fruits of creation, his fate was sealed.

Jesus would not be crucified today. The prophets would not be stoned. Socrates would not drink the hemlock. They would instead be banned from the Sunday talk shows and op-ed pages by the sentries of establishment thinking who guard against dissent with the one weapon of mass destruction most cleverly designed to obliterate democracy—the rubber stamp.

A stock broker who makes bad picks doesn't last too long. A baseball player in an extended slump gets traded. A worker made redundant by cheaper labor abroad or by a new machine—well, she's done for, too. But four years after the invasion of Iraq—the greatest blunder in foreign policy since Vietnam—the public apologists and advocates of the war flourish in the media, while the costs of their delusions accrue in body counts and lost treasure. A public that detests the war is relegated to the bleachers, fated to watch from afar the playing out by political and media elites of a game that has been rigged.

Yet the salvation of democracy requires a public aroused by the knowledge of what is being done to them in their name. Here is the crisis of the times as I see it: We talk about problems, issues, policies, but we don't talk about what democracy means—what it bestows on us—the revolutionary idea that it isn't just about the means of governance but the means of dignifying people so they become fully free to claim their moral and political agency. "I believe in Democracy because it releases the energies of every human being." So spoke Woodrow Wilson, the namesake of your foundation and, I would suggest, still your guiding spirit.

The only PhD ever to reach the White House was a public intellectual and genuine reformer who understood what a major battleground higher education was. He learned what the political struggle was about while a professor and later the president of Princeton, where he lost his share of institutional battles with wealthy alumni who largely controlled the university's development, and the nation beyond.

In his forgotten political testament The New Freedom (1913), Wilson took up something of the ancient, critical task of the public intellectual, a fact all the more remarkable in that he was president at the time. Louis Brandeis, the people's lawyer, was his inspiration and the source of this vision, but Wilson stood for it, right there at the center of power. "Don't deceive yourselves for a moment as to the power of the great interests which now dominate our development." "No matter that there are men in this country big enough to own the government of the United States. They are going to own it if they can." But "there is no salvation," he said, "in the pitiful condescensions of industrial masters. Guardians have no place in a land of freemen. Prosperity guaranteed by trustees has no prospect of endurance." From his stand came progressive income taxation, the federal estate tax, tariff reform, and a resolute spirit "to deal with the new and subtle tyrannies according to their deserts."

Wilson described his reformism in plain English no one could fail to understand: "The laws of this country do not prevent the strong from crushing the weak." That was true in 1800, it was true in 1860, in 1892, in 1912, and 1932; it was true in 1964, and it is true today. We have often been pressed to the limit, the promise of the Declaration and the ideals of the Gettysburg Address ignored or trampled upon and our common interests brought low. But every time there came a great wave of reform, and I believe one is coming again, helped along by the bright young people this foundation is nurturing.

We cannot build a political consensus or a nation across the vast social divides that mark our country today. Consensus arises from bridging that divide and making society whole again, the fruits of freedom and prosperity made available to the least among us. What we have to determine now, as Wilson said in his day, "is whether we are big enough . . . whether we are free enough, to take possession again of the government which is our own. We haven't had free access to it, our minds have not touched it by way of guidance, in half a generation, and now we are engaged in nothing less than the recovery of what was made with our own hands, and acts only by our delegated authority."

As we face that challenge even today, a story about Helen Keller is worth remembering. Toward the end of her career, as she was speaking at a Midwestern college, a student asked: "Miss Keller, is there anything that could have been worse than losing your sight?" Helen Keller replied: "Yes, I could have lost my vision."

BILL MOYERS is chairman of the Schumann Center for Media and Democracy and an independent journalist with his own production company. On February 7, the Woodrow Wilson National Fellowship Foundation presented Judith and Bill Moyers the first Frank E. Taplin, Jr. Public Intellectual Award for "extraordinary contributions to public cultural, civic and intellectual life." This is an excerpt of his remarks.

From *Tom.Paine.common sense,* Copyright © 2007 by Institute for America's Future. Reprinted by permission.

Article 3

Off Course

How the hip and ambitious coverage of pop culture at our most influential newspaper manages to miss half the story.

MICHAEL MASSING

Not too many years ago, *The New York Times* was so thoroughly high-minded in its approach to culture, so consumed with opera and museums and classical music, that it let critical trends in popular culture pass by unremarked. With the entertainment business expanding into a huge global combine reaching into every corner of the American psyche, however, the *Times* has recognized that, as a world-class newspaper—and one in need of younger readers—it must approach the subject with the same intensity and sense of purpose it brings to politics and economics, and for the last decade it has been moving in that direction. More recently, the paper has been reorganizing its coverage of culture—adding staff, mapping out new beats, and better coordinating coverage among the relevant sections, Arts & Leisure, The Arts, and Business Day. Now, with a culture staff of nearly one hundred reporters, critics, and editors, the *Times* can ferret out news about pop culture like few other publications.

Yet in boosting its coverage of this subject, the paper at times seems to have careened toward the opposite extreme, eagerly chronicling every up-and-down tick in the great fame-and-ambition sweepstakes. Its reports on TV, movies, pop music, video games, publishing, and advertising brim with news about boardroom struggles, mogul rivalries, high-stakes dealmaking, ratings shares, marketing strategies, publicity blitzes, technological innovations, branding, and franchising. The paper is drawn to the hot and the hip, to glamour and buzz, to the Weinsteins and Eisners, the Spielbergs and Bronfmans. With its heavy reliance on sources inside the media business, the paper's coverage at times seems indistinguishable from that of *Billboard, Variety, Advertising Age*, and other publications aimed at industry insiders.

In the process, the *Times* has neglected a critical aspect of pop culture—its effects on society. With the entertainment world grown so pervasive, with its products so thoroughly infiltrating the nation's households, its influence on kids, families, and communities has intensified as well. Yet the *Times*, like most mainstream news media, pays all that only sporadic attention. When Janet Jackson exposes her nipple during a halftime show, or desperate housewife Nicollette Sheridan drops her towel during an NFL promo, the paper will jump on the story. When TV stations refuse to air *Saving Private Ryan* for fear of being sanctioned, or the secretary of education blasts PBS for distributing a show about an animated rabbit who visits a friend with lesbian parents, the *Times* is faithfully there.

But public concerns about popular culture run much deeper than such incidents, and point to stories that are not being written. In a poll of 1,001 parents conducted last year by the Kaiser Family Foundation, only 17 percent expressed high levels of concern about the Janet Jackson incident. But 63 percent said they were "very concerned" that children are being exposed to too much inappropriate content in entertainment media, and another 26 percent said they were "somewhat concerned." As these figures show, it's not just conservatives who feel this way. "The vast majority of parents," said the foundation, "believe that sexual and violent content on TV contributes to children's behavior."

As to what to do about it, Americans are much more conflicted. A survey of 1,505 adults conducted earlier this year by the Pew Research Center for the People and the Press found that 48 percent believe that government control of entertainment poses a greater danger than harmful programming, compared to 41 percent who felt the reverse. Yet when asked about specific control measures, they were far more supportive. For instance, 75 percent said they favored stricter enforcement of government rules about TV content when children are likely to be watching; 69 percent said they supported steeper fines for violations of indecency guidelines.

To some, all this might seem like yesterday's news. It has been nearly twenty years since Tipper Gore launched a campaign urging recording companies to place warning labels on records containing explicit language. And it has been six years since the shootings at Columbine generated a rash of articles on the effects of violent programming on kids. Yet far from ebbing, the issue has intensified as pop culture grows ever more invasive, polymorphous, and perverse. On an episode of Fox's short-lived *Keen Eddie*, three men trafficking in horse semen hire a prostitute to arouse their stud. In the plastic surgery drama *Nip/Tuck*, a character has sex with a life-sized doll of a porn star and has a threesome with a hooker and a guy named Christian. On MTV's *I Want a Famous Face*, young women undergo nose jobs, breast implants, and other forms of surgery to look like their favorite celebrities. On shows like *Survivor* and *The Bachelor*, lying, deceiving, and sheer meanness are not only tolerated but celebrated. (In the Pew study, 38 percent of those surveyed expressed serious concern over reality shows in which people "are made fun of or tricked.") On *The Sopranos*, one character beats his girlfriend (a stripper) to death and is later killed by Tony Soprano, who chops off his head and stuffs it in a bowling-ball bag. The Internet, meanwhile, gives youngsters access to all sorts of lewd and grotesque material at the stroke of a key.

The journalistic questions such fare provokes seem endless, and they extend far beyond the usual ones about sex and violence into the realms of sociology, politics, and religion. Consider, for instance, the surge of religious fervor across the country. Is it linked in any way to the growing reach, and grossness, of popular culture? To what extent does the spread of evangelical Christianity represent a reaction to the language on *South Park* and the lifestyles on *Sex and the City*? With so many TV shows built around the imperfections of women's bodies and the urgent need to correct them, what effect has this had on the health (both physical and psychological) of young women? Even more urgent are the questions raised by last November's postelection exit polls showing that "moral values" were a top concern for many voters. Many journalists automatically assumed that this finding referred to such traditional issues as abortion, gay rights, and school prayer, but might it not also have reflected mounting discomfort with ads showing preteens in low-rider jeans and kids miming the garb and gestures of gangsta rap? In March, Hillary Clinton, citing studies on the impact of violent images on children, denounced violent video games, including one that encourages players "to have sex with prostitutes and then murder them." How is such a stand likely to play with voters and with the entertainment executives who have traditionally backed her?

Is the surge in religious fervor across the country linked to the growing penetration, and grossness, of popular culture?

Answering these kinds of questions requires an approach no different from that involved in investigating other social issues like welfare reform and school vouchers—sending reporters into the field. It requires talking to parents and teachers, youth counselors and Little League coaches, young children and teenagers. It requires speaking with psychologists and sociologists and drawing on studies and statistics that can help provide context for the anecdotes gathered from the field. Finally, it requires fashioning all this into a lively and insightful report.

With such a large culture staff and newshole, the *Times* would seem in an ideal position to address the impact of pop culture. And over the years it has—in book reviews, op-eds, the magazine, and the style section, as well as in the culture pages. Yet actual reported pieces on the subject appear only rarely, making the paper's culture coverage seem strangely out of balance.

Now would seem a good time to address this imbalance, for the *Times* has just named a new culture editor, Sam Sifton. From 1990 to 1998, Sifton worked at *New York Press*, then left to become a founding editor of *Talk* magazine. Arriving at the *Time* in 2002, he became the deputy dining editor. For the last year, he has participated in a "bakeoff" with Jim Schachter, formerly an editor in the business section, for the top culture job. As the winner, the thirty-eight-year-old Sifton will oversee what executive editor Bill Keller recently called, in a memo, "quite simply the finest staff of culture journalists working anywhere, and working at the top of their game." Sifton is no doubt being pelted with ideas and suggestions, but, here, unsolicited, are some of my own.

Monday, May 23, was a typical day in the life of culture at the *Times*. The Arts section offered a rumination on three new museum exhibitions on the Jewish presence in early New York, plus reviews of dance, theater, classical music, world music, and the "tribal & textile arts show" at the Seventh Regiment Armory—an indication of the paper's deep commitment to covering the arts. Top billing, though, went to a long feature titled SKATEBOARDING'S UPSTART DAYS, by Sharon Waxman, one of the paper's Hollywood correspondents. It recounted the tale of Catherine Hardwicke, an up-and-coming director in Venice, California, who managed to convince Sony Pictures Entertainment to let her direct a movie about the early history of skateboarding. In SO LONG, GARAGE. LAPTOPS ROCK, David Carr described how musicians "are using powerful laptop tools to produce music that in an earlier age might have wailed out of a garage." Inside, another Waxman article noted that *Star Wars: Episode III* had become the "year's first movie blockbuster," breaking box-office records for a four-day opening.

This being a Monday, much of the day's media action was in Business Day. (For ten years now, the Monday business section has featured stories on the entertainment and media industries.) ON FALL TV, THE NETWORKS ARE PLANNING SOMETHING BORROWED, ran the headline across the section's front page. It was the latest in a series of *Times* pieces on the new fall TV lineups. The article cited the usual array of media buyers and strategists, one of whom declared that it was "shocking" that NBC "was leaving intact its sagging lineup on Thursday, the biggest night of the week for advertising." A column along the left-hand side of the front page, also by David Carr, described how two "very wealthy young men" were seeking to break Hollywood's habit of being "hooked on the big opening weekend" by releasing movies in DVD and on cable on the same day as their theatrical release. Inside were articles about the disappearance of the comedian Dave Chappelle; a new wrinkle in the feud between the rap stars Ja Rule and 50 Cent; Nintendo's efforts to bolster its market share in the video game console business; and Google's recent introduction of a service that lets users build a customized home page.

It was quite a yeasty mix for a single day, leavened with dashes of celebrity and gossip. The harvest on other days looks little different. Here's a brief sampler, culled from April and May:

- DVD producers "climbing up the Hollywood food chain"
- the revival of *Radar* as a magazine for the hip
- the move from New York to Los Angeles of the publishing industry "trend-setter" Judith Regan
- Hollywood's welcoming of a "new crop of moguls"
- PARIS INC., on Paris Hilton's burgeoning business empire
- *Gawker*, the "flagship chronicle of Manhattan's news and gossip" (offering blogs that are "sexy, irreverent, a tad elitist, and unabashedly coastal.")
- a deal by the founders of Miramax (i.e., the Weinsteins) to distribute video programs
- how CBS is planning to fill the void left in its lineup by *Everybody Loves Raymond*
- how ABC, celebrating a ratings comeback, "won't rest on its laurels"
- how ABC's schedule "emits that 'Housewives' vibe"
- how Fox and UPN are aiming for young viewers, and how Fox, in its fall lineup, is sticking with the "tried and true" (no surprise, given that Fox finished the season "as the top-rated network among those aged 18 to 49, the category most desired by advertisers")

That last reference, to 18- to 49-year-old viewers, is a fixture of TV stories in the *Times*. According to a Nexis search, the phrase appeared more than 200 times in the two-year period ending in April 2005. A variant, "18 to 34," appeared more than a hundred times, often accompanied by the words "most desirable," "coveted," and "sought after" by advertisers. Back in October 2002, the *Times Magazine* ran an article, headlined THE MYTH OF '18 TO 34,' by Jonathan Dee, that disputed the idea that this age group is of special value to advertisers; members of the aging baby-boom generation, he argued, have much more disposable income and so make up a more lucrative market. It remains true that many advertisers continue to pay a premium for younger viewers. But the frequency with which the *Times* mentions this demographic, and the reflexive, almost unthinking way it's cited, captures the extent to which the paper's culture coverage has been penetrated by the jargon and thinking of Madison Avenue and Hollywood.

In that same April–May period, meanwhile, I found little reporting on the social or political effects of culture. The closest entry seemed a March 30 article by Julie Salamon (HAS BIG BIRD SOLD OUT?) on a new deal to distribute PBS children's shows on a 24-hour commercial cable network, and the debate over whether or not that was good for children. Amid the outpouring of reports on ratings sweeps and marketing campaigns, though, this piece was easy to overlook.

How might pop culture be covered differently? One place to begin looking for an answer is Orlando, Florida, which is in the heart of the Bible Belt and has a burgeoning population of evangelical Christians. Mark I. Pinsky has covered religion for the *Orlando Sentinel* for ten years, and he says he has been struck by how many evangelicals "feel besieged by a toxic popular culture. It's public enemy number one. They see it as hypersexual and ultraviolent, and out of their control. These people are stuck in middle-class or lower-middle-class tract houses, and they can't get away from it."

Interestingly, Pinsky, the author of a forthcoming first-person book titled *A Jew Among the Evangelicals*, says he often finds himself in agreement with the evangelical critique of pop culture. He has a seventeen-year-old son and a fourteen-year-old daughter, and they are not allowed to watch TV on school nights. "I don't believe kids hear or see something and then go out and do it," he observes. "I don't think that if they see a murder on TV, they're going to go out and kill somebody." But the literature "does suggest a desensitizing and normalizing of behavior that takes place," he says, adding, "A friend gave me a DVD of *Deadwood*. I have no problem with my son watching that. But I won't let him watch a dumb-ass sitcom. We're not prudish people at all, but I won't let the stupidity on such shows seep into their minds. It's attitudinal. Twelve-year-olds who watch TV begin talking like thirty-year-olds to their parents. You can see it immediately."

Pinsky referred me to a recent article by a fellow *Sentinel* reporter, Linda Shrieves, about "sitcom kids"—children who mimic the behavior they see on TV. "Though most TV watchdog groups fret about violence and sex on television," Shrieves wrote, "some parents say they're increasingly concerned about TV's attitude problem. From cartoons to sitcoms, the stars are now sassy children who deliver flip one-liners, put down authority figures and revel in a laugh track. And their attitudes are contagious. Formerly polite kids are smart-aleck, eye-rolling and harrumphing, just like the kids on television." Douglas Gentile of the National Institute on Media and the Family was quoted as saying that "psychologists love to slice it up many different ways, but it boils down to this: Kids copy what they see on TV."

Gentile's institute, based in Minneapolis, is one of several nonpartisan groups in the United States that seeks to guide parents on pop culture. The groups are far less political than, say, the Parents Television Council, which is headed by the right-wing activist L. Brent Bozell and which generates many of the indecency complaints that flood the FCC. On its Web site, the National Institute on Media posts reviews of movies and video games, assessing their suitability for kids. Some are truly eye-opening. Of the video game "Grand Theft Auto: San Andreas," it writes, "Raunchy, violent and portraying just about every deviant act that a criminal could think of in full, living 3D graphics.... There are no redeeming qualities in this game for children. From glorifying drive-by-shootings to delivering prostitutes to their johns, this game teaches just about everything you wouldn't even want your kids to see." In the game, players are rewarded for stealing guns and squad cars from police officers and brutally murdering them. On the Web site, readers are urged to sign a petition to tell the makers of "Grand Theft Auto," Take Two Interactive Software, to "do the only decent thing: publicly apologize and STOP KILLING COPS AS ENTERTAINMENT!"

Last year, "Grand Theft Auto: San Andreas" was the top-selling video game in the United States, with 5.1 million units sold. Its popularity and violence raise obvious questions about its possible effects on kids. On the occasions when the *Times* runs articles about such questions, it's usually in its specialized Circuits section (recently reduced to a weekly page), which guarantees that many *Times* readers will not read them. In *The Washington Post*, by contrast, the subject has twice this year made page one. In March, for instance, the *Post* ran a front-page article about the popular game "Postal" (named after shootings by postal workers). While violence has always been vital to the game's success, Ariana Eunjung Cha wrote, things have reached the point where even the game's creative team worries about excessive gore. Steve Wik, the team's creative director, is quoted as saying that "too many games have become dependent on violence for violence's sake, and that has made violence boring." A colleague feels that "some games are too dark for even his taste." The article goes on to note that the surging popularity of video games has "prompted a backlash," with a number of states introducing bills to ban the sale of violent games to minors.

The market for pop culture no doubt includes many of the same people who express backlash outrage. This contradiction seems worth exploring.

The *Post* piece suggests another approach to writing about pop culture—probing the attitudes of entertainment executives about the products they create. A pioneer of the genre is Ken Auletta's "What Won't They Do?" Published in *The New Yorker* back in 1993, it recounts his exchanges with various Hollywood figures about movies and TV shows that push the edge on violence and sex. His subjects range from Oliver Stone, who suggests that some criticism of violent programming "borders on censorship," to Debra Winger, who, as the mother of a young boy, lashes out at movies with gratuitous violence and kinky sex and who won't even let her son see *Home Alone* because the parents "are idiots" and because the son, played by Macaulay Culkin, takes too much joy in committing acts of violence.

Most revealing is Auletta's conversation with Rupert Murdoch, the chairman of 20th Century Fox. Murdoch tells Auletta of his contempt for the liberal group-think of Hollywood and its reflexive suspicion of ideas like "family values." Auletta then asks him whether *A Current Affair*, a nightly stew of sex, scandal, and rumor produced by Murdoch's Fox network, has had a coarsening effect on American life. "Coarsening?" Murdoch says, seemingly caught off-guard. "I don't know. If you were to say there had been occasions when *A Current Affair* has treated some subjects sleazily in the past, I'd have to say yes." He adds, "If you want me to get up and defend every film, every program, I don't do it."

Since then, of course, Murdoch has started up the Fox News Channel. There, hosts like Bill O'Reilly and John Gibson inveigh against "Hollywood" and the "liberal media elite" for inflicting lurid movies and vulgar sitcoms on the upstanding folks of middle America. Needless to say, they almost never mention the part that Murdoch's own companies play in this. Nor do they acknowledge that much of the proliferating junk they so strenuously condemn is served up by entertainment corporations seeking to maximize their profits according to the principles of the unfettered market—the same market that these conservatives so noisily champion. This contradiction within conservatism is rarely examined by the *Times* or other newspapers.

One writer who has probed this issue is Thomas Frank. In his book, *What's the Matter with Kansas?*, he writes, "The truth is that the culture that surrounds us—and that persistently triggers new explosions of backlash outrage—is largely the product of business rationality."

> It is made by writers and actors, who answer to editors and directors and producers, who answer to senior vice presidents and chief executive officers, who answer to Wall Street bankers, who demand profits above all else. From the megamergers of the media giants to the commercial time-outs during the football game to the plots of the Hollywood movies and to the cyberfantasies of *Wired* and *Fast Company* and *Fortune*, we live in a free-market world.... It is because of the market that our TV is such a sharp-tongued insulter of "family values" and such a zealous promoter of every species of social deviance.

Frank does not dwell much on who makes up that market. It no doubt includes many of the same people who express backlash outrage. This contradiction, too, would seem worth exploring. Those who produce toxic products often argue that they're simply giving the market what it wants. Even if one accepts that defense, it's still possible that such fare could have undesirable effects or feed a sense of insecurity and dismay. Last November, the *Times* ran a lively and informative piece on how the ratings of shows like *Desperate Housewives* are as high in conservative red states as in liberal blue ones. The piece quoted experts noting that those who most strenuously denounce salacious programs on TV are often those most drawn to them. Unfortunately, the article did not quote any viewers, nor did it seek to go inside any real communities to see what ordinary Americans might have to say about these shows. (By the way, *Desperate Housewives* was the eleventh-most-watched show among two-to-eleven-year-olds last year.)

Despite that oversight, Frank's account is refreshing, because, unlike many journalists, he takes seriously the anger and frustration that many ordinary Americans feel about the culture around them. His central thesis is that corporate elites have effectively taken the backlash outrage of ordinary people and directed it at liberals, thus helping those elites win electoral office, which they then use to adopt economic policies that further enrich corporations at the expense of these same ordinary people. Whether or not one agrees with this analysis, Frank convincingly shows that it's impossible to grasp the current political dynamic in

America without understanding pop culture and how ordinary Americans view it.

The same is true for the rest of the world. American movies, TV shows, and pop music have conquered foreign lands with far more ease than have American armies. (In *From Beirut to Jerusalem*, Thomas Friedman describes how two journalists traveling by taxicab in Beirut were stopped by a bunch of fierce-looking militiamen. When the militiamen learned that one of the journalists was from the *Dallas Times Herald*, they pointed their guns at him as if to shoot, then demanded to know, "Who shot J.R.?" Breaking into howls of laughter, they let the car pass.) But all those satellite dishes pulling down the signals of Howard Stern and *The Real World* have no doubt generated much reaction and animosity. And what about all those sadistic action pics churned out by Hollywood and avidly marketed abroad? To what degree have they fed the bloodlust of jihadis and suicide bombers? You rarely read about this in our top papers.

In early June, as I was completing this article, the *Times* finally ran a piece that took a serious look at the issue of culture and its impact. Written by Bruce Weber, it described a bitter dispute at a high school in the town of Muhlenberg, Pennsylvania, over *The Buffalo Tree*, a novel set in a juvenile detention center that includes a scene in a communal shower in which an adolescent boy becomes sexually aroused. After a sixteen-year-old student complained at a school board meeting about having to read this, the board voted to ban the book, and by the next morning all classroom copies had been collected and stored in a vault in the principal's office. As Weber noted, Muhlenberg, while conservative politically and with a growing evangelical population, "is not militantly right wing," and "even the more vociferous opponents of the book did not insist it come off the school library shelves." The school board's vote set off a period of "unusual activism," with students circulating petitions, teachers preparing defenses of the book, and letters on both sides appearing in the local paper. The schools' superintendent tried to broker a compromise, but as one teacher observed, "*The Buffalo Tree* isn't coming back anytime soon." Overall, the piece provided a sensitive and insightful look at a knotty cultural issue.

No doubt a thorough search of *Times* coverage in recent years would turn up other stories like this. But they remain rare. Now that the paper has a new culture editor, might we see more of them? Sam Sifton declined to be interviewed for this article, but I did speak with the man who, by all accounts, remains the real power in culture at the *Times*: Frank Rich. Like his mentor Arthur Gelb, who for decades dictated the paper's tastes in the arts, Rich is the *Times*'s culture czar, though he exercises his power with far more discretion. In Rich's weekly columns, he routs the indecency police, roasts right-wing politicians, and flays religious hypocrites, creating the ideological climate in which the culture staff operates. After more than two years on the front page of the Arts & Leisure section, his column in April returned to the op-ed page. Rich himself was assigned a new office on the tenth floor of the *Times*, where the opinion pages are housed, but he will also retain his old office on the fourth floor, where culture roosts, and from which he has played an instrumental part in the remaking of the culture department.

That process began under Howell Raines. On becoming executive editor of the *Times*, Raines had ambitious plans for building its circulation. The goal was to corral more readers, and two of the largest potential pools were affluent readers nationwide and the young. The key to getting both, Raines believed, was improving the *Times*'s "back of the book" sections. In his long, self-aggrandizing retrospective in the *Atlantic* in May 2004, Raines wrote that to get readers between the ages of twenty and forty, "you have to penetrate the worlds of style and popular culture." For national readers, he mentioned those same two subjects plus entertainment and travel as critical. Improving the coverage of these areas, he wrote, would help "to lure national readers who wanted to use the *Times* to experience the New Yorkness of New York—which is to say a point of view that could not be found in their local papers."

Do most *Times* readers really need to know which network delivers the most 18- to 49-year-olds to advertisers?

Among the decisions Raines faced after taking over the paper was naming a new editor for Arts & Leisure. For suggestions, he turned to Frank Rich. Rich, in turn, mentioned Jodi Kantor as someone to watch for the department. The New York editor of *Slate*, Kantor was only twenty-seven, but she had the hip, edgy sensibility that was seen as the route to young readers, and she was hired in March 2003. Before Raines could proceed, Jayson Blair intervened, but Bill Keller, his successor, decided to pursue the process. To prepare a culture plan, Keller appointed a committee that included Rich, Kantor, Adam Moss, Steve Erlanger, and Michael Kimmelman, among others. The blueprint they produced called for restructuring beats, improving coordination between the various sections responsible for culture, and increasing the emphasis on reporting.

"We wanted to beef up our reporting of culture, especially at a time when culture coverage is in decline almost everywhere in journalism," Rich told me. "We've had a huge expansion in our coverage." As the reporting on culture has been strengthened, so has the reporting on its business side. As Rich noted, it's become hard to "separate the coverage of show business from the coverage of the show. There's been a complete changeover in every cultural field. When I began as a theater critic, Broadway shows were produced by rich people like David Merrick and Alexander Cohen. Now Broadway is dominated by Clear Channel and Disney. Look at independent movies—today they're produced by companies like New Line, which is owned by Time Warner, the biggest media company in the world. As big money and large corporations take over the business, that becomes part of the story."

I asked Rich about the idea of doing more reporting from the field about the social impact of culture. He sounded dubious. Such reporting, he said, "has to be done very carefully." He cited the Columbine shootings and the initial reports that the perpetrators were influenced by *The Matrix*. "That turned out not to be true." He went on: "I'm skeptical of determinist correspondences. Michael Medved, the conservative critic, has observed that the generation raised on *Father Knows Best* produced the sixties." Rich cited the case of his own two sons: "All they did in high school was listen to hip hop and watch video games. They saw Quentin Tarantino at a young age. I rarely censored what they did. Now one at the age of twenty-five has just had a book published by a division of *The New York Review of Books*. Another is studying fiction at Harvard and wants to be a novelist." I did not have the presence of mind to suggest that the kids of a renowned cultural critic like Rich might have one or two more cultural advantages over most kids in the country.

But pursuing the point, I asked, Wouldn't the *Times*'s coverage benefit from sending reporters into local communities to talk with parents, teachers, and counselors? "It's all anecdotal," Rich said. "No one seems able to agree on what it all means."

I wondered, though, if reporting on culture and its effects would be any more anecdotal than, say, reporting on class in America, a subject on which the *Times* just published a very extended series, most of it consisting of anecdotes about individuals, backed up by occasional citations from studies and experts. Given those nearly one hundred people on the *Times* culture staff, would it hurt to spare one or two to visit Florida or Kansas or Colorado and report back on the debates over pop culture taking place there? Is it really necessary to run all those stories about the new fall TV lineups? Do most *Times* readers really need to know which network wins the ratings war or delivers the most 18- to 49-year-olds to advertisers? Do they really need to be apprised of the every move of Paris Hilton and Harvey Weinstein? The *Times* does a good job of giving its readers around the country a taste of New York. Isn't it time it gave its New York readers more of a taste of what's going on in the rest of the country?

If it did, the *Times* could help spark a debate about pop culture and its consequences. And that in itself would be healthy. Looming over every discussion of this subject is the threat of censorship. That threat is serious. But contrary to Oliver Stone's fear, the mere discussion of whether some forms of pop culture hurt society does not constitute censorship. Given its vast influence, the *Times*, by covering pop culture more fully, could help get a national discussion going. That, in turn, might give entertainment executives new incentives—apart from FCC fines or congressional intervention—to consider the social effects of what they produce.

MICHAEL MASSING, a contributing editor to *CJR*, is the author of *Now They Tell Us: The American Press and Iraq*.

Reprinted from *Columbia Journalism Review*, July/August 2005, pp. 28–34. Copyright © 2005 by Columbia Journalism Review, Columbia University.

Article 4

Reel to Real: Psychology Goes to the Movies

Grab some popcorn, find a seat, and watch as psychologists uncover the behavioral impact of film.

ERIC JAFFE

One of the first films ever made, *Arrivée d'un train à La Ciotat,* was first shown in France in 1896. The silent, black-and-white, minute-long picture, produced by Louis Lumière, showed a train rushing toward the foreground. As legend has it, when the train started chugging, the audience leapt from their seats and fled the theater.

Apocryphal or not, the era of film had begun, and this new medium's impact on behavior seemed ripe for research. Some 20 years after Lumière's film, a Harvard psychologist named Hugo Munsterberg challenged researchers to figure out the depth of, and reason for, cinema's influence:

"For the first time the psychologist can observe the starting of an entirely new esthetic development, a new form of true beauty in the turmoil of a technical age, created by its very technique and yet more than any other art destined to overcome outer nature by the free and joyful play of the mind," Munsterberg wrote in *The Photoplay: A Psychological Study,* considered by many to be the first important behavioral look at film.

But though the research gauntlet had been thrown down, what followed is what one would expect when looking for artistry in a Pauly Shore flick: nothing. Or, at least, very little, says Stuart Fischoff, founder of the *Journal of Media Psychology,* who in 2003 retired from the psychology department at California State University, Los Angeles. Between 1916, when Munsterberg wrote *The Photoplay,* and the 1950s, perhaps the most influential psychological research on cinema was L. L. Thurstone's 1928 Payne Fund report—a study whose purpose was to indict, not investigate, the role of film on behavior, Fischoff says.

In fact, for much of the 20th century, the psychological study of film was considered "lightweight stuff," says Dolf Zillmann, University of Alabama, one of the field's pioneers. Film study was approached with a Freudian mindset, and few empirical studies took place. But in the past decade or so, such research has experienced a resurgence—the rare sequel that outperforms the original. "There's really a new psychology of film in the making," says Zillmann. Film study from a psychological perspective now takes place in campuses around the country, combining interdisciplinary approaches from several areas, with an increasing focus on the neuroscience of viewer response. Cinematic research also deals with the effectiveness of product placement, the therapeutic role of movies, even the impact that inaccurate portrayals of psychologists can have on the public's attitude toward the profession.

"It's incredibly more sophisticated," says Fischoff of film study. "We're looking at the different dimensions of film experience, at the cognitive component of film, as the human mind mediates what comes out in terms of behavior."

As psychological science has developed, particularly in the cognitive realm, the study of film has progressed beyond a purely psychoanalytical pursuit, says Ira Konigsberg, a Professor Emeritus of Film and Video Studies at the University of Michigan. And it will continue to grow as technology advances—both in terms of creating films and studying them.

"We are in an amazing age of technology, in which the image itself plays a paramount part in shaping the way we think," says Konigsberg, who is editing a new journal in the field, *Projections,* which will publish its first issue this summer. That issue will reflect the full spectrum of interdisciplinary science and cinema: Cognitive psychologist Patrick Hogan will write on the way the mind processes a movie; Norman Holland will discuss the relationship between neuroscience and film; Torben Grodal will touch on the silver screen's emotional impact.

"Film [was] the art form of the 20th century, and maintains a significant hold on our imagination and culture," Konigsberg says. "It offers immense opportunity to understand individual and social psychology."

Under Siege

Zillmann still remembers walking into the living room and finding his son, then six years old, distressed by a brutal fist fight in the film *Gunsmoke.* "He swung his head to me and said, 'Is this real?'" Zillmann recalls. He explained to his son that the fighters were pretending—that their job was to make the brawl appear, but not be, vicious—until the boy felt relieved.

Zillmann has long studied why films arouse certain types of behavioral responses. Decades worth of literature, including a 2003 *Psychological Science in the Public Interest* report, have argued that viewing violent media increases both short- and long-term aggression and violence. But the jury remains out on the impact of violent media, Zillman says, despite arguments for its widespread role in aggressive behavior. Violent media can create aggression, Zillmann says, but it affects certain types of people differently.

"We have committed mistakes by thinking that everybody will be affected [in an equal fashion]" by violent films, he says. "I've been an advocate of stratifying the public. You can't believe all people are equal in the way in which they respond to media violence."

In general, women and sensitive men do not react to violent pictures. Hostile or physically aggressive men, on the other hand, are two subsets of this stratification that do react strongly. To further test the impact of such movies on people with these traits, Zillmann recently collected data on 120 male subjects. Some had scored high on behavioral tests measuring hostility or physical aggression, some had scored low.

Zillmann and his coauthor, James B. Weaver III, played an eight-minute film clip for each subject. Some subjects watched an innocuous scene from *Driving Miss Daisy,* others watched a violent scene from *Falling Down*. Afterward, the subjects took part in a cooperation task: They each had to teach a research confederate to assemble red and green blocks in a certain pattern. (To the film buff, this experiment evokes a scene from *The Royal Tenenbaums,* in which Bill Murray's psychologist character asks the same of his colorblind patient, to hilarious ends.)

The subjects communicated with these learners via video. As a teaching motivator, the subjects had access to a button that, they were told, would apply a painful amount of pressure to the learner's arm. A phony monitor showed how many volts of pressure were being applied, from zero to 10. In fact, the learner was not actually there at all; he had been tape-recorded to finally solve the puzzle with 20 seconds to go, maximizing the potential for teacher frustration—as well as the number of chances to hurt the learner.

Highly hostile subjects behaved more aggressively than low-hostility subjects regardless of which film they watched, Zillmann and Weaver report in an upcoming *Journal of Research in Personality.* But only the subjects who scored high on physical aggression behaved more aggressively after watching the violent clip; those who scored low did not. So, the type of person who is typically high in physical aggressiveness might be particularly susceptible to behavioral changes after watching a violent film.

In addition to a viewer's personality, the type of violence shown on-screen makes a behavioral difference, Zillmann argues. Old West films are considered minimally violent by today's standards. And horror films are usually perceived as more funny than aggressive (in fact, they can even prompt romance under the "snuggle theory," when a couple pretends to be scared).

It's the gratuitous but realistic films that have the greatest affect on aggressive behavior, those of Jean-Claude Van Damme, Steven Seagal, and, more recently, Jet Li. And with the line between reality and fiction becoming blurrier—with "based on a true story" used to describe many a matinee and ordinary people producing real-time films on devices like camcorders and cell phones—the violence has a potentially stronger effect.

"You can discount [a film] and initiate getting rid of a strong emotion by discounting reality," Zillmann says. "But if it's based on reality, you cannot discount it."

The importance of being able to discount reality has become clearer with research by neuroscientist Joseph LeDoux of Columbia University. LeDoux has found that violent images elicit an immediate response in the amygdala, the brain's emotional hub, before the information being processed reaches the cognitive center. The more realistic a film, says Zillmann, the harder it is for this cognitive center to reason with the amygdala's natural response.

"If you can't discount [reality], you're aroused longer," Zillmann says. "This time discrepancy is important in new film research. . . . This is the new psychology; it's neuropsychology, in a way."

The Game

The mind games played by violent movies can at least be rationalized as part of a film's greater aesthetic value (or, in the case of Van Damme and Seagal, as necessary plot progression). But other, perhaps equally powerful, head games are being played behind the scenes by movie advertisers.

Such games began in 1982, when Reese's Pieces made its commercial debut during the film *ET*. Since that time, product placement in movies has become far more pervasive. Sometimes, as in *Lethal Weapon II,* entire scenes are written around the chance to grab ad dollars from a vendor (in that case, Subway restaurants). But modern audiences are savvy enough to spot a blatant marketing ploy; it's the subtler references—the ones, like Reese's Pieces, that are embedded in the plot—that stand a chance of having a behavioral impact.

When people are exposed to ads during movies, "they don't have a chance to put up sensors, their shields, it gets through," says Fischoff. "It's not coming in the same door as advertisers typically have to come through—it's the front door, and people are less armed than they would be in a commercial."

Still, evidence has shown that people don't simply rush out and purchase whatever product appears in a film. In a recent test of the effectiveness of subliminal product placement, psychologist Johan Karremans of Radboud University Nijmegen in the Netherlands showed some 60 subjects a screen that showed slides of random letters. Half of the subjects occasionally saw a brief blip displaying "Lipton Ice." Half the subjects saw a blip with a nonsense word. None of the subjects realized that "Lipton Ice" or the nonsense word had ever appeared on the screen.

Flashing "Lipton Ice" did increase a subject's likelihood of choosing that drink over a different drink, but only if that subject had been thirsty to begin with, Karremans and his

> **Psychologists' Favorite Films**
>
> Stuart Fischoff: *Random Harvest*. "It's a fantastic, romantic, psychological drama." But it's not the best film ever made, he says. That distinction goes to *The Godfather* and *The Godfather Part II*.
>
> Birgit Wolz: *Whale Rider*. "It's about a little girl in the Pacific, who convinces her grandfather to become the leader of the tribe there."
>
> Lindsay M. Orchowski: All of the *Rocky* movies. "Which has nothing to do with psychotherapy."
>
> John Flowers: *Forbidden Games*. "That floored me. Probably because of when I saw it [in the 1950s]." (The film is about World War II.)
>
> Dolf Zillmann: "I don't have a favorite. I enjoy anything."

colleagues report in the November *Journal of Experimental Social Psychology*.

This research reflects other social-cognitive findings by psychologists like APS Fellows and Charter Members John Bargh and Bob Zajonc, Karremans says. But the effectiveness of such subliminal advertising in real-life scenarios is debatable. "These stimuli should be goal-relevant," Karremans says. "Subliminally presenting an ad [for Apple computers] would probably not affect a person to buy a Macintosh if the person does not even want to buy a computer."

Good Will (Toward Psychologists) Hunting

Early in the film *Good Will Hunting*, the character Will, played by Matt Damon, visits psychotherapist Sean Maguire, played by Robin Williams. Will notices a painting on Sean's wall of a solitary man at sea struggling to row his boat amid a tempest. It turns out that Sean painted the picture. To Will, the picture suggests something haunting in Sean's past. "Maybe you married the wrong woman," Will says. Sean, whose wife we'll later learn died after a long bout with cancer, thrusts Will against the wall by the throat and threatens to "end" him should such a comment be repeated.

To APS Charter Member John V. Flowers, Chapman University, Williams' portrayal of a mental health professional is extremely damaging to the public's understanding of psychological therapy. Flowers has written a historical reference book on films depicting psychologists dating back to 1899. Since that time, less than a quarter of some thousand films featuring psychologists portray them in a positive light, he says. The remainder of the films can't be taken seriously, he thought; otherwise, "the profession would be clobbered." So Flowers began one of the only empirical studies to investigate which types of portrayals cause the most harm to psychology's reputation.

Flowers split all negative portrayals into three categories: evil or manipulative, such as the nurse in *One Flew Over the Cuckoo's Nest*; goofy, as in *What About Bob*; and flawed or unethical, like Sean Maguire. Flowers measured subjects' skin conductance, respiration, and heart rate as they viewed clips of one of these three films. After a single viewing, subjects respond greatly to evil portrayals. Each time the same clip is repeated, however, this response softens. But flawed portrayals elicit a strong response even after five viewings, says Flowers, who has tested more than 100 subjects for each type of portrayal. "We get more response from flawed than evil," he says, "and it does not die out."

Such depictions of psychologists might have a negative influence on therapy, says Lindsay M. Orchowski, who is working on her doctoral degree at Ohio University's psychology department. Orchowski and her colleagues reviewed the literature of psychologist portrayal in the October 2006 *Professional Psychology: Research and Practice*. They concluded that, in the emotional sea of viewer perception, psychologists are lonely boat-rowers struggling against the elements.

"The general public is not well socialized to know what psychotherapy's like," Orchowski says, adding that many students she helps counsel still walk in and wonder where the couch is. "The amount [of psychologists in films] is increasing, and we want to make sure those portrayals out there are valid."

But while some films might hinder psychological therapy, Birgit Wolz, a clinical practitioner in Oakland, has harnessed the power of film to help counsel her clients. Wolz' method, called cinema therapy, uses movies to familiarize patients with emotional problems they have a hard time identifying in themselves but can spot more easily in film characters.

The method has yet to receive adequate empirical testing, admits Wolz, but, when used as an adjunct, it can enhance traditional therapeutic methods. "There's a lot of talk about mirror neurons," says Wolz. "The whole idea is that we experience things internally, subjectively, if we experience them for real. But the emotional response can be exactly the same in real life as in reel life."

Zillmann, who says he has not seen convincing data of cinema therapy, takes a different approach to capturing the psychological benefits of film. Instead of trying to cure psychological illnesses with movies, he would rather simply change a person's mood. Such mood-management studies have shown that movies can help a person escape from a bad mood, he says. This work might not help a person suffering from serious mental or emotional conditions, but it does get back to the core of the power of film.

"If you can change people's mood by film exposure in a desirable direction, then you can say this is the therapeutic effect, but you don't talk about healing illnesses," he says. "You talk about making people feel better. And that's what entertainment is for."

ERIC JAFFE is an *Observer* contributor and Associate Web Editor of *Smithsonian* magazine.

Are Newspapers Doomed?

JOSEPH EPSTEIN

"Clearly," said Adam to Eve as they departed the Garden of Eden, "we're living in an age of transition." A joke, of course—but also not quite a joke, because when has the history of the world been anything other than one damned transition after another? Yet sometimes, in certain realms, transitions seem to stand out with utter distinctiveness, and this seems to be the case with the fortune of printed newspapers at the present moment. As a medium and as an institution, the newspaper is going through an age of transition *in excelsis*, and nobody can confidently say how it will end or what will come next.

To begin with familiar facts, statistics on readership have been pointing downward, significantly downward, for some time now. Four-fifths of Americans once read newspapers; today, apparently fewer than half do. Among adults, in the decade 1990–2000, daily readership fell from 52.6 percent to 37.5 percent. Among the young, things are much worse: in one study, only 19 percent of those between the ages of eighteen and thirty-four reported consulting a daily paper, and only 9 percent trusted the information purveyed there; a mere 8 percent found newspapers helpful, while 4 percent thought them entertaining.

From 1999 to 2004, according to the Newspaper Association of America, general circulation dropped by another 1.3 million. Reflecting both that fact and the ferocious competition for classified ads from free online bulletin boards like craigslist.org, advertising revenue has been stagnant at best, while printing and productions costs have gone remorselessly upward. As a result, the New York Times Company has cut some 700 jobs from its various papers. The *Baltimore Sun*, owned by the *Chicago Tribune*, is closing down its five international bureaus. Second papers in many cities have locked their doors.

This bleeding phenomenon is not restricted to the United States, and no bets should be placed on the likely success of steps taken by papers to stanch the flow. *The Wall Street Journal*, in an effort to save money on production costs, is trimming the width of its pages, from 15 to 12 inches. In England, the once venerable *Guardian*, in a mad scramble to retain its older readers and find younger ones, has radically redesigned itself by becoming smaller. London's *Independent* has gone tabloid, and so has the once revered *Times*, its publisher preferring the euphemism "compact."

For those of us who grew up with newspapers in our daily regimen, sometimes with not one but two newspapers in our homes, it is all a bit difficult to take in. As early as 1831, Alexis de Tocqueville noted that even frontier families in upper Michigan had a weekly paper delivered. A.J. Liebling, the *New Yorker's* writer on the press, used to say that he judged any new city he visited by the taste of its water and the quality of its newspapers.

The paper to which you subscribed, or that your father brought home from work, told a good deal about your family: its social class, its level of education, its politics. Among the five major dailies in the Chicago of my early boyhood, my father preferred the *Daily News*, an afternoon paper reputed to have excellent foreign correspondents. Democratic in its general political affiliation, though not aggressively so, the *Daily News* was considered the intelligent Chicagoan's paper.

My father certainly took it seriously. I remember asking him in 1952, as a boy of fifteen, about whom he intended to vote for in the presidential election between Dwight Eisenhower and Adlai Stevenson. "I'm not sure," he said. "I think I'll wait to see which way Lippmann is going."

The degree of respect then accorded the syndicated columnist Walter Lippmann is hard to imagine in our own time. In good part, his cachet derived from his readers' belief not only in his intelligence but in his impartiality. Lippmann, it was thought, cared about what was best for the country; he wasn't already lined up; you couldn't be certain which way he would go.

Of the two candidates in 1952, Stevenson, the intellectually cultivated Democrat, was without a doubt the man Lippmann would have preferred to have lunch with. But in the end he went for Eisenhower—his reason being, as I recall, that the country needed a strong leader with a large majority behind him, a man who, among other things, could face down the obstreperous Red-baiting of Senator Joseph McCarthy. My father, a lifelong Democrat, followed Lippmann and crossed over to vote for Eisenhower.

My father took his paper seriously in another way, too. He read it after dinner and ingested it, like that dinner, slowly, treating it as a kind of second dessert: something at once nutritive and entertaining. He was in no great hurry to finish.

Today, his son reads no Chicago newspaper whatsoever. A serial killer could be living in my apartment building, and I would be unaware of it until informed by my neighbors. As for the power of the press to shape and even change my mind, I am in the condition of George Santayana, who wrote to his sister in 1915 that he was too old to "be influenced by newspaper argument. When I read them I form perhaps a new opinion of the newspaper but seldom a new opinion on the subject discussed."

I do subscribe to the *New York Times*, which I read without a scintilla of glee. I feel I need it, chiefly to discover who in my cultural world has died, or been honored (probably unjustly), or has turned out some new piece of work that I ought to be aware of. I rarely give the daily *Times* more than a half-hour, if that. I begin with the obituaries. Next, I check the op-ed page, mostly to see if anyone has hit upon a novel way of denigrating President Bush; the answer is invariably no, though they seem never to tire of trying. I glimpse the letters to the editor in hopes of finding someone after my own heart. I almost never read the editorials, following the advice of the journalist Jack Germond who once compared the writing of a newspaper editorial to wetting oneself in a dark-blue serge suit: "It gives you a nice warm feeling, but nobody notices."

The arts section, which in the *Times* is increasingly less about the arts and more about television, rock 'n' roll, and celebrity, does not detain me long. Sports is another matter, for I do have the sports disease in a chronic and soon to be terminal stage; I run my eyes over these pages, turning in spring, summer, and fall to see who is pitching in that day's Cubs and White Sox games. And I always check the business section, where some of the better writing in the *Times* appears and where the reporting, because so much is at stake, tends to be more trustworthy.

Finally—quickly, very quickly—I run through the so-called hard news, taking in most of it at the headline level. I seem able to sleep perfectly soundly these days without knowing the names of the current presidents or prime ministers of Peru, India, Japan, and Poland. For the rest, the point of view that permeates the news coverage in the *Times* is by now so yawningly predictable that I spare myself the effort of absorbing the facts that seem to serve as so much tedious filler.

A m I typical in my casual disregard? I suspect so. Everyone agrees that print newspapers are in trouble today, and almost everyone agrees on the reasons. Foremost among them is the vast improvement in the technology of delivering information, which has combined in lethal ways with a serious change in the national temperament.

The technological change has to do with the increase in the number of television cable channels and the astonishing amount of news floating around in cyberspace. As Richard A. Posner has written, "The public's consumption of news and opinion used to be like sucking on a straw; now it's like being sprayed by a fire hose."

The temperamental change has to do with the national attention span. The critic Walter Benjamin said, as long ago as the 1930's, that the chief emotion generated by reading the newspapers is impatience. His remark is all the more pertinent today, when the very definition of what constitutes important information is up for grabs. More and more, in a shift that cuts across age, social class, and even educational lines, important information means information that matters to *me*, now.

And this is where the two changes intersect. Not only are we acquiring our information from new places but we are taking it pretty much on our own terms. The magazine *Wired* recently defined the word "egocasting" as "the consumption of on-demand music, movies, television, and other media that cater to individual and not mass-market tastes." The news, too, is now getting to be on-demand.

Instead of beginning their day with coffee and the newspaper, there to read what editors have selected for their enlightenment, people, and young people in particular, wait for a free moment to go online. No longer need they wade through thickets of stories and features of no interest to them, and least of all need they do so on the websites of newspapers, where the owners are hoping to regain the readers lost to print. Instead, they go to more specialized purveyors of information, including instant-messaging providers, targeted news sites, blogs, and online "zines."

Much cogitation has been devoted to the question of young people's lack of interest in traditional news. According to one theory, which is by now an entrenched cliché, the young, having grown up with television and computers as their constant companions, are "visual-minded," and hence averse to print. Another theory holds that young people do not feel themselves implicated in the larger world; for them, news of that world isn't where the action is. A more flattering corollary of this is that grown-up journalism strikes the young as hopelessly out of date. All that solemn good-guy/bad-guy reporting, the taking seriously of *opéra-bouffe* characters like Jesse Jackson or Al Gore or Tom DeLay, the false complexity of "in-depth" television reporting à la *60 Minutes*—this, for them, is so much hot air. They prefer to watch Jon Stewart's *The Daily Show* on the Comedy Central cable channel, where traditional news is mocked and pilloried as obvious nonsense.

Whatever the validity of this theorizing, it is also beside the point. For as the grim statistics confirm, the young are hardly alone in turning away from newspapers. Nor are they alone responsible for the dizzying growth of the so-called blogosphere, said to be increasing by 70,000 sites a day (according to the search portal technorati.com). In the first half of this year alone, the number of new blogs grew from 7.8 to 14.2 million. And if the numbers are dizzying, the sheer amount of information floating around is enough to give a person a serious case of Newsheimers.

Astonishing results are reported when news is passed from one blog to another: scores if not hundreds of thousands of hits, and, on sites that post readers' reactions, responses that can often be more impressive in research and reasoning than anything likely to turn up in print. Newspaper journalists themselves often get their stories from blogs, and bloggers have been extremely useful in verifying or refuting the erroneous reportage of mainstream journalists. The only place to get a reasonably straight account of news about Israel and the Palestinians, according to Stephanie Gutmann, author of *The Other War: Israelis, Palestinians, and the Struggle for Media Supremacy*, is in the blogosphere.

The trouble with blogs and Internet news sites, it has been said, is that they merely reinforce the reader's already established interests and views, thereby contributing to our much-lamented national polarization of opinion. A newspaper, by contrast, at least compels one to acknowledge the existence of other subjects and issues, and reading it can alert one to affecting or important matters that one would never encounter if left to one's own devices, and in particular to that primary device of our day, the computer. Whether or not that is so, the argument has already been won, and not by the papers.

Another argument appears to have been won, too, and again to the detriment of the papers. This is the argument over politics, which the newspapers brought upon themselves and which, in my view, they richly deserved to lose.

One could put together an impressive little anthology of utterances by famous Americans on the transcendent importance of the press as a guardian watchdog of the state. Perhaps the most emphatic was that of Thomas Jefferson, who held that freedom of the press, right up there with freedom of religion and freedom of the person under the rights of habeas corpus and trial by jury, was among "the principles [that] form the bright constellation which has gone before us, and guided our steps through an age of revolution and reformation." Even today, not many people would disagree with this in theory; but like the character in a Tom Stoppard play, many would add: "I'm with you on the free press. It's the damned newspapers I can't stand."

The self-proclaimed goal of newsmen used to be to report, in a clear and factual way, on the important events of the day, on subjects of greater or lesser parochialism. It is no longer so. Here is Dan Rather, quoting with approval someone he does not name who defines news as "what somebody doesn't want you to know. All the rest is advertising."

"What somebody doesn't want you to know"—it would be hard to come up with a more concise definition of the target of the "investigative journalism" that has been the pride of the nation's newspapers for the past three decades. Bob Woodward, Carl Bernstein, Seymour Hersh, and many others have built their reputations on telling us things that Presidents and Senators and generals and CEO's have not wanted us to know.

Besides making for a strictly adversarial relationship between government and the press, there is no denying that investigative journalism, whatever (very mixed) accomplishments it can claim to its credit, has put in place among us a tone and temper of agitation and paranoia. Every day, we are asked to regard the people we elect to office as, essentially, our enemies—thieves, thugs, and megalomaniacs whose vicious secret deeds it is the chief function of the press to uncover and whose persons to bring down in a glare of publicity.

All this might have been to the good if what the journalists discovered were invariably true—and if the nature and the implications of that truth were left for others to puzzle out. Frequently, neither has been the case.

Much of contemporary journalism functions through leaks—information passed to journalists by unidentified individuals telling those things that someone supposedly doesn't want us to know. Since these sources cannot be checked or cross-examined, readers are in no position to assess the leakers' motives for leaking, let alone the agenda of the journalists who rely on them. To state the obvious: a journalist fervently against the U.S. presence in Iraq is unlikely to pursue leaks providing evidence that the war has been going reasonably well.

Administrations have of course used leaks for their own purposes, and leaks have also become a time-tested method for playing out intramural government disputes. Thus, it is widely and no doubt correctly believed that forces at the CIA and in the State Department have leaked information to the *New York Times* and the *Washington Post* to weaken positions taken by the White House they serve, thereby availing themselves of a mechanism of sabotage from within. But this, too, is not part of the truth we are likely to learn from investigative journalists, who not only purvey slanted information as if it were simply true but then take it upon themselves to try, judge, and condemn those they have designated as political enemies. So glaring has this problem become that the *Times*, beginning in June, felt compelled to introduce a new policy, designed, in the words of its ombudsman, to make "the use of anonymous sources the 'exception' rather than 'routine.'"

No wonder, then, that the prestige of mainstream journalism, which reached perhaps an all-time high in the early 1970's at the time of Watergate, has now badly slipped. According to most studies of the question, journalists tend more and more to be regarded by Americans as unaccountable kibitzers whose self-appointed job is to spread dissension, increase pressure on everyone, make trouble—and preach the gospel of present-day liberalism. Aiding this deserved fall in reputation has been a series of well-publicized scandals like the rise and fall of the reporter Jayson Blair at the *New York Times*.

The politicization of contemporary journalists surely has a lot to do with the fact that almost all of them today are university-trained. In *Newspaper Days*, H.L. Mencken recounts that in 1898, at the age of eighteen, he had a choice of going to college, there to be taught by German professors and on weekends to sit in a raccoon coat watching football games, or of getting a job on a newspaper, which would allow him to zip off to fires, whorehouse raids, executions, and other such festivities. As Mencken observes, it was no contest.

Most contemporary journalists, by contrast, attend schools of journalism or study the humanities and social sciences. Here the reigning politics are liberal, and along with their degrees, and their sense of enlightened virtue, they emerge with locked-in political views. According to Jim A. Kuypers in *Press Bias and Politics*, 76 percent of journalists who admit to having a politics describe themselves as liberal. The consequences are predictable: even as they employ their politics to tilt their stories, such journalists sincerely believe they are (a) merely telling the truth and (b) doing good in the world.

Pre-university-educated journalists did not, I suspect, feel that the papers they worked for existed as vehicles through which to advance their own political ideas. Some among them might have hated corruption, or the standard lies told by politicians; from time to time they might even have felt a stab of idealism or sentimentality. But they subsisted chiefly on cynicism, heavy boozing, and an admiration for craft. They did not treat the news—and editors of that day would not have permitted them to treat the news—as a trampoline of which to bounce their own tendentious politics.

To the degree that papers like the *New York Times*, the *Washington Post*, and the *Los Angeles Times* have contributed to the political polarization of the country, they much deserve their fate of being taken less and less seriously by fewer and fewer people. One can say this even while acknowledging that the cure, in the form of on-demand news, can sometimes seem as bad as the disease, tending often only to confirm users, whether liberal or conservative or anything else, in the opinions they already hold. But at least the curious or the bored can, at a click, turn elsewhere on the Internet for variety or relief—which is more than can be said for newspaper readers.

Nor, in a dumbed-down world, do our papers of record offer an oasis of taste. There were always a large number of newspapers in America whose sole standard was scandal and entertainment. (The crossword puzzle first appeared in Joseph Pulitzer's *New York World*.) But there were also some that were dedicated to bringing their readers up to a high or at least a middling mark. Among these were the *New York Times*, the *St. Louis Post-Dispatch*, the *Washington Post*, the *Milwaukee Journal*, the *Wall Street Journal*, the now long defunct *New York Herald-Tribune*, and the *Chicago Daily News*.

These newspapers did not mind telling readers what they felt they ought to know, even at the risk of boring the pajamas off them. The *Times*, for instance, used to run the full text of important political speeches, which could sometimes fill two full pages of photograph-less type. But now that the college-educated are writing for the college-educated, neither party seems to care. And with circulation numbers dwindling and the strategy in place of whoring after the uninterested young, anything goes.

What used to be considered the serious press in America has become increasingly frivolous. The scandal-and-entertainment aspect more and more replaces what once used to be called "hard news." In this, the serious papers would seem to be imitating the one undisputed print success of recent decades, *USA Today*, whose guiding principle has been to make things brief, fast-paced, and entertaining. Or, more hopelessly still, they are imitating television talk shows or the Internet itself, often mindlessly copying some of their dopier and more destructive innovations.

The editor of the *London Independent* has talked of creating, in place of a newspaper, a "viewspaper," one that can be viewed like a television or a computer. The *Los Angeles Times* has made efforts to turn itself interactive, including by allowing website readers to change the paper's editorials to reflect their own views (only to give up on this initiative when readers posted pornography on the page). In his technology column for the *New York Times*, David Carr speaks of newspapers needing "a podcast moment," by which I take him to mean that the printed press must come up with a self-selecting format for presenting on-demand news akin to the way the iPod presents a listener's favorite programming exactly as and when he wants it.

In our multitasking nation, we already read during television commercials, talk on the cell-phone while driving, listen to music while working on the computer, and much else besides. Some in the press seem in their panic to think that the worst problem they face is that you cannot do other things while reading a newspaper except smoke, which in most places is outlawed anyway. Their problems go much deeper.

In a speech given this past April to the American Society of Newspaper Editors, the international publisher Rupert Murdoch catalogued the drastic diminution of readership for the traditional press and then went on to rally the troops by telling them that they must do better. Not different, but better: going deeper in their coverage, listening more intently to the desires of their readers, assimilating and where possible imitating the digital culture so popular among the young. A man immensely successful and usually well anchored in reality, Murdoch here sounded distressingly like a man without a plan.

Not that I have one of my own. Best to study history, it is said, because the present is too complicated and no one knows anything about the future. The time of transition we are currently going through, with the interest in traditional newspapers beginning to fade and news on the computer still a vast confusion, can be likened to a great city banishing horses from its streets before anyone has yet perfected the automobile.

Nevertheless, if I had to prophesy, my guess would be that newspapers will hobble along, getting ever more desperate and ever more vulgar. More of them will attempt the complicated mental acrobatic of further dumbing down while straining to keep up, relentlessly exerting themselves to sustain the mighty cataract of inessential information that threatens to drown us all. Those of us who grew up with newspapers will continue to read them, with ever less trust and interest, while younger readers, soon enough grown into middle age, will ignore them.

My own preference would be for a few serious newspapers to take the high road: to smarten up instead of dumbing down, to honor the principles of integrity and impartiality in their coverage, and to become institutions that even those who disagreed with them would have to respect for the reasoned cogency of their editorial positions. I imagine such papers directed by editors who could choose for me—as neither the Internet nor I on my own can do—the serious issues, questions, and problems of the day and, with the aid of intelligence born of concern, give each the emphasis it deserves.

In all likelihood a newspaper taking this route would go under; but at least it would do so in a cloud of glory, guns blazing. And at least its loss would be a genuine subtraction. About our newspapers as they now stand, little more can be said in their favor than that they do not require batteries to operate, you can swat flies with them, and they can still be used to wrap fish.

JOSEPH EPSTEIN contributed *"Forgetting Edmund Wilson"* to last month's COMMENTARY. His new book, *Friendship, An Exposé,* will be published by Houghton Mifflin in July.

Reprinted from *Commentary,* January 2006, by permission of Commentary and Joseph Epstein. Copyright © 2006 by Commentary, Inc. All rights reserved.

Article 6

Research on the Effects of Media Violence

Whether or not exposure to media violence causes increased levels of aggression and violence in young people is the perennial question of media effects research. Some experts, like University of Michigan professor L. Rowell Huesmann, argue that fifty years of evidence show "that exposure to media violence causes children to behave more aggressively and affects them as adults years later." Others, like Jonathan Freedman of the University of Toronto, maintain that "the scientific evidence simply does not show that watching violence either produces violence in people, or desensitizes them to it."

Many Studies, Many Conclusions

Andrea Martinez at the University of Ottawa conducted a comprehensive review of the scientific literature for the Canadian Radio-television and Telecommunications Commission (CRTC) in 1994. She concluded that the lack of consensus about media effects reflects three "grey areas" or constraints contained in the research itself.

First, media violence is notoriously hard to define and measure. Some experts who track violence in television programming, such as George Gerbner of Temple University, define violence as the act (or threat) of injuring or killing someone, independent of the method used or the surrounding context. Accordingly, Gerber includes cartoon violence in his data-set. But others, such as University of Laval professors Guy Paquette and Jacques de Guise, specifically exclude cartoon violence from their research because of its comical and unrealistic presentation.

Second, researchers disagree over the type of relationship the data supports. Some argue that exposure to media violence causes aggression. Others say that the two are associated, but that there is no causal connection. (That both, for instance, may be caused by some third factor.) And others say the data supports the conclusion that there is no relationship between the two at all.

Third, even those who agree that there is a connection between media violence and aggression disagree about how the one effects the other. Some say that the mechanism is a psychological one, rooted in the ways we learn. For example, Huesmann argues that children develop "cognitive scripts" that guide their own behaviour by imitating the actions of media heroes. As they watch violent shows, children learn to internalize scripts that use violence as an appropriate method of problem-solving.

Other researchers argue that it is the physiological effects of media violence that cause aggressive behaviour. Exposure to violent imagery is linked to increased heart rate, faster respiration and higher blood pressure. Some think that this simulated "fight-or-flight" response predisposes people to act aggressively in the real world. Still others focus on the ways in which media violence primes or cues pre-existing aggressive thoughts and feelings. They argue that an individual's desire to strike out is justified by media images in which both the hero and the villain use violence to seek revenge, often without consequences.

In her final report to the CRTC, Martinez concluded that most studies support "a positive, though weak, relation between exposure to television violence and aggressive behaviour." Although that relationship cannot be "confirmed systematically," she agrees with Dutch researcher Tom Van der Voot who argues that it would be illogical to conclude that "a phenomenon does not exist simply because it is found at times not to occur, or only to occur under certain circumstances."

What the Researchers Are Saying

The lack of consensus about the relationship between media violence and real-world aggression has not impeded ongoing research. Here's a sampling of conclusions drawn to date, from the various research strands:

> Research strand: Children who consume high levels of media violence are more likely to be aggressive in the real world.

In 1956, researchers took to the laboratory to compare the behaviour of 24 children watching TV. Half watched a violent episode of the cartoon *Woody Woodpecker,* and the other 12 watched the non-violent cartoon *The Little Red Hen.* During play afterwards, the researchers observed that the children who watched the violent cartoon were much more likely to hit other children and break toys.

Article 6. Research on the Effects of Media Violence

Six years later, in 1963, professors A. Badura, D. Ross and S.A. Ross studied the effect of exposure to real-world violence, television violence, and cartoon violence. They divided 100 pre-school children into four groups. The first group watched a real person shout insults at an inflatable doll while hitting it with a mallet. The second group watched the incident on television. The third watched a cartoon version of the same scene, and the fourth watched nothing.

When all the children were later exposed to a frustrating situation, the first three groups responded with more aggression than the control group. The children who watched the incident on television were just as aggressive as those who had watched the real person use the mallet; and both were more aggressive than those who had only watched the cartoon.

Over the years, laboratory experiments such as these have consistently shown that exposure to violence is associated with increased heartbeat, blood pressure and respiration rate, and a greater willingness to administer electric shocks to inflict pain or punishment on others. However, this line of enquiry has been criticized because of its focus on short term results and the artificial nature of the viewing environment.

Other scientists have sought to establish a connection between media violence and aggression outside the laboratory. For example, a number of surveys indicate that children and young people who report a preference for violent entertainment also score higher on aggression indexes than those who watch less violent shows. L. Rowell Huesmann reviewed studies conducted in Australia, Finland, Poland, Israel, Netherlands and the United States. He reports, "the child most likely to be aggressive would be the one who (a) watches violent television programs most of the time, (b) believes that these shows portray life just as it is, [and] (c) identifies strongly with the aggressive characters in the shows."

A study conducted by the Kaiser Family Foundation in 2003 found that nearly half (47 per cent) of parents with children between the ages of 4 and 6 report that their children have imitated aggressive behaviours from TV. However, it is interesting to note that children are more likely to mimic positive behaviours—87 per cent of kids do so.

Recent research is exploring the effect of new media on children's behaviour. Craig Anderson and Brad Bushman of Iowa State University reviewed dozens of studies of video gamers. In 2001, they reported that children and young people who play violent video games, even for short periods, are more likely to behave aggressively in the real world; and that both aggressive and non-aggressive children are negatively affected by playing.

In 2003, Craig Anderson and Iowa State University colleague Nicholas Carnagey and Janie Eubanks of the Texas Department of Human Services reported that violent music lyrics increased aggressive thoughts and hostile feelings among 500 college students. They concluded, "There are now good theoretical and empirical reasons to expect effects of music lyrics on aggressive behavior to be similar to the well-studied effects of exposure to TV and movie violence and the more recent research efforts on violent video games."

Research Strand: Children who watch high levels of media violence are at increased risk of aggressive behaviour as adults.

In 1960, University of Michigan Professor Leonard Eron studied 856 grade three students living in a semi-rural community in Columbia County, New York, and found that the children who watched violent television at home behaved more aggressively in school. Eron wanted to track the effect of this exposure over the years, so he revisited Columbia County in 1971, when the children who participated in the 1960 study were 19 years of age. He found that boys who watched violent TV when they were eight were more likely to get in trouble with the law as teenagers.

When Eron and Huesmann returned to Columbia County in 1982, the subjects were 30 years old. They reported that those participants who had watched more violent TV as eight-year-olds were more likely, as adults, to be convicted of serious crimes, to use violence to discipline their children, and to treat their spouses aggressively.

Professor Monroe Lefkowitz published similar findings in 1971. Lefkowitz interviewed a group of eight-year-olds and found that the boys who watched more violent TV were more likely to act aggressively in the real world. When he interviewed the same boys ten years later, he found that the more violence a boy watched at eight, the more aggressively he would act at age eighteen.

Columbia University professor Jeffrey Johnson has found that the effect is not limited to violent shows. Johnson tracked 707 families in upstate New York for 17 years, starting in 1975. In 2002, Johnson reported that children who watched one to three hours of television each day when they were 14 to 16 years old were 60 per cent more likely to be involved in assaults and fights as adults than those who watched less TV.

Kansas State University professor John Murray concludes, "The most plausible interpretation of this pattern of correlations is that early preference for violent television programming and other media is one factor in the production of aggressive and antisocial behavior when the young boy becomes a young man."

However, this line of research has attracted a great deal of controversy. Pulitzer Prize-winning author Richard Rhodes has attacked Eron's work, arguing that his conclusions are based on an insignificant amount of data. Rhodes claims that Eron had information about the amount of TV viewed in 1960 for only 3 of the 24 men who committed violent crimes as adults years later. Rhodes concludes that Eron's work is "poorly conceived, scientifically inadequate, biased and sloppy if not actually fraudulent research."

Guy Cumberbatch, head of the Communications Research Group, a U.K. social policy think tank, has equally harsh words for Johnson's study. Cumberbatch claims Johnson's group of 88 under-one-hour TV watchers is "so small, it's aberrant." And, as journalist Ben Shouse points out, other critics say that Johnson's study "can't rule out the possibility that television is just a marker for some unmeasured environmental or psychological influence on both aggression and TV habits."

Research Strand: The introduction of television into a community leads to an increase in violent behaviour.

Researchers have also pursued the link between media violence and real life aggression by examining communities before and after the introduction of television. In the mid 1970s, University of British Columbia professor Tannis McBeth Williams studied a remote village in British Columbia both before and after television was introduced. She found that two years after TV arrived, violent incidents had increased by 160 per cent.

Researchers Gary Granzberg and Jack Steinbring studied three Cree communities in northern Manitoba during the 1970s and early 1980s. They found that four years after television was introduced into one of the communities, the incidence of fist fights and black eyes among the children had increased significantly. Interestingly, several days after an episode of *Happy Days* aired, in which one character joined a gang called the Red Demons, children in the community created rival gangs, called the Red Demons and the Green Demons, and the conflict between the two seriously disrupted the local school.

University of Washington Professor Brandon Centerwall noted that the sharp increase in the murder rate in North America in 1955 occurred eight years after television sets began to enter North American homes. To test his hypothesis that the two were related, he examined the murder rate in South Africa where, prior to 1975, television was banned by the government. He found that twelve years after the ban was lifted, murder rates skyrocketed.

University of Toronto Professor Jonathan Freedman has criticized this line of research. He points out that Japanese television has some of the most violent imagery in the world, and yet Japan has a much lower murder rate than other countries, including Canada and the United States, which have comparatively less violence on TV.

Research Strand: Media violence stimulates fear in some children.

A number of studies have reported that watching media violence frightens young children, and that the effects of this may be long lasting.

In 1998, Professors Singer, Slovak, Frierson and York surveyed 2,000 Ohio students in grades three through eight. They report that the incidences of psychological trauma (including anxiety, depression and post-traumatic stress) increased in proportion to the number of hours of television watched each day.

A 1999 survey of 500 Rhode Island parents led by Brown University professor Judith Owens revealed that the presence of a television in a child's bedroom makes it more likely that the child will suffer from sleep disturbances. Nine per cent of all the parents surveyed reported that their children have nightmares because of a television show at least once a week.

Tom Van der Voort studied 314 children aged nine through twelve in 1986. He found that although children can easily distinguish cartoons, westerns and spy thrillers from reality, they often confuse realistic programmes with the real world. When they are unable to integrate the violence in these shows because they can't follow the plot, they are much more likely to become anxious. This is particularly problematic because the children reported that they prefer realistic programmes, which they equate with fun and excitement. And, as Jacques de Guise reported in 2002, the younger the child, the less likely he or she will be able to identify violent content as violence.

In 1999, Professors Joanne Cantor and K. Harrison studied 138 university students, and found that memories of frightening media images continued to disturb a significant number of participants years later. Over 90 per cent reported they continued to experience fright effects from images they viewed as children, ranging from sleep disturbances to steadfast avoidance of certain situations.

Research Strand: Media violence desensitizes people to real violence.

A number of studies in the 1970's showed that people who are repeatedly exposed to media violence tend to be less disturbed when they witness real world violence, and have less sympathy for its victims. For example, Professors V.B. Cline, R.G. Croft, and S. Courrier studied young boys over a two-year period. In 1973, they reported that boys who watch more than 25 hours of television per week are significantly less likely to be aroused by real world violence than those boys who watch 4 hours or less per week.

When researchers Fred Molitor and Ken Hirsch revisited this line of investigation in 1994, their work confirmed that children are more likely to tolerate aggressive behaviour in the real world if they first watch TV shows or films that contain violent content.

Research Strand: People who watch a lot of media violence tend to believe that the world is more dangerous than it is in reality.

George Gerbner has conducted the longest running study of television violence. His seminal research suggests that heavy TV viewers tend to perceive the world in ways that are consistent with the images on TV. As viewers' perceptions of the world come to conform with the depictions they see on TV, they become more passive, more anxious, and more fearful. Gerbner calls this the "Mean World Syndrome."

Gerbner's research found that those who watch greater amounts of television are more likely to:

- overestimate their risk of being victimized by crime
- believe their neighbourhoods are unsafe
- believe "fear of crime is a very serious personal problem"
- assume the crime rate is increasing, even when it is not

André Gosselin, Jacques de Guise and Guy Paquette decided to test Gerbner's theory in the Canadian context in 1997. They surveyed 360 university students, and found that heavy television viewers are more likely to believe the world is a more dangerous place. However, they also found heavy viewers are not more likely to actually feel more fearful.

Research Strand: Family attitudes to violent content are more important than the images themselves.

A number of studies suggest that media is only one of a number of variables that put children at risk of aggressive behaviour.

For example, a Norwegian study that included 20 at-risk teen-aged boys found that the lack of parental rules regulating what the boys watched was a more significant predictor of aggressive behaviour than the amount of media violence they watched. It also indicated that exposure to real world violence, together with exposure to media violence, created an "overload" of violent events. Boys who experienced this overload were more likely to use violent media images to create and consolidate their identities as members of an anti-social and marginalized group.

On the other hand, researchers report that parental attitudes towards media violence can mitigate the impact it has on children. Huesmann and Bacharach conclude, "Family attitudes and social class are stronger determinants of attitudes toward aggression than is the amount of exposure to TV, which is nevertheless a significant but weaker predictor."

From *www.media-awareness.ca*, 2008. Copyright © 2008 by Media Awareness Network. Reprinted by permission.

Article 7

Japan, Ink

In a nation obsessed with comics, the big publishers get rich. But now amateur rip-offs are taking over, making fan fiction the hottest thing on the street. Inside the manga industrial complex.

DANIEL H. PINK

When the chimes sound at 10:30 AM, the young men pour through the doors. First a few dozen. Then a few hundred. Then, in a matter of minutes, a few thousand. Mobile phones pressed to their ears, empty backpacks flapping on their skinny shoulders, they tear across the floor of the Tokyo Big Sight convention center as if pursued by demons.

"*Hashiranaide!*" cry the blue-shirted security officials. "*Hashiranaide!*" Don't run!

But it's no use. The collective force of so many men fed on a combo platter of anticipation and desire is unstoppable. Call it the running of the *otaku*. For what has stoked their fires isn't flesh or cash but stack upon precious stack of manga.

As you may have noticed, Japanese comics have gripped the global imagination. Manga sales in the US have tripled in the past four years. Titles like *Fruits Basket, Naruto,* and *Death Note* have become fixtures on American best-seller lists. Walk into your local bookstore this afternoon and chances are the manga section is bigger than the science fiction collection. Europe has caught the bug, too. In the United Kingdom, the Catholic Church is using manga to recruit new priests. One British publisher, in an effort to hippify a national franchise, has begun issuing manga versions of Shakespeare's plays, including a *Romeo and Juliet* that reimagines the Montagues and Capulets as rival *yakuza* families in Tokyo.

Yet in Japan, its birthplace and epicenter, manga's fortunes are sagging. Circulation of the country's weekly comic magazines, the essential entry point for any manga series, has fallen by about half over the last decade. Young people are turning their attention away from the printed page and toward the tiny screens on their mobile phones.

Fans and critics complain that manga—which emerged in the years after World War II as an edgy, uniquely Japanese art form—has become as homogenized and risk-averse as the limpest Hollywood blockbuster. Pervading the nation's $4.2 billion-a-year industry is a sense that its best days have passed.

Which ought to make what's happening here at Comic Ichi—a manga market the size of several airplane hangars that will attract some 25,000 buyers—so heartening. The place is pulsing with possibility, full of inspired creators, ravenous fans, and wads of yen changing hands. It represents a dynamic force that could reverse the industry's decline.

There's just one hitch, one teensy roadblock on the manga industry's highway to rejuvenation: Nearly everybody here is breaking the law.

This spring I spent two months in Japan looking under the hood of the manga industry. I met with key players in the supply chain—from the artists who create the work and the editors who polish it to the retailers who sell it and the fans who devour it. I argued with manga critics in Tokyo, hung out at the country's only college manga department in Kyoto, and paid homage to the God of manga in Osaka. I was hoping to get a sense of why Japanese comics have become so insanely popular around the world. What I got instead was a tantalizing peek into what might be the future business model of music, movies, and media of every kind.

To understand manga's place in Japan, you must begin with its ubiquity. Even though the popularity of manga has fallen in recent years, it still comprises about 22 percent of all printed material in Japan. In many parts of Tokyo, you can't walk more than two or three blocks without encountering comics. (Trust me. I checked.) Most omnipresent are the magazines—*Weekly Shonen Magazine, Weekly Shonen Jump, Young King Ours, Shojo Comic,* and countless others. They're teetering in messy piles at convenience stores, stacked in neat slabs at every subway station, and for sale just about anywhere someone might be inclined to pull a couple hundred yen ($2 to $4) from their pocket. Published on flimsy newsprint and often as thick as a Baltimore phone book, these magazines can contain 25 different serialized stories that run about 20 pages each. The most popular series then get repackaged as paperback graphic novels. These books dominate long stretches of Japanese bookstores, and their sales figures would make American authors and publishers weep with envy. One example among many: The paperback editions of *Bleach,* a series about a ghost-spotting teenager that has been running in *Weekly Shonen Jump* for the past six years, have sold some 46 million copies (in a country of 127 million people).

And manga, unlike most American comics, isn't reserved for freaks, geeks, and pip-squeaks. Ride the Tokyo subway and you'll see passengers peering at their mobiles. But you'll also inevitably spot gray-haired businessmen, twentysomething hipsters, and Japanese schoolgirls alike paging through a manga weekly or a graphic novel. The city of Hiroshima even has a bustling public library devoted entirely to manga.

Yet the role of manga in the broader economic ecosystem is perhaps more important than its actual sales figures. Japan's vaunted pop culture apparatus, it turns out, is really a manga industrial complex. Nearly every aspect of cultural production—which is now Japan's most influential export—is rooted in manga. Most anime (animated) movies and television series, as well as many videogames and collectible figures, began life as comics. *Dragonball*—now a multibillion-dollar international franchise comprising movies, games, and cards—debuted as an installment in *Weekly Shonen Jump* in 1984. Uzumaki Naruto, the protagonist of the mega-property that bears his name, first showed his blond ninja head in the pages of the same magazine eight years ago. Trace any of Japan's most successful media franchises back to their origins and you'll likely end up inside a colorful brick of newsprint, where 20 pages of exquisitely matched words and drawings tell the inaugural story.

But manga has become a bit like network television in the US. It reaches a wide but inexorably shrinking audience. Weekly magazine circulation is on a steep and steady downward slope; book sales are no higher than they were a decade ago despite a rise in population. Still, manga is more influential in Japan than network television is in the US. Comics occupy the center, feeding the rest of the media system. If they dry up, other media players risk losing their deepest and most vital source of material. If manga gets creaky, and by all accounts it is heading that way, it could undermine Japan's entire pop culture machine. What the industry needs is something that can rescue it from decline—a force that can reenergize its fans, restock its talent pools, and revive its creative mojo. The sound of those flapping backpacks may herald the arrival of that savior.

A few days after visiting Comic Ichi, I returned to Tokyo Big Sight for Super Comic City, another manga market, this one held over two days to accommodate even larger crowds. Although Comic Ichi was from Mars—the male to-female ratio, by my rough count, was about 300 to 1—and Super Comic City was from Venus, with several hundred women for every man, both markets were selling material from the same planet: nonprofessional self-published manga known as *dojinshi*. At Super Comic City, for instance, 33,000 amateur artists stuffed themselves into six huge halls, each the size of a professional basketball arena, stationed themselves behind card tables, and sold their own home-brewed comics.

Markets like these started to appear in 1975, when a few hundred fans with an artistic bent gathered to trade their work. Today, dojinshi has become a sprawling enterprise. The comics markets—comikets, for short—held in December and August attract about a half-million people. Most of the material for sale at those markets, as well as the ones I visited, have the look and feel of professional work. Their creators often spend weeks meticulously drawing and inking their comics. Then they typically scan those pages onto computers and refine them with Photoshop and other software. Finally, using one of an array of print shops that cater to dojinshi, they produce limited editions of the work (as few as 20 copies, as many as several thousand) on high-quality paper, bound between glossy covers.

I spent two days at Super Comic City. But an American intellectual property lawyer probably would not have lasted more than 15 minutes. After cruising just one or two aisles, he would have thudded to the floor in a dead faint. About 90 percent of the material for sale—how to put this—borrows liberally from existing works. Actually, let me be blunter: The copyright violations are flagrant, shameless, and widespread. For example, in both Japan and the US, one of the past decade's most successful manga series is *Fullmetal Alchemist*. The story pivots around a group of people with the ability to transmute matter into new substances. The main character is Edward Elric, a young man who possesses these powers. Another character is a father-figure type named Colonel Roy Mustang. At Super Comic City, there were at least 30 tables where amateurs were selling 20- or 30-page stories in which perfectly drawn, instantly recognizable Elrics and Mustangs discover their forbidden love for each other. (In all, 1,100 Full Metal Alchemist dojinshi groups had registered to sell their wares.) In many of these comics, the drawings are so precisely rendered that the characters are indistinguishable from the originals. Some of these tales portray chaste affairs full of yearning and unrealized passion. Others depict sexual encounters grunting and graphic enough to make Larry Flynt blush. Though nobody was merely reproducing existing *Fullmetal Alchemist* stories, everybody—by swiping the characters without consent and selling the resulting work to others—was trampling intellectual property rights. And Japanese copyright law is just as restrictive as its American cousin, if not more so.

It was the same everywhere I went: acres of territory in which the basic tenets of intellectual property seemed not to apply. True, some dojinshi collectives, which are known as "circles" even if they have only one member, were selling works based on their own original characters. At Comic Ichi, one of the longest lines was for drawings of a rabbit-eared maid created by Ice and Choco, a circle made up of one woman named Naru Nanao. But most offerings plucked characters from popular manga series and dropped them into new scenarios. The authors told me they were uncovering hidden potential in their favorite stories—revealing themes, relationships, and plot lines that were gurgling just beneath the surface of the official narrative.

At the edge of one hall, I saw a young woman wearing a short skirt, white shoes, and stylish blue leggings pulled over her knees. She was sitting on a folding chair behind a card table greeting a modest but steady stream of customers. She is 24 years old and lives with her parents in the Kyushu region of southern Japan, about 500 miles away. She works at a bank. "It's a lame job," she said with one of her frequent giggles, "which is why I'm spending my life drawing these comics." Nobody at work or at home knows about her hobby; her parents think she came to Tokyo to visit friends. Because of that, she asked me to use only the first letter of her last name.

Three years ago Ms. O produced her first work, a story about Chibi Maruko-Chan, a sassy third grader—think Sally from *Peanuts* inflected with Lisa Simpson—who's a mainstay in a long-running kids' series. Since then, she has created nine more short books that reveal what happens in the alternative universe where the series characters actually age. Much of Ms. O's oeuvre concerns an up-and-down love affair between a late-teen version of Chibi Maruko-Chan and another character. "It's so bizarre that Chibi Maruko could be grown up and think about women's things in the first place," she told me. "But we all know deep in her heart that she longs for this." Does Ms. O aspire to be a professional manga artist? "No. I'm happy just to draw." Is she making lots of money? "I don't make any money." What's driving her? "Nobody else is doing this. I had to show this aspect of Chibi Maruko and get it out there."

Guided by a 440-page catalog with tiny blurbs about each circle, buyers—many of them pulling wheeled suitcases—could find all manner of reimagined, copyright-defying manga peddled by people like Ms. O. *Yaoi*, or "boys' love," was popular among women. Hetero porn remixes were popular among the men. And although sex and romance titles predominated, buyers could also choose from action, adventure, supernatural, and other genres, most selling for 500 to 1,000 yen (about $4 to $8) apiece.

Now think back to our American lawyer—the one lying on the cement floor. After the smelling salts arrived, he no doubt would have picked himself off the ground, thumbed a cease-and-desist letter on his BlackBerry, and phoned in a temporary injunction to close down the joint. Imagine Disney's response if some huge comics convention in St. Louis or Houston were selling exquisitely rendered, easily identifiable comic book versions of Mickey Mouse and Goofy falling in love. Picture the legal department at United Feature Syndicate hearing about someone selling $6 books that show a buxom teenage Sally and a husky teenage Linus canoodling on a beach. The violations at Super Comic City were so brazen and the scale so huge—by day's end, some 300,000 books sold in cash transactions totaling more than $1 million—that just about any US media company would have launched a full-metal lawsuit to shut the market for good.

Why aren't Japanese publishers doing the same? I posed that question to two of the main organizers of Japan's dojinshi gatherings, Kouichi Ichikawa and Keiji Takeda.

"Obviously, there are copyright issues at play here," Ichikawa said. When the markets expanded beyond the clutch of early adopters in the 1980s and 1990s, publishers and authors made threatening noises, and some accused successful dojinshi circles of violating copyright law. But lately, as the markets have reached such enormous scale, the big publishing houses have taken a different approach.

"This is something that satisfies the fans," Ichikawa said. "The publishers understand that this does not diminish the sales of the original product but may increase them. So they don't come down here and shut it down."

"Is that something publishers have told you?" I asked.

No, he said, not exactly. "This is something very Japanese. It's an ancient sensibility—like the *wabi-sabi* of the tea ceremony."

In case you missed the wabi-sabi lecture back in high school, it means something like "aesthetic transience." I asked Takeda about it.

As recently as a decade ago, he told me, creators of popular commercial works sometimes cracked down on their dojinshi counterparts at Super Comic City. "But these days," he said, "you don't really hear about that many publishers stopping them."

"Why not?" I asked.

They have an understanding, he said, using a phrase I'd encounter again and again: *anmoku no ryokai*, meaning essentially "unspoken, implicit agreement."

"The dojinshi are creating a market base, and that market base is naturally drawn to the original work," he said. Then, gesturing to the convention floor, he added, "This is where we're finding the next generation of authors. The publishers understand the value of not destroying that." And as the manga weeklies falter and decline, new talent is more important than ever. Meanwhile, Takeda said, the dojinshi creators honor their part of this silent pact. They tacitly agree not to go too far—to produce work only in limited editions and to avoid selling so many copies that they risk cannibalizing the market for original works.

> **"In Japan, everything can be rendered in manga. Now some enterprising outfits in the West are picking up on that idea—and putting comics to some surprising uses."**
>
> —Manga Does Shakespeare

"Obviously," Takeda said, "this is something that no one comes out with a bullhorn and states."

What's less obvious is that *anmoku no ryokai* isn't just a deft way to avoid conflict. It's also a business model, one that's exportable to the US.

If you want to snag your own little piece of Japanese cool, come to Mandarake. This chain of 11 retail stores sells tons (literally) of used artifacts—manga, trading cards, figures, games, posters, costumes, and dojinshi—that can satisfy the deepest pop culture urges. At the helm of Mandarake is its founder, a failed manga artist named Masuzo Furukawa. By Japanese standards, Furukawa is an iconoclast. His black hair is kinked into curls and colored brownish red. He wears a shiny tracksuit rather than a salaryman's coat and tie. He jokes about his many failures. He opened Mandarake 27 years ago, well before the dojinshi markets began growing more popular—in part to provide another sales channel for the work coming out of them.

At first, publishers were none too pleased with his new venture. "You think I didn't hear from them?" he tells me in a company conference room. But in the past five years, he says, as the scale and reach of the markets has expanded, the publishers' attitude "has changed 180 degrees." It's all a matter of business, he says.

To illustrate what he means, he reaches across the conference-room table and takes my notebook. On a blank page he draws a large triangle. "You have the authors up there at this tiny little tip at the top. And at the bottom," he says, drawing a line just above the widening base of the triangle, "you have the readers. The *dojin* artists are the ones connecting them in the middle."

In other words, where there was once a clear divide between producers and consumers and between pros and amateurs, the boundaries are now murky. The people selling their wares at the comics markets are consumers *and* producers, amateurs *and* pros. They nourish both the top and the bottom. If publishers were to squash the emerging middle, they would disrupt, and perhaps destroy, this delicate new triangular ecosystem. And remember: If manga craters, it could drag the entire Japanese pop culture industry down with it.

However, because permitting—let alone encouraging—dojinshi runs afoul of copyright law, the agreement remains implicit: The publishers avert their eyes, and the dojinshi creators resist going too far. This *anmoku no ryokai* business model helps rescue the manga industrial complex in at least three ways.

First, and most obviously, it's a customer care program. The dojinshi devotees are manga's fiercest fans. "We're not denying the viability or importance of intellectual property," says Kazuhiko Torishima, an executive at the publishing behemoth Shueisha. "But when the numbers speak, you have to listen."

Second, as Takeda put it at Super Comic City, "this is the soil for new talent." While most dojinshi creators have no aspirations to become manga superstars, several artists have used the comic markets to springboard into mainstream success. The best example is Clamp, which began as a circle of a dozen college women selling self-published work at comics markets in the Kansai region. Today, Clamp's members are manga rock stars; they have sold close to 100 million books worldwide.

Third, the *anmoku no ryokai* arrangement provides publishers with extremely cheap market research. To learn what's hot and what's not, a media company could spend lots of money commissioning polls and conducting focus groups. Or for a few bucks it could buy a Super Comic City catalog and spend two days watching 96,000 of its best customers browse, gossip, and buy in real time. These settings often provide early warnings of the shifting fan zeitgeist. For instance, a few years ago several circles that had been creating dojinshi for the series *Prince of Tennis* switched to *Bleach*, an indication that one title was falling out of favor and another was on the rise. "The publishers are seeing the market in action," Ichikawa says. "They're seeing the successes and the failures. They're seeing the trends."

Taking care of customers. Finding new talent. Getting free market research. That's a pretty potent trio of advantages for any business. Trouble is, to derive these advantages the manga industry must ignore the law. And this is where it gets weird. Unlike, say, an industrial company that might increase profits if it skirts environmental regulations imposed to safeguard the public interest, the manga industrial complex is ignoring a law designed to protect its *own* commercial interests.

This odd situation exposes the conflict between what Stanford law professor (and *Wired* contributor) Lawrence Lessig calls the "read only" culture and the "read/write" culture. Intellectual property laws were crafted for a read-only culture. They prohibit me from running an issue of *Captain America* through a Xerox DocuColor machine and selling copies on the street. The moral and business logic of this sort of restriction is unassailable. By merely photocopying someone else's work, I'm not creating anything new. And my cheap reproductions would be unfairly harming the commercial interests of Marvel Comics.

But as Lessig and others have argued, and as the dojinshi markets amply confirm, that same copyright regime can be inadequate, and even detrimental, in a read/write culture. Amateur manga remixers aren't merely replicating someone else's work. They're creating something original. And in doing so, they may well be helping, not hindering, the commercial interests of the copyright holders. Yet they're treated no differently from me and my hypothetical *Captain America* photocopies. The result is a misalignment between the emerging imperatives of smart business and the lagging sensibilities of old laws.

It's hard to imagine the US media industry ditching legal protections to tap the creativity of a super-empowered fan base.

How to bring matters into alignment, without undercutting the "read only" protections, has been a vexing issue for American music producers and music studios as well as platforms like YouTube. One possibility, of course, is to change copyright law to make it flexible enough for a read/write culture. Good luck. In the past few decades, the copyright winds in the US have been blowing in the opposite direction—toward longer and stricter protections. It is hard to imagine Hollywood, Nashville, and New York agreeing to scale back legal protection in order to release the creative impulses of super-empowered fans, when the gains from doing so are for now only theoretical.

Another possibility is something akin to Lessig's Creative Commons licenses. Copyright holders could voluntarily reserve only some of their rights or perhaps create a special dojinshi license that allows fans to reproduce and remix works in limited ways. That's probably the ideal option. And perhaps some day Big Media will see its virtues. But the use of Creative Commons licenses so far has been extremely limited. Again, it's difficult to envision large publishers or giant movie and music studios relinquishing control over their products when the benefits are indirect, distant, and as yet unproven.

In *anmoku no ryokai*, manga publishers might have found a tentative, imperfect, but ultimately more promising answer—a business model that could help media companies in both Japan and the US begin to navigate these potentially treacherous new waters. Instead of rewriting a national statute or hashing out separate individual contracts or crafting special licenses, it leaves everything unsaid in order to simply give the new arrangement a test drive. It takes the situation out of the realm of law and plops it into the realm of economics and game theory. It places the established publishers and the dojinshi creators in something resembling the prisoners' dilemma: If they cooperate—that is, if they honor the terms of *anmoku no ryokai*—they both gain. But if one overreaches—if publishers crack down aggressively or if dojinshi creators go too far—they both suffer.

Instead of negotiating a formal pact, both parties can advance their interests through the deterrent of mutually assured destruction. What that accommodation lacks in legal clarity, it makes up for in commercial pragmatism. If the experiment fails, then everyone reverts back to the legal status quo. But if it endures, and if everyone comes to realize that the interests of the copyright holders and the fans are aligned, it could become the prelude to wider adoption of Creative Commonsstyle licenses and a more coherent set of rules for a remix culture around the world.

One afternoon in May, I walked into K-Books, a third-floor bookshop in Akihabara, a neighborhood of flashing lights and moving bodies that is the epicenter of Tokyo's otaku culture. In one section of the store, I found graphic novels by Clamp, that circle of women who went from amateurs to best-selling pros. I bought a copy of *Chobits,* their series about a young man who has a friendly female android assistant; a volume of *xxxHolic,* about a high school student who works for a witch (despite the trio of x's in the title, it's not porn); and a hardcover edition of *Card Captor Sakura,* about a girl with magical powers. And in a nearby section of the store, I bought dojinshi versions of those same titles. For 210 yen ($1.80), I picked up *Hacker Chobits,* in which the female android expands the frontiers of "friendliness." For 630 yen ($5.40) I bought a *yuri,* or lesbian, version of *xxxHolic* featuring the two main female characters of that series. And for another 630 yen, I purchased the 70-page, sprightly illustrated *Sakura Remix,* wherein the heroine encounters a strangely amorous frog and later discovers a hidden video camera in her classroom at an especially inopportune moment.

The official versions and the remixed versions weren't side by side. But they were for sale perhaps 10 yards away from each other. *In the same store.* Think about that in a US context. You walk in to Barnes & Noble and walk out with a copy of *Harry Potter and the Deathly Hallows*—as well as an unauthorized remix of a May-December romance between Hermione Granger and Professor Minerva McGonagall. Our American IP lawyer is starting to get woozy again.

A few weeks later, I tossed these books into my backpack, hopped on a train to the outskirts of Tokyo, and entered a castle-like building that is the headquarters of Clamp's media empire. There I met with Ageha Ohkawa, the very smart and refreshingly down-to-earth head of this monumentally successful manga machine. In the late 1980s, before they started to create original work, she and her colleagues produced some remixed versions of *Captain Tsubasa,* a series about a soccer team, and sold them at dojinshi markets. Today, she's on the other end of the *anmoku no ryokai* détente.

During our conversation, I reached into my backpack to show her the three Clamp dojin titles I'd bought at K-Books. Her handlers—a few managers and a guy from legal—winced and exchanged worried looks. But Ohkawa burst into a delighted laugh and then flipped through *Sakura Remix* and *Hacker Chobits.* "Any popular manga is going to have this treatment done," she told me. "It is by people who are truly in love with the work, and you have to respect that."

So, I asked, is *Hacker Chobits* actually good for the real Chobits?

She paused. "I think it's good because they are expressing love for the work. And, of course, we come from the dojinshi world, so I understand this." Fans even sometimes send her their dojinshi, and what she admires about these works is the dedication and the innovation they show. "There is originality here. There are new stories. It's not a copy."

Still, she's not entirely comfortable having the black-and-white world of manga governed by the gray zone of *anmoku no ryokai.* "It's very vague," she says. "It's always pushing the edge of whether it should be forbidden. Should someone actually make a pirate version instead of a remix, this whole thing could collapse." Yet she can't think of a better approach. Holding up a copy of *Hacker Chobits,* she says, "It's not something I'm going to stand up and rail against."

The manga industrial complex has seen the future. And it works. For now.

Contributing editor **DANIEL H. PINK** (dp@danpink.com) was a 2007 Japan Society Media Fellow. His next book, a manga called *The Adventures of Johnny Bunko,* will be published in the spring of 2008. (For a crash course on manga, visit wired.com/extras.)

Originally Published in Wired, November 2007, pp. 217-235. Copyright © 2007 by Daniel H. Pink. Reprinted by permission of the author.

Chica Lit: Multicultural Literature Blurs Borders

Marie Loggia-Kee

With chick lit, it's all about the attitude: Think of the original *Diary of Bridget Jones,* a tell-all of the dating life of a singleton. Chica lit takes that sass and combines it with culture.

> **There has been a rich tradition of Latina literature out there, most of it quite literary and heavy. Chica lit, by contrast, is bubbly, fun, irreverent, modern, and fashionable.**

Alisa Valdes-Rodriguez, author of the genre-setting bestseller *The Dirty Girls Social Club,* quickly dismisses the term "Latina lit." That's not what her novels are. They're *Chica lit.* "There has been a rich tradition of Latina literature out there, most of it quite literary and heavy. Chica lit, by contrast, is bubbly, fun, irreverent, modern, and fashionable," Valdes-Rodriguez says. "I think of Chica lit as being like the *Seinfeld* show, whereas traditional Latina literature is more like *ER.*"

In May 2006 Valdes-Rodriguez joined Mary Castillo, author of *Hot Tamara: What's Life Without a Little Spice,* among others, in Miami Beach at the first Chica Lit Club. While Valdes-Rodriguez usually sets her novels on the East Coast, Castillo captures the essence of Los Angeles. Together the two authors are helping to define a new genre of writing.

When Castillo submitted her manuscript for publication, editors told her the same thing over and over again: "It's not Latina enough." Often Chica literature breaks the traditional roles and forges a new identity; the protagonist of the new fiction is not just a woman of Latina heritage, she's a strong, and strongly identified, Latina-American woman.

In *Hot Tamara's* closing notes, Castillo said that she learned more about herself and her heritage while working on the book:

> Writing *Hot Tamara* was a journey for me to realize how much of a Latina I really am. In my family we didn't speak Spanish or even identify ourselves as Mexican. I was a fourth-generation American on my dad's side, who happened to be Mexican. ("Avon's Little Black Book on Mary Castillo," cited in *Hot Tamara*)

Castillo and other writers reach a segment of the population eager for role models that reflect some of the realities and obstacles they face in real life. Authors such as Valdes-Rodriguez and Castillo touch a growing mainstream population that often relates to more than one culture.

Industry Trends

One way to distinguish the direction of the publishing industry is to look at what the major houses solicit. Chica lit is showing up on the request list. Selina McLemore, a former editor at HarperCollins Publishers who now acquires for Harlequin, credits not only literary writers such as Isabel Allende and Sandra Cisneros for changing the voice of the literature, but contemporary writers such as Valdes-Rodriguez and Castillo as well.

"We're seeing fiction that is truly intended for the commercial market," McLemore explains. "These writers and books are a reflection of the way Latino culture has become, in the last ten years, a much more accepted part of mainstream pop culture, as has been proven in music, movies, and TV."

Rather than assimilating her characters into mainstream culture, Valdes-Rodriguez notes that they and their stories reflect the lives of her readers. "I had no idea my work would resonate with so many people—more than half a million books sold to date," Valdes-Rodriguez says. "Again and again I hear that my work has affirmed the life choices many Latinas have made, like college and a professional career, choices that none of us have yet seen reflected in the mainstream media very well."

Cultural Identity

The recently published anthology *Border-Line Personalities: A New Generation of Latinas Dish on Sex, Sass and Cultural Shifting* explores the concept of self-defining that surfaces in many of the Chica lit novels. Michelle Herrera Mulligan, one of the anthology's editors, said that her mother accused her of not staying true to the culture. "Even though I'm half white," she said, "I though I'd bridged the gap between my mother and me. If I didn't fit into her world, where did I belong?" (xxvi). Through the process of putting together the anthology, Herrera Mulligan said that the contributors developed a "pathology of being Latina" (xxxi):

> We realized that ultimately, it is up to us to decide if we are Latina, to individually determine what the term means. We grappled with the implications of this on our greater cultures, and argued about the word's ability to entirely define us. At the end of this process, we realized that no matter how loaded, conflicted, and difficult the term may be, we are Latinas. Through heritage and by choice. (xxxi)

Hot Latinas

Rather than falling victim to the traditions of its readers' heritage, Chica lit forges new ground. The female characters in the literature follow their dreams and take on new roles: Women can be strong, and they don't have to be dependent on or subservient to a man. McLemore says that current stories are "more reflective of real Latina women."

The female characters in the literature follow their dreams and take on new roles.

"We're not just maids anymore, nor the salacious vixens of telenovelas," McLemore explains. "These stories often reflect the lives of first- and second-generation Latinas who have grown up in the United States, who may or may not even speak Spanish. They are about blending cultures, living in what can sometimes seem to be two very different worlds."

In the opening of Castillo's debut novel, *Hot Tamara*, the protagonist forgoes the traditional values of settling down with the "right" guy—by her family's standards—in order to pursue her dream of working for an art gallery. Like Tamara, the characters of Chica lit are not necessarily disrespectful, but that doesn't mean that their elders see them as respectful. In *Hot Tamara*, Tamara's mother expresses her feelings about modern girls:

> "You're so self-centered that you can't see how your idiotic decisions hurt everyone around you." Her mom's voice cracked. "We do these things for you because you can't. You're making a mistake, and as far as I'm concerned, I want nothing to do with it. You want to move to L.A.? Fine. Go. There's nothing for you here, and when you fall on your face, don't bother to come running to us."(72)

But Tamara is willing to go against the wishes of her mother and pursue her interests. Rather than taking the safe choice, this Latina embraces the diversity within her own heritage and the wider culture that enables her freedom.

Described by *New York* magazine as "the Hispanic version of *Waiting to Exhale*" (on the back cover of the book), *The Dirty Girls Social Club* also breaks through the multicultural barrier to address stereotypes about identity and gender roles. *The Dirty Girls* follows six Latina women who come from different cultural backgrounds. Lauren, the opening narrator, is a Cuban woman who learned Spanish for a reporting job; Amber is Californian Mexican; Usnavys is Puerto Rican; Rebecca aligns herself as "Spanish," not "Mexican"; Sara is Cuban; and Elizabeth is a black Colombian. Valdes-Rodriguez shows the cultural diversity of the characters' milieu in her descriptions, but although all of these women hail from a different heritage, they are still considered "Latina" women.

While Valdes-Rodriguez says she's very much in touch with her own heritage, she admits that she learned much while writing her novel. "I'm not Colombian, but for Elizabeth's character, [I] had to learn about Colombia. In that sense, writing has broken down a lot of barriers for me," she explains. "I think all writers should stretch to include people whose backgrounds are different from their own. Just because I'm Latina doesn't mean I speak for all Latinas. We are a diverse group. The books that succeed will be those that reflect this diversity."

Fiction also touches on some of the same language and terminology issues addressed in the nonfiction anthologies; even though the women are "Latinas," they don't truly know what the word encompasses. In *The Dirty Girls Social Club*, Valdes-Rodriguez writes, "Nobody knew that we had no idea what a Latina was supposed to be, that we just let the moniker fall over us and fit in the best we could" (34).

In a recent interview, Castillo said that the new Chica fiction doesn't necessarily get pigeonholed into the "often hard-to-find Latino" section at Barnes & Noble. Instead, her readers vary from those who happen to be Mexican Americans to those who are not. At its heart, Chica fiction touches on a reality shared by many cultures. While the market has seen changes with the acceptance of a more "mainstream" Latina lit, Castillo implied that there is still a ways to go.

"I think they need to be honest portrayals of Latinas in all their cultural, racial, and economic diversity. Readers aren't dumb and they can sniff out a faker and stereotypes," Castillo said. "This is where authors and publishing houses can experience some tension. A friend of mine was asked to make the title of her new book 'more ethnic.' That is not only confusing to us authors, but also a bit demeaning. How much do you want to bet that Janet Evanovich isn't asked to make her titles 'more white' or 'more New Jersey'?"

Chica lit shows the main characters not only embracing their culture, but also accepting the diversity that comes along with it. Rather than following the traditional roles imposed within the Hispanic culture, writers such as Castillo show that sometimes a woman's got to stay true to herself.

"Chica lit is filling a void in commercial women's fiction in the United States and elsewhere by portraying Latinas as diverse, modern, funny, smart, educated, independent, and professional," Valdes-Rodriguez offers. "Many of my Latina readers also enjoy Sophie Kinsella and Jennifer Weiner, so in a sense it's not imperative that a reader identify with the ethnicity of a character. Many of my readers, too, are not Latina at all. The most important thing a writer can offer readers is believable characters who are fundamentally human, flawed like the rest of us."

"It is the universal appeal of character that hooks readers," she continues, "regardless of the racial, cultural, or ethnic background of the reader, writer or characters. That said, it is of course important for people to feel like their own life is somehow validated and accepted in popular culture."

Works Cited

Castillo, Mary. "Re: Answers to your questions." E-mail to the author. May 23, 2005.

Castillo, Mary. *Hot Tamara*. New York: HarperCollins, 2005.

McLemore, Selina. "Re: Latina Lit Trends." E-mail to the author. May 18, 2005.

Moreno, Robyn and Michelle Herrera Mulligan, eds. *Border-Line Personalities: A New Generation of Latinas Dish on Sex, Sass and Cultural Shifting.* New York: HarperCollins, 2004.

Valdes-Rodriguez, Alisa. *The Dirty Girls Social Club.* New York: HarperCollins, 2003.

Valdes-Rodriguez, Alisa. E-mail to the author. October 26, 2005.

With a mother who was adopted from Mexico at the age of 12 and an Italian-American father, **MARIE LOGGIA-KEE** understands growing up between cultures. In addition to writing, she teaches English and popular culture at the University of Phoenix and National University.

From *Multicultural Review*, Spring 2007, pp. 46–48. Copyright © 2007 by MultiCultural Review. Reprinted by permission of The Goldman Group, Inc.

Cheap Thrills

It doesn't take much to enthrall the prepubescent audience.

JOHN PODHORETZ

What are we to make of the fact that the most successful work of popular entertainment made in this decade for children between the ages of five and 12 is a profoundly inoffensive trifle about a jock boy and a brainiac girl who find themselves starring in their high school's musical?

According to some conservative critiques of popular culture, the astounding success of *High School Musical* and *High School Musical 2* shouldn't have been possible. For decades, conservatives have decried the corrupting effect of popular culture—a sexualized, hyperviolent, commercialized pop culture that dictates the clothing habits, speaking patterns, and behavior of impressionable young Americans who do not have the ability to resist its siren song. The central contention of those who make this argument is that these trends in popular culture mirror eating patterns: Just as the combination of sugar and carbs and transfats has created addictively tasty potions that are causing childhood obesity levels to spike, the sex-and-violence mash-up has an addictive allure that quashes all attempts to provide American youth with more acceptable, or at least more anodyne, entertainment.

So how, exactly, did the Disney Channel's two little musicals aimed at prepubescent kids emerge squeakyclean and jam-packed with wholesome goodness to capture the imaginations of kids from California to Kathmandu? The makers and distributors of popular culture just haven't been trying hard enough to find something of appeal to these kids. Or trying at all.

Certainly Disney didn't try very hard when it came to *High School Musical*. When the Disney Channel debuted the original movie in January 2006, it was merely one in a series of monthly movies made for the channel. Others in the series include a thing about a boy who discovers he's part fish, a tale about a boy's basketball team at a Jewish day school and its involvement with a homeless man, and the saga of a girl who wants to play hockey on a boy's team. It's clear from how amateurish these pictures are that no one at the channel or anywhere else gave much creative thought or attention to them. *HSM* was just another throwaway product, if a more elaborate one—as evidenced by the fact that Disney hired a man named Kenny Ortega to direct it. Disney would never have engaged Ortega to direct a project it considered significant, since it had made the disastrous mistake of giving Ortega the responsibility of helming two colossally bad musicals in the 1990s (*Newsies* and *Hocus Pocus*) that both tanked at the box office.

As it happens, I watched *High School Musical* on the evening of its premiere, since as a parent of a very young child I had seen a few preview commercials for it, thought it had an engaging premise, and wondered whether it might be an unexpected sleeper. After an hour or so, I shut off the TV. *High School Musical* is so cheaply made that its set designer barely even bothered to throw a little tinsel and lights around in its opening scene, supposedly set at a resort on New Year's Eve. The whole movie is slapdash in this way, with an under-populated high school setting and scenes so hurried and false that one can almost hear Ortega shouting offscreen, "Come on, people, we have to get this whole thing shot in 24 days."

The wretched numbers—written by no fewer than 12 people—evoke not Broadway show tunes but latter-day pop music. But they are so generic and feeble they make songs like Avril Lavigne's "Sk8ter Boi" and Justin Timberlake's "SexyBack" sound like Vivaldi by comparison. The routine dancing, choreographed by the egregious Ortega, would not pass muster in summer stock in Alaska. The script was written by Peter Barsocchini, whose prior claim to fame was that he helped produce the late Merv Griffin's talk show. Evidently, Barsocchini learned everything he knew about dialogue from Griffin's infamously inane exchanges with celebrity guests.

I approached *HSM* with goodwill and exited with grave disappointment. And yet I was one of the few people in America to turn the television off that night. *High School Musical* was a sensation from the moment it aired. An estimated 8 million people watched it all the way through on the evening of its debut, making it not only the highest-rated program ever to air on the Disney Channel but one of the most highly-rated programs in the history of cable television. Every time the Disney Channel has aired a repeat of the movie in the 19 months since, its ratings have soared. Disney says *High School Musical* has been viewed 70 million times in the United States since its first broadcast. The soundtrack album was the best-selling CD of 2006. More than 5 million DVDs have been sold. Disney has earned in excess of $70 million from a movie that it has aired, repeatedly, for free.

As the weeks ticked down toward the airing of the sequel, *High School Musical 2*, I began to feel optimistic again. After all, the star of both movies, 19-year-old Zac Efron, does a splendid job playing a teen heartthrob in the big-screen version of the Broadway musical *Hairspray*. But once again, I could only last an hour. *HSM 2* is, if anything, even worse than its predecessor. Set during summer vacation, the sequel tells the bland story of the jock boy's temptation away from his hardworking girlfriend toward the rich country-club owner's daughter—with the action culminating in a country-club amateur talent show.

Disney spent a few more dollars on the new one than on the last, and so the cinematography came out a little brighter and the settings better dressed. But everything else is as it was: horrible songs, lamentable choreography, and dreadful overacting from all concerned. But when the sequel debuted in the middle of August, it became the highest-rated program ever to air on cable television.

It's not enough to explain away my critical reaction to the two *HSM*s by saying they were not intended for adult viewing. That's certainly true; but most of my daughter's picture books aren't intended for me, either, and I am able to see what's cute about them. No, the success of the *High School Musicals* is a mark not of their quality but of how starved little kids are for entertainments that don't require them to assume a false affect of sophistication—a sophistication they do not possess, and whose assumption is both tiring and confusing to them.

High School Musical is a movie for little kids about teenagers. It's a depiction of the high school years as a young child would wish them to be: Snazzy and colorful, playful and unthreatening. The cute couple never even exchanges a kiss in the first one, and there's a running gag in the second one about how they keep getting interrupted in their efforts to smooch. The atmosphere is so desexualized that we are supposed to accept the idea that a brother and sister can play the leads in school musicals together—a virtual impossibility, as the leads in musicals are always romantically entwined.

This is an easy formula to duplicate. The fact that no one has duplicated it since January 2006, except for the Disney Channel in making *High School Musical 2*, is indicative of a massive blind spot in Hollywood. One always hears that Hollywood makes its choices based not on ideology or a set of fashionable ideas but on what will sell. Now we know that appealing to the presexual fantasies of prepubescent children about the easy and uncomplicated nature of life after puberty is the path to a guaranteed blockbuster. And nobody in Hollywood is making bank on it because, I think, they just can't imagine it's actually true.

JOHN PODHORETZ, a columnist for the New York Post, is *The Weekly Standard's* movie critic.

From *The Weekly Standard*, September 3, 2007, pp. 42–43. Copyright © 2007 by Weekly Standard. Reprinted by permission.

Article 10

The Diana/Whore Complex

Lovelorn stars are out. Today's celebs are prized for their bad behavior.

LAKSHMI CHAUDHRY

"We've all seen her . . . as a princess, as a loving and dedicated mother and as one of the great, great, great icons of giving," declared Kiefer Sutherland, one of the many bright shiny celebrities who gathered at a concert in July to commemorate Diana—or, more accurately, to canonize her—on the tenth anniversary of her death. Yet in the pantheon of female icons, Diana was more Marilyn Monroe than Mother Teresa, a woman best known not for her "giving" but for what Joyce Carol Oates described in her 1997 obituary as "her often desperate search for love."

Looking back, the people's princess appears a strange anachronism, perhaps the last of an extinct breed of tragic Cinderellas whose romantic failures and heartbreak were essential ingredients of their mystique. In the ten years since Diana's death, female celebrities have indeed come a long way, baby. Whatever the failings of the brat pack who dominate the tabloid headlines today, they represent a new generation of stars—including the likes of Lindsay Lohan, Nicole Richie and Tara Reid—who no longer feel the need to hide their appetite for pleasure, status and attention behind a giggle or a teary smile.

"I think every decade has an iconic blonde—like Marilyn Monroe or Princess Diana—and right now, I'm that icon," Paris Hilton told the *Sunday Times* of London last year, at the height of her notoriety as the tabloids' favorite party girl. Her remark drew jeers of derision, but as Matt Haber observed on *Radar Online,* Paris wasn't entirely wrong about her importance as a cultural signifier of her time: "Journalists reach for her name first when seeking an easy phrase signifying unearned fame, inherited wealth, propensity for sexual indiscretion or a penchant for cheap publicity."

While Diana and Marilyn shared a number of qualities with today's female celebs—notably a lack of sexual discretion and an appetite for public attention—Paris is, for better or worse, a new variety of feminine icon, defined not by victimhood and suffering but by self-sufficiency and self-gratification. In many ways, the "skank posse" represents the pop incarnation of a certain brand of Gen-X feminism that places sexual gratification and independence at the top of the agenda. It's the kind of "party girl" power that was daring and cool back in the '90s but now represents the new "normal"—as made painfully evident by the shallow young Hilton wannabes who populate MTV's reality shows.

In a *Guardian* article written nearly a year after Diana's car crash, Joan Smith bemoaned our fascination with tragic love goddesses who are willing to bare every detail of their calamitous personal lives to earn our sympathy and regard. "Our appetite for stories of female misery, it seems, can never be sated," Smith wrote. "What we want to know about rich, beautiful, successful women is that they are, in spite of all their advantages, lonely and miserable." Or, more precisely, that their success and fame are a poor substitute for the love of a good man.

Likewise, Sarah Churchwell wrote in *The Many Lives of Marilyn Monroe* of the mythology inspired by the ultimate blond victim: "Unmarried, childless, a professional success, she will still be branded a personal failure. The prospect of the most desirable woman in the world becoming a spinster is finally what will kill her. She will die when the men have left the tale. She will die because she was a woman alone on a Saturday night—a fate worse than death."

The plot line of this fairy tale is always the same: Deprived childhood creates lifelong craving for love, which she seeks in the arms of various unsuitable men and, failing that, in public adulation, which cannot, however, save her from a tragic, usually lonely and always untimely death. Cinderella gets to be princess but never finds Prince Charming, and that's why we love her. The more she bares her scars—her rejected, needy, self-loathing self—the closer we press her to our hearts.

Describing a grab bag of Monroe memorabilia, a Christie's auctioneer summed up the secret of their allure: "All these things reflect Marilyn's vulnerability. Vulnerability was part of Marilyn Monroe's irresistible appeal." Just as irresistible is the suffering of the woman who would emerge two decades later as the rightful heir to Marilyn's mantle of thorns. Diana "used her big blue eyes to their fullest advantage, melting the hearts of men and women through an expression of complete vulnerability. Diana's eyes, like those of Marilyn Monroe, contained an appeal directed not to any individual but to the world at large. Please don't hurt me, they seemed to say," gushed Ian Buruma in his 1999 write-up for *Time,* which featured both women in its list of the twenty greatest heroes and icons of the twentieth century.

In her biography of Monroe, Churchwell takes to task the relentless mythomania of her admirers and critics, who are equally invested in nurturing the legend of a hapless beautiful woman consumed by her desire for celebrity and love. What they carefully ignore, she argues, is Marilyn's own role in using the media and men to catapult what was at best an unexceptional acting career into the heights of enduring stardom. Behind the image was a complicated, intelligent, damaged woman, no doubt, but hardly desperate, fragile or even particularly love-struck.

Although Diana's connection to Marilyn Monroe would not be cemented in the public mind until her death—when Elton John did the needful by rewriting "Candle in the Wind"—the people's princess proved herself to be a worthy heir to Marilyn's legacy from the moment she stepped into the public spotlight. In her book *The Diana Chronicles,* Tina Brown reveals a determined 19-year-old who employed her considerable skills of self-invention and public relations to seduce the British press and pave her ascension to Buckingham Palace. Tabloid photographer Ken Lennox told Brown of those early days, "The shy Di is a myth. That came about because she would put her head down and her hair would fall over her face and she would glance up every now and then to see where we were."

When her fairy-tale wedding turned into a domestic nightmare—what with Charles unhelpfully refusing to play his assigned role—Diana simply discarded one mythic narrative in favor of another, this time in order to secure her postdivorce future outside the palace. The "true story" that she leaked to Andrew Morton in 1992 in a pre-emptive strike against her husband and in-laws contained all the ingredients for her posthumous canonization as the new Marilyn. The details seemed shocking and yet carefully selected to renarrate her life to fit her new role as tragic Cinderella: Her tawdry sexual escapades skillfully recast as romantic tragedies, appetite for publicity as a desperate cry for recognition and real bouts of bulimia and invented suicide attempts as signs of deep emotional pain.

The Joyce Carol Oates obituary, penned for *Time* magazine, is stirring testimony to Diana's PR success. Shrill in her indignation at the endless indignities heaped on her hapless heroine by "the Establishment," "human jackals known as paparazzi," the philandering husband and the parade of caddish lovers, Oates concludes with a paean to Diana's "significance for women that approaches the mystical. In Diana, the fairy-tale princess who was cruelly awakened to the world of hurt, betrayal and humiliation, women of all ages found a mirror image of themselves, however magnified and glamorized." In one fell swoop, this feminist author who should surely have known better reduced not only Diana but also her many female fans to the worst kind of feminine stereotype: frail, dependent and easily abused.

In a June 17 column, Naomi Wolf complained about a culture that "seems increasingly obsessed with showcasing images of glamorous young women who are falling apart," citing the spectacle of Britney Spears's meltdown, Paris Hilton's arrest and Lindsay Lohan's various stints in rehab. The more women advance in the real world, Wolf argues, the more "the broken, out-of-control ingenue—who clearly can't manage without lots of help—is reassuring. And, I'd say, seductive." In other words, Paris may be no Marilyn or Diana, but she serves exactly the same purpose: to assure us of feminine vulnerability.

It would be a convincing argument, except these young women present themselves as neither broken nor fragile. Where Diana made much of her indifferent mother, Lindsay plays down her far more dysfunctional family life, which includes an ex-convict dad. Like Paris, these young women position themselves as overindulged princesses rather than scarred little waifs. Peddling emotional pain is just not their thing.

"[Paris is] too rich, skinny, blond, nude, slutty, drunk, spoiled and famous. She ignores the law and openly flouts our social mores, as if they don't apply to her," writes Cintra Wilson in *Salon.* Hilton, Lohan and their peers represent a radically new generation of celebrities who receive attention—or more precisely notoriety—because they violate rather than perform traditional modes of femininity, especially when it comes to matters of the heart.

Unlike the media narratives about previous female celebrities, stories about today's stars center less on their dating travails than on their partying ways. Almost all of these women seem less interested in Mr. Right than Mr. Right Now. "They certainly aren't sitting at home, crying into their beer, saying, 'If I only had the right man,'" points out Bella DePaulo, author of *Singled Out.* "They seem to take for granted what women before them have worked for, which is to lead lives independent of men."

There is, however, a price to pay for their transgressions. "I find of particular interest the amount of hatred people have, especially male commentators, for Paris Hilton," says Karen Hollinger, author of *The Actress: Hollywood Acting and the Female Star.* "She isn't portrayed as looking for love—and finding or not finding it—but as beautiful and rather wild. On the other hand, Diana fit so well into the model of the beautiful woman searching and suffering for love that men were falling all over themselves to celebrate this 'candle in the wind.'"

Paris is no more of a "media whore" than were Diana or Marilyn, but unlike them, her narcissism is brazen and unapologetic rather than eager to please, and therefore despicable. What hasn't changed is the age-old double standard that shapes tabloid press coverage of female stars. "There doesn't seem to be the same obsession with catching male celebrities in these disreputable acts—which would be perfectly easy to do—as there is with these young women," says Charles Ponce de Leon, author of *Self-Exposure: Human-Interest Journalism and the Emergence of Celebrity in America, 1890–1940.* "The spotlight is harsh and unforgiving on these women because they seem to be wantonly violating conventional norms."

The public's appetite for feminine suffering once fed by tales of heartbreak is now sated by a stint in rehab or behind bars. What was once a self-satisfied desire to protect is now an urgent need to punish. As Wilson observes, "We are engaging in our new favorite dysfunctional love-hate relationship: Public stoning of the celebrity hooker."

Take, for example, Britney Spears. People were on her side after she kicked her deadbeat husband to the curb, but she felt the wrath of her fans at her nightclub shenanigans, which were deemed inappropriate for a new mother. We may be OK with our stars being single, but they're still not free of their womanly duty to "behave."

The news isn't all bad, however. We may not care much for the "skank posse," but the demise of the love-obsessed tragic Cinderella is good reason to celebrate. Today's dominant feminine imperative is not to suffer but to prevail over emotional adversity. Female stars emerge from their divorces looking radiant and liberated, à la Nicole Kidman, whose career soared after being publicly dumped by her husband. Even Diana's story is being revised to suit a twenty-first-century sensibility. The book jacket of Andrew Morton's revised iteration of Diana's life in 2004 touts her "courageous evolution from life as a downtrodden wife and reluctant royal fashion plate to a self-confident and independent modern woman."

A primary reason for our newfound tolerance is also a significant shift in demographics. Dedicating your life to the so-called "desperate search for love" increasingly seems absurd in a culture where relationships often don't last forever and in which—as DePaulo points out—Americans, on average, will spend more years of their adult lives single than married, partly because they're marrying later and living longer as widows. No wonder a recent Pew survey found that 79 percent of Americans believe a woman can lead a complete and happy life if she remains single. (The figure for men was actually lower, at 67 percent.)

Our vision of a happy life for a single female star, however, still requires a continual stream of love affairs, temporary though they may be, and the various Hollywood accoutrements—low body fat, plastic surgery, fabulous wardrobe—that establish her "hotness." In other words, the women we admire are like Diana, sans the self-pity and desperation. It is progress—of a sort.

LAKSHMI CHAUDHRY, a *Nation* contributing writer, is a Puffin Foundation Writing Fellow at The Nation Institute.

Reprinted by permission from the August 27/September 3, 2007, pp. 22–25 issue of *The Nation*. Copyright © 2007 by The Nation. For subscription information, call 1-800-333-8536. Portions of each week's Nation magazine can be accessed at www.thenation.com

Article 11

The Beauty of Simplicity

I'm snuggled under the covers with Jon Stewart and the remote. The "Evolution/Schmevolution" skit is funny, but it's been a long day, and I'm fading fast. The promise of technology is that I'm one click away from slumberland. I hit the power button. The picture disappears, but the TV is still glowing a creepy blue that will haunt my dreams if I don't make it go away. I try the TV button. Nothing. The cable button. Nothing. What the %$*&?? I kick off the blankets and trudge over to turn off the miserable box at the source. I can't help but wonder, as I lie there, now wide awake, how it is that all the things that were supposed to make our lives so easy instead made them more complex. Why is so much technology still so hard?

LINDA TISCHLER

It is innovation's biggest paradox: We demand more and more from the stuff in our lives—more features, more function, more power—and yet we also increasingly demand that it be easy to use. And, in an Escher-like twist, the technology that's simplest to use is also, often, the most difficult to create.

Marissa Mayer lives with that conundrum every day. As Google's director of consumer Web products, she's responsible for the search site's look and feel. Mayer is a tall, blond 30-year-old with two Stanford degrees in computer science and an infectious laugh. She's also Google's high priestess of simplicity, defending the home page against all who would clutter it up. "I'm the gatekeeper," she says cheerfully. "I have to say no to a lot of people."

The technology that powers Google's search engine is, of course, anything but simple. In a fraction of a second, the software solves an equation of more than 500 million variables to rank 8 billion Web pages by importance. But the actual experience of those fancy algorithms is something that would satisfy a Shaker: a clean, white home page, typically featuring no more than 30 lean words; a cheery, six-character, primary-colored logo; and a capacious search box. It couldn't be friendlier or easier to use.

Here is how Mayer thinks about the tension between complexity of function and simplicity of design: "Google has the functionality of a really complicated Swiss Army knife, but the home page is our way of approaching it closed. It's simple, it's elegant, you can slip it in your pocket, but it's got the great doodad when you need it. A lot of our competitors are like a Swiss Army knife open—and that can be intimidating and occasionally harmful."

It would be lovely if Google's corporate mythology included an enchanting tale to account for the birth of this pristine marvel. But the original home-page design was dumb luck. In 1998, founders Sergey Brin and Larry Page were consumed with writing code for their engine. Brin just wanted to hack together something to send queries to the back end, where the cool technology resided. Google didn't have a Web master, and Brin didn't do HTML. So he designed as little as he could get away with.

The accident became an icon, of course, and a key reason the company enjoys a commanding lead. Google's design has been mimicked on the search pages of MSN and Yahoo, whose portals are messy throwbacks to the "everything but the kitchen sink" school of Web design. But they're poor imitations; according to Hitwise, Google controls 59.2% of the search market, up from 45% a year ago; MSN's share is down to 5.5% and Yahoo's is 28.8%.

No surprise that a site easy enough for a technophobe to use has caught the public imagination. Like desperate Gullivers, we're pinned down by too much information and too much stuff. By one estimate, the world produced five exabytes (one quintillion bytes) of content in 2002—the same amount churned out between 25,000 B.C. and A.D. 2000. Little wonder that *Real Simple* has been the most successful magazine launched in a decade, and the blogosphere is abuzz over the season's hottest tech innovation—the Hipster PDA: 15 index cards held together by a binder clip.

The Simple, and the Simply Awful

A pantheon of technology products that marry great performance with simplicity of design—and those that miss the mark

Products we love . . .

TiVo, by TiVo. It's not often that owners refer to their pet technology as "life changing," but the ability to watch 24 at 3 A.M. surely counts as one of the decade's greatest humanitarian breakthroughs. The remote, the intuitive menus, the crisp instructions—everything about it can make even your parents feel smart.

iPod, by Apple. You don't have to be a hipster to love iPod, which plays Henry Mancini as easily as it blasts Cannibal Corpse.

Skype's Voice-over-Internet service. Cheap long distance? Without having to deal with the phone company? What's not to love?

Google's search engine. So good it's a verb. The real question is, How did we find anything in the pre-Google era?

BlackBerry by RIM. Love 'em or hate 'em, their ubiquity speaks for itself. Sure beats lugging around an eightpound laptop just to get email.

. . . and love to hate

Universal remote. So many buttons, so little time—and more complicated than the flight deck of the starship *Enterprise*. If you're an engineering prof (or a 14-year-old), it's heaven on earth. For the rest of us, it's easier to haul our weary bodies out of the La-Z-Boy than to figure out how to turn of the TV with this thing.

PeopleSoft software. The product most likely to induce a bout of Tourette's syndrome in the office.

LG VX6100 cell phone. Why is it so hard to make it shut up? Finding the MUTE button requires digging through the innards of the user's manual.

HP Officejet 7110 printer. It does it all—printing, scanning, copying, faxing—and does it all badly.

Sony Synthesized Radio. One aggravated owner complained, "It's impossible to program. You can't get the clock to stop blinking . . . and the antenna is useless." But it looks cool.

With Google's extraordinary trajectory and the stratospheric success of Apple's iPod—itself a marvel of simplicity and, with 20 million units sold, a staggering hit—we seem to be nearing a seminal moment. Whereas endless Sunday Styles stories may have failed to get its attention, the tech industry's interest is invariably galvanized by cash. If the equation T(technology) + E(ease of use) = $ can be proven, the time may be right for the voice of the technologically challenged who can't operate their remotes to be heard.

In a 2002 poll, the Consumer Electronics Association discovered that 87% of people said ease of use is the most important thing when it comes to new technologies. "Engineers say, 'Do you know how much complexity we've managed to build in here?' But consumers say, 'I don't care. It's just supposed to work!' " says Daryl Plummer, group vice president at Gartner Group.

It's often that tension—between the desire to cram in cool new features and the desire to make a product easy to use—that makes delivering on the simplicity promise so hard, particularly in companies where engineers hold sway. At Google, it's an ongoing battle. As developers come up with ever sexier services—maps! news alerts! scholarly papers!—the pressure to lard on links is fierce. Mayer holds them at bay with a smile and strict standards.

To make it to the home page, a new service needs to be so compelling that it will garner millions of page views per day. Contenders audition on the advanced-search page; if they prove their mettle—as image search did, growing from 700,000 page views daily to 2 million in two weeks—they may earn a permanent link. Few make the cut, and that's fine. Google's research shows that users remember just 7 to 10 services on rival sites. So Google offers a miserly six services on its home page. By contrast, MSN promotes more than 50, and Yahoo, over 60. And both sell advertising off their home pages; Google's is a commercial-free zone.

I want to figure out how to combine simplicity, which is basic human life, with this thing—technology—that's out of control.

So why don't those sites simply hit the DELETE button and make theirhome pages more Googlesque? Hewing to the simplicity principle, it turns out, is tougher than connecting with tech support, particularly if you try it retrospectively. "Once you have a home page like our competitors'," Mayer says, "paring it back to look like Google's is impossible. You have too many stakeholders who feel they should be promoted on the home page." (MSN says more than half its customers are happy with its home page—but it's experimenting with a sleeker version called "start.com.")

Google understands that simplicity is both sacred and central to its competitive advantage. Mayer is a specialist in artificial intelligence, not design, but she hits on the secret to her home page's success: "It gives you what you want, when you want it, rather than everything you could ever want, even when you don't."

That, says Joe Duffy, founder of the award-winning Minneapolis design firm Duffy & Partners and author of *Brand Apart*, is a pretty good definition of good design. He quotes a famous line from the eminent designer Milton Glaser: "Less isn't more; just enough is more." Just enough, says Duffy, contains an aesthetic component that differentiates one experience from another.

It's just that holding the line on what constitutes "just enough" is harder than it looks.

It's early September, and the streets of Cambridge, Massachusetts, are teeming with young technorati in flip-flops and shorts. But there is calm at the MIT Media Lab, just upstairs from the List Visual Arts Center, the university's preeminent gallery. It's a fitting juxtaposition, a place where art and technology seek common ground.

John Maeda runs the Media Lab's Simplicity Consortium. His goal is to find ways to break free from the intimidating complexity of today's technology and the frustration of information overload. He is a gentle, soft-spoken man, dressed elegantly in a crisp, white collarless shirt and black pants. And he is an unusual amalgam: having the mathematical wizardry of a computer geek with the soul of an artist. Indeed, in 1990, he left MIT for four years to study art. "My whole life changed," he says. "I thought, this is a great way to live." But rather than throwing over his digital life entirely, he conceived a mission. "I came back to MIT to figure out how you could combine simplicity, which is basic human life, with this thing—technology—that's out of control."

Maeda's ability to toggle back and forth between right brain and left affords him unusual insight into how we got stuck in this technological quagmire. On one level, he says, the problem is simply one of scale. Before computer technology, small things were simple; big things were more likely complex. But the microchip changed that. Now small things can be complex, too. But small objects have less room for instruction—so we get cell phones with tip calculators buried deep in submenus and user manuals the size of the Oxford English Dictionary to help us figure it all out.

Blame the closed feedback loop among engineers and industrial designers, who simply can't conceive of someone so lame that she can't figure out how to download a ringtone; blame a competitive landscape in which piling on new features is the easiest way to differentiate products, even if it makes them harder to use; blame marketers who haven't figured out a way to make "ease of use" sound hip. "It's easier," says Charles Golvin, principal analyst with Forrester Research, "to market technology than ease of use."

Across the river from MIT, in the Boston suburb of West Newton, Aaron Oppenheimer runs the product behavior group of Design Continuum, one of the country's preeminent design firms. He is the sympathetic counselor who gently points out that for each feature clients want to include—"Hey, if we've got a microprocessor in there, let's add an alarm clock!"—they're trading off a degree of ease of use. It's a never-ending battle. "I spend a lot of time talking clients out of adding features," he says with a sigh. "Every new feature makes things more complicated, even if you never use them."

In the past, he says, adding features usually meant adding costs. Put a sound system or power windows into a car, and you've upped the price, so you better make sure consumers really want what you're peddling. But in the digital world, that cost-benefit calculus has gone awry. "The incremental cost to add 10 features instead of one feature is just nothing," says Oppenheimer. "Technology is this huge blessing because we can do anything with it, and this huge curse because we can do anything with it."

But the issue is also our conflicted relationship with technology. We want the veneer of simplicity but with all the bells and whistles modern technology can provide. "The market for simplicity is complex," says Dan Ariely, a business-school professor who is spending a year off from MIT figuring out how to quantify the value of simplicity at Princeton's Institute for Advanced Study. "If I offer you a VCR with only one button, it's not all that exciting, even if when you use it, it's likely to be easier."

We also want our devices to talk to each other—cell phone to the Web, digital camera to printer. That requires a level of interoperability that would be difficult to attain in a perfect world, but is well nigh impossible in one where incompatibility is a competitive strategy. "In business, it's all about war," says Maeda. "I hate to sound like a hippie, but if there were just some sense of peace and love, products would be much better."

In his quiet way, Maeda hopes to right the balance between man and machine. He and his students are working on software, code-named OPENSTUDIO, that would create an "ecosystem of design"—connecting designers with customers on a broad scale. That could lead to bespoke products—a cell phone, for example, with 30 features for Junior, 3 for Gran. "You can't make the world simpler unless you can get in touch with design," he says, "and the only way you can do that is to get in touch with designers."

How do you make your company's products simpler? You can start by simplifying your company.

In the late 1990s, Royal Philips Electronics was a slow footed behemoth whose products, from medical diagnostic imaging systems to electric shavers, were losing traction in the marketplace. By 2002, a new CEO, Gerard Kleisterlee, determined that the company urgently needed to address the dynamic global marketplace and become more responsive to consumers' changing needs.

Philips deployed researchers in seven countries, asking nearly 2,000 consumers to identify the biggest societal issue that the company should address. The response was loud and urgent. "Almost immediately, we hit on the notion of complexity and its relationship to human beings," says Andrea Ragnetti, Philips's chief marketing officer. Consumers told the researchers that they felt overwhelmed by the complexity of technology. Some 30% of home-networking products were returned because people couldn't get them to work. Nearly 48% of people had put off buying a digital camera because they thought it would be too complicated.

Strategists recognized a huge opportunity: to be the company that delivered on the promise of sophisticated technology without the hassles. Philips, they said, should position itself as a simple company. Ragnetti was dumbstruck. "I said, 'You must be joking. This is an organization built on complexity, sophistication, brainpower.' " But he and Kleisterlee responded with an even more audacious plan. Rather than merely retooling products, Philips would also transform itself into a simpler, more market-driven organization.

The market for simplicity is complex. If I offer you a VCR with only one button, it's not all that exciting, even if when you use it, it's likely to be easier.

That initiative has been felt from the highest rungs of the organization to the lowest. Instead of 500 different businesses, Philips is now in 70; instead of 30 divisions, there are 5. Even things as prosaic as business meetings have been nudged in the direction of simplicity: The company now forbids more than 10 slides in any PowerPoint presentation. Just enough, they decided, was more.

The campaign, christened "Sense and Simplicity," required that everything Philips did going forward be technologically advanced—but it also had to be designed with the end user in mind and be easy to experience. That ideal has influenced product development from conception—each new product, like the ShoqBox, an MP3 mini-boom box, must be based on a user need that's tested and validated—to packaging. Philips invited 15 customers to its Consumer Experience Research Centre in Bruges, Belgium, to see how they unpacked and set up a Flat TV. After watching people struggle to lift the heavy set from an upright box, designers altered the packaging so the TV could be removed from a carton lying flat on the ground.

While many of the new products have yet to hit the market, early results of the business reorganization, particularly in North America, have been dramatic. Sales growth for the first half of 2005 was up 35%, and the company was named Supplier of the Year by Best Buy and Sam's Club. Philips's Ambilight Flat TV and GoGear Digital Camcorder won European iF awards for integrating advanced technologies into a consumer-friendly design, and the Consumer Electronics Association handed the company 12 Innovation Awards for products ranging from a remote control to a wearable sport audio player.

Maeda, who, as a member of Philips's Simplicity Advisory Board has had a front-row seat for this transformation, is impressed. "The best indication of their sincerity is that they're embracing the concept at a management level," says Maeda. "It isn't just marketing to them. That's quite a radical thing."

Designing products that are easy to use is nothing new for Intuit, the big tax- and business-software company. Indeed, it's been the mantra since founder Scott Cook developed Intuit's first product, Quicken, back in 1983 after listening to his wife complain about writing checks and managing bills.

But even by Intuit's standards, Simple Start, a basic accounting package that debuted in September 2004, was a leap. For one thing, the target market was tiny businesses that used no software at all. "These were people who said, 'I have a simple business, and I don't want the complexity of having to learn this. I don't want to use the jargon, I don't want the learning curve, and besides, I'm afraid of it,' " says project manager Terry Hicks.

But the potential was huge: some 9 million microbusiness owners that Intuit wasn't reaching with its current line. So Hicks's team first tried a knockoff of Intuit's QuickBooks Basic, with a bunch of features turned off. Then they confidently took the product out for a test-drive with 100 potential customers.

And it bombed. It was still too hard to use, still riddled with accounting jargon, still too expensive. They realized they had to start from scratch. "We had to free ourselves and say, 'Okay, from an engineering point of view, we're going to use this code base, but we need to design it from a customer's point of view,' " says Lisa Holzhauser, who was in charge of the product's user interface.

The designers followed more customers home. They heard more complaints about complexity, but also anxiety that things in their business might be falling through the cracks. So the team distilled two themes that would guide their development: The product had to be simple, and it had to inspire confidence. Terms such as "aging reports" and "invoicing" were edited out, and the designers drew on the experience of the SnapTax division, which had hired an editor from *People* magazine to help translate accountant-speak into real-world language. Accounts receivable became "Money In," accounts payable, "Money Out." They pared back 125 setup screens to three, and 20 major tasks to six essentials. They spent days worrying about the packaging, knowing that to this audience, something labeled "Simple Accounting" was an oxymoron.

Above all, they subjected their work to the demanding standards of Intuit's usability lab, run by Kaaren Hanson. To get a product by her, users must be able, 90% of the time, to accomplish the tasks deemed most critical. It's a draconian standard. But "if our goal was to make it 'as easy as we can,' " Hanson says, "we wouldn't be as successful as if we had set a concrete number."

The Simple Start team thought they had nailed the user-interface problem after their third iteration of the product got rave reviews for its look and feel. But task completion results from the lab were dismal. The launch was delayed for months while the team reengineered the tools until they measured up.

The additional time was worth it. Simple Start—a product with 15 years of sophisticated QuickBooks code lurking behind an interface even a Luddite could love—sold 100,000 units in its first year on the market. Even better, reviews from target customers indicate that Intuit hit the mark. Ken Maples, owner of a tiny flight-instruction school in Cupertino, California, summed it up: "It's easy to use. It's got everything I need and nothing more." Ah . . . just enough. Good. Somewhere, Milton Glaser is smiling.

LINDA TISCHLER (ltischler@fastcompany.com) is a *Fast Company* senior writer. TiVo changed her life, but she can't find the mute button on her new phone. Jennifer Reingold contributed to this story.

From *Fast Company,* issue 100, November 2005, pp. 54, 56, 59–60. Copyright © 2005 by Mansueto Ventures LLC. Reprinted by permission via the Copyright Clearance Center.

UNIT 2
Telling Stories

Unit Selections

12. **Whatever Happened to Iraq?: How the Media Lost Interest in a Long-running War with No End in Sight,** Sherry Ricchiardi
13. **"You Don't Understand Our Audience": What I Learned about Network Television at Dateline NBC,** John Hockenberry
14. **What the Mainstream Media Can Learn from Jon Stewart,** Rachel Smolkin
15. **Other Voices,** Kiera Butler
16. **Return of the Sob Sisters,** Stephanie Shapiro
17. **Climate Change: Now What?,** Cristine Russell
18. **Myth-Making in New Orleans,** Brian Thevenot
19. **Double Whammy,** Raquel Christie
20. **Wonderful Weeklies,** Julia Cass
21. **Beyond News,** Mitchell Stephens
22. **Rocketboom!,** Paul Farhi
23. **Epidemic,** Trudy Lieberman

Key Points to Consider

- What is your take on media coverage of war and politics? What are your primary sources of information on these topics?

- Analyze an issue of a news magazine. Rate each page of editorial copy on a 1 (hard news) to 5 (soft news) scale. Note examples of editorial viewpoints and/or subjectivity in the selection and presentation of information. If you were the editor, what would you do differently? Why?

- Watch newscasts on two different networks on the same evening (in many markets, you can find one network's early evening news airing on the half hour and another on the hour, or you can videotape one network while watching another). Record the stories covered, in the order in which they are reported, and the time devoted to each. Did you notice any patterns in the reporting? Were there any differences in the way stories on the same topic were presented? Did you note any instances in which editorial or entertainment values were reflected in the story selection or coverage? What conclusions do you draw from your findings?

- To what extent do you agree with the criticisms of news and information media? What do you think accounts for the American public's increasing disinterest in hard news topics? Is it the media's fault? Should making news more interesting/appealing be a media priority? Why or why not?

Student Web Site
www.mhcls.com

Internet References

Cable News Network
http://www.cnn.com
Fairness and Accuracy in Reporting
http://www.fair.org
Organization of News Ombudsmen (ONO)
http://www.newsombudsmen.org
Television News Archive
http://tvnews.vanderbilt.edu

The reporting of news and information was not, in the beginning, considered an important function within broadcast media organizations. Television news was originally limited to 15-minute commercial-free broadcasts, presented as a public service. Over the years, however, the news business has become big business. News operations are intensely competitive, locked in head-to-head popularity races, in which the loss of one ratings point can translate into a loss of millions of dollars in advertising revenue, and in which, smaller-market media are aware that alienating a major advertiser can spell financial disaster.

News, by definition, is timely: It is "news," not "olds." Decisions regarding what stories to play and how to play them are made under tight deadlines. Media expert Wilbur Schramm has noted that "hardly anything about communication is so impressive as the enormous number of choices and discards and interpretations that have to be made between [an] actual news event and the symbols that later appear in the mind of a reporter, an editor, a reader, a listener, or a viewer. Therefore, even if everyone does his job perfectly, it is hard enough to get the report of an event straight and clear and true." Schramm's comments point to the tremendous impact of selectivity in crafting news messages. The process is called *gatekeeping*.

Gatekeeping is necessary. News operations cannot logistically cover or report every event that happens in the world from one edition or broadcast to the next. The concerns associated with the reality of gatekeeping relate to whether or not the gatekeepers abuse the privilege of deciding what information or viewpoints the mass audience receive. Simply being selected for media coverage lends an issue, an event, or an individual a certain degree of celebrity—the "masser" the medium, the greater the effect.

Traditional news media are under enormous pressure to remain competitive in a changing media environment. Daily U.S. newspaper circulation peaked at 62.3 million in 1990. Circulation today is about 50 million, close to what it was in 1950, when the total population was half of what it is now. Some 50,000 news industry employees lost their jobs between 2001 and 2006. Between 1970 and 2006, the percentage of U.S. homes with televisions turned on at news time and tuned to the nightly news (in Nielsen terms, the combined news "share") declined from 75% to 35%. The average age of viewers of prime-time television is 42, about the median age of the population as a whole; the median age of network evening news viewers is 60. The percentage of people who report that they never watch a nightly news broadcast has more than doubled.

In his novel *The Evening News*, Arthur Hailey observed: "People watch the news to find out the answers to three questions, Is the world safe? Are my home and family safe? and, Did anything happen today that was interesting?" Given cursory answers to those questions, viewers are satisfied that they are "keeping up," although the total amount of news delivered in a half-hour newscast would, if set in type, hardly fill the front page of a daily newspaper. Many adults report that they are too busy to follow the news, or are suspicious of the media, or find the news too depressing. In one recent study, 27% of television viewers described themselves as "stressed" while watching the evening news (51% reported feeling "stressed" watching Martha Stewart). Availability and consumption of *information*, however, is on the rise. Knowledge of sports and celebrities has increased, while knowledge of local and national politics has decreased.

The articles in this section explore the changing landscape of contemporary news and information coverage and consumption. The first two articles discuss gatekeeping. "Whatever Happened to Iraq?" suggests reasons for the declining coverage of the Iraq War. "'You Don't Understand Our Audience': What I Learned about Network Television at Dateline NBC" provides former *Dateline NBC* correspondent John Hockenberry's views on tensions among the editorial, technical, and business decisions in television news. "What the Mainstream Media Can Learn from Jon Stewart" proposes "lessons for newspapers and networks struggling to hold on to fleeting readers, viewers, and advertisers in a tumultuous era of transition for old media." Jon Stewart aficionados fare well. "Return of the Sob Sisters" analyzes the appeal of long-format feature stories that frequently become "less about providing information and more about manipulating emotions."

The next two articles take on questions of bias or spin in the reporting on global warming. "Climate Change: Now What?" takes the position that media have appropriately moved beyond debating the presence of global warming to advocating for political, economic, and consumer actions to mitigate its progress. "Double Whammy" presents a case study of news coverage of race and racism by the national media. "Epidemic" provides perspective on the business-media partnership between hospitals and television news channels.

"Beyond News" and "Rocketboom!" focus on new media, and what has been called, differentiation of news product. "Beyond News" suggests that mainstream news is on the brink of being pushed out of prominence by the capabilities of the Internet. The article recommends current news organizations to "flip" from reporting to analyzing information, rather than trying to compete with the Web. "Rocketboom!" explores the quirky creativity and expanding reach of videoblogs. Blogs take many forms; some are personal, some devoted to celebrities, some to hobbies, some to politics and news. Of the latter, a handful have achieved bona fide influence as alternative news sources. With that influence comes questions of conduct, ethics, and regulation.

Communicating news and information is a critical function of mass media; the degree to which media perform, and are perceived to perform, and their gatekeeping and watchdog functions are of critical importance. In his book *Tuned Out: Why Americans Under 40 Don't Follow the News,* David T.Z. Mindich writes, "Robert Putnam's 2000 book, *Bowling Alone,* charted the decay of what the author called 'social capital,' the important resource of public and quasi-public dialogue. For example, Putnam discovered that more people bowl than ever before, but fewer bowl in leagues; hence, the title of his book. But bowling is just the start. The last half century has seen a decline in membership in unions, Elks clubs, and PTAs; fewer people give dinner parties, speak in public, go to church, and attend the theater . . . . Putnam convincingly demonstrated a correlation between the lack of social capital and news consumption. The same people who join groups and write their representatives also read newspapers. The same people who have trust in the system, and their ability to change it, use the news for ammunition. The same people who distrust each other, drop out of society, and become isolated, find news irrelevant to their lives." It is arguable that a decline in careful and credible coverage of important events and issues among media has contributed to decline in social capital. However, in a market-driven media climate, it is difficult for news media to sustain an economically viable hard news orientation when a declining number of consumers express interest in that product.

Article 12

Whatever Happened to Iraq?
How the Media Lost Interest in a Long-running War with No End in Sight

SHERRY RICCHIARDI

Armando Acuna, public editor of the Sacramento Bee, turned a Sunday column into a public flogging for both his editors and the nation's news media. They had allowed the third-longest war in American history to slip off the radar screen, and he had the numbers to prove it.

The public also got a scolding for its meager interest in a controversial conflict that is costing taxpayers about $12.5 billion a month, or nearly $5,000 a second, according to some calculations. In his March 30 commentary, Acuna noted: "There's enough shame ... for everyone to share."

He had watched stories about Iraq move from 1A to the inside pages of his newspaper, if they ran at all. He understood the editors' frustration over how to handle the mind-numbing cycles of violence and complex issues surrounding Operation Iraqi Freedom. "People feel powerless about this war," he said in an interview in April.

Acuna knew the Sacramento Bee was not alone.

For long stretches over the past 12 months, Iraq virtually disappeared from the front pages of the nation's newspapers and from the nightly network newscasts. The American press and the American people had lost interest in the war.

The decline in coverage of Iraq has been staggering. During the first 10 weeks of 2007, Iraq accounted for 23 percent of the newshole for network TV news. In 2008, it plummeted to 3 percent during that period. On cable networks it fell from 24 percent to 1 percent, according to a study by the Project for Excellence in Journalism.

The numbers also were dismal for the country's dailies. By Acuna's count, during the first three months of this year, front-page stories about Iraq in the Bee were down 70 percent from the same time last year. Articles about Iraq once topped the list for reader feedback. By mid-2007, "Their interest just dropped off; it was noticeable to me," says the public editor.

A daily tracking of 65 newspapers by the Associated Press confirms a dip in page-one play throughout the country. In September 2007, the AP found 457 Iraq-related stories (154 by the AP) on front pages, many related to a progress report delivered to Congress by Gen. David Petraeus, the top U.S. commander in Iraq. Over the succeeding months, that number fell to as low as 49. A spike in March 2008 was largely due to a rash of stories keyed to the conflict's fifth anniversary, according to AP Senior Managing Editor Mike Silverman.

During the early stages of shock and awe, Americans were glued to the news as Saddam Hussein's statue was toppled in Baghdad and sweat-soaked Marines bivouacked in his luxurious palaces. It was a huge story when President Bush landed on the aircraft carrier USS Abraham Lincoln on May 1, 2003, and declared major combat operations were over.

By March 2008, a striking reversal had taken place. Only 28 percent of Americans knew that 4,000 military personnel had been killed in the conflict, according to a survey by the Pew Research Center for the People & the Press. Eight months earlier, 54 percent could cite the correct casualty rate.

TV news was a vivid indicator of the declining interest. The three broadcast networks' nightly newscasts devoted more than 4,100 minutes to Iraq in 2003 and 3,000 in 2004. That leveled off to 2,000 annually. By late 2007, it was half that, according to Andrew Tyndall, who monitors the nightly news (tyndall report.com).

In broadcast, there's a sense that the appetite for Iraq coverage has grown thin.

"In broadcast, there's a sense that the appetite for Iraq coverage has grown thin. The big issue is how many people stick with it. It is not less of a story," said Jeffrey Fager, executive producer of "60 Minutes," during the Reva and David Logan Symposium on Investigative Reporting in late April at the Graduate School of Journalism at the University of California, Berkeley. The number of Iraq-related stories aired on "60 Minutes" has been consistent over the past two years. The total from April 2007 through March 2008 was 15, one fewer than during the same period the year before.

Despite the pile of evidence of waning coverage, news managers interviewed for this story consistently maintained there was no conscious decision to back off. "I wasn't hearing that in our newsroom," says Margaret Sullivan, editor of the Buffalo News. Yet numbers show that attention to the war plummeted at the Buffalo paper as it did at other news outlets.

Why the dramatic drop-off? Gatekeepers offer a variety of reasons, from the enormous danger for journalists on the ground in

Iraq (see "Obstructed View," April/May 2007) to plunging newsroom budgets and shrinking news space. Competing megastories on the home front like the presidential primaries and the sagging economy figure into the equation. So does the exorbitant cost of keeping correspondents in Baghdad.

No one questioned the importance of a grueling war gone sour or the looming consequences for the United States and the Middle East. Instead, newsroom managers talked about the realities of life in a rapidly changing media market, including smaller newsholes and, for many, a laser-beam focus on local issues and events.

Los Angeles Times' foreign editor Marjorie Miller attributes the decline to three factors:

The economic downturn and the contentious presidential primaries have sucked oxygen from Iraq. "We have a woman, an African American and a senior running for president," Miller says. "That is a very big story."

With no solutions in sight, with no light at the end of the tunnel, war fatigue has become a factor. Over the years, a bleak sameness has settled into accounts of suicide bombings and brutal sectarian violence. Insurgents fighting counterinsurgents are hard to translate to an American audience.

The sheer cost of keeping correspondents on the ground in Baghdad is trimming the roster of journalists. The expense is "unlike anything we've ever faced. We have shouldered the financial burden so far, but we are really squeezed," Miller says. Earlier, the L.A. Times had as many as five Western correspondents in the field. The bureau is down to two or three plus Iraqi staff.

Other media decision-makers echo Miller's analysis.

When Lara Logan, the high-profile chief senior foreign correspondent for CBS News, is rotated out of Iraq, she might not be replaced, says her boss, Senior Vice President Paul Friedman. The network is sending in fewer Westerners from European and American bureaus and depending more on local staff, a common practice for media outlets with personnel in Iraq. "We won't pull out, but we are making adjustments," Friedman says.

Friedman defends the cutbacks: "One of the definitions of news is change, and there are long periods now in Iraq when very little changes. Therefore, it's difficult for the Iraq story to fight its way on the air against other news where change is involved," such as the political campaign, he says.

John Stack, Fox News Channel's vice president for newsgathering, has no qualms about allotting more airtime to the presidential campaign than to Iraq. "This is a very big story playing out on the screen every night.... The time devoted to news is finite," Stack says. "It's a matter of shifting to another story of national interest."

Despite diminished emphasis on the war, Fox has no plans to cut back its Baghdad operation. "We still have a full complement of people there, operating in a very difficult environment. That hasn't gone down at all," he says. Fox has two full reporting teams in Iraq as well as a bureau chief and some local staff, for a total of 25 to 30 people, according to Stack.

In late 2007, the networks—CBS, NBC, ABC, CNN and Fox—entertained the notion of pooling resources in Iraq to cut expenses. After much discussion, the idea was tabled. "It turned out not to be possible," Friedman says. "To some extent, our needs are very different." Cable TV is all about constant repetition; even during lulls it features correspondents standing in front of cameras making reports. "The networks don't do that and don't need the same kind of facilities," Friedman says.

McClatchy Newspapers maintains a presence in Baghdad—a bureau chief, a rotating staffer generally from one of the chain's papers and six local staffers—but the decline in violence since the U.S. troop buildup last year has resulted in fewer daily stories, says Foreign Editor Roy Gutman. "We produce according to the news. During the [Iraqi] government's offensive in Basra [in March], we produced lengthy stories every day." To add another dimension to the coverage, McClatchy tapped into its Iraqi staff for compelling first-person accounts posted on its Washington bureau's Web site (mcclatchydc.com—see "A Blog of Heartbreak," April/May 2007).

New York Times Foreign Editor Susan Chira says she is content to run fewer stories than in the past. "But we want them to have impact. And, of course, when there are big running stories, we will stay on them every day."

Midsize dailies around the country face a different set of challenges. Many operate under mandates from their bosses to push local stories over national or international news in hope of boosting readership and advertising. In those publications, it often takes a strong community tie to propel Iraq onto page one.

Case in point: During the first week of February, the one story about Iraq that made 1A in the Buffalo News was headlined, "Close to home while far off at war." It told how the latest gadgetry helps local service members stay in touch with loved ones. During the same week a year ago, four Iraq-related stories made 1A. None appeared to have a local angle.

"There is strong local interest because we have a lot of service members over there and we have had quite a few deaths of local soldiers," Editor Sullivan says. "In my mind, there is no bigger nonlocal story. It's the expense, the lives, the policy issues, and what it means to the country's future. There is a general feeling that the media have tired of Iraq, but I have not."

At Alabama's Birmingham News, it takes a significant development to get an Iraq-related story prominent play without a local link, says Executive Editor Hunter George. During the first week in February, the Birmingham paper ran only one story related to the war. The topic: "Brownies send goodies, cards to troops in Iraq."

Editors did not sit in a news budget meeting and make a conscious decision to cut back on Iraq coverage, George says. He believes the repetitiveness of the storyline has something to do with the decline. "I see and hear it all the time. It seems like a bad dream, and the public's not interested in revisiting it unless there is a major development. If I'm outside the newsroom and Iraq comes up, I hear groans. People say, 'More bad news,' Stories about the economy are moving up the news scale."

It was big news for Pennsylvania's Reading Eagle when a wounded soldier came home from Iraq and was met by some 50 bikers at the airport. The "Patriot Guard," as they are called, provided an escort. Townspeople slapped together a carnival to help raise money for a wheelchair ramp. "For us, it comes down to the grassroots level," says Eagle reporter Dan Kelly.

Earlier that day, Kelly's editor had handed him an assignment about a Marine from nearby Exeter Township who rushed home from the war zone to visit his ailing grandfather. By the time he got there, he was facing a funeral instead. "We look for special circumstances like this," Kelly says. "We pick our battles."

The Indianapolis Star ramped up coverage in January when the 76th Infantry Brigade Combat Team from the Indiana National Guard was redeployed to Iraq. The newspaper created a special Web page to help readers stay in touch with the more than 3,000 soldiers from around the state, including graphics showing their hometowns and how the combat gear they wear works in the war zone.

"I don't want to mislead you and say our coverage has been consistent over the past 12 months. It has rolled and dipped. We have had calls from people who believe we underplay events like bombings where several people are killed," says Pam Fine, the Star's managing editor until early April. Front-page coverage of Iraq was the same in the first three months of 2007 and 2008. A total of 23 stories ran in each period. Fine left the paper to become the Knight Chair in News, Leadership and Community at the University of Kansas.

The reader representative for the San Francisco Chronicle doesn't think placement of stories about Iraq makes much difference. He reasons that five years in, most readers have formed clear opinions about the war. They're not likely to change their minds one way or another if a story runs on page one or page three, says Dick Rogers. "The public has become accustomed to the steady drumbeat of violence out of Iraq. A report of 20 or 30 killed doesn't bring fresh insight for a lot of people."

Americans might care if they could witness more of the human toll. That's the approach the Washington Post's Dana Milbank took in an April 24 piece titled, "What the Family Would Let You See, the Pentagon Obstructs."

When Lt. Col. Billy Hall was buried in Arlington National Cemetery in April, his family gave the media permission to cover the ceremony—he is among the highest-ranking officers to be killed in Iraq. But, according to Milbank, the military did everything it could to keep the journalists away, isolating them some 50 yards away behind a yellow rope.

The "de facto ban on media at Arlington funerals fits neatly" with White House efforts "to sanitize the war in Iraq," and that, in turn, has helped keep the bloodshed out of the public's mind, Milbank wrote in his Washington Sketch feature. There have been similar complaints over the years about the administration's policy that bans on-base photography of coffins returning from Iraq and Afghanistan. (See Drop Cap, June/July 2004.)

Despite the litany of reasons, some journalists still take a "shame on you" attitude toward those who have relegated the Iraq war to second-class status.

Sig Christenson, military writer for the San Antonio Express-News, has made five trips to the war zone and says he would go back in a heartbeat. "This is not a story we can afford to ignore," he says. "There are vast implications for every American, right down to how much gasoline costs when we go to the pump."

Christenson, a cofounder of the organization MRE—Military Reporters and Editors—believes the media have an obligation to provide context and nuance and make clear the complexities of the war so Americans better understand its seriousness. "That's our job," he says.

Along the same lines, Greg Mitchell, editor of Editor & Publisher, faults newsroom leaders for shortchanging "the biggest political and moral issue of our time."

"You can forgive the American public for being shocked at the recent violence in Basra [in March]. From the lack of press coverage that's out there, they probably thought the war was over," says Mitchell, who wrote about media performance in the book "So Wrong for So Long: How the Press, the Pundits—and the President—Failed on Iraq."

Both journalists point to cause and effect: The public tends to take cues from the media about what is important. If Iraq is pushed to a back burner, the signal is clear—the war no longer is a top priority. It follows that news consumers lose interest and turn their attention elsewhere. The Pew study found exactly that: As news coverage of the war diminished, so too did the public interest in Iraq.

Ellen Hume, research director at the MIT Center for Future Civic Media and a former journalist, believes the decline in Iraq news could be linked to a larger issue—profits. "The problem doesn't seem to be valuing coverage of the war; it's more about the business model of journalism today and what that market requires," Hume says.

"There is no sense that [the media] are going to be able to meet the numbers that their corporate owners require by offering news about a downer subject like Iraq. It's a terrible dilemma for news organizations."

Still, there has been some stunningly good reporting on Iraq over the past year.

Two of the Washington Post's six Pulitzer Prizes were war-related. Anne Hull and Dana Priest won the public service award for revealing the neglect of wounded soldiers at Walter Reed Army Medical Center (see Drop Cap, April/May 2007). Steve Fainaru won in the international reporting category for an examination of private security contractors in Iraq.

McClatchy's Baghdad bureau chief, Leila Fadel, collected the George R. Polk Award for outstanding foreign reporting. Judges offered high praise for her vivid depictions of the agonizing plight of families in ethnically torn neighborhoods.

CBS took two Peabody Awards, one for Scott Pelley's report on the killings of civilians in the Iraqi city of Haditha (see "A Matter of Time," August/September 2006) on "60 Minutes," another for Kimberly Dozier's report about two female veterans who lost limbs in Iraq on "CBS News Sunday Morning." Dozier herself was wounded in Iraq in May 2006.

ABC News correspondent Bob Woodruff, who was injured in Iraq in January 2006, received a Peabody Award for "Wounds of War," a series of reports about injured veterans.

There have been a series of groundbreaking investigations over the past year. In one of the most recent, the New York Times' David Barstow documented how the Pentagon cultivated military analysts to generate favorable news for the Bush administration's wartime performance. Many of the talking heads, including former generals, were being coached on what to tell viewers on television.

The Times continues to have a dominant presence on the ground in Iraq, sinking millions into maintaining its Baghdad complex, home and office to six or seven Western correspondents and a large Iraqi staff. Foreign Editor Chira says it has been more challenging to recruit people to go to Baghdad, but "we remain completely committed to maintaining a robust presence in Iraq."

Those are notable exceptions; no doubt there are more. But overall, Iraq remains the biggest nonstory of the day unless major news is breaking.

Mark Jurkowitz, associate director of the Project for Excellence in Journalism, points to May 24, 2007, as a major turning point in the coverage of U.S. policy toward Iraq. That's the day Congress voted to continue to fund the war without troop withdrawal timetables, giving the White House a major victory in a clash with the Democratic leadership over who would control the purse strings and thus the future of the war. Democrats felt they had a mandate from Americans to bring the troops home. President Bush stuck to a hard line and came out the victor. "The political fight was over," Jurkowitz says. "Iraq no longer was a hot story. The media began looking elsewhere."

Statistics from a report by Jurkowitz released in March 2008 support his theory. From January through May 2007, Iraq accounted for 20 percent of all news measured by PEJ's News Coverage Index. That period included the announcement of the troop "surge."

"But from the time of the May funding vote through the war's fifth anniversary on March 19, 2008, coverage plunged by about 50 percent. In that period, the media paid more than twice as much attention to the presidential campaigns than the war," according to PEJ.

"You could see the coverage of the political debate [over Iraq] shrink noticeably. The drop was dramatic," says Jurkowitz, who believes the press has an obligation to cover stories about Iraq even when the political landscape changes. "It is hard to say that the media has spurred any meaningful debate in America on this."

Is there anything to the concept of war fatigue or a psychological numbing that comes with rote reports of violence? Susan Tifft, professor of journalism and public policy at Duke University, believes there is.

She reasons that humans do adapt when the abnormal gradually becomes normal, such as a bloody and seemingly endless conflict far from America's shores. Tifft explains that despite tensions of the Cold War, America's default position for many years had been peace. Now the default position—the environment in which Americans live—is war. "And somehow we have gotten used to it. That's why it seems like wallpaper or Muzak. It's oddly normal and just part of the atmosphere," she says.

Does an acceptance of the status quo indicate helplessness or rational resignation on the part of the public and the press? Is it a survival mechanism?

Harvard University Professor Howard Gardner, a psychologist and social scientist, has explored what it is about the way humans operate that might allow this to happen.

Gardner explains that when a news story becomes repetitive, people "habituate"—the technical term for what happens when they no longer take in information. "You can be sure that if American deaths were going up, or if there was a draft, then there would not be acceptance of the status quo," Gardner wrote in an April 17 e-mail.

"But American deaths are pretty small, and the children of the political, business and chattering classes are not dying, and so the war no longer is on the radar screen most of the time. The bad economy has replaced it, and no one has yet succeeded in tying the trillion-dollar war to the decline in the economy."

New York Times columnist Nicholas D. Kristof is one who has tried. In a March 23 op-ed column, he quoted Nobel Prize-winning economist Joseph Stiglitz as saying the "present economic mess" is very much related to the Iraq war, which also "is partially responsible for soaring oil prices." Stiglitz calculated the eventual total cost to be about $3 trillion.

Kristof tossed out plenty of fodder for stories: "A congressional study by the Joint Economic Committee found that the sums spent on the Iraq war each day could enroll an additional 58,000 children in Head Start or give Pell Grants to 153,000 students to attend college . . . . [A] day's Iraq spending would finance another 11,000 border patrol agents or 9,000 police officers."

In Denver, Jason Salzman has been thinking along the same lines. The media critic for the Rocky Mountain News suggested in a February 16 column that news organizations "treat the economic costs of the war as they've treated U.S. casualties." After the death of the 3,000th American soldier, for instance, his newspaper printed the names of all the dead on the front page. To mark economic milestones, Salzman would like to see page one filled with graphics representing dollars Colorado communities have lost to the war.

"It's hard for me to realize why more reporters don't do these stories about the impact of the cost of the war back home," he said in an interview.

Another aspect of the war that could use more scrutiny is the Iraqi oil industry: Where is the money going? Who is benefiting? Why isn't oil money paying for a fair share of reconstruction costs?

Similarly, much more attention could be paid to the ramifications of stretching America's military to the limit.

And what about the impact of the war on the lives of ordinary Iraqis (see "Out of Reach," April/May 2006)? In April, Los Angeles Times correspondent Alexandra Zavis filed a story about a ballet school in Baghdad that had become an oasis for children of all ethnic and religious backgrounds.

"Now, more than ever," Zavis wrote in an e-mail interview, it "is the responsibility of journalists to put a name and a face on the mind-numbing statistics, to take readers in to the lives of ordinary Iraqis, and to find ways to convey what this unimaginable bloodshed means to the people who live it."

Jurkowitz's March 2008 report cited the "inverse relationship between war coverage and the coverage of the 2008 presidential campaign—an early-starting, wide-open affair that has fascinated the press since it began in earnest in January 2007. As attention to Iraq steadily declined, coverage of the campaign continued to grow in 2007 and 2008, consuming more of the press' attention and resources.

"Moreover, the expectation that Iraq would dominate the campaign conversation proved to be wrong," the report said. It was the economy instead. Jurkowitz cites what he calls an eye-catching statistic: In the first three months of 2008, coverage of the campaign outstripped war coverage by a ratio of nearly 11 to 1, or 43 percent of newshole compared with 4 percent.

But all that soon could change. "The [Iraq] story, we believe, remains as important as ever, and the debate about the future conduct of the war and the level of American troop presence in Iraq during the presidential campaign makes it crucial for the American public to be well informed," says the New York Times' Chira.

Jurkowitz agrees. That's why he's predicting a renaissance in Iraq coverage in the coming months. Battle lines already have been drawn: Sen. John McCain, the presumed Republican candidate, has vowed to stay the course in Iraq until victory is achieved. The Democrats favor withdrawing U.S. forces, perhaps beginning as early as six months after taking the oath of office.

"When we get in the general election mode, Iraq will be a big issue. The candidates will set the agenda for the discussion and the media will pick it up. This could reinvigorate the debate," Jurkowitz says. "The war will be back in the headlines."

Senior contributing writer **Sherry Ricchiardi** (sricchia@iupui.edu), who writes frequently about international coverage for *AJR*, assessed reporting on Iran in the magazine's February/March issue. Editorial assistant Roxana Hadadi (rhadadi@ajr.umd.edu) contributed research to this report.

Article 13

"You Don't Understand Our Audience"
What I Learned about Network Television at Dateline NBC

The most memorable reporting the author has encountered on the conflict in Iraq was delivered in the form of confetti exploding out of a cardboard tube. The falling confetti transported him back three years to the early days of the war in Iraq, when the bombs intended to evoke shock and awe were descending on Baghdad. In the New York offices of NBC News, one of his video stories was being screened. If it made it through the screening, it would be available for broadcast later that evening. Networks are built on the assumption that audience size is what matters most. Content is secondary; it exists to attract passive viewers who will sit still for advertisements. Life at the Media Lab has reminded him once again that technology is most exciting when it upsets the status quo. Technology as it has done through the ages, is freeing communication, and this is good news for the news.

JOHN HOCKENBERRY

The most memorable reporting I've encountered on the conflict in Iraq was delivered in the form of confetti exploding out of a cardboard tube. I had just begun working at the MIT Media Lab in March 2006 when Alyssa Wright, a lab student, got me to participate in a project called "Cherry Blossoms." I strapped on a backpack with a pair of vertical tubes sticking out of the top; they were connected to a detonation device linked to a Global Positioning System receiver. A microprocessor in the backpack contained a program that mapped the coördinates of the city of Baghdad onto those for the city of Cambridge; it also held a database of the locations of all the civilian deaths of 2005. If I went into a part of Cambridge that corresponded to a place in Iraq where civilians had died in a bombing, the detonator was triggered.

When the backpack exploded on a clear, crisp afternoon at the Media Lab, handfuls of confetti shot out of the cardboard tubes into the air, then fell slowly to earth. On each streamer of paper was written the name of an Iraqi civilian casualty. I had reported on the war (although not from Baghdad) since 2003 and was aware of persistent controversy over the numbers of Iraqi civilian dead as reported by the U.S. government and by other sources. But it wasn't until the moment of this fake explosion that the scale and horrible suddenness of the slaughter in Baghdad became vivid and tangible to me. Alyssa described her project as an upgrade to traditional journalism. "The upgrade is empathy," she said, with the severe humility that comes when you suspect you are on to something but are still uncertain you aren't being ridiculous in some way.

The falling confetti transported me back three years to the early days of the war in Iraq, when the bombs intended to evoke "shock and awe" were descending on Baghdad. Most of the Western press had evacuated, but a small contingent remained to report on the crumbling Iraqi regime. In the New York offices of NBC News, one of my video stories was being screened. If it made it through the screening, it would be available for broadcast later that evening. Producer Geoff Stephens and I had done a phone interview with a reporter in Baghdad who was experiencing the bombing firsthand. We also had a series of still photos of life in the city. The only communication with Baghdad in those early days was by satellite phone. Still pictures were sent back over the few operating data links.

Our story arranged pictures of people coping with the bombing into a slide show, accompanied by die voice of Melinda Liu, a *Newsweek* reporter describing, over the phone, the harrowing experience of remaining in Baghdad. The outcome of the invasion was still in doubt. There was fear in the reporter's voice and on the faces of the people in the pictures. The four minute piece was meant to be the kind of package that would run at the end of an hour of war coverage. Such montages were often used as "enders," to break up the segments of anchors talking live to field reporters at the White House or the Pentagon, or retired generals who were paid to stand on in-studio maps and provide analysis of what was happening. It was also understood that without commercials there would need to be taped pieces on standby in case an anchor needed to use the bathroom. Four minutes was just about right.

At the conclusion of the screening, there were a few suggestions for tightening here and clarification there. Finally, an NBC/GE executive responsible for "standards" shook his head and wondered about die tone in die reporter's voice. "Doesn't it seem like she has a point of view here?" he asked.

There was silence in the screening room. It made me want to twitch, until I spoke up. I was on to something but uncertain I wasn't about to be handed my own head. "Point of view? What exactly do you mean by *point of view?*" I asked. "That war is bad? Is that the *point of view* that you are detecting here?"

The story never aired. Maybe it was overtaken by breaking news, or maybe some pundit-general went long, or maybe an anchor was able to control his or her bladder. On the other hand, perhaps it was never aired because it contradicted the story NBC was telling. At NBC that night, war was, in fact, not bad. My remark actually seemed to have made the point for the "standards" person. Empathy for the civilians did not fit into the narrative of shock and awe. The lesson stayed with me, exploding in memory along with the confetti of Alyssa Wright's "Cherry Blossoms." Alyssa was right. Empathy was the upgrade. But in the early days of the war, NBC wasn't looking for any upgrades.

"This Is London"

When Edward R Murrow calmly said those words into a broadcast microphone during the London Blitz at the beginning of World War II, he generated an analog signal that was amplified, sent through a transatlantic cable, and relayed to transmitters that delivered his voice into millions of homes. Broadcast technology itself delivered a world-changing cultural message to a nation well convinced by George Washington's injunction to resist foreign "entanglements." Hearing Murrow's voice made Americans understand that Europe was close by, and so were its wars. Two years later, the United States entered World War II, and for a generation, broadcast technology would take Americans ever deeper into the battlefield, and even onto the surface of the moon. Communication technologies transformed America's view of itself, its politics, and its culture.

One might have thought that the television industry, with its history of rapid adaptation to technological change, would have become a center of innovation for the next radical transformation in communication. It did not. Nor did the ability to transmit pictures, voices, and stories from around the world to living rooms in the U.S. heartland produce a nation that is more sophisticated about global affairs. Instead, the United States is arguably more isolated and less educated about the world than it was a half-century ago. In a time of such broad technological change, how can this possibly be the case?

In the spring of 2005, after working in television news for 12 years, I was jettisoned from NBC News in one of die company's downsizings. The work that I and others at *Dateline NBC* had done—to explore how the Internet might create new opportunities for storytelling, new audiences, and exciting new mechanisms for the creation of journalism—had come to naught. After years of timid experiments, NBC News tacitly declared that it wasn't interested. The culmination of *Dateline's* Internet journalism strategy was the highly rated pile of programming debris called *To Catch a Predator.* The TCAP formula is to post offers of sex with minors on the Internet and see whether anybody responds. *Dateline's* notion of New Media was the technological equivalent of etching "For a good time call Sally" on a men's room stall and waiting with cameras to see if anybody copied down the number.

Networks are built on the assumption that audience size is what matters most. Content is secondary; it exists to attract passive viewers who will sit still for advertisements. For a while, that assumption served the industry well. But the TV news business has been blind to the revolution that made the viewer blink: the digital organization of communities that are anything but passive. Traditional market-driven media always attempt to treat devices, audiences, and content as bulk commodities, while users instead view all three as ways of creating and maintaining smaller-scale communities. As users acquire the means of producing and distributing content, the authority and profit potential of large traditional networks are directly challenged.

In the years since my departure from network television, I have acquired a certain detachment about how an institution so central to American culture could shift so quickly to the margins. Going from being a correspondent at *Dateline*—a rich source of material for *The Daily Show*—to working at the MIT Media Lab, where most students have no interest in or even knowledge of traditional networks, was a shock. It has given me some hard-won wisdom about the future of journalism, but it is still a mystery to me why television news remains so dissatisfying, so superficial, and so irrelevant. Disappointed veterans like Walter Cronkite and Dan Rather blame the moral failure of ratings-obsessed executives, but it's not that simple. I can say with confidence that Murrow would be outraged not so much by the networks' greed (Murrow was one of the first news personalities to hire a talent agent) as by the missed opportunity to use technology to help create a nation of engaged citizens bent on preserving their freedom and their connections to the broader world.

I knew it was pretty much over for television news when I discovered in 2003 that the heads of NBC's news division and entertainment division, the president of the network, and the chairman all owned TiVos, which enabled them to zap past the commercials that paid their salaries. "It's such a great gadget. It changed my life," one of them said at a corporate affair in the *Saturday Night Live* studio. It was neither the first nor the last time that a television executive mistook a fundamental technological change for a new gadget.

Setting the Table for *Law and Order*

On the first Sunday after the attacks of September 11, pictures of the eventual head of NBC littered the streets and stuffed the garbage cans of New York City; Jeff Zucker was profiled that week in the *New York Times Magazine.* The piles of newspapers from the weekend were everywhere at 30 Rockefeller Center. Normally, employee talk would have been about how well or badly Zucker had made out in the *Times.* But the breezy profile was plainly irrelevant that week.

The next morning I was in the office of David Corvo, the newly installed executive producer of *Dateline,* when Zucker entered to announce that the network was going to resume the prime-time schedule for the first time since the attacks. The long stretch of commercial-free programming was expensive, and Zucker was certain about one thing: "We can't sell ads around pictures of Ground Zero." At the same time, he proceeded to explain that the restoration of the prime-time shows *Friends, Will and Grace,* and *Frasier* was a part of America's return to normalcy, not a cash-flow decision. He instructed Corvo that a series of news specials would be scattered through the next few days, but as it was impossible to sell ads for them, scheduling would be a "day to day" proposition.

Normally I spent little time near NBC executives, but here I was at the center of power, and I felt slightly flushed at how much I coveted the sudden proximity. Something about Zucker's physical presence and bluster made him seem like a toy action figure from *The Simpsons* or *The Sopranos.* I imagined that he could go back to his office and pull mysterious levers that opened the floodgates to pent-up advertisements and beam them to millions of households. Realistically, though, here was a man who had benefited from the timing of September 11 and also had the power to make it go away. In a cheap sort of way it was delirious to be in his presence.

At the moment Zucker blew in and interrupted, I had been in Corvo's office to propose a series of stories about al-Qaeda, which was just emerging as a suspect in the attacks. While well known in security circles and among journalists who tried to cover international Islamist movements, al-Qaeda as a terrorist organization and a story line was still obscure in the early days after September 11. It had occurred to me and a number of other journalists that a core mission of NBC News would now be to explain, even belatedly, the origins and significance of these organizations. But Zucker insisted that *Dateline* stay focused on the firefighters. The story of firefighters trapped in the crumbling towers, Zucker said, was the emotional center of this whole event. Corvo enthusiastically agreed. "Maybe," said Zucker, "we ought to do a series of specials on firehouses where we just ride along with our cameras. Like the show *Cops,* only with firefighters." He told Corvo he could make room in the prime-time lineup for firefighters, but then smiled at me and said, in effect, that he had no time for any subtitled interviews with jihadists raging about Palestine.

With that, Zucker rushed back to his own office, many floors above *Dateline*'s humble altitude. My meeting with Corvo was basically over. He did ask me what I thought about Zucker's idea for a reality show about firefighters. I told him that we would have to figure a way around the fact that most of the time very little actually happens in firehouses. He nodded and muttered something about seeking a lot of "back stories" to maintain an emotional narrative. A few weeks later, a half-dozen producers were assigned to find firehouses and produce long-form documentaries about America's rediscovered heroes. Perhaps two of these programs ever aired; the whole project was shelved very soon after it started. Producers discovered that unlike September 11, most days featured no massive terrorist attacks that sent thousands of firefighters to their trucks and hundreds to tragic, heroic deaths. On most days nothing happened in firehouses whatsoever.

This was one in a series of lessons I learned about how television news had lost its most basic journalistic instincts in its search for the audience-driven sweet spot, the "emotional center" of the American people. Gone was the mission of using technology to veer out onto the edge of American understanding in order to introduce something fundamentally new into the national debate. The informational edge was perilous, it was unpredictable, and it required the news audience to be willing to learn something it did not already know. Stories from the edge were not typically reassuring about the future. In this sense they were like actual news, unpredictable flashes from the unknown. On the other hand, the coveted emotional center was reliable, it was predictable, and its story lines could be duplicated over and over. It reassured the audience by telling it what it already knew rather than challenging it to learn. This explains why TV news voices all use similar cadences, why all anchors seem to sound alike, why reporters in the field all use the identical tone of urgency no matter whether the story is about the devastating aftermath of an earthquake or someone's lost kitty.

It also explains why TV news seems so archaic next to the advertising and entertainment content on the same networks. Among the greatest frustrations of working in TV news over the past decade was to see that while advertisers and entertainment producers were permitted to do wildly risky things in pursuit of audiences, news producers rarely ventured out of a safety zone of crime, celebrity, and character-driven tragedy yarns.

Advertisers were aggressive in their use of new technologies long before network news divisions went anywhere near them. This is exactly the opposite of the trend in the 1960s and '70s, when the news divisions were first adopters of breakthroughs in live satellite and video technology. But in die 1990s, advertisers were quick to use the Internet to seek information about consumers, exploiting the potential of communities that formed around products and brands. Throughout the time I was at the network, GE ads were all over NBC programs like *Meet the Press* and CNBC's business shows, but they seemed never to appear on *Dateline.* (They also had far higher production values than the news programs and even some entertainment shows.) Pearl Jam, Nirvana, and N.W.A were already major cultural icons; grunge and hip-hop were the soundtrack for commercials at the moment networks were passing on stories about Kurt Cobain's suicide and Tupac Shakur's murder.

Meanwhile, on *60 Minutes,* Andy Rooney famously declared his own irrelevance by being disgusted that a spoiled Cobain could find so little to love about being a rock star that he would kill himself. Humor in commercials was hip—subtle, even, in its use of obscure pop-cultural references—but if there were any jokes at all in news stories, they were telegraphed, blunt visual gags, usually involving weathermen. That disjunction remains: at the precise moment that Apple cast John Hodgman and Justin Long as dead-on avatars of the PC and the Mac, news anchors on networks that ran those ads were introducing people to multibillion-dollar phenomena like MySpace and Facebook with the cringingly naïve attitude of "What will those nerds think of next?"

Entertainment programs often took on issues that would never fly on *Dateline*. On a Thursday night, *ER* could do a story line on the medically uninsured, but a night later, such a "downer policy story" was a much harder sell. In the time I was at NBC, you were more likely to hear federal agriculture policy discussed on *The West Wing*, or even on Jon Stewart, than you were to see it reported in any depth on *Dateline*.

Sometimes entertainment actually drove selection of news stories. Since *Dateline* was the lead-in to the hit series *Law & Order* on Friday nights, it was understood that on Fridays we did crime. Sunday was a little looser but still a hard sell for news that wasn't obvious or close to the all-important emotional center. In 2003, I was told that a story on the emergence from prison of a former member of the Weather Underground, whose son had graduated from Yale University and won a Rhodes Scholarship, would not fly unless it dovetailed with a story line on a then-struggling, soon-to-be-cancelled, and now-forgotten Sunday-night drama called *American Dreams*, which was set in the 1960s. I was told that the Weather Underground story might be viable if *American Dreams* did an episode on "protesters or something." At the time, *Dateline's* priority was another series of specials about the late Princess Diana. This blockbuster was going to blow the lid off the Diana affair and deliver the shocking revelation that the poor princess was in fact even more miserable being married to Prince Charles than we all suspected. Diana's emotional center was coveted in prime time even though its relevance to anything going on in 2003 was surely out on some voyeuristic fringe.

To get airtime, not only did serious news have to audition against the travails of Diana or a new book by Dr. Phil, but it also had to satisfy bizarre conditions. In 2003, one of our producers obtained from a trial lawyer in Connecticut video footage of guards subduing a mentally ill prisoner. Guards themselves took the footage as part of a safety program to ensure that deadly force was avoided and abuses were documented for official review. We saw guards haul the prisoner down a greenish corridor, then heard hysterical screaming as the guard shooting the video dispassionately announced, "The prisoner is resisting." For 90 seconds several guards pressed the inmate into a bunk. All that could be seen of him was his feet. By the end of the video the inmate was motionless. Asphyxiation would be the official cause of death.

This kind of gruesome video was rare. We also had footage of raw and moving interviews with this and another victim's relatives. The story had the added relevance that one of the state prison officials had been hired as a consultant to the prison authority in Iraq as the Abu Ghraib debacle was unfolding. There didn't seem to be much doubt about either the newsworthiness or the topicality of the story. Yet at the conclusion of the screening, the senior producer shook his head as though the story had missed the mark widely. "These inmates aren't necessarily sympathetic to our audience," he said. The fact that they had been diagnosed with schizophrenia was unimportant. Worse, he said that as he watched the video of the dying inmate, it didn't seem as if anything was wrong.

"Except that the inmate died," I offered.

"But that's not what it looks like. All you can see is his feet."

"With all those guards on top of him."

"Sure, but he just looks like he's being restrained."

"But," I pleaded, "the man died. That's just a fact. The prison guards shot this footage, and I don't think their idea was to get it on *Dateline*."

"Look," the producer said sharply, "in an era when most of our audience has seen the Rodney King video, where you can clearly see someone being beaten, this just doesn't hold up."

"Rodney King wasn't a prisoner," I appealed. "He didn't die, and this mentally ill inmate is not auditioning to be the next Rodney King. These are the actual pictures of his death."

"You don't understand our audience."

"I'm not trying to understand our audience," I said. I was getting pretty heated at this point—always a bad idea. "I'm doing a story on the abuse of mentally ill inmates in Connecticut."

"You don't get it," he said, shaking his head.

The story aired many months later, at less than its original length, between stories that apparently reflected a better understanding of the audience. During my time at *Dateline*, I did plenty of stories that led the broadcast and many full hours that were heavily promoted on the network. But few if any of my stories were more tragic, or more significant in news value, than this investigation into the Connecticut prison system.

Networks have so completely abandoned the mission of reporting the news that someone like entrepreneur Charles Ferguson, who sold an Internet software company to Microsoft in 1996 *[and whose writing has appeared in this magazine; see "Whats Next for Google," January 2005—Ed.]*, can spend $2 million of his own money to make an utterly unadorned documentary about Iraq and see it become an indie hit. Ferguson's *No End in Sight* simply lays out, without any emotional digressions or narrative froth, how the U.S. military missed the growing insurgency. The straightforward questions and answers posed by this film are so rare in network news today that they seem like an exotic, innovative form of cinema, although they're techniques that belong to the Murrow era. In its way, Ferguson's film is as devastating an indictment of network television as it is of the Bush administration.

Misfires

Even when the networks do attempt to adopt new technology, they're almost as misguided as when they don't. As the nation geared up for the invasion of Iraq back in 2002 and 2003, NBC seemed little concerned with straightforward questions about policy, preparedness, and consequences. It was always, on some level, driven by the unstated theme of 9/11 payback, and by the search for the emotional center of the coming conflict. From the inside, NBC's priority seemed to be finding—and making sure the cameras were aimed directly at—the September 11 firefighters of the coming Iraq invasion: the soldiers. To be certain, the story of the troops was newsworthy, but as subsequent events would reveal, focusing on it so single-mindedly obscured other important stories.

In 2002 and 2003, NBC news spent enormous amounts of time and money converting an army M88 tank recovery vehicle into an armored, mobile, motion-stabilized battlefield production studio. The so-called Bloom-mobile, named for NBC correspondent David Bloom, brought a local, Live-at-5, "This is London" quality to armed conflict. Using a microwave signal, the new vehicle beamed pictures of Bloom, who was embedded with the Third Infantry Division, from the Iraqi battlefield to an NBC crew a few miles behind, which in turn retransmitted to feed via satellite to New York, all in real time. While other embeds had to report battlefield activities, assemble a dispatch, and then transport it to a feed point at the rear of the troop formation, Bloom could file stories that were completely live and mostly clear. He became a compelling TV surrogate for all the soldiers, and demand for his "live shots" was constant

But Bloom's success in conveying to the viewing audience the visual (and emotional) experiences of the advancing troops also meant that he was tethered to his microwave transmitter and limited in his ability to get a bigger picture of the early fight. Tragically, Bloom died of a deep-vein blood clot. The expensive Bloom-mobile remote transmitter eventually came home and spent time ghoulishly on display outside 30 Rockefeller Center. It was used once or twice to cover hurricanes in the fall of 2004, to little success, and was eventually mothballed. The loss of one of NBC's most talented journalists was folded into the larger emotional narrative of the war and became a way of conveying, by implication, NBC's own casualty count in the war effort.

The focus on gadgetry meant once again that the deeper story about technology and the war was missed. Technology was revolutionizing war reporting by enabling combat soldiers to deliver their own dispatches from the field in real time. In 2004, I pitched *Dateline* on the story of how soldiers were creating their own digital networks and blogging their firsthand experiences of the war. The show passed. My story appeared in *Wired* a year later.

Six Sigma in the Newsroom

Perhaps the biggest change to the practice of journalism in the time I was at NBC was the absorption of the news division into the pervasive and all-consuming corporate culture of GE. GE had acquired NBC back in 1986, when it bought RCA. By 2003, GE's managers and strategists were getting around to seeing whether the same tactics that made the production of turbine generators more efficient could improve the production of television news. This had some truly bizarre consequences. To say that this *Dateline* correspondent with the messy corner office greeted these internal corporate changes with selfdestructive skepticism is probably an understatement.

Six Sigma—the methodology for the improvement of business processes that strives for 3.4 defects or fewer per million opportunities—was a somewhat mysterious symbol of management authority at every GE division. Six Sigma messages popped up on the screens of computers or in e-mail in-boxes every day. Six Sigma was out there, coming, unstoppable, like a comet or rural electrification. It was going to make everything better, and slowly it would claim employees in glazed-eyed conversions. Suddenly in the office down the hall a coworker would no longer laugh at the same old jokes. A grim smile suggested that he was on the lookout for snarky critics of the company. It was better to talk about the weather.

While Six Sigma's goal-oriented blather and obsession with measuring everything was jarring, it was also weirdly familiar, inasmuch as it was strikingly reminiscent of my college Maoism I class. Mao seemed to be a good model for Jack Welch and his Six Sigma foot soldiers; Six Sigma's "Champions" and "Black Belts" were Mao's "Cadres" and "Squad Leaders."

Finding such comparisons was how I kept from slipping into a coma during dozens of NBC employee training sessions where we were told not to march in political demonstrations of any kind, not to take gifts from anyone, and not to give gifts to anyone. At mandatory, hours-long "ethics training" meetings we would watch in-house videos that brought all the drama and depth of a driver's-education film to stories of smiling, swaggering employees (bad) who bought cases of wine for business associates on their expense accounts, while the thoughtful, cautious employees (good) never picked up a check, but volunteered to stay at the Red Roof Inn in pursuit of "shareholder value."

To me, the term "shareholder value" sounded like Mao's "right path," although this was not something I shared at the employee reëducation meetings. As funny as it seemed to me, the idea that GE was a multinational corporate front for Maoism was not a very widespread or popular view around NBC. It was best if any theory that didn't come straight from the NBC employee manual (a Talmudic tome that largely contained rules for using the GE credit card, most of which boiled down to "Don't") remained private.

I did, however, point out to the corporate-integrity people unhelpful details about how NBC News was covering wars in Iraq and Afghanistan that our GE parent company stood to benefit from as a major defense contractor. I wondered aloud, in the presence of an integrity "team leader," how we were to reconcile this larger-scale conflict with the admonitions about free dinners. "You make an interesting point I had not thought of before," he told me. "But I don't know how GE being a defense contractor is really relevant to the way we do our jobs here at NBC news." Integrity, I guess, doesn't scale.

Other members of the "GE family" had similar doubts about their relevance to the news division. In early 2002, our team was in Saudi Arabia covering regional reaction to September 11. We spent time on the streets and found considerable sympathy for Osama bin Laden among common citizens at the same time that the Saudi government expressed frustration that Americans seemed not to consider it an ally in the war on terror. We tracked down relatives of the September 11 hijackers, some of whom were deeply shocked and upset to learn what their family members had done. We wanted to speak with members of Osama bin Laden's family about their errant son's mission to bring down the Saudi government and attack the infidel West. We couldn't reach the bin Ladens using ordinary means, and the royal family claimed that it had no real clout with the multibillion-dollar bin Laden construction giant that built mosques, roads, and other infrastructure all over the world.

But GE had long done business with the bin Ladens. In a misguided attempt at corporate synergy, I called GE headquarters in Fairfield, CT, from my hotel room in Riyadh. I inquired at the highest level to see whether, in the interest of bringing out all aspects of an important story for the American people, GE corporate officers might try to persuade the bin Ladens to speak with *Dateline* while we were in the kingdom. I didn't really know what to expect, but within a few hours I received a call in my hotel room from a senior corporate communications officer who would only read a statement over the phone. It said something to the effect that GE had an important, long-standing, and valuable business relationship with the Bin Laden Group and saw no connection between that relationship and what *Dateline* was trying to do in Saudi Arabia. He wished us well. We spoke with no bin Laden family member on that trip.

In the end, perhaps the work that I was most proud of at NBC marginalized me within the organization and was my undoing. I had done some of the first live Internet audio and video webcasts on MSNBC. I anchored live Web broadcasts from the political conventions in 2000 when such coverage was just beginning. I helped produce live interactive stories for *Dateline* where the audience could vote during commercial breaks on how a crime mystery or a hostage situation would turn out. I loved what we could do through the fusion of TV and the Internet During one interactive broadcast I reported the instant returns from audience surveys live in the studio, with different results for each time zone as *Dateline* was broadcast across the country. Sitting next to me, Stone Phillips (not a big fan of live TV) would interact with me in that chatty way anchors do. Stone decided that rather than react naturally to the returns from the different time zones, he would make a comment about how one hostage-negotiator cop character in the TV story reminded him of Dr. Phil. He honed the line to the point that he used the exact same words for each time zone. "I think the Dr. Phil line is working, don't you?" he asked, as though this was his reporting-from-the-rooftops-of-London moment. "Sure, Stone." I said. "It's working great."

Phillips was hardly alone in his reaction to the new technology that was changing television, and in die end we were both dumped by NBC anyway. When I got die word that I'd been axed, I was in the middle of two projects that employed new media technology. In the first, we went virtually undercover to investigate the so-called Nigerian scammers who troll for the gullible with (often grammatically questionable) hard-luck stories and bogus promises of hidden millions. We descended into the scammers' world as a way of chasing them down and also illustrating how the Internet economy works. With search techniques and tracing strategies that reveal how Internet traffic is numerically coded, we chased a team of con artists to a hotel in Montreal, where we nailed them on hidden camera. With me playing the patsy, the story showed, in a very entertaining and interesting way, how the mechanics of die Internet worked to assist criminals. The second story unearthed someone who spammed people with porn e-mails. It was a form of direct-mail advertising that paid decent money if you had the right e-mail lists. The spammers didn't get involved with the porn itself; they just traded in e-mail lists and hid behind their digital anonymity. We exposed one of these spammers and had him apologize on camera, without spectacle, to a Dallas housewife to whom he had sent hard-core e-mails. The story wasn't merely about porn and spammers; it showed how electronic media gave rise to offshore shadow companies that traded e-mail lists on a small but very effective scale. The drama in the story was in seeing how we could penetrate spammers' anonymity with savvy and tenacity while educating people about technology at the same time. It was admittedly a timid effort that suggested the barest glimpse of new media's potential, but it was something.

Dateline started out interested but in the end concluded that "it looks like you are having too much fun here." David Corvo asked us to go shoot interviews of random people morally outraged by pornographic e-mails to "make it clear who the bad guys are." As might have been predicted, he was sending us back to find the emotional center after journalistic reality, once again, had botched the audition. I had long since cleaned out my office when the stories finally aired. *Dateline* eventually found the emotional center with *To Catch a Predator,* which had very little to do with Internet technology beyond 1990s-era chat rooms. What it did have was a supercharged sense of who the bad guys were (the upgrade for my spammer's simple apology was having the exposed predators hauled off to jail on camera) and a superhero in the form of grim reaper Chris Hansen, who was now a star.

I moved on. My story for *Wired* on bloggers from the Iraq War landed me an appearance on *The Daily Show.* Jon Stewart blundy asked me what it's like to be at *Dateline* for nine years: "Does it begin to rot you from the inside?" The audience seemed not entirely convinced that this was a joke. They were actually interested in my answer, as though I were announcing the results of a medical study with wide implications for human health. I had to think about this rotting-from-the-inside business. I dodged the question, possibly because it was the one I had been asking myself for most of those nine years. But the answer is that I managed not to rot.

Life at the Media Lab has reminded me once again that technology is most exciting when it upsets the status quo. Big-screen TVs and downloadable episodes of *Late Night with Conan O'Brien* are merely more attempts to control the means of distribution, something GE has been doing since the invention of the light bulb. But exploding GPS backpacks represent an alien mind-set; they are part of the growing media insurgency that is redefining news, journalism, and civic life. This technological insurgency shouldn't surprise us: after all, it's wrapped up in language itself, which has long defied any attempt to commodify it. Technology, as it has done through the ages, is freeing communication, and this is good news for the news. A little empathy couldn't hurt.

What the Mainstream Media Can Learn from Jon Stewart

No, not to be funny and snarky, but to be bold and to do a better job of cutting through the fog.

RACHEL SMOLKIN

When Hub Brown's students first told him they loved "The Daily Show with Jon Stewart" and sometimes even relied on it for news, he was, as any responsible journalism professor would be, appalled.

Now he's a "Daily Show" convert.

"There are days when I watch 'The Daily Show,' and I kind of chuckle. There are days when I laugh out loud. There are days when I stand up and point to the TV and say, 'You're damn right!'" says Brown, chair of the communications department at Syracuse University's S.I. Newhouse School of Public Communications and an associate professor of broadcast journalism.

Brown, who had dismissed the faux news show as silly riffing, got hooked during the early days of the war in Iraq, when he felt most of the mainstream media were swallowing the administration's spin rather than challenging it. Not "The Daily Show," which had no qualms about second-guessing the nation's leaders. "The stock-in-trade of 'The Daily Show' is hypocrisy, exposing hypocrisy. And nobody else has the guts to do it," Brown says. "They really know how to crystallize an issue on all sides, see the silliness everywhere."

Whether lampooning President Bush's disastrous Iraq policies or mocking "real" reporters for their credulity, Stewart and his team often seem to steer closer to the truth than traditional journalists. The "Daily Show" satirizes spin, punctures pretense and belittles bombast. When a video clip reveals a politician's backpedaling, verbal contortions or mindless prattle, Stewart can state the obvious—ridiculing such blather as it deserves to be ridiculed—or remain silent but speak volumes merely by arching an eyebrow.

Stewart and his fake correspondents are freed from the media's preoccupation with balance, the fixation with fairness. They have no obligation to deliver the day's most important news, if that news is too depressing, too complicated or too boring. Their sole allegiance is to comedy.

Or, as "The Daily's Show's" Web site puts it: "One anchor, five correspondents, zero credibility. If you're tired of the stodginess of the evening newscasts, if you can't bear to sit through the spinmeisters and shills on the 24-hour cable news networks, don't miss The Daily Show with Jon Stewart, a nightly half-hour series unburdened by objectivity, journalistic integrity or even accuracy."

That's funny. And obvious. But does that simple, facetious statement capture a larger truth—one that may contain some lessons for newspapers and networks struggling to hold on to fleeing readers, viewers and advertisers in a tumultuous era of transition for old media?

Has our slavish devotion to journalism fundamentals—particularly our obsession with "objectivity"—so restricted news organizations that a comedian can tell the public what's going on more effectively than a reporter? Has Stewart, whose mission is to be funny, sliced through the daily obfuscation more effectively than his media counterparts, whose mission is to inform?

This is, perhaps, a strange premise for a journalism review to explore. AJR's mission is to encourage rigorous ethical and professional standards, particularly at a time when fake news of the non Jon Stewart variety has become all too prevalent. Stewart's faux news is parody, a sharp, humorous take on the actual events of the day, not to be confused with fake news of the Jayson Blair, Jack Kelley, National Guard memos or even WMD variety, based only loosely on actual events yet presented as real news.

As I posed my question about lessons of "The Daily Show" to various journalism ethicists and professionals, some carefully explained why mainstream news organizations should refrain from engaging in such whimsy.

Ed Fouhy, who worked for all three broadcast networks in his 22-year career as a producer and network executive before retiring in 2004, is a regular "Daily Show" watcher. "Sometimes conventional journalism makes it difficult for a journalist to say what he or she really thinks about an incident. Sometimes you can cut closer to the bone with another form, another creative form, like a novel or a satire on television," Fouhy says. "I think what we're seeing is just a daily dose of it. You think back to 'Saturday Night Live,' and they've satirized the news for a long time with their 'Weekend Update.' 'That Was the Week That Was' was an early television satire on the news."

But Fouhy cringes at the idea that real journalists should model themselves after such a show. When readers pick up a newspaper or viewers turn on a news broadcast, they're looking for serious information, and they should be able to find it. "When you begin to blur the line . . . to attract more viewers and younger viewers, I think that's a lousy idea," he says.

Adds Robert Thompson, director of the Bleier Center for Television and Popular Culture at Syracuse University, "Journalists have a really inconvenient thing they've got to go through: a process of trying to get [the story] right. . . . I don't think journalists should try to be more hip. Journalists have to learn the one lesson which is important, which is to try to get it right."

Fouhy and Thompson are correct, of course. But Thompson's colleague Hub Brown and some others interviewed for this piece believe the lesson of "The Daily Show" is not that reporters should try to be funny, but that they should try to be honest.

"Stop being so doggone scared of everything," Brown advises journalists. "I think there is much less courageousness than there needs to be. There are people out there who stick out because of their fearlessness. Somebody like Lara Logan at CBS," the network's chief foreign correspondent who has reported extensively from Iraq and Afghanistan, "is a great example who is fearless about saying the truth."

In the hours and days following Hurricane Katrina, state and federal officials dithered while New Orleanians suffered inside the filth and chaos of the Louisiana Superdome. Many journalists, notably CNN's Anderson Cooper, jettisoned their usual care in handling all sides equally. They were bewildered, appalled and furious, and it showed.

"We saw a lot of that during Hurricane Katrina, but it shouldn't take a Hurricane Katrina to get journalists to say the truth, to call it as they see it," Brown says. "The thing that makes 'The Daily Show' stick out is they sometimes seem to understand that better than the networks do." He adds: "I think it's valuable because when the emperor has no clothes, we get to say the emperor has no clothes. And we have to do that more often here. . . . The truth itself doesn't respect point of view. The truth is never balanced. . . . We have to not give in to an atmosphere that's become so partisan that we're afraid of what we say every single time we say something."

Venise Wagner, associate chair of the journalism department at San Francisco State University, argues with her students over whether "The Daily Show" is real journalism. They think it is; she tells them it isn't, explaining that journalism involves not just conveying information but also following a set of standards that includes verification, accuracy and balance.

But she says "The Daily Show" does manage to make information relevant in a way that traditional news organizations often do not, and freedom from "balance" shapes its success.

"'The Daily Show' doesn't have to worry about balance. They don't have to worry about accuracy, even. They can just sort of get at the essence of something, so it gives them much more latitude to play around with the information, to make it more engaging," Wagner says. "Straight news sometimes places itself in a box where it doesn't allow itself—it doesn't give itself permission to question as much as it probably should question." Instead, the exercise becomes one of: "I'm just going to take the news down and give it to you straight."

But what exactly is straight news, and what is balance? Is balance a process of giving equal weight to both sides, or of giving more weight to the side with more evidence? Does accuracy mean spelling everybody's name right and quoting them correctly, or does it also mean slicing to the heart of an issue? "Nowhere is the comedy show balanced," says Wagner, "but it allows them more balance in showing what is really going on."

As journalists, by contrast, "We've presented a balanced picture to the public. But is it accurate? Is it authentic?" She cites coverage of the global warming debate, which, until recently, often was presented as an equal argument between scientists who said global warming was occurring and scientists who denied it. "That reality was not authentic. There were very few scientists who refuted the body of evidence" supporting global warming, Wagner says, yet the coverage did not always reflect that.

Martin Kaplan, associate dean of the University of Southern California's Annenberg School for Communication, dislikes journalists' modern perception of balance. "Straight news is not what it used to be," he says. "It has fallen into a bizarre notion that substitutes something called 'balance' for what used to be called 'accuracy' or 'truth' or 'objectivity.' That may be because of a general postmodern malaise in society at large in which the notion of a truth doesn't have the same reputation it used to, but, as a consequence, straight journalists both in print and in broadcast can be played like a piccolo by people who know how to exploit that weakness.

"Every issue can be portrayed as a controversy between two opposite sides, and the journalist is fearful of saying that one side has it right, and the other side does not. It leaves the reader or viewer in the position of having to weigh competing truth claims, often without enough information to decide that one side is manifestly right, and the other side is trying to muddy the water with propaganda."

Kaplan directs USC's Norman Lear Center, which studies how journalism and politics have become branches of entertainment, and he has worked in all three worlds: former editor and columnist for the now-defunct Washington Star; chief speechwriter for Vice President Walter Mondale; deputy presidential campaign manager for Mondale; Disney studio executive and motion picture and television producer.

He borrows Eric Alterman's phrase "working the ref" to illustrate his point about balance. Instead of "reading a story and finding out that black is black, you now read a story and it says, 'Some say black is black, and some say black is white'. . . . So whether it's climate change or evolution or the impact on war policy of various proposals, it's all being framed as 'on the one hand, on the other hand,' as though the two sides had equal claims on accuracy."

Therein lies "The Daily Show's" appeal, he says. "So-called fake news makes fun of that concept of balance. It's not afraid to have a bullshit meter and to call people spinners or liars when they deserve it. I think as a consequence some viewers find that helpful and refreshing and hilarious."

In addition to the user-generated satire on YouTube, Kaplan thinks the Web is bursting with commentators, including Alterman and Salon's Glenn Greenwald, who brilliantly penetrate the fog—sometimes angrily, sometimes amusingly, sometimes a bit of both.

Broadcasters have tackled this least successfully, he says, citing CBS' ill-fated "Free Speech" segment. Launched on and then discarded from "The CBS Evening News with Katie Couric," the segment gave personalities such as Rush Limbaugh uninterrupted airtime to trumpet their views. And "the challenge for the great national papers," Kaplan adds, "is to escape from this straightjacket in which they're unable to say that official A was telling the truth, and official B was not."

Part of "The Daily Show's" charm comes from its dexterity in letting public figures from Bush to House Speaker Nancy Pelosi (D-Calif.) speak for—and contradict—themselves, allowing the truth to emanate from a politician's entanglement over his or her own two feet. It's one way to hold government officials accountable for their words and deeds. Some might even call it fact-checking.

Brooks Jackson directs FactCheck.org, a project of the Annenberg Public Policy Center of the University of Pennsylvania, which monitors the accuracy of prominent politicians' statements in TV ads, debates, speeches, interviews and press releases. Jackson himself is a former reporter for the Associated Press, Wall Street Journal and CNN who pioneered "ad watch" coverage at the cable network during the '92 presidential race.

"I'm totally buying it," he told me after I stumbled through my fake-news-gets-at-the-truth-better premise. "I am in awe of the ability of Stewart and however many people he has working for him to cull through the vast wasteland of cable TV and pick out the political actors at their most absurd. They just have an unerring eye for that moment when people parody themselves. And I guess while the cable news hosts are obliged to take those moments of idiocy seriously, Jon Stewart can give us that Jack Benny stare—Does anybody remember Jack Benny?—give us that Jon Stewart stare and let the hilarity of the moment sink in, often without saying a word."

Does this qualify as fact-checking? Not exactly, Jackson replies, but "one thing he does do that is fact-checking: If somebody says, 'I never said that,' and next thing you know, there's a clip of the same guy three months ago saying exactly that, that's great fact-checking," and a great lesson for journalists. Jackson thinks NBC's Tim Russert is the master of that art in the mainstream media, confronting his subjects as he puts their quotes on-screen and reading them verbatim. "Stewart does it for laughs, and Russert does it for good journalistic reasons, and we all can learn from the two of them."

The form has its limits as a fact-checking technique. Jackson doesn't envision Stewart giving a State of the Union address rigorous ad-watch-type treatment, complete with statistical analysis of the president's proposed budget. Why would he? He'd put his audience to sleep. "Not every misleading statement can be debunked out of the person's own mouth," notes Jackson. "That's a particular kind of debunking that's very effective as comedy. . . . There's plenty that needs debunking that isn't funny."

Asked about Stewart's influence on mainstream reporters, Jackson says: "Jon's been holding up the mirror to them for quite a while without any particular effect. The forces that are making the news more trivial and less relevant are frankly much more powerful than a show like Jon Stewart's can change."

Much of the allure of Stewart's show lies in its brutal satire of the media. He and his correspondents mimic the stylized performance of network anchors and correspondents. He exposes their gullibility. He derides their contrivances.

On March 28, the broadcast media elite partied with their government sources at the annual Radio and Television Correspondents' Association dinner. The disquieting spectacle of White House adviser Karl Rove rapping in front of a howling audience of journalists quickly appeared on YouTube. Quipped Stewart, only too accurately, the next night: "The media gets a chance to, for one night, put aside its cozy relationship with the government for one that is, instead, nauseatingly sycophantic."

His 2004 textbook satire, "America (The Book): A Citizen's Guide to Democracy Inaction," devotes a section to media in the throes of transformation and punctures this transition far more concisely, and probably more memorably, than the millions of words AJR has devoted to the subject:

"Newspapers abound, and though they have endured decades of decline in readership and influence, they can still form impressive piles if no one takes them out to the trash. . . . Television continues to thrive. One fifteen-minute nightly newscast, barely visible through the smoky haze of its cigarette company benefactor, has evolved into a multi-channel, twenty-four hour a day infotastic clusterfuck of factish-like material. The 1990s brought the advent of a dynamic new medium for news, the Internet, a magnificent new technology combining the credibility of anonymous hearsay with the excitement of typing."

Phil Rosenthal, the Chicago Tribune's media columnist, thinks part of the reason "The Daily Show" and its spinoff, "The Colbert Report," resonate is that they parody not only news but also how journalists get news. "It's actually kind of a surefire way to appeal to people because if the news itself isn't entertaining, then the way it's covered, the breathless conventions of TV news, are always bankable," Rosenthal says. "You can always find something amusing there."

He adds that "so much of the news these days involves managing the news, so a show like Stewart's that takes the larger view of not just what's going on, but how it's being manipulated, is really effective. I think there's general skepticism about the process that this plays into. . . . The wink isn't so much we know what's really going on. The wink is also we know you know what we're doing here. It's down to the way the correspondents

Article 14. What the Mainstream Media Can Learn from Jon Stewart

stand [in front of] the green screen, offering commentary and intoning even when their commentary may not be important."

Irony-deficient journalists have rewarded Stewart over the last five years by devoting more than 150 newspaper articles alone to his show and to studies about his show. Most have discussed the program's popularity. ("The Daily Show" attracted an average 1.5 million viewers nightly from January 1 through April 19, according to Nielsen Media Research. Couric's beleaguered CBS newscast, by contrast, netted an average 7.2 million viewers nightly during the same period.)

Many stories have pondered whether "The Daily Show" has substance and credibility; mourned young people's alleged propensity to rely on such lighthearted fare for news; brooded over what this reliance says about the state of the news media; and grieved that the show poisons young people's outlook on government, leaving them cynical and jaded. Stewart, who declined to be interviewed for this article, has patiently explained that his show is supposed to be funny.

That hasn't stopped the onslaught of serious discourse and research about "The Daily Show." A 2004 survey by the Pew Research Center for the People and the Press found that 21 percent of people age 18 to 29 cited comedy shows such as "The Daily Show" and "Saturday Night Live" as places where they regularly learned presidential campaign news, nearly equal to the 23 percent who regularly learned something from the nightly network news or from daily newspapers.

Even if they did learn from his show, a more recent study indicates Stewart's viewers are well-informed. An April 15 Pew survey gauging Americans' knowledge of national and international affairs found that 54 percent of regular viewers of "The Daily Show" and "Colbert Report" scored in the high-knowledge category, tying with regular readers of newspaper Web sites and edging regular watchers of "The NewsHour with Jim Lehrer." Overall, 35 percent of people surveyed scored in the high-knowledge category.

In October, Julia R. Fox, who teaches telecommunications at Indiana University, and two graduate students announced the results of the first scholarly attempt to compare Stewart's show with traditional TV news as a political information source. Their study, which will be published this summer by the Journal of Broadcasting & Electronic Media, examined substantive political coverage in 2004 of the first presidential debate and political conventions on "The Daily Show" and the broadcast television networks' nightly newscasts. Fox concluded Stewart's show is just as substantive as network news.

Fox says she wasn't surprised by the study results, but she was surprised by the general lack of surprise. "People have e-mailed me and said, 'I think you're absolutely wrong. I think 'The Daily Show' is more substantive.'"

Beyond the debate over whether Stewart's show is a quality source of information or whether wayward young fans have lost their minds, the media have treated him with admiration bordering on reverence. In early 2005, press reports handicapped his chances of landing on the "CBS Evening News," which, like Comedy Central, was then owned by Viacom. After Dan Rather had announced his abrupt retirement following revelations that alleged memos about President Bush's National Guard Service had not been authenticated, CBS chief Leslie Moonves said he wanted to reinvent the evening news to make it more relevant, "something that younger people can relate to." Asked at a news conference whether he'd rule out a role for Stewart, Moonves took a pass, fueling more speculation.

In 2004, the Television Critics Association bestowed the outstanding achievement in news and information award not on ABC's "Nightline" or PBS' "Frontline," but on "The Daily Show." Stewart, who had won for outstanding achievement in comedy the previous year, seemed bemused by the honor. Instead of accepting in person, he sent a tape of himself sitting at "The Daily Show" anchor desk. "We're fake," he informed the TV critics. "See this desk? . . . It folds up at the end of the day, and I take it home in my purse."

But Melanie McFarland, the critic who presented Stewart's award, calls him a "truth teller" who speaks plainly about the news and offers a "spoonful of sugar that helps the medicine, the news, go down."

That sugar is not just delightful; it's provocative. "Any comedian can do sort of a 'Saturday Night Live' presentation and just do the punch line," says McFarland, who writes for the Seattle Post-Intelligencer. "He actually gives you some stuff to consider in addition to the punch line. He and his staff show an awareness of the issues and [are] able to take a longer view than a 24-hour news cycle can, which is funny because it's also a daily show." Other news programs and journalists, including "Frontline" and Bill Moyers, do this also, she says, but not as often. "So much of the news is not digestion but regurgitation. He's sort of looking at the raw material and making a commonsense assessment of what it means."

McFarland says Stewart's mockery of the media should galvanize journalists to perform better. "If there's a guy who's making great headway in giving people information by showing people what you're not doing in giving them information, let's try to do our jobs."

For serious news organizations, change is easier advised than enacted. Take Stewart's imitation of the stylized anchor persona, which—with precious little exaggeration—makes TV personalities look silly and stilted. Altering that persona is no easy task, as Katie Couric discovered when she tried to make the nightly news chattier.

"While Jon Stewart is a guy in a suit pretending to be a newscaster, and he acts like a guy in a suit pretending to be a newscaster, there's a certain formality and rigidity we've come to expect from our news, so much so that when Katie Couric opens the news with 'Hi,' or now I think it's 'Hello,' this is thought of as some kind of breakdown in the proper etiquette of newscasting," says the Chicago Tribune's Rosenthal. He thinks perhaps the time has come to abandon the old formality of newscasting but says such a process will be evolutionary.

In other broadcast formats, incorporating a more sardonic tone can work well. Rosenthal cites MSNBC's "Countdown with Keith Olbermann" as one news program that does a pretty good job incorporating the same sorts of elements that make "The Daily Show" successful. "Keith Olbermann gets a lot of attention for his editorializing, but the meat of that show is this hybrid blend of the news you need to know, the news that's entertaining, with a little bit of perspective [in] taking a step back from what the news is and what the newsmakers want it to be," he says. (See "Is Keith Olbermann the Future of Journalism?" February/March.)

Rosenthal thinks ABC's quirky overnight show, "World News Now," also has achieved a more detached, looser tone, and says it's no accident that the program has been "such a fertile breeding ground for unorthodox newspeople," including Anderson Cooper and Aaron Brown.

Public radio, known for its sober (and sometimes stodgy) programming, is experimenting with a more freewheeling search for truth as well. In January, Public Radio International launched "Fair Game from PRI with Faith Salie," a one-hour satirical news and entertainment show that airs on weeknights. The Sacramento Bee's Sam McManis likened the new show to "the quirky love child of 'The Daily Show With Jon Stewart' and 'All Things Considered.' It's smart enough to slake the traditional public-radio fans' thirst for intellectual programming but satiric enough to catch the attention of the prematurely cynical Gen X and Gen Y sets."

Salie is a comedian and a Rhodes Scholar with a bachelor's degree from Harvard and a master of philosophy from Oxford in modern English literature. "I'm not a journalist, and I don't have to pretend to be one," she says, describing herself as her listeners' proxy. When she interviews newsmakers—topics have included the Taliban, Hillary Clinton and the Dixie Chicks—"I don't feel like I have to mask my incredulousness. I can say, 'For real? Are you kidding me?' That leads to spontaneity."

Sometimes humor results from a certain framing of the news. Each Monday, the show revisits metaphors from the Sunday morning news shows. On "Fox News Sunday" on April 8, Juan Williams first compared Republican presidential hopeful John McCain to a "deflated balloon," then declared the Arizona senator was on the "wrong path" with his Iraq policy and concluded that he shouldn't be "tying his tail" to such an albatross. On NBC's "Meet the Press," Judy Woodruff in January described the administration's Iraq policy as akin to "putting a fist in a sink full of water, leaving it there for a few minutes and taking it out."

Salie says "The Daily Show" has demonstrated that young people are savvier than many elders believe, and the mainstream media should learn from that. Young people "are aware of the news and can recognize the preposterousness of some of it." But don't try too hard to be funny, she cautions. "I don't think real news shows should try the scripted, cutesy, pithy banter. It gives me the heebie-jeebies. It makes me feel sad for them, and it feels pathetic."

For an informal, satirical or even humorous take on the news to work in a mainstream newspaper, the format must be exactly right. Gene Weingarten, the Washington Post humor writer, thinks the media would do their jobs better if they had more fun, and he cringes whenever editors insist on labeling his pieces as satire. "Nothing could be worse for satire than labeling it satire," he laments.

But he concedes his editors may have a point. In August, Paul Farhi, a reporter for the Post's Style section (and an AJR contributor), reviewed the debut of colleague Tony Kornheiser on ESPN's "Monday Night Football." The critique was not flattering, and an apoplectic Kornheiser retaliated by publicly trashing Farhi as "a two-bit weasel slug," whom he would "gladly run over with a Mack truck."

The smackdown drew national attention, and Weingarten decided he wanted a piece of the action. So he skewered Kornheiser's second show with an outrageous, over-the-top rant on the front of Style about the "failed Kornheiser stewardship" taking "yet another bumbling misstep toward its inevitable humiliating collapse."

"It was patently unfair," Weingarten says of his tongue-in-cheek diatribe, which was not labeled as satire. "A child would have understood this piece. No one could have misunderstood this."

And yet they did. Weingarten got hundreds, possibly thousands, of complaints from sports lovers pummeling him for attacking Kornheiser unfairly. (Kornheiser himself called Weingarten, unsure how to interpret the piece.) "The mail I got was just absolutely hilarious," Weingarten says. "There is a problem of applying irony, humorous satire, in a newspaper when readers are not accustomed to seeing it there."

Did he learn from the experience? "No," he replies. "Because my reaction was, 'These people are idiots.'"

Perhaps the hardest lesson to take away from "The Daily Show" is the most important one. How can journalists in today's polarized political climate pierce the truth, Edward R. Murrow-style, without a) being ideological, or b) appearing ideological?

Olbermann's show, cited in several interviews as a serious news program that excels in revealing hypocrisy, is unabashedly liberal, and "The Daily Show" itself is frequently tagged with that label. In February, Fox News Channel debuted "The 1/2 Hour News Hour," billed as the conservative riposte to Stewart's liberal bent; after two pilot shows, the network has agreed to pick up 13 additional episodes.

"Unfortunately, people are heading for news that sort of reinforces their own beliefs," says Washington Post reporter Dana Milbank. "That may be Jon Stewart on the left, or that may be Rush Limbaugh on the right. . . . Limbaugh isn't funny, but he's starting with something that has a kernel of truth and distorting it to the point of fakery as well, so I think they are parallel."

Milbank is the author of Washington Sketch, an experiment at slashing through the hazy words and deeds of federal power players. Milbank pitched the idea, based on British newspapers' parliamentary sketches, and argued for a few years before getting the green light in early 2005. "There was a lot of sort of figuring out the place, and first it really floated in the news section," he says. "I think we fixed that problem [by] putting it consistently on page two, and it's labeled more clearly."

Occasionally, Washington Sketch has appeared on page one, as it did March 6 when Milbank tartly contrasted the style of two generals who testified before Congress on the deplorable conditions at Walter Reed Army Medical Center. Then and at other times, Milbank's acerbic take has proved more enlightening than the longer, more traditional accompanying news story.

The column lacks a consistent ideology. Milbank says his goal is a "pox on both their houses sort of thing," and adds, "I'm not trying to be 50-50, particularly. The goal is to pick on all of them. . . . It's observational as opposed to argumentative." Too often, he says, "We seem to make the mistake of thinking that if you're not being ideological, you therefore have to be boring, and all sort of 50-50 down the middle and follow the inverted pyramid."

Jeff Jarvis, the blogger behind BuzzMachine.com, says journalists should engage in more open, honest conversations with readers. "I think what Stewart et al do is remind us of what our mission and voice used to be and should be," says Jarvis, who also is a media consultant and head of the interactive journalism program at the City University of New York Graduate School of Journalism. He notes that Stewart is "very much a part of the conversation. He's joking about things we're talking about. And then the next day, we're talking about him talking about it."

Jarvis wants journalists to unleash their inner Stewart. "After enough drinks, reporters talk like Stewart: 'You won't BELIEVE what the mayor said today!' Why don't we talk to our readers that way?" he asks, and then acknowledges: "OK. There's a lot of arguments: 'The mayor won't talk to us again.' 'It's biased.' 'We don't want to turn everything into blogs.'"

Jarvis doesn't mean that every story should become a first-person diatribe, and obviously the mainstream media can't fall back on Stewart's I'm-just-joking excuse after they've infuriated a thin-skinned politician. But there are instances when a little unorthodoxy may be appropriate, and speaking frankly may enhance credibility.

Eric Deggans, the TV and media critic for the St. Petersburg Times, also wants to see a little more pluck. "'The Daily Show' is pushing us to be less traditional about how we deliver people information," Deggans says. "Are we going to turn around and turn into the Onion?" (The cult publication parodies news in print and online; its facetious Onion News Network debuted on March 27.) "Of course not. But if you've got a longtime state capitol bureau chief, and they see something go down in the capitol, and they have a great, acerbic take on it, why not let them go at it in a column?"

Or, he suggests, experiment just a bit with the sacred space on page one. "Sometimes editors have really rigid ideas about what can go on the front page," he says. "If somebody has a really good column on [Don] Imus, why wouldn't you put it on the front page, as long as you label it clearly as opinion? There are some editors who would say your first next-day story about Don Imus has to be traditional. Why? Why does it have to be traditional? As long as the reader isn't fooled, why do you let yourself be handcuffed like that?"

Deggans is quick to add some caveats, including the importance of fairness. "You always have to be careful because there's a good reason why we had those rules," Deggans says. "But we have to challenge ourselves to subvert them more often. You have to be subversive in a way that maintains your credibility. When you have smart, capable people who want to write in a different way, let them try it."

The mainstream media can not, should not and never will be "The Daily Show." The major news of our time is grimly serious, and only real news organizations will provide the time, commitment and professionalism necessary to ferret out stories such as the Washington Post's exposé of neglected veterans at Walter Reed or the New York Times' disclosures of secret, warrantless wiretapping by the federal government.

But in the midst of a transition, our industry is flailing. Our credibility suffers mightily. The public thinks we're biased despite our reluctance to speak plainly. Our daily newspapers often seem stale. Perhaps "The Daily Show" can teach us little, but remind us of a lot: Don't underestimate your audience. Be relevant. And be bold.

Says Deggans: "In a lot of news organizations, it's the fourth quarter. It's fourth down, man. It's time to show a little pizzazz. It's time to reinvent what's going on, so people get engaged."

RACHEL SMOLKIN (rsmolkin@ajr.umd.edu) is *AJR*'s managing editor. *AJR* editorial assistant Emily Groves contributed research to this report.

Other Voices
The Hunger for Personal Narrative in a Fragmenting World

KIERA BUTLER

Even in New Orleans's French Quarter, where one expects a certain amount of weirdness, the StoryCorps mobile booth looked out of place. Something like a cross between a gypsy wagon and a futuristic pod, it is about the size of your average RV, but its gleaming silver exterior is rounded like a capsule. The tinted windows let those inside look out but passersby can't see in (this doesn't seem to discourage curious people from knocking on the door all day and asking about StoryCorps). Inside, the booth has two rooms: one is a soundproof recording studio, where all kinds of people come, usually in pairs, to record interviews with loved ones; the other, a kind of business area with a table and chairs, where the booth's facilitators can make calls and work on their laptops.

Sitting at the table and wearing a pair of wireless headphones, I listened to six interviews during my eight-hour day in the booth. Although Katrina was not everyone's main focus, it was clear that it's hard for New Orleanians *not* to think about the hurricane; it loomed at the edges of almost every conversation I heard. A woman asked her mother about retired life—and what it had been like to evacuate to Florida during the storm. A few Vietnamese-American waitresses from Café du Monde talked about their boss—and what it had been like to ready the café for reopening after the storm.

StoryCorps is difficult to describe and, on paper, it sounds like a pretty strange idea. A set of instructions for someone who wants to participate in the program but knows nothing about it might go something like, "First you choose someone—anyone—who you think has interesting things to say. Then you take them to a soundproof booth, pay ten dollars, and ask your chosen person about whatever you want for forty minutes. You will receive a recording of the interview, and so will the Library of Congress. And also, if you and your interviewee are interesting, funny, or poignant enough, there is a small chance that a portion of your interview might end up on public radio."

With little else to go on besides his faith in stories, David Isay, a radio documentary producer, founded StoryCorps in 2003. After a decade of listening to ordinary people record extraordinary stories, Isay knew that most people had something not only worth saying, but worth preserving. "We believe that the stories of everyday people are as interesting as Donald Trump and TomKat," Isay told me. "StoryCorps tells people they matter and they won't be forgotten."

We believe that the stories of everyday people are as interesting as Donald Trump and TomKat. StoryCorps tells people they matter and they won't be forgotten.

A quirky concept, perhaps, but Isay was able to secure a handful of grants to support StoryCorps. Almost seven thousand people have participated in the program so far, and last year, StoryCorps expanded. In addition to the original two New York City booths (one in Grand Central Station and another at Ground Zero), two new mobile booths now travel with a crew of four facilitators, stopping for weeks at a time in cities and towns across the country. When a mobile booth pulled into New Orleans a few weeks ago, all the interview spots were filled within a week of the booth's arrival.

In part, StoryCorps is successful because it generates its own publicity. The program is familiar to the millions of people who hear the segments from the interviews that air on the National Public Radio program *Morning Edition*, some of whom then sign up to participate when they find out a booth will make a stop nearby. But the fact that so many people arrive confident that their stories are worthwhile is indicative of something that has changed only in the past few years.

"People used to be surprised when you wanted to record them," says Michael Taft, who runs the Archive of Folk Culture at the Library of Congress, where the StoryCorps recordings are archived. No more. The idea of the recorded personal narrative has settled into the public consciousness. Public Radio International's *This American Life* draws more than 1.7 million listeners every week. More than fifty public radio stations nationwide have picked up WNYC's *Radio Lab*, another new narrative-heavy program. And public-radio programmers keep finding ways to incorporate the stories of ordinary people into regular programs, hoping to capture an audience that craves personal stories. As a result, it has occurred to more and more people that they—or people they know—have tales to tell that are just as moving as those they hear on the radio. Taft reported that the number of requests he gets from people hoping to archive recordings they've made of their family members has increased tenfold in the past several years. The veteran radio producer Jay Allison, who runs the radio documentary community Web site *Transom*, says thousands of people each month view the part of the site that offers how-to advice on equipment and technique.

Still, the narrative renaissance has deeper roots. National Public Radio first employed the "everyday person" narrative form in the early seventies, when the network was born, and when historians in the United States were in the midst of a major paradigm shift. From the civil rights movement, student antiwar protests, and the women's movement, the nation learned that ordinary people—not just the rich and powerful—make history. Historians like Howard

Zinn and Eric Foner revolutionized the field by considering politics and culture from the point of view of the poor. In the eighties and nineties an academic backlash against bottom-up history took away some of the revolution's momentum, but today, some historians are again finding reasons to focus on ordinary people. Roy Rosenzweig, a history professor at George Mason University, has spent the last several years collecting personal stories for the online digital history archive he created. "Some people might see bottom-up history as old-fashioned," says Rosenzweig. "On the other hand it remains a pretty powerful strand." Although many historians these days are mostly focused on global powers, Rosenzweig says there's another new contingent that's interested in "micro-history"—the study of the minutiae that get lost in the din of twenty-first-century life. Individual voices are some of the "grains of sand" that interest these micro-historians.

Intellectual and broadcasting trends aside, storytelling is such a timeless and basic human activity that it exists, in many ways, outside the world of zeitgeist. Henry Jenkins, a professor of media studies at MIT, recently pointed out to me that even as communities grow more fractured, people *still* seek out opportunities to hear stories—and to tell them. "The twentieth-century history of mass media should have destroyed the storytelling tradition," says Jenkins. "But it didn't." He's right. There has never been a time when people *haven't* needed personal stories. We don't want stories any less than we did ten thousand years ago. In fact, we may want them more. "We are social beings, and our lives got kind of fragmented—our media lives, our civic lives, our personal lives," says Rob Rosenthal, director of the radio program at the Salt Institute for Documentary Studies. "Listening to these kinds of stories on the radio can connect us to one another."

If you ask radio-savvy people why there are so many personal narratives on the air these days, many will respond with just one word: Ira. And in some ways, they're right. Ira Glass, host of *This American Life*, has single-handedly brought personal narrative radio—and public radio in general—to a level of hip no one ever thought possible. Among a certain set a kind of Ira-mania has taken hold. "The Sex Pistols were to punk rock as *This American Life*," says Rosenthal.

Ira Glass didn't invent the personal narrative radio form (one could credit the oral historian Studs Terkel with that). But since the early nineties, largely because of a core group of freelance radio documentarians, the genre has gathered momentum. In 1993, long before he started StoryCorps, David Isay gave tape recorders to two kids on Chicago's South Side. They documented their experiences growing up in the projects, and the result was the widely aired documentary, *Ghetto Life 101*, one of many pieces Isay made with his production company, Sound Portraits. For the past decade, Joe Richman, a freelance radio documentarian, has been producing pieces that let people like residents of a retirement home, prison inmates, and a teenager with AIDS in South Africa tell their stories in their own voices. And Dan Collison, who in 1994 founded his documentary company, now called Long Haul Productions, has followed his "everyday" subjects (a woman trying to adopt, a senior citizen moving on to a retirement community, a profoundly terrible high school football team) for months, sometimes years. During the nineties, the work of these documentarians and others like them quietly amassed, airing here and there on public radio. But after *This American Life* gained popularity the others became more visible as well. In fact, Ira Glass says that people have a way of giving him credit for every radio narrative they hear. Recently, a woman came up to him and told him how much she loved his piece about people living on the Bowery. A nice compliment, but it was Isay's story.

Some guy's cheating on his girl and they force them to encounter each other on stage? That's the stuff of life, man.

There's something to the Cult of Ira, but his skills are not what make personal narratives compelling. Glass himself agrees, and not just because he is famously self-effacing. The actual subject matter of his shows, he told me, is "very basic human drama": relationships between parents and children, say, or husbands and wives; expectations set too high, expectations set too low. "It's kind of hard to turn away from that stuff," says Glass. "I feel the same way about that that I do about the first time you see *The Jerry Springer Show*. Snobby people will say, 'How can you be interested in that?' And it's like, if you can't be interested in that, who *are* you? Some guy's cheating on his girl and they force them to encounter each other on stage? That's the stuff of life, man."

Perhaps I am a snobby person, but I wasn't sure I bought it. The lurid spectacle of Jerry Springer seemed a far cry from the subtle, respectful *This American Life*. It was only after I spent a day in the StoryCorps mobile booth in New Orleans that I began to understand what Glass meant.

About halfway through that day, Cynthia Scott, a local artist, interviewed her fifty-eight-year-old fiancé, Les Colonello, a jazz musician. Colonello had remained in the couple's house during the storm, and he described both the harrowing few hours when his house literally began to fall apart around him and the days immediately following the storm, when he and a few neighbors banded together to survive.

It was clear from the beginning of the interview that Colonello knew how to tell a story—his memory for details was impressive, and his language was specific and descriptive. He described, for example, how he and a neighbor, in a boat they had grabbed as it floated down their street, took food for the neighborhood from a pitch-black, flooded Winn Dixie.

But as I listened, I realized that Colonello's story was most compelling during the moments when some small detail struck a chord in a way that made the disaster understandable on a human scale. One of those moments came when Colonello described climbing up into the rafters of his house to repair the roof. From the rafters, he saw that the wind had destroyed the local horse-racing track, and trees littered the streets. "All the neat property lines the neighbors worked so hard on were gone," he said. "There was no 'this is my territory, that's your territory' anymore." In a few sentences, Colonello had made me understand the chaos after the storm in a way that I hadn't before.

At the end of my day in the booth, I visited the StoryCorps Web site and listened to clips of interviews that had aired on *Morning Edition*. I wanted to get a sense of which kinds of interviews made it onto the radio, and what made them work. On first listen, the clips didn't seem to have much in common. A twelve-year-old boy with Asperger's Syndrome interviewed his mother. Two cousins remembered their neighbor and Sunday school teacher. A woman told her husband about what it had been like to beat cancer. But as I listened, I realized that part of the appeal of the clips was that in less than five minutes, each of the interviews gave a real sense of someone else's experience. We are storytellers and listeners by nature, but we are also, by nature, curious about other people.

And just as Glass suggested with his Jerry Springer comparison, we go to great lengths to satisfy that curiosity. Later that same evening, the concierge at my hotel in New Orleans told me that guests often sheepishly ask her where they can go to see hurricane damage. Most of the tour companies in New Orleans, she said, had started to offer

Katrina packages: tours through some of the city's hardest-hit areas. Understandably, the tours disgust more than a few locals who suspect that a little schadenfreude is what's motivating the gawkers. But while it's unlikely that a few hours of cruising through the wreckage in an air-conditioned bus will substantially enlighten anyone, it's possible that the basic urge that compels tourists to see the damage for themselves is related to what made me want to keep listening to Colonello's hurricane survival story.

In the days following Katrina, we learned what it meant for a levee to break, saw maps of flooding, and heard about the extent of the damage. But after a news event of that magnitude the sheer volume of print, broadcast, and Internet coverage can be hard to digest. Stories like Colonello's help make sense of the information overload by making us feel closer to the people who are affected.

Whether or not Colonello's story makes it onto the radio is up to the programmers at the New Orleans public radio station, WWNO. StoryCorps partners with public radio stations near each of the mobile booths' stops, and the facilitators provide transcripts and tape for the station to edit into short segments. At the time I was in New Orleans, none of the StoryCorps interviews had aired yet. But when I spoke to WWNO's programming director, Fred Kasten, he told me that when he begins to select material from StoryCorps, he will probably look for stories—not necessarily all about the hurricane—that tease meaning from the mundane. "The minutiae of daily life can be very interesting, particularly in the hands of a good raconteur," says Kasten.

For the past hundred years of broadcast history we have depended on a small group of good raconteurs to bring us our news, but recently it has become increasingly true that getting a story to an audience does not require the blessing of a network. The larger context of the personal-narrative renaissance has to do with the democratization of news-bringing, and the fact that perhaps right now we are remembering something that we have always known: good raconteurs are everywhere.

And with new technology, for those who want to give their stories a better chance at traveling further than an archive at the Library of Congress, the equipment is more affordable and easier to use than ever before. When Isay, Richman, and Collison started out, producing a radio piece required an entire studio full of expensive gear. Now, anyone with a few basics—a mini-disc recorder, a decent microphone, a computer, and a copy of the free version of the editing program ProTools—can make a documentary.

And an audience is easier to come by, too. Not even a decade ago, the only way for an amateur radio producer to get a piece distributed to public radio stations was to subscribe to an expensive satellite-feed system. The system still exists, but it is no longer the only place that programmers look for material. In 2002, radio producers Jay Allison and Jake Shapiro founded PRX (www.prx.org), a sort of Internet sounding board for radio pieces. Anyone can post a piece, and both a review board and community members review submissions. Public radio stations often troll PRX for content and, after paying a licensing fee, a programmer can pick up a story from the site and air it. According to Shapiro, more than 8,000 pieces have been licensed by more than 220 stations.

Another of Allison's Web projects is *Transom* (www.transom.org), a site that provides tips and advice to radio documentarians, and showcases a new documentary each month. Some of the work that *Transom* features comes from people with radio training, but a good bit comes from novices with extraordinary stories—and the drive to put in the long hours necessary to perfect a radio piece.

One of those novices with a story was Sue Mell, whose documentary, "Girl Detectives," was featured on *Transom* in December 2003. Mell originally hoped to attract the attention of Ira Glass, but she knew that a wide gulf of technical expertise stood between her and *This American Life*, so she turned to *Transom*. Mell now describes herself as "the *Transom* poster girl"—she produced the first version of her draft by following *Transom's* advice on equipment and editing technique. Later, after Allison expressed interest in featuring "Girl Detectives" on the site, she worked with a *Transom* editor to polish the piece into a radio-ready documentary. Of course, Mell had a particularly compelling story. She had been working as a stand-up comedian in San Francisco in 2003 when her friend Laura's husband, Jay, was found dead, his throat slit, in a movie theater parking lot. The police ruled his death a suicide, claiming that he had planned to make it look like a murder so his family could collect on an insurance policy. But Laura was sure that her husband wouldn't have killed himself. "Girl Detectives" tells the story of how, without the help of the police, Laura and a few close friends tried in vain to solve Jay's murder.

On Allison's recommendation I visited the archive section on *Transom* and listened to "Girl Detectives" in MP3 format. Mell lays out the story in simple language, but from the beginning it's clear that, just as Colonello's story was not just about a hurricane, "Girl Detectives" is not just about a murder. Rather, it makes a subtle point about what it means to feel not just bereft, but also frustrated. "We're all so helpless in the face of death, and even more so in the face of an unsolved crime, of a murder," Mell says at the beginning of the piece. "And women, women are always relegated to the role of providing comfort where really, there isn't any to be had. We make phone calls, we make coffee, we hand out Kleenex, and we're advised, over and over again, not to antagonize the police. The police will find the answers. This, after all, is their job."

After it aired on *Transom*, Mell came pretty close to getting "Girl Detectives" on *This American Life*. But Glass wanted to take the story in a different direction; among other things, he wanted Laura's voice in the piece, and Mell knew that speaking on air would make her friend uncomfortable. So in the end, there was no *This American Life* for "Girl Detectives." Nevertheless, the piece has slowly found a substantial audience. A version aired on the San Francisco public radio program *Invisible Ink*, and it's exposed to *Transom's* roughly two thousand daily viewers as well. Through "Girl Detectives," Mell has found that these days, an important story doesn't necessarily need an important radio show to carry it. And when that story is about what it feels like to be voiceless and powerless, it is especially important to know that people are listening.

KIERA BUTLER is an assistant editor at *CJR*.

Reprinted from *Columbia Journalism Review*, July/August 2006. Copyright © 2006 by Columbia Journalism Review, Columbia University.

Return of the Sob Sisters

Newspapers have fallen in love with long narratives about fatal illnesses and disfiguring ailments, particularly when they involve children. Many readers respond powerfully to these emotional sagas that, like the work of the sob sisters years ago, often offer lessons in spiritual stamina and redemption.

STEPHANIE SHAPIRO

In June 2005, the Boston Globe ran a three-part, 10,000-word series about a Harvard University freshman who as a child was left legally blind and partially paralyzed by brain tumors. In December, the Denver Post devoted 11,500 words in a special section to the saga of a young boy with cerebral palsy whose parents made the choice to let him die. In January, the Los Angeles Times ran a 4,400-word story about a mother who gave birth to her son knowing he would only live for a matter of hours.

Newspapers can't resist the urge to go long when it comes to tales of fatal illnesses, disfiguring ailments and accidents, particularly when they strike children. In recent decades, the drama underlying these anguishing accounts has led to the creation of a subgenre of narrative journalism that often vies with hard news for A1 recognition in the country's most prestigious newspapers.

Such human interest stories, molded by the techniques of fiction, put a face on the bewildering universe of medical ethics, risky procedures and end-of-life choices. Like the harrowing tales that yellow journalism's Nellie Bly and her sob sister descendants became known for, they also are calculated to snag readers by the emotions and not let them go until they burst, on cue, into tears.

Reader responses such as this one are typical: "Thank you for your magical story about Dylan," wrote a Denver Post reader regarding Kevin Simpson's account of the little boy with cerebral palsy. "I broke into tears several times reading it. The mystical connections were stunning and, as the mother of a handicapped child, comforting to me."

Ambitious newspaper narratives showcasing "coping with adversity" themes are hardly a recent innovation. But the expanding role played by these narratives merits scrutiny, particularly in a climate in which news stories double as infotainment and in which the James Frey "memoir" debacle highlighted the vanishing line between truth and fiction.

When does a news story become less about providing information and more about manipulating emotions? When does it become more voyeuristic than revealing? At what point does an effort to elucidate slide hopelessly into pathos? And are such stories as much about reinforcing cultural and religious beliefs as about shedding light on medicine's triumphs and limitations?

These narrative stories are lengthy by design, often warrant a dedicated editor and photographer, and receive top billing in newspaper promotions. They usually are worth the effort, as far as recognition goes. Such touching tales routinely receive plaudits and Web visitors galore and frequently nab illustrious prizes. A study of trends in Pulitzer Prize-winning feature stories, published in the Winter 2005 edition of the Newspaper Research Journal, found that "a significant number of winning stories involved a death by murder or illness." Authors Chris Lamb at the College of Charleston in South Carolina and Jeanie McAdams Moore, who completed the study as a graduate student at American University in Washington, D.C., continued: "A second review indicated that 10 of the 31 winning stories—nearly one in three—involved a death."

Poignant newspaper accounts of children facing life-threatening conditions or challenging odds often have been expanded into books. Tom Hallman Jr.'s "Sam: The Boy Behind the Mask," based on his Pulitzer-winning series in Portland's Oregonian, appeared in 2002. Boston Globe reporter Mitchell Zuckoff's "Choosing Naia," a series about a married couple who decide to have a child with Down syndrome, was published in book form in 2002. Mark Patinkin's "Up and Running," based on his Providence Journal series about a boy who lost his legs to bacterial meningitis, appeared in 2005.

Garnering grateful responses from readers and laurels from professional organizations, such stories have become largely impervious to criticism. Even the most cynical of editors may consider it impolitic to question heartrending accounts of illness and death. (Moore says she was accused of being "overly critical" in her Pulitzer study.) And yet, in the search for emotional copy, writers may neglect the nuances that fully describe a story if they appear to detract from its narrative flow.

Prior to her analysis of Pulitzer winners, Moore says she had planned to become a feature writer. But the fact that many of journalism's most highly lauded human interest stories dealt with death helped lead to her disenchantment with the field. "I was disappointed by the tone in the articles and by the general impression I had that to be successful, I had to focus on that kind of story," says Moore, now a public affairs consultant for a Washington, D.C., defense contractor.

"It's very easy to go out and find a sad story," she says. "But that doesn't really stretch the author [as would] an issue that's really worthy of explaining in detail and putting before the public."

When does a news story become less about providing information and more about manipulating emotions?

Emotional journalism didn't always prevail in the elite press. By the end of the 19th century, the sensational and mawkish tales of misfortune that were a hallmark of yellow journalism were yielding to the refined sensibilities of those such as Adolph Ochs, owner of the New York Times.

In his book "Just the Facts," David T. Z. Mindich writes that Ochs and other members of the elite press dismissed "the yellows" as newspapers with "little breeding or dignity." Ochs' insistence in the late 1890s on aloof, impartial reportage set the standard for decades to come.

As recently as 30 years ago, "Newspapers used to be a lot more macho," says Kyrie O'Connor, deputy managing editor for features at the Houston Chronicle. When she entered journalism in the late 1970s, "There wasn't any appetite for that kind of emotional story. It was all facts." Editors said, " 'Write about the town sewer board meeting.' You couldn't really tell the story of someone who has just had a double mastectomy."

As literary journalism came into vogue in the 1960s and '70s, though, the standards of dispassionate journalism were loosened, and feature stories were released from the purgatory of the "women's pages." Legitimized by Pulitzer recognition in 1979, features, including increasingly graphic accounts of illness and disability, gained traction in much of the daily press.

The long-form chronicle of disease or disability is one legacy of New Journalism's stylistic verve. The work of Tom Wolfe and others made the narrative form "acceptable and useful again," says Carolyn Kitch, associate professor of journalism at Temple University in Philadelphia. "Now what we have been left with is narrative form without the deeper stuff it was used for in the 1960s and '70s."

In her book "Everyman News: How and Why American Newspapers Changed Forever," set for publication in 2007, Michele Weldon argues that since 9/11, personal features have transformed front pages across the nation. In an analysis of 20 daily newspapers, the assistant professor of journalism at the Medill School at Northwestern University measured a 43 percent increase in A1 features from 2001 (pre 9/11) to 2004.

The rise stems in part from what Weldon calls the "post 9/11 sensitivity" that engendered the Pulitzer-winning "Portraits of Grief" series in the New York Times. She also speaks of the "cultural sanctity of stories." Whether found in blogs, documentaries, reality TV, advertising or any other form of communication, personal stories are the perennial vehicle of choice for conveying information and compelling belief.

As new media play to their strengths, including 24-hour news coverage, one of the sole remaining roles for newspapers is to tell stories, Weldon says. "I think a lot of it has to do with the fact that a consumer can find the news anywhere else faster, so newspapers must deliver a product that's different."

But critics say that in capitulating to the demand for personal stories, newspapers have surrendered to the competition. "Journalism today is built on these kinds of stories," Joe Saltzman, director of the Image of the Journalist in Popular Culture project at the University of Southern California's Annenberg School for Communication, said in an e-mail interview. "There doesn't seem much room left in the newspapers and on television for news coverage on the major events and trends unless that story can be cloaked as an article on an individual braving great odds or suffering great misfortune or achieving superhuman success."

As did sob stories more than a century ago, today's sentimental tales offer lessons in spiritual stamina and redemption, particularly comforting in a period of anxiety.

Tales of sorrow and woe are primarily motivated by "the desire of print to get readers any way they can, and one way to do it is to tell stories the way TV does," New York Times op-ed columnist Frank Rich wrote in an e-mail interview. "I can't say strongly enough that the triumph of television over print has brought about many of these changes—newspapers need to compete, and this is one way to do it." Whether award-winning feature writers are "more like yellow-journalism sentimentalists of old than the New Journalist ideal" may have to be determined on a case-by-case basis, Rich says.

Matthew T. Felling, media director at the Center for Media and Public Affairs, also attributes the trend to a "weep creep" from television to print. The "sob stories that have become standard fare in the electronic media and People magazine knockoff shows have conditioned news consumers to look for them in every news product," he says.

These features have the power to lure readers indifferent to dry subjects such as farm subsidies but who may think, " 'That pregnant mother breaks my heart,' " Felling says. "Newspapers were not constructed to attract the less interested reader, but now they are, to maintain profit margins."

Such narrative accounts of suffering characteristically make readers privy to intimate secrets, explicit physical details and excruciating deliberations that inform life-and-death decisions. In stories about ailing or injured children, writers also tend to accept without question their subjects' religious faith, the supernatural portents they see in ordinary occurrences and the meanings they struggle to find in their trials.

The analysis of Pulitzer features by Moore and Lamb notes "the frequency with which Christian references appeared, while other religions were almost completely absent. It seemed that Christianity often served as a reader's guide to right and wrong," the researchers observe. They single out "Angels and Demons," the 1998 Pulitzer winner by Tom French of the St. Petersburg Times, for the headline itself, which "told the reader to expect a battle between good and evil, with clearly defined heroes and villains." In French's account of the murder of three Ohio tourists, including a 13-year-old girl, Christian imagery was "used consistently as a tool for pointing out 'good' forces," Moore and Lamb write.

The researchers suggest that "Christian symbolism has become inextricably woven into the fabric of American metaphor and has become an easy means of painting a picture without requiring the audience to think too hard. Thus, although the stories are highly readable and beautifully written, readers learned nothing new; accepted values and plots are simply recycled because they confirm the readers' own views and beliefs."

As did sob stories more than a century ago, today's sentimental tales offer lessons in spiritual stamina and redemption, particularly comforting in a period of anxiety. "It seems like Americans have been experimenting with redemptive stories for a long time," says Dan P. McAdams, a professor of human development and social policy at Northwestern University and author of "The Redemptive Self: Stories Americans Live By." "The recent flap with James Frey—that was a redemptive narrative about recovery. It's almost like we've played out every possible redemptive narrative out there," McAdams says.

Perhaps stories about the loss of children—"the worst thing that could possibly happen to you"—are the ultimate spiritual test, McAdams suggests. "If you can find meaning in that, [that would constitute] the last bastion of redemptive hope."

In a scene from Denver Post reporter Kevin Simpson's account of how parents Kerri Bruning and Dave Walborn grapple with whether to withdraw life support from their son, Dylan, God becomes an active character:

A little past 8 A.M. Oct. 18, Pastor Buddy Conn came calling at Kerri's apartment.

Together, they prayed.

Pastor Buddy, on the staff of a large non-denominational congregation, knew Kerri and Dave from previous hospital visits in which he'd prayed with them and Dylan. This time, he asked the Lord to give the parents clear understanding of what they were supposed to do later that day; he did not presume to know the answer.

He prayed for Dylan's healing—whether on earth or in heaven.

"Mom just wanted to know, 'Boy, have I fought the good fight, have I finished the race?'" the pastor says. "She felt she had. She's a believer, so she leans on God for her day-to-day guidance. I believe God gave her an answer in the afternoon."

Seeking solace in one's religious beliefs, particularly in the aftermath of a death or other tragedy, was once a private matter, McAdams notes. Now, "there's more leeway" for journalists as prayer and proclamation of one's faith have become commonplace in public discourse. "More people want to hear this," McAdams says. "We sort of value this talking about our pain much more than we used to. When stories get told, it gives them a reality they didn't have before. In the telling, they get expanded."

The "need to find positive meaning in suffering is so strong, sometimes we can go overboard on it," he adds. "Sometimes you're deluding yourself if you're going to find meaning in the Holocaust, 9/11 or when a child dies."

And yet Americans, staunchly pragmatic in their faith, live by such stories, McAdams says. "We want something to come out of suffering. We have a really difficult time with the idea that we wouldn't be able to move forward. The idea that some things are so bad that we would not be able to find meaning in them is anathema. It's something Americans don't want to think about."

The spiritual dimension underlying Kevin Simpson's story about Dylan was impossible to ignore, says Denver Post Editor Gregory Moore. "I think any time you're talking about life and death, then religion and faith and God come into play," he says. To give up hope that their son's life would improve if he were kept alive was a "tremendously difficult thing for [Dylan's parents]. To the extent that they could do it, their faith had a lot to do with it," Moore says.

He has no plans to run similar stories simply because they evince sympathy and compliments from readers. "The key to this type of narrative journalism is to find the right story that's worth telling," Moore says. "They don't come along every day or every week or every month. I see us as having the commitment to do these stories when they present themselves."

But others argue that these types of pieces gloss over thorny details. "In struggling to make real stories fit the conversion/redemption narrative, all sorts of inconvenient facts get left out. Like the fact that autism isn't a 'disease' and can't be 'cured,'" says Mitzi Waltz, an American lecturer in journalism and media studies at the University of Sunderland in Great Britain who is completing a dissertation on the cultural history of autism. "Parents whose own experiences don't match these well-retailed tales feel a huge amount of guilt," she wrote in an e-mail interview.

The author of numerous books about developmental disorders, Waltz also studies how people with disabilities are portrayed in popular culture. Articles that give the impression that autism is curable are partly to blame for the dearth of services available to adults with the disorder, Waltz says. And yet "editors will buy a cure story, but have little interest in the less dramatic 'muddling through' story that's far more common."

In a 1998 paper, Beth A. Haller, an associate professor of journalism at Towson University in Maryland, found that inspiring narratives about people with disabilities often earn prizes. The evergreen "coping with adversity" theme allows for "easy cultural cues" that convey the impression that disability and chronic illness are by definition tragedies, Haller says. "A lot of people don't define these things in their lives as tragedy; a lot of people say their lives turned out differently after disability or a car accident."

Many of these accounts are "very, very well-written pieces," Haller says. "It's hard not to have these things affect you emotionally and feel the pull of the story. [Readers] don't realize it's the good writing. The story's the same story. It's been told over and over. You're not really learning anything new."

A story's poignant subject matter doesn't automatically consign it to the sob sister files. With astute editing and a willingness to defy literary conventions by incorporating sometimes messy nuances and other narrative anomalies, such tales can be both enthralling and informative.

The "need to find positive meaning in suffering is so strong, sometimes we can go overboard on it."

If editors were to "turn it around and demand that reporting be at the core of the story as opposed to the writing, it would be a totally different style of story, and well-written as well," Haller says.

With health care becoming an increasingly prominent issue, the proliferation of illness-related stories can serve a purpose, the Times' Rich wrote in an e-mail interview. "Health care—and medicine in general—are far bigger issues now than they ever were in American history, especially as Americans live longer and longer. Today—as was not the case in the '30s or '50s or even '60s—journalists can cover disease candidly, without euphemisms (even the word cancer was once verboten), and personal narratives are a way of breaking through or explaining the science."

People's "struggle with illness and the medical system may be of more interest to readers than any other single issue," Rich says. "In this sense, the assignment of these stories and their proliferation reflect the news, because the medical system is in an intractable crisis that affects nearly every American and business."

Dylan's story departed from pure melodrama because it addressed crucial ethical questions that influence end-of-life decisions, says the Denver Post's Moore. "I think the thing that made this story different was the commitment these parents had and the decision they made in a post-Terri Schiavo world," he says. "There was all this hullabaloo over Terri Schiavo, and every day hundreds of lives are ended, and we don't know much about that."

Whether such stories serve an important social function or are merely crowd-pleasers must be decided story by story, says Felling of the Center for Media and Public Affairs. In part, intent can be determined by tone, he says. "How is the story written? Is it maudlin or straightforward? What is the adjective per 100 word rate? How often does the journalist imagine what might be going through someone's head?"

The Providence Journal's Mark Patinkin was mindful of the potential pitfalls when he wrote the series that became "Up and Running: The Inspiring True Story of a Boy's Struggle to Survive and Triumph."

"I didn't want it to just be one more inspirational, dramatic story about overcoming an illness, and so the approach I actually took was to bend over as far as I could in the direction of understatement," says Patinkin, who is a columnist. "I found it was an interesting exercise as a journalist. So often when we're trying to find the drama in stories, I think readers pick up that you're forcing [the story] when you're doing that."

The "kind of drama that came out of that understatement was even more powerful," Patinkin says. He didn't shy away from addressing the role faith played in the lives of his subjects. "I decided to ask a question I almost never ask: 'Did you pray?' And I asked that of everybody, including the doctors. Some of them thought it was a question out of left field," he says. "In a case like this, it's just as important to describe the patient as being anointed as being intubated."

As the media turn dying children and cancer victims into heroes, it is "not necessarily a sign that journalism has gone bad. It's a sign that journalism has been moving toward 'public journalism,'" Temple's Kitch says. "The ordinary person, meaning the reader, has become a symbolically elevated figure in the news as [important as] the president or official sources."

In a similar vein, Northwestern's Weldon says that as more ordinary people become the sources quoted in news coverage, readers increasingly regard them as just as credible as public officials. A greater number of stories tend to revolve around individuals as well and take on a more intimate tone, she says. Today, readers want news "up close and personal, humanistic."

Editors are mindful that personal stories can be a boon for newspapers languishing in the new-media climate. A 2005 series by a young San Francisco Chronicle copy editor, Alicia Parlette, about her cancer diagnosis generated thousands of mostly favorable responses that have vindicated the paper's venture into pathos, says Managing Editor Robert J. Rosenthal. "We can be the glue or the connector for communities and stories about triumphs and tragedy, and sometimes they are very mundane. But they really resonate with people," Rosenthal says. "They can see themselves in these stories."

The steady stream of inspiring yet depressing stories can leave the impression that joy and humor are scarce commodities. In the view of the Houston Chronicle's O'Connor, that is unfortunate. "Making people cry seems a lot more serious than making people laugh," she says. "I'm really fond of humor, and I love stories that make people laugh. But those don't seem to have the same intellectual heft in the eyes of a lot of people."

If the press persists in running stories about disabilities, it is possible to tell them in fresh, unpredictable ways, O'Connor says. Now that "newspapers have somewhat belatedly caught up to the idea that emotional stories and stories that speak from the heart are a way to connect with the readers, the challenge for an editor and a writer is to find a way to tell the story that appears to be going in one direction and make it go slightly to the left or to the right, to take a person to an unexpected place."

She cites a story by Chronicle reporter Jeannie Kever about a high school student with Down syndrome elected homecoming queen. Kever "did not pump up the emotional value, didn't inflate it," O'Connor says. "But the story was very sweet and had no villains, no nothing. It was a lovely story. What it turned out to be about was this generation of high-school kids and how it's no big deal to them, about her complete acceptance. This was not a story of tragedy at all; it was more a story of kids who are mainstreamed their whole life, and this was fine."

The "deeper you go into one person's unique story, the more the uniqueness of the story emerges," O'Connor says. "You can have a hypothesis, but if the hypothesis isn't overturned, you've failed," she says.

"People rarely conform to some type. It's not a question of sneering or trying to find an edge; it's a question of really, really trying to find the story."

STEPHANIE SHAPIRO (Stephanie.Shapiro@baltsun.com) is a features reporter for the *Baltimore Sun* and the author of "Reinventing the Feature Story: Mythic Cycles in American Literary Journalism."

Article 17

Climate Change: Now What?

Scientists agree it's real, but there's no consensus on solutions. Readers need a guide to the options.

CRISTINE RUSSELL

Media coverage of climate change is at a crossroads, as it moves beyond the science of global warming into the broader arena of what governments, entrepreneurs, and ordinary citizens are doing about it. Consider these recent examples: a decade from now, Abu Dhabi hopes to have the first city in the world with zero carbon emissions. In a windswept stretch of desert, developers plan to build Masdar City, a livable environment for fifty thousand people that relies entirely on solar power and other renewable energy. Science correspondent Joe Palca reported from Masdar's construction site as part of National Public Radio's yearlong project "Climate Connections."

The *Christian Science Monitor*'s Peter N. Spotts went to the Biesbosch, a small inland delta near the Netherlands' city of Dordrecht, to research "How to Fight a Rising Sea." In an effort that could be instructive for others, the Dutch are developing ways to protect their small country's vulnerable coast against rising sea levels that could result from climate change.

Wang Suya lives in Japan but sends a YouTube greeting to fellow visitors at Dot Earth, the innovative blog started by Andrew C. Revkin, the *New York Times* environment reporter. Having traveled the globe to cover global warming, Revkin now posts and exchanges ideas on Dot Earth about climate and sustainability issues, particularly the energy, food, and water demands on a planet that may house nine billion people by mid-century.

These reporters are in the advance guard of an army of journalists around the world who are covering what *Time* magazine has dubbed the "War on Global Warming." Journalists will play a key role in shaping the information that opinion leaders and the public use to judge the urgency of climate change, what needs to be done about it, when and at what costs. It is a vast, multifaceted story whose complexity does not fit well with journalism's tendency to shy away from issues with high levels of uncertainty and a time-frame of decades, rather than days or months.

In 2009, climate-change coverage will grow in significance on a number of domestic and international fronts:

In science, the impact of global warming will be followed closely at the two poles as well as Pacific island hot spots, like the low-lying islands of Papua New Guinea, that are in the greatest danger.

In politics, after eight years of relative inaction by the Bush administration, the new U.S. president and Congress will be under pressure to pass legislation to curb emissions of greenhouse gases.

Internationally, the United Nations has scheduled key conferences—in Poznan, Poland, in December 2008 and in Copenhagen in December 2009—to hammer out a new international treaty that is practically and politically feasible. Shortages and high prices are bringing the role of biofuels in the global food crisis under added scrutiny.

Meanwhile, the efforts of countries, businesses, communities, and even individuals to reduce their "carbon footprints" will increasingly be examined.

Climate change will require thoughtful leadership and coordination at news organizations. Editors will need to integrate the specialty environment, energy, and science reporters with other beats that have a piece of the story—everything from local and national politics to foreign affairs, business, technology, health, urban affairs, agriculture, transportation, law, architecture, religion, consumer news, gardening, travel, and sports. "News organizations are increasingly asking what other beats are going to be affected by climate," says veteran environment reporter Bud Ward, who edits a respected online journalism site, The Yale Forum on Climate Change & The Media. He notes that even *Sports Illustrated* has tackled climate change and its potential impact on everything from cancelled games to baseball bats. But, Ward worries, "it will be extremely difficult to explain the policy side of the debate" in the months ahead. Unless editors push hard for it, "there's generally not the time or space for that kind of explanatory coverage."

To that end, Ward has organized media workshops on global warming for top editors as well as reporters. A daylong meeting last fall at Stanford University attracted heavy hitters like Washington Post executive editor Leonard Downie Jr. and top editors from *The New York Times,* the *Los Angeles Times,* and metropolitan papers from Detroit to Des Moines. Eighteen news executives spent the morning with leading scientists, who emphasized the strong agreement among international experts that the earth is warming and that man-made greenhouse gas emissions are largely to blame. The UN Intergovernmental Panel on Climate Change (IPCC) last year issued a widely publicized report (in four parts) that provided the most comprehensive scientific agreement to date on the causes and potentially devastating impact of global warming. Yet, recalls Stephen H. Schneider, a Stanford climatologist, "several editors were surprised there was so much consensus."

In the afternoon session, the consensus dissipated when it came to a discussion of the potential economic impact of climate actions. One expert saw climate change as a profitable business opportunity; another warned that solutions would be difficult and costly: "There are no silver bullets . . . only silver birdshot." Ward says that one editor later commented: "It looks like economists are going to need their own IPCC."

Daniel P. Schrag, a climate geologist who directs the Harvard University Center for the Environment, says, "We're in a transition in which the climate science is no longer the primary issue. More and more it's about how we stop it, not whether it is happening."

And Matthew C. Nisbet, an American University communications professor, says, "We have had more science coverage on climate change than at any time in history. The next challenge is to find ways to cover the story across news beats and in ways that engage new readers."

Here are some thoughts as to how coverage might be sharpened in the year ahead in the broad areas of science, politics, and business.

Science and Technology

The ongoing science story. After several years of stumbling, mainstream science and environmental coverage has generally adopted the scientific consensus that increases in heat-trapping emissions from burning fossil fuels and tropical deforestation are changing the planet's climate, causing adverse effects even more rapidly than had once been predicted.

The process of science often involves studies that contradict one another along the way. . . . Journalists should avoid 'yo-yo' coverage with each new study and try to put the latest findings in context.

But the devil is in the details. New findings on why, where, how fast, and with what impact climate change might occur will take time to assess, and there is a danger that the subtleties of the science, and its uncertainty, might be missed by reporters unfamiliar with the territory. The process of science often involves studies that contradict one another along the way; scientists look for consistency among several reports before concluding that something is true. Journalists should avoid "yo-yo" coverage with each new study and try to put the latest findings in context.

Scientists are debating, for example, how global warming may affect hurricanes, with an "ongoing tempest among meteorologists and climatologists spouting off at one another on whether hurricane activity in the Atlantic is up due to a warming ocean," noted Charles Petit in the MIT Knight Science Journalism Tracker. He cited a recent computer simulation of late twenty-first-century hurricane patterns by National Oceanic and Atmospheric Administration scientists that predicted *fewer* tropical storms and hurricanes in the Atlantic. Experienced journalists reported the findings cautiously, noting that some studies have suggested *more* and *more powerful* hurricanes due to global warming. Jim Loney, a Reuters reporter, concluded his story with a scientist's caveat: "We don't regard this as the last word on this topic."

You can't see climate change out the window. "Weather is what you get; climate is what you expect," says Stanford's Schneider. "Weather is the day-to-day fluctuations; climate is the long-term averages, the patterns and probability of extremes." The basic difference is time: weather equals short-term, climate the long haul. Ward uses a clothes analogy—weather helps us decide what to wear each day; climate influences the wardrobe we buy.

"The earth is getting hotter," says John P. Holdren, a Harvard scientist and international climate-policy leader who has addressed the UN—and been on the *Late Show with David Letterman*. He cites climate patterns showing that twenty-three out of twenty-four of the hottest years on record have occurred since 1980. The thirteen hottest all have occurred since 1990, with 2005 the hottest ever recorded. But "the heating is not uniform geographically," cautioned Holdren, who uses the term "global climate disruption" because some regions may experience more extreme—and less predictable—environmental changes than others.

This message was echoed in a landmark Agriculture Department report, released in late May and signed by three Cabinet secretaries, that Juliet Eilperin, the national environment and politics reporter for *The Washington Post,* called the "most detailed look in nearly eight years at how climate change is reshaping the American landscape." It concluded that the West is already vulnerable to forest fires, reduced snow pack, and drought.

It is a good rule of thumb to avoid attributing any specific weather event directly to climate change. A single summer heat wave may or may not be part of a long-term climate trend. A cold winter in New England does not mean that global warming is not happening.

Environmental forces may also interact in ways that can be hard to explain. German researchers, writing recently in *Nature,* used a new climate model to suggest that natural variation in ocean circulation might "temporarily offset" temperature increases from human-caused global warming in Europe and North America over the next decade. Some misleading media reports turned the preliminary forecast into a definitive statement that, as a British *Telegraph* reporter put it, "global warming will stop until at least 2015."

Watch out for techno-optimism. Proponents of new energy technologies often hype the potential benefits—without knowing the effectiveness, cost, time frame (always longer than expected), risks, or potential impact on the larger energy picture. It's a reporter's duty to explain the potential downside as well as conflicts of interests.

Renewable energy sources, such as solar, wind, and geothermal, have garnered enthusiastic publicity. But it will take time for them to make a dent in the overall U.S. energy marketplace because of higher costs, lower scale, and public opposition to sitings of wind farms and solar grids. Nuclear power is popular in France but still largely radioactive in the American public's mind. Another area for further media follow-up is the touted technology for carbon capture and storage at coal-burning power plants, which has stalled in the U.S. because of political squabbling and unexpected cost overruns.

In a related vein, beware the law of unintended consequences. The biofuel ethanol was ballyhooed as a big win for U.S. energy security, farmers, and the environment, but a funny thing happened on the way to the fuel tank. A February 2008 study in *Science* magazine concluded that producing ethanol from corn may exceed or match the greenhouse gas emissions from fossil fuels.

More recently, of course, ethanol has been blamed for contributing to the world food crisis, since farm acreage previously used for food is now devoted to lucrative fuel-producing corn. Suddenly many elected officials want to cut back on congressional mandates to produce far more ethanol. Once again, the public is left wondering what happened. An excellent April 30 front-page piece from Charles City, Iowa, by *Washington Post* energy reporter Steven Mufson, explored the links between "food and fuel prices." But where were the skeptical scientists, politicians, and journalists earlier, when ethanol was first being promoted in Congress?

Choose your experts carefully. Experts are always a minefield, so the *Times*'s Revkin has a simple rule: when writing about climate science, seek comments from respected scientific experts who have published in major journals in the field, not the experts offered by various policy think tanks and interest groups with axes to grind.

The era of "equal time" for skeptics who argue that global warming is just a result of natural variation and not human intervention seems to be largely over—except on talk radio, cable, and local television. Last year, a meteorologist at CBS's Chicago station did a special report entitled "The Truth about Global Warming." It featured local scientists discussing the hazards of global warming in one segment, well-known national skeptics in another, and ended with a cop-out: "What is the truth about global warming? . . . It depends on who you talk to." Not helpful, and not good reporting.

As the climate issue moves further into public policy, journalists will need to sort out the political and economic interests of experts with a dizzying array of opinions about costs and benefits.

As the climate issue moves further into public policy, journalists will face new challenges in sorting out the political and economic interests of experts with a dizzying array of opinions about the costs and benefits of combating global warming. The he-said, she-said reporting just won't do. The public needs a guide to the policy, not just the politics.

Politics and Policy

After the horse race. A Gallup election poll in early February about what issues would influence Americans' votes put the economy, Iraq, education, health care, and gas prices in the top five considered "extremely or very important." Environment and global warming weighed in at number thirteen.

Politicians pay attention to public opinion, of course. In the 2008 presidential race, Obama and McCain both favor mandatory caps to reduce greenhouse gas emissions—though McCain's plan is not as strict on this—and both candidates push nuclear power, though McCain pushes it more aggressively and with fewer caveats.

In Congress, a groundbreaking cap-and-trade "climate security" bill to reduce key greenhouse gas emissions by about 70 percent by 2050 came to the Senate floor for the first time in June. GOP critics argued that it would raise energy costs further, and the bill was blocked. The debate foreshadowed the difficulties such measures may face in the next Congress.

Think China. Estimates suggest China has passed the U.S. for the dubious distinction as the world's leader in total greenhouse gas emissions. Its rising emissions are fueled by coal-burning power plants—on average, about one new one fires up each week—to meet the energy demands of a growing middle class. But the Pew Center on Global Climate Change said that, on a per-capita basis, U.S. carbon emissions are still about five times greater than those of China, whose enormous 1.3 billion population dwarfs America's three-hundred million.

Neither the U.S. nor China has agreed to international restrictions on greenhouse gas emissions. While the conventional wisdom is that China will wait for the U.S. to act first, a recent opinion piece in the *San Francisco Chronicle* predicted that "China just might surprise the U.S. on climate change" because of growing domestic concerns about pollution, droughts, flooding, and other environmental hazards. The University of California authors predicted that China could also take the lead in the development of clean-energy technology—a good area for journalists to track, in addition to coal and cars.

Business and Commerce

Costs and benefits. Evaluating economic forecasts is even tougher than evaluating the science and precipitates fierce debate. A seven-hundred-page report for the British government in 2006 by economist Nicholas Stern said the costs of enacting global measures to reduce greenhouse gas emissions could amount to about 1 percent of world economic output annually. But not doing so, he said, might ultimately lead to a massive global "market failure," ranging from five to more than twenty times that amount. It drew international coverage for its methods and both praise and criticism from fellow economists. Yale economist William D. Nordhaus's new book concludes that the

Stern approach is too "ambitious" in requiring "extreme immediate action" and is therefore not cost-effective. He favors global carbon taxes that ramp up more gradually.

Many players are weighing in on the how-to-fix-it political issue. A May Reuters story, that ran before the Senate floor debate on cap-and-trade legislation, cited environmental groups as saying "the cost of doing nothing would be far higher" than taking action, while *Washington Post* columnist George Will called the bill a "radical government grab for control of the American economy." A *New York Times* editorial noted that despite Bush administration contentions that "mandatory cuts in carbon dioxide would bankrupt the country," every "serious study" has found that a market-based program "could yield positive economic gains" and that the "costs of inaction will dwarf the costs of acting now."

Times science writer Cornelia Dean wrote last year about the Interface Corporation, a Georgia carpet tile manufacturer that went on a full-court sustainability press by cutting waste, recycling, lowering energy use, and reducing greenhouse gas emissions—and saved money in doing so. "We have made the point in everybody's mind that the cost of reducing carbon emissions will be painful," Dean noted. But "it can also work to your advantage."

Track "green" promises. In the absence of federal action, more than 850 mayors have signed the U.S. Conference of Mayors Climate Protection Agreement to reduce local carbon emissions by using goals set by signatories to the international Kyoto Protocol. States like California and regional efforts in New England have also led in climate-change initiatives. Some corporations, too, have set ambitious goals for reducing their carbon footprints. Reporters need to hold private and public enterprises accountable by analyzing and comparing how well all of these bodies are doing in carrying out their bold promises.

In the meantime, there's a great risk of green fatigue in the media. The number of articles in U.S. newspapers mentioning "going green" in the first quarter of 2008 was about twelve times greater than the comparable period in 2005, according to LexisNexis. Worse, it is also the darling of the advertising business, and the mixing of news and commercial messages is starting to give the phrase a sour green-apple taste.

Still, the trend does give reporters an opportunity to expose examples of "green-washing" that promise eco-friendliness but don't deliver.

As climate change encompasses virtually all aspects of contemporary life, reporters need to tell the story on their watch. A number of Web sites provide helpful information (see the list posted with this story on CJR.org). In the meantime, here is a starter set of possible stories for reporters to consider and readers to request:

In the realm of science, what is the stability of ice sheets in Greenland and West Antarctica, and how will this affect rising sea-level estimates? What plants and animals are at most risk of extinction, and what can be done about that?

What about adaptation to climate change, both here and abroad? Regardless of new control efforts, greenhouse gas emissions already in the pipeline will continue to have warming-related impacts for decades to come. How will Americans cope with changing conditions?

In land use and transportation, what efforts are under way to push auto makers to improve gas mileage? What can drivers do today? Hint: it's not just what you drive, it's how often and how far (eco-driving anyone?). How does air travel compare? How can city planners encourage compact living to reduce a community's carbon footprint? What else can consumers do?

In technology, what are the R&D prospects for biofuel alternatives like cellulosic ethanol, made from grass, wood chips, and other inedible plants? What about futuristic ideas like genetically engineered carbon-eating trees?

In policy, what lessons does the European Union's experience have for the U.S. about possible carbon cap-and-trade schemes? How are the world's countries doing at meeting their Kyoto Protocol targets, which expire in 2012, and how do they compare to the U.S.?

In economics, what can be done to make tough emission caps in the U.S. more cost-efficient? How can developing countries balance economic growth and better living conditions against rising greenhouse gases?

Internationally, what is being done to slow deforestation in the tropics, from Indonesia to the Amazon, which is estimated to cause almost one-fifth of human-induced global carbon emissions? What about population growth and the increasing number of environmental refugees forced to flee because of flooding, drought, or other problems? How will global health be affected by climate change?

How will climate negotiations affect the geopolitics of energy, and what does "energy security" really mean?

There are countless such questions for reporters to tackle on a story that is only going to get bigger and more complicated in the decades (yes, decades) ahead.

And there is some urgency. Despite increased coverage of climate change, it is still not at the top of the media or public priority list. "If you don't have climate change as a headline in the press," says Nisbet, who writes the blog Framing Science, "it's unlikely to be a top-tier issue in the public or among policy makers." A 2007 ranking by the Project for Excellence in Journalism found that among all media, environmental coverage ranked nineteenth, at 1.7 percent of the newshole—just behind sports and celebrity coverage.

There is some urgency. A Gallup report last year found that just one in four Americans believes there will be extreme effects from global warming in fifty years without immediate, drastic action.

A Gallup report last November found that only about four in ten Americans believes that immediate, drastic action is needed to deal with global warming, and just one in four says there will be "extreme" effects of global warming in fifty years if efforts are not increased. Is this a failure of the experts and politicians to communicate the situation or a failure of journalists to dig and report?

Yet journalists should not be cheerleaders. As climate change moves further into the policy and political arena, the traditional wall between analytical reporting and advocacy is in danger. The issue is coming to the fore at a time of major change in mainstream journalism and the growth of opinionated Web sites and blogs that have helped to blur the old lines.

Nisbet, for one, sees a dramatic shift in media rhetoric on climate change. In the spring of 2006, fear was at the heart of Al Gore's documentary film, *An Inconvenient Truth,* which jump-started media coverage of global warming after years on the back burner. Suddenly, climate change—that term is gaining ground over global warming, by the way—was on front pages and magazine covers, including *Time*'s iconic image of a lone polar bear and the warning, "Be Worried. Be Very Worried."

Today, says Nisbet, "the underlying appeal is a moral message: 'We're all in this together.' It's a moral call to arms." Gore's new $300-million "We" media campaign seeks to cross the partisan divide with the optimistic motto: "We Can Solve It." The cover of *Time*'s Spring 2008 environment issue, bordered in green instead of *Time*'s customary red, took the famous World War II photo of Marines raising a U.S. flag on Iwo Jima and substituted a tree to illustrate its bold headline: "How to Win the War on Global Warming."

Did *Time* cross the line into environmental cheerleading? It would seem so, perhaps reflecting the magazine's more general shift into opinion and away from pure news. Managing editor Richard Stengel called the cover story "our call to arms to make this challenge—perhaps the most important one facing the planet—a true national priority."

Others are feeling their way more carefully. "Sure, I care about the environment," says Steve Curwood, host of "Living on Earth," a weekly environmental show on more than three hundred public radio stations. "But it's not our job to decide what should be done. It's our job to inform the citizenry. Right now we have an alarmed citizenry, but still not a very well-informed one," he said at a recent journalism forum.

"We don't set policy, we tell stories," says David Ledford, executive editor of *The News Journal* in Wilmington, Delaware, and president of The Associated Press Managing Editors. "But it's important to not just throw out that the earth is on fire without giving a sense of what they can do."

"It's very simple. The job of a professional journalist is to give the audience information that is a good thing for them to know," says seasoned ABC News correspondent Bill Blakemore, who has led the network's new multiplatform approach to global warming. Yet he finds that the momentous nature of the climate-change story carries even more of a responsibility and psychological burden than the dozen wars he has covered. "The unprecedented nature of this story," says Blakemore, "is quite grave."

CRISTINE RUSSELL is a freelance science journalist, president of the Council for the Advancement of Science Writing and a senior fellow at Harvard's Belfer Center for Science and International Affairs. She is a former Shorenstein Center fellow and *Washington Post* reporter, and writes regularly for *The Observatory,* the science desk on CJR.org.

Reprinted from *Columbia Journalism Review,* July/August 2008, pp. 45–49. Copyright © 2008 by Columbia Journalism Review, Columbia University.

Article 18

Myth-Making in New Orleans

The impressive media coverage of Hurricane Katrina was marred by the widespread reporting—sometimes attributed to public officials—of murders and rapes that apparently never took place. What can news outlets learn from this episode to prevent similar problems in the future?

BRIAN THEVENOT

As I walked briskly through the dimly lit area inside the food service entrance of New Orleans' Ernest N. Morial Convention Center, the thought of pulling back the sheets covering the four stinking, decomposing corpses in front of me seemed wrong, even perverse. Before I'd even thought to ask, one of the two soldiers who escorted me, Arkansas National Guardsman Mikel Brooks, nixed the prospect of looking inside the freezer he and another soldier said contained "30 or 40" bodies.

"I ain't got the stomach for it, even after what I saw in Iraq," he said.

I didn't push it. Now I wish I had, as gruesome as that may seem. The soldiers might have branded me a morbid fiend and run me the hell out of there, but my story in the September 6 edition of the Times-Picayune would have been right, or at least included a line saying I'd been denied the opportunity to lay eyes on the freezer.

Instead, I quoted Brooks and another soldier, by name, about the freezer's allegedly grim inventory, including the statement that it contained a "7-year-old with her throat cut."

Neither the mass of bodies nor the allegedly expired child would ever be found. As I later reported, an internal review by Arkansas Guard Lt. Col. John Edwards found that Brooks and others who repeated the freezer story had heard it in the food line at Harrah's Casino, a law enforcement and military staging area a block away. Edwards told me no soldier had actually seen bodies in a freezer.

I retell this story not to deflect blame—factual errors under my byline are mine alone—but as an example of how one of hundreds of myths got reported in the early days of Hurricane Katrina's aftermath.

I retell this story not to deflect blame—factual errors under my byline are mine alone—but as an example of how one of hundreds of myths got reported in the early days of Hurricane Katrina's aftermath. I corrected the freezer report—along with a slew of other rumors and myths transmitted by the media—in a September 26 Times-Picayune story coauthored by my colleague Gordon Russell. In that piece, we sought to separate fact from fiction on the narrow issue of reported violence at the Louisiana Superdome and the Convention Center.

We hadn't anticipated the massive shockwave of self-correction that story would send through the international media. The examination of myths of violence—and their confirmation by New Orleans Mayor C. Ray Nagin and then-Police Superintendent Eddie Compass—became *the* story for days on end, a moment of mass-scale media introspection that ultimately resulted in a healthy revision of history's first draft.

The Los Angeles Times, the New York Times and the Washington Post followed up with similar, well-researched efforts debunking myths and coming to essentially the same conclusion we had: While anarchy indeed reigned in the city, and subhuman conditions in the Dome and the Convention Center shocked the nation's conscience, many if not most of the alarmist reports of violence were false, or at least could not be verified. Dozens of other newspapers and television outlets joined in, offering news and opinion pieces, many doggedly questioning what they and others had earlier reported.

Our myth-debunking story put me in the eye of the debate's swirling storm. National television outlets praised our work, quoted it frequently and sought me out for interviews as their latest instant expert. A few bloggers had the opposite reaction, hanging me in virtual effigy as a symbol of the failings of the dreaded "MSM"—the mainstream media, that evil monolith—and concocting conspiracy theories to explain the media's errant early reports. Questions of race and class pervaded the debate in all media: Did the reporting of violence stem from journalists' willingness to believe the worst about poor African Americans?

What role did the refugees themselves, along with local black public officials—both of whom served as sources for many of the false stories—play in creating the myths?

The New York Times tempered its assessment of false reports, writing "some, though not all, of the most alarming stories that coursed through the city appear to be little more than figments of frightened imaginations." But the Times' piece differed in scope from ours, assessing reports of crime citywide instead of only at the Dome and the Convention Center. The Times also reported on property crimes such as widespread looting—definitely not a myth, I can confirm as an eyewitness—as part of the paper's exhaustive review. We concentrated exclusively on violent crime.

Jim Dwyer, one of the lead reporters on the Times' story, says he came to Louisiana for two weeks specifically to ascertain the truth of early wild reports of crime. As we did at the Picayune, Dwyer says he had taken an interest when the tenor of some reports, many unattributed, relayed nightmarish scenes that seemed to defy common sense.

"I just thought that some of the reports were so garish, so untraceable and always seemed to stop short of having actual witnesses to the atrocities... like a galloping mythical nightmare had taken control," Dwyer told me.

The paper also dispatched stringers to shelters in Houston and Austin, Dwyer says, where they found no shortage of secondhand or thirdhand accounts of rape and murder—but none that seemed credible enough to discount Dwyer's original thesis. "Nobody could say they saw rapes and murders. It was always three or four steps removed, like 'my sister's uncle's cousin'" had seen the violence, he says.

Dwyer also reviewed his own paper's reporting, but found that, while the Times had reported unconfirmed accounts of treachery, as did many others, its reporters had generally couched them with the caveat that they couldn't be confirmed.

"I read all of it. We certainly reported stuff that Compass said, that Nagin said, but with pretty clear markers that it couldn't be verified," he says. "Also, the reports hadn't taken over our coverage in as powerful a way [as they did in some other media]. The atrocities didn't become the story. The paper kept its eye on the perilous conditions the people were in."

By the time the Times-Picayune's story ran—followed quickly by the L.A. Times' and the New York Times' pieces—nearly a month after the storm, there was no shortage of reports to second-guess. Many were attributed to refugees, cops and soldiers and even top public officials. Others appeared with weak attribution or none at all. Consider one example, this unattributed September 1 exchange on Fox News Channel between host John Gibson and correspondent David Lee Miller, live from New Orleans:

Gibson: "These are pictures of the cops arriving on the scene, armed and ready to take on the armed thugs.... Thugs shooting at rescue crews..."

Miller: "Hi, John, as you so rightly point out, there are so many murders taking place. There are rapes, other violent crimes taking place in New Orleans."

Kicking it up a notch and taking it worldwide, the normally staid Financial Times of London offered this September 5 description of the Convention Center, attributed to unnamed refugees: "Girls and boys were raped in the dark and had their throats cut and bodies were stuffed in the kitchens while looters and madmen exchanged fire with weapons they had looted."

The story went on to quote some flood victims by name: "Geraldine Lavy said her son protected four Australian tourists from rapists in the convention centre. 'Can you imagine? Four white women on their own?'" A man named Larry Martin told the Times that looters and gunmen "were shooting at buses, the rapes, the murders, the sodomy." The piece also reported, with no attribution, the apocryphal tale that "several hundred corpses are reported to have been gathered by locals in one school alone" in St. Bernard Parish, the badly flooded community just east of the city.

That one struck me as familiar: The Picayune's small team of reporters in New Orleans—most of the staff had been forced to evacuate to Baton Rouge after our headquarters nearly flooded—heard a similar report of up to 300 bodies piled at Marion Abramson High School in Eastern New Orleans. We dispatched two reporters to the school in a delivery truck, which got stuck while driving through high water. The reporters then canoed to the school, went inside—and found no bodies, and had nothing to write for their trouble.

Immediately after our story broke, we found ourselves making the rather jarring transition from reporter to source. The cable networks—CNN, MSNBC and Fox—needed to act immediately. It had taken me and Russell a full week to research our piece. So they sought members of our rag-tag "New Orleans bureau" for interviews.

The day the story ran, I went on CNN's "NewsNight with Aaron Brown." Our on-the-ground editor, David Meeks, had appeared on the cable channel along with reporter Michael Perlstein earlier that evening with Paula Zahn. The next morning, I went on MSNBC while being trailed by a French television reporter, and appeared again that afternoon on CNN Headline News.

We came away with differing assessments of how the television media had handled the revision. Meeks and Perlstein felt Zahn, in the live interview, had tried to pile the entirety of the blame at the foot of the New Orleans mayor and police chief, fully exonerating the media and street-level sources.

Zahn started the interview by asking Perlstein: "So, Michael, how is it that the mayor got all of this wrong?"

Perlstein didn't bite, explaining that the mayor—along with much of the media—had gotten somewhat understandably engulfed in the hysteria that spread like wildfire through a city with a devastated communications apparatus. "I think that the mayor was caught up in the same thing that a lot of people were caught up, reporters, officials and everyone else here included, and that there was a communications blackout," Perlstein said. "He was getting reports from pretty credible sources. But, by then, it had been passed along four or five different times, the story exaggerated each time along the way."

Zahn didn't appear interested in spreading the blame.

Zahn: "So, Michael in the end, what do you think is the most egregious exaggeration the mayor made?" she asked.

Perlstein responded that Nagin would have been wise to wait for a more official review of the violence at the Dome and the Convention Center.

Apparently still unsatisfied, Zahn served up another mayor-bashing opportunity to Meeks.

"Clearly, there was a great sensitivity to race in covering this story. But you had an African American mayor. You had the head of the police department being an African American. And, clearly, they had to be sensitive that what they were saying was going to have some tremendous impact. You're not suggesting, David, that they intentionally exaggerated this story?"

Neither Meeks nor anyone reasonable had suggested anything of the kind.

"I really don't think they did," Meeks told her. "I think they got caught up in hysteria."

After Meeks and Perlstein prepped me on the line of questioning, I went on CNN later that night with Aaron Brown. Standing under a tent in front of the Baton Rouge emergency management center, I stood nervously fidgeting with my earpiece, listening to Brown's introduction.

"We often remind you, when reporting breaking news stories, that the first reports are often wrong," Brown started. "With Katrina, it turns out that some of those reports, and not just the early ones, were really wrong. Some were fueled by people who were tired and hungry and clearly desperate. But some were fueled by the people in charge."

Knowing I had little time to make a point, I made sure to shift some focus away from the criticism of Nagin and Compass and turn the attention forward, toward correcting the record rather than finger-pointing.

"I have some sympathy for their initial reporting of supposed atrocities at the Dome and the Convention Center," I said of the city leaders. "Their communication apparatus had completely broken down . . . I also think that the media, in some sense, has to take responsibility for this and to come back to check, to verify some of these stories, basically just to finish the job, as I think we tried to do today."

Brown took the point and moved the conversation toward explaining how confusion created misinformation. "It sounds like there was almost a giant game of post office being played," he said. "One person believes to have seen one thing, tells someone else, and as it goes down the line, it keeps getting bigger and bigger and bigger. Before you know it, you have hundreds of deaths."

One guy saw six bodies. Then another guy saw six bodies. And another guy saw the same six and all of a sudden, it become 18.

I concurred. "There was a quote in the story today, I think a smart one, from deputy chief Warren Riley," I told Brown.

"He says, 'One guy saw six bodies. Then another guy saw six bodies. And another guy saw the same six and all of a sudden, it becomes 18.'"

The broadcasters had a point about public officials fueling the rumor mill, a point we had made, but not dwelled on, in our original story. In the most extreme case, Nagin told Oprah Winfrey that people in the Dome had sunk to an "almost animalistic state" after "five days watching dead bodies, watching hooligans killing people, raping people."

Then-Police Chief Eddie Compass—pushed into retirement by Nagin immediately after our story broke—spoke of "babies" being raped.

Still, Brown got past the public-official bashing and grasped the point of our story that many others missed: It hadn't been an "investigation," as some termed it, but rather an explanatory piece. We never intended to write "gotcha" journalism or declare ourselves the holier-than-thou hometown paper, preaching to the rest of the media and the public officials we all quoted. We just wanted to get the story right, and explain, to the extent possible, how it came to be wrong.

Dwyer expressed a similar goal. In his story, he didn't explicitly challenge any early reporting from the Times or any other outlet. Instead, he referred generally to widespread reports of violence and concentrated on the story itself: what really happened.

"My purpose wasn't to flay the New York Times or anybody else. This wasn't another Jayson Blair or Judith Miller situation, although it seems like sometimes these days your integrity is judged on how much you beat yourself like a pious Shiite," he says. "Whatever people reported from there in the early days, getting cold, hard facts was no easy task. They were doing the best they could, while trying to find electricity every 30 minutes just to be able to file, or in the Times-Picayune's case, struggling just to publish a paper on the Web."

Keith Woods, dean of faculty at the Poynter Institute, as well as a former Times-Picayune reporter, city editor and opinion writer and a New Orleans native, takes an even harder line on what he describes as a fashionable but destructive self-flagellation by media outlets—particularly television—that amounts to the media undercutting their already fragile credibility with the public. The press has had its legitimate reporter-writing-fiction scandals—Jayson Blair, Stephen Glass, Mike Barnicle—and in those instances, the media should indeed police themselves—brutally, Woods says. But early Katrina reporting, in which reporters often attributed tales and/or couched stories of violence with qualifiers, isn't even in the same ballpark, much less the same league, as making up stories out of thin air.

Some television outlets' willingness to put media-haters on air to bash the press only made the problem worse. "It was the typical self-abuse that follows media mistakes, and it became an equally unhelpful debate, an 'are not! are too!' debate over whether the media are biased or whatever," Woods says. "This sort of cannibalization is of great concern to me. If we just continue to stick our fingers in the wind, and then when we feel the hot breath of the public, we continue this self-abuse, then we'll just continue to hold up this unrealistic expectation that we're perfect . . . If we're walking around expecting that every time somebody goes off and does their job that it's done perfectly, then, first of all, we wouldn't have jobs in journalism, and second, public officials wouldn't need term limits."

Woods, who has been interviewed several times about Katrina reporting, found himself silently boiling with anger during one television panel discussion. He had agreed to go on PBS' "The NewsHour with Jim Lehrer" for a discussion of hurricane coverage, hoping for the fair, reasonable treatment for which Lehrer and PBS have been long respected. Instead, he found himself in the midst of a near food fight between NBC reporter Carl Quintanilla—in one corner, defending the media—and conservative radio talk show host Hugh Hewitt in the other corner, clubbing them.

"They'd go to the NBC reporter, who I thought made reasonable comments, to Hewitt, whose message was basically, 'Shoot the media,' then turn to me and say, 'Keith, what do you think?' " Woods says. "I was incensed."

Av Westin, a former vice president and executive producer for ABC News, says television reporters' and anchors' repeating of mythical violence, with sloppy attribution, marred otherwise remarkable journalism that aggressively reported the catastrophic damage of Katrina. He chalked it up to a lesson the television media should already have learned in the era of 24-hour news: Journalism requires thoughtful editing often absent in the competitive rush to air emotional breaking news.

"When I was at ABC, nothing got on the air without having the piece read in to us," he says. "Now, they're on the air 24-7 and they have to fill airtime, and that leads frequently to the reporting of rumor and speculation . . . Rather than saying, 'Let's wait five minutes,' they just go with it because it's in front of them. They keep learning that lesson and forgetting that lesson."

Then the mistakes feed off one another and multiply, Westin says. "There's something I call the 'out there syndrome'—it's okay for us to publish it because someone else already has, so it's 'out there,'" he says, rather than each media outlet confirming its own facts. "With 24-7 news, the deadline is always now, you go with whatever you've got, you stick it on the air."

Even as I became temporarily famous (for the standard 15 minutes) in the television news world, I was taken aback to find myself vilified by a few bloggers. In the blogosphere, I served as a target for a seemingly unquenchable disdain for the MSM.

Some branded me a hypocrite for writing about myth-making after I'd earlier reported one of the myths, the "30 or 40" bodies. But what's curious about much of the criticism is that reporters from the dreaded MSM often did a more thorough and sober job of correcting mainstream reports than did their sworn enemies in the blogosphere. Indeed, because most bloggers do little or no original reporting, they used my story about myths, along with those of the L.A. Times and New York Times, as the tools with which to beat us about the ears. They clubbed us with our own sticks.

Some blogs offered fair criticism, but others hyperventilated with unchecked rage that contributed little or nothing to the larger public good of finding out what had really happened. Some simply piled myth upon myth, developing media conspiracies out of what in the vast majority of cases were honest mistakes.

Article 18. Myth-Making in New Orleans

Lester Dent of ChronWatch, a San Francisco-based "media watchdog and conservative news site," went so far as to compare me to Jayson Blair. Dent asserted I "obviously" had never even been at the Convention Center and then demanded my head on a platter.

"Thevenot should be disciplined, up to and including being fired," Dent wrote.

I asked Dent about his allegation in an e-mail. He sent pages of further criticism in response, but somewhat reluctantly dropped the charge that I hadn't been at the scene, along with the Blair comparison.

"I will accept that you were on site making the report," he wrote in an e-mail response. "So no Jayson Blair moment."

As New Orleanians, playing a key role in correcting the international image of our own citizens gave us a deep satisfaction. Mostly poor, overwhelmingly African American, flood victims in the two shelters had been, in the most egregious cases, portrayed as beasts, raping and killing one another and even shooting at rescue workers trying to save them.

As journalists, reporting myths and later correcting them offers vital lessons on ramping up skepticism in initial reporting from chaotic environments—even if the sources are authoritative ones. We have three basic tools to use here, one during the reporting, the other during publishing, the third during any needed correction of initial reports.

The first is the persistent questioning of sources—about their sources: How do you know that? Did you see it? Who told you this? Are you 100 percent sure this happened? Who else can confirm it?

The second, wisely suggested in a column by former Washington Post Ombudsman Michael Getler, is careful and frequent qualification: "There is a journalistic device that is informative, accurate and protective, but that too often doesn't get used. It is a simple sentence that says: 'This account could not be independently verified.'"

The second time I wrote about the bodies in the freezer, as part of a narrative piece I penned for this magazine, I added just such a qualification (see "Apocalypse in New Orleans," October/November). At the time, a few days after I'd been to the Convention Center, I still had no higher-level confirmation of a body count—because no official count had been taken. So I added a sentence saying the presence and number of bodies at the center was "still unconfirmed amid a swirl of urban myths churned up by the storm."

The revision came as a result of a conversation with an editor in which I initially recommended cutting the mention of 40 bodies altogether unless I could confirm it independently before deadline. We compromised, adding the qualifier and strict attribution of the number to the guardsmen.

The third tool, which lately has been on display by many, though not all, media outlets, is an attitude that embraces the correcting of major news stories as news itself, not something to be buried in a corrections box.

"I think you treat it as a separate story, and it should have A1 prominence," says Hub Brown, an associate professor of broadcast journalism at the S.I. Newhouse School of Public Communications at Syracuse University. "Of course, print journalists are so much more meticulous at correcting their mistakes... Why not have a segment in the newscast that says, 'We've reported this through the past day, and it turned out to be wrong'?"

That sort of record correction would be a lot less painful—indeed, not painful at all—if journalists' initial dispatches contained detailed attribution, especially for high-temperature reports out of disaster zones. With stories like Katrina, in which rock-solid information in many cases proved so elusive, that should extend even to the point of publishing exactly how official sources came to know the information in question.

David Carr, a media columnist for the New York Times, was one of the first to question some of the early Katrina reporting in a September 19 column headlined: "More Horrible Than Truth: News Reports."

While Carr, in his column and in an interview, asserted that the media should shoulder their share of the blame, he was stunned at the degree to which public officials solidified the myths. "In New Orleans, that's what set this apart" from other examples of misinformation reported by the media, he says. "I was actually prepared a week before and had a column set to go, but then I realized the top police official and the top elected official were confirming these rumors. So how could I go after reporters on the ground receiving confirmation that this happened?"

Carr revised the column to address public officials' roles. Many have given Nagin and Compass a pass, saying they probably repeated exaggerations by mistake in a desperate attempt to get help for a truly desperate situation. Carr, however, suggests they were driven in part by political motives.

"Usually the first reaction of officials in crisis is to obfuscate and tamp down the rumors," he says. "Nagin and Compass stood there with a can of gasoline... In part what they were trying to do was explain that they had a mess on their hands—and that the feds had dropped the ball—by communicating an atmosphere of chaos that rendered their inability understandable."

In the worst of the storm reporting, tales of violence, rapes, murders and other mayhem were simply stated as fact with no attribution at all.

I am among those who committed this sin. In my previous AJR piece, although I attributed the account of bodies in the freezer and added that it could not be confirmed, I got loose with the attribution at another point in the story, describing the Convention Center as "a nightly scene of murders, rapes and regular stampedes."

What I later confirmed is that occasional gunfire, stampedes and terror did indeed plague the Convention Center. But only one death could be called a suspected homicide, a body with a gunshot wound, according to Kristen Meyer, spokeswoman for the state Department of Health and Hospitals. Meyer also confirmed that four bodies were retrieved from just inside the food service entrance, the same place I witnessed the four bodies lying under sheets. Widespread reports of rapes could not be confirmed.

Only one of those bodies has since been identified by name by her family, that of 79-year-old Clementine Eleby, who was not the gunshot victim, Meyer says.

While the media should learn lessons from Katrina, appropriate caution can't lead to paralysis. Backing off aggressive reporting of scenes where "official" information and sources, in some cases, literally don't exist isn't an option.

While the media should learn lessons from Katrina, appropriate caution can't lead to paralysis. Backing off aggressive reporting of scenes where "official" information and sources, in some cases, literally don't exist isn't an option. The many early Katrina stories marred by exaggerations or errors still stand out as a point of pride for the media. The quick reaction to the storm by reporters put accounts—most of them true and confirmed—of dire suffering in the faces of the public and authorities, prompting them to take action that saved lives.

As the debate about misreported Katrina violence rolled though blogs and more mainstream outlets, a conventional wisdom emerged: White middle-class reporters only believed and reported atrocities because they were predisposed to accept the worst about poor, black flood victims.

The race and class dynamics here are far more complicated. Many of the worst stories were attributed to poor, black flood victims themselves, along with African American public officials.

Brown, the Syracuse professor and an African American who teaches about diversity in the media, says that's no surprise. Black people are sometimes unconsciously biased against black people, too. "The fact that racism exists in the country doesn't mean everybody of one race feels one way, and everybody of another race feels the other," he says. "Sometimes victims of racism believe the worst about themselves. That's part of what makes it so harmful."

Poynter's Woods, an African American who has been writing and teaching about reporting on racial issues for years, doesn't buy the charge that the reports were driven largely by racial bias. It's not necessarily a gigantic leap in logic, he says, to believe that New Orleanians would murder one another in desperate times—they murder one another with regularity during normal times.

"I spent most of my life in the city of New Orleans, and when I left, it was the murder capital of the country," Woods says. "If you were to tell me a bunch of people murdered each other in the Dome and Convention Center, why wouldn't I believe it? ... Race played a role, but it's an indecipherable role. It's useless trying to spend a lot of time trying to figure it out because you have to climb into the psyche of the people who were there."

You also have to deal in hypothetical comparisons. What would the media have reported if the Dome had been packed with white people?

The reality of being white in New Orleans and most of America, of course, substantially increases the likelihood of being middle class, and thus substantially decreases the likelihood of being anywhere near a shelter of any kind during a disaster of Katrina proportions.

I'll offer another hypothetical comparison that takes class out of the issue and leaves only race: If Katrina had hit a poor, white trailer-park town in, say, the Florida Panhandle, and white refugees and white public officials had offered the media tales of rape and murder, would any of us have doubted their "eyewitness" or "official" accounts?

There's no simple answer. White trailer-park towns don't typically include a Dome that might end up packed with about 30,000 people, with no power, no working toilets and scant medical care.

While the role of race can't be definitively measured, I have little doubt that, consciously or unconsciously, some white reporters and probably a smaller number of black ones found it more plausible that babies had been raped and children knifed in a black crowd than they would in a theoretical white one.

But I don't think race was the overriding factor.

I'm more inclined to go with an expanded version of Aaron Brown's gossip-line theory: that stories that may have started with some basis in fact got exaggerated and distorted as they were passed orally—often the only mode of communication—through extraordinarily frustrated and stressed multitudes of people, including refugees, cops, soldiers, public officials and, ultimately, the press.

The confusion was created by a titanic clash of communications systems. Stone-age storytelling got amplified by space-age technology.

A person might have seen a man passed out from dehydration in the Superdome, for instance, and assumed he was dead, then assumed there must be more dead. In the retelling, it becomes, "There's bodies in the Dome." Retold a few more times by stressed and frightened people—all the way up to the mayor—and it became, "There's so many bodies in the Dome you can't count them."

Then the media arrived, with satellite phones and modems, BlackBerrys, television trucks with the ability to broadcast worldwide and the technology to post on the Internet in an instant—and most of them not realizing that normal rules of sourcing no longer ensured accuracy.

The gossip line then circled the globe, as officials, hurricane victims, and rescue and security personnel began to confirm nightmarish scenarios, sincerely believing what they were saying and wanting desperately to get the word out—and get help on the way.

I can assure you that Mikel Brooks and his fellow guardsman sincerely believed what they told me. They talked to me out of disgust at the horrors, real and imagined. They did not "lie," which implies intent. They were consumed with a more important job at the time than nailing down every report they heard and believed: giving food and water to the living to keep them from joining the dead. It was my job to make sure what they said was true.

Ultimately, I followed up and did that job, as did many others. What Woods finds curious about the media-bashing on the Katrina story is that critics don't credit the media for doing the research to prove their early reports wrong.

"Don't forget, the journalists kept reporting—the reason you know that things were reported badly is because the journalists told you."

BRIAN THEVENOT, a reporter at New Orleans' *Times-Picayune*, can be reached at brianthevenot@hotmail.com.

From *American Journalism Review*, December 2005/January 2006. Copyright © 2006 by the Philip Merrill College of Journalism at the University of Maryland, College Park, MD 20742-7111. Reprinted with permission.

Article 19

Double Whammy

It took an awfully long time for the national media to catch up to the racial turmoil in Jena, Louisiana. When they did, the results were not exactly a clinic in precision journalism.

RAQUEL CHRISTIE

To think of excellent reporting on racial issues, Gene Roberts must reach back 40 years, back to the Orangeburg massacre, when South Carolina State Police shot more than 20 students protesting segregation outside a bowling alley. Three students died. Surviving students insisted the police were the aggressors, but police swore they were attacked by the students.

Public opinion and the press sided with the officers—it was seen as an unfortunate side effect of upholding the law. And so the story went, until Jack Nelson decided there must be more to it than that. The Los Angeles Times reporter went to the local hospital and got a hold of the medical records.

Virtually all the students had been shot in the back, and some had bullets in the bottom of their feet. They weren't attacking the police—they were running away.

Such dogged, skeptical reporting, so common in the civil rights era, is what's missing from racial reportage today, says Roberts, Pulitzer Prize-winning author of "The Race Beat" and former executive editor of the Philadelphia Inquirer. It is an absence that has come back to haunt us in the case of the Jena 6.

The turmoil in Jena, Louisiana, began in late August 2006, when a black student asked at an assembly if he could sit under what some refer to as the "white tree" at Jena High School. The next day, nooses were strung from that tree—black and gold nooses, school colors. The students responsible for the nooses were disciplined but not expelled.

The atmosphere at the school grew tense. In November, the school's main building was severely damaged by a fire. Then a white kid beat up a black kid at a party and a white kid pulled a shotgun on black kids at a convenience store. Black on white, white on black, black on white, white on black, but the presses were largely silent.

Then, on December 4, 2006, white Jena High School student Justin Barker was beaten up by black students and knocked unconscious; three days later, six black students were charged with attempted second-degree murder. That day, 35 area religious leaders from black and white churches gathered to promote peace, and less than a week later 600 Jena residents filled the Guy Campbell Memorial Football Stadium for a prayer service.

And for five more months, the presses were silent.

Until last spring, until a May 20 article appeared in the Chicago Tribune, not a single story, not one column or comment, was published in the national media about the racial incidents in Jena. In a search for Jena on LexisNexis, "Jena Malone" pops up plenty, as does a "Jena" band of Choctaw Indians, but the town is entirely absent until mid-2007.

The Washington Post's first story on the situation ran on August 4, 2007. The New York Times and the Los Angeles Times published their initial pieces on September 15, 2007—a day after defendant Mychal Bell's second-degree battery conviction was overturned because, the court said, he was improperly tried as an adult.

U.S. News & World Report weighed in on September 20. Newsweek first mentioned Jena on June 4, but only as a blip in its "Perspectives: Quotes in the News" section. (The magazine didn't publish a story on Jena until August 20.) Time magazine first mentioned Jena in a September 27 story on Barack Obama.

Television missed out, too. CNN first addressed Jena on "Paula Zahn Now" on June 25, 2007. CBS News waited until September 15 to do its first segment, a 567-word interview with some of the parents of the defendants and a school board member. ABC News waited until the same day, and reporter Ron Claiborne almost acknowledged the folly: "[M]ostly by word of mouth, by e-mail, and yes, by the Internet, the case of the Jena Six, six black high school students originally charged with attempted murder in the beating of a white teenager, has been bubbling, or more like boiling for months, provoking accusations of racism and unequal justice."

Yet the story was out there. From September 7, 2006, to October 12, 2007, the Associated Press distributed 74 stories about the Jena nooses, 52 on state wires, 38 on national wires, 22 on North American wires and five on southern regional wires. In the same time period, "Jena High School" appeared in AP stories 77 times. Three AP stories covered the high school arson. Mychal Bell first appeared in an AP story on May 3, 2007—more than

Jena Timeline

2006

Late August/early September—A black student asks at an assembly if he can sit under a tree known as a gathering spot for white students in the high school courtyard. Two or three nooses are then found hanging from the tree.

The principal recommends expulsion for three white students, but the LaSalle Parish School District instead imposes a series of suspensions and detentions. Several black parents and students attend a meeting at a local church to discuss the noose incident. The local daily newspaper reports on the meeting, and area television stations follow up. Law enforcement officers are posted at the school after reports of tensions.

September 7—The Associated Press runs its first Jena report.

November 30—The main building of Jena High School is badly damaged by a fire determined to be arson and is later demolished. In December 2007, the sheriff-elect says the fire was unrelated to the turmoil at the school; instead, it was set to destroy records of bad grades. Eight people, black and white, are charged with arson.

December 1–2—Several fights occur that police say are racial in nature.

December 4—On the first day back after the fire, black students beat up a white male student who is knocked unconscious and treated in the emergency room. Six are later charged with conspiracy to commit second-degree murder and attempted second-degree murder. Five are expelled from school. The attack victim also is later expelled for having a firearm in his truck on school grounds.

December 7—About 35 religious leaders from black and white area churches meet. Prayer services are held at Jena schools a few days later.

December 13—Approximately 600 Jena residents fill the football stadium for a unity and prayer service.

2007

March 8 and May 2—Rallies for the Jena 6 are held at the LaSalle Parish Courthouse in Jena and draw a few dozen people each, including representatives of the national ACLU and state NAACP.

May 20—The Chicago Tribune runs its first article on Jena.

June 25–28—Mychal Bell, 17, is the first of the Jena 6 to go to trial, in adult court because of the nature of the charges. He is convicted of reduced charges of aggravated second-degree battery and conspiracy to commit that crime. Eventually charges against the remaining five also will be reduced to battery. CNN first reports the story on June 25.

Mid-July—The tree in the school courtyard is cut down.

July 31—About 300 people from around the country rally for the Jena 6 at the courthouse.

August 4—The Washington Post publishes its first Jena story.

August 5—Rev. Al Sharpton visits Jena. Martin Luther King III joins him there on August 14.

Late August to mid-September—Bell retains new attorneys, working pro bono, who seek to move his case to juvenile court and to free Bell on bond. The judge denies bond, citing Bell's prior criminal record involving battery and criminal damage, and sends the conspiracy case to juvenile court. He upholds the battery conviction. Rev. Jesse Jackson visits Jena and calls for a major rally for September 20, the sentencing date for Bell's battery conviction. An appellate court overrules the judge, vacating the battery conviction and sending that case to juvenile court.

September 15—The New York Times, Los Angeles Times, ABC and CBS run their first reports on Jena.

September 20—An estimated 20,000 people from around the nation hold peaceful rallies and marches in Jena.

December—Bell pleads guilty to second-degree battery in juvenile court and agrees to testify in upcoming Jena 6 cases. He is sentenced to 18 months, to be reduced by time already served, in state juvenile custody. He is also serving a separate, partially concurrent 18-month sentence for three earlier crimes.

2008

A white-power group has sued the town of Jena to march against the Jena 6, the civil rights movement and Martin Luther King Jr. Day. The rally had been planned for January 21, when Jena residents hold a march to honor King.

The parents of the December 4 attack victim have filed a civil lawsuit seeking unspecified damages from the school board, the Jena 6 parents, the defendants who are legal adults and a seventh student who was not charged.

---

two weeks before the mainstream media bothered to mention the person who became the most recognized member of the Jena 6.

All this awful bait, but the national media didn't bite. The story, instead, was the property of black bloggers and radio hosts, two local papers and activists. Only after they had interpreted it, only after they had dissected it, only after they had decided the right and the wrong of it—and dedicated a movement, the Afrospear, to it—only after big names like Al Sharpton and Jesse Jackson stepped into the fray last summer did the news media give it to us.

And when the media got it, they often took it as it was told to them. They let the citizens do much of the journalism, instead of piecing it together for themselves. They took Jena as a handout, not as an opportunity. They ignored the shades of gray, and kept what could have been the most complex, most challenging racial story, the one that would drive thousands to march and thousands to question the media and thousands to question the American justice system, black and white.

Why? What happened to the race beat?

"Race is still an issue in society, but it's difficult for newspapers to get handles on it," says Roberts, who now teaches journalism at the University of Maryland. "These usually aren't the kinds of events that lead to sort of inverted-pyramid, hard news kinds of stories. They're more ooze-and-seep racial stories. And it requires a lot of time and attention to do them with the nuance they deserve. And a lot of papers, in an era of cutbacks and short staffs, are shortchanging the race story."

Last summer, Jena became a major national story, inspiring a thousands-strong march, protests, calls for equal justice and a flooding of the national media.

But not before Alan Bean got to it.

Bean is not a journalist. He's the cofounder and executive director of Friends of Justice, a grassroots organization designed "to create media scandals around questionable prosecutions as they unfold," according to its Web site (friendsofjustice.wordpress.com/). In January 2007, Bean began receiving phone calls from a few parents in the small Louisiana town, complaining of racial injustice in the case of six young black men.

Bean researched. He read the local papers. He visited Jena and met the defendants and their parents. He developed a sense of mission. "It became clear that if business as usually practiced was going to play out . . . then these kids were going to be dragging felony convictions for the rest of their lives," Bean says. "That would probably mean they'd never go to college, never have a professional job, never have a chance at the American Dream. The Jena defendants had a lot of support, but [there was also] a lot of fear, and a lot of people felt they didn't want to speak up."

After more than a month, Bean spoke up for them. He wrote a six-page, "media-friendly" report titled "RESPONDING TO THE CRISIS IN JENA, LOUISIANA." Here is some of what it says.

- "The competence and independence of investigators is seriously in doubt."
- "The behavior of school officials and school board members reflects a breathtaking insensitivity to the mixture of anger, intimidation and horror inspired by the hate crime of late August."
- "The ethical lapses and flawed professional judgment of LaSalle Parish District Attorney Reed Walters call for strong remedial action."

Bean concedes he connected many events: the noose hangings, the December assault on Barker, the fight between black and white students. He also says he set out clear characters in his story. Walters, who charged the boys with attempted murder, and the school officials, who Bean says did not give the white students harsh enough punishments, are cast as the villains. The six defendants are described as "good kids."

"I made it very clear that I tried to present this as a human drama," Bean says.

In April 2007, he sent his report directly to those he thought would cover Jena the way he wanted it covered: Howard Witt of the Chicago Tribune, Tom Mangold of the BBC and Jordan Flaherty of Left Turn Magazine. Shortly after, Witt broke the story in the national media on May 20; Mangold broadcast "This World: 'Stealth racism' stalks deep South" four days later.

Flaherty's first Jena piece, on May 9 (leftturn.org/?q=node/649), begins with a quote from Alan Bean: "'The highest crime in the Old Testament,' he declared, 'is to withhold due process from poor people. To manipulate the criminal justice system to the advantage of the powerful, against the poor and the powerless.'" It continues with emotional quotes from the Jena defendants' parents: "When asked how her life has changed, [Bryant] Purvis' mother described the sadness of having her son taken away from her without warning. 'You wake up in the morning and your son is there. You lay down at night and he's there. Then all of a sudden he's gone. That's a lot to deal with.'"

"Racial demons rear heads," reads the headline over Witt's story, and the story begins: "The trouble in Jena started with the nooses. Then it rumbled along the town's jagged racial fault lines. Finally, it exploded into months of violence between blacks and whites."

"Now the 3,000 residents of this small lumber and oil town deep in the heart of central Louisiana are confronting Old South racial demons many thought had long ago been put to rest."

From "Stealth racism" by Tom Mangold: "The bad old days of the 'Mississippi Burning' 60s, civil liberties and race riots, lynchings, the KKK and police with billy clubs beating up blacks might have ended."

"But in the year that the first serious black candidate for the White House, Barack Obama, is helping unite the races in the north, the developments in the tiny town of Jena are disturbing." It goes on to recount many examples of a so-called "stealth" racism in Jena: a barber who won't cut black people's hair but insists he's not racist; the fact that Caseptla Bailey, mother of Jena defendant Robert Bailey, can't get a job as a bank teller. And it echoes Martin Luther King Jr. in calling Sunday mornings "perhaps one of the most segregated times in all of America," noting that a church in a white Jena neighborhood only has one black member.

Soon, the blogs were afire with cries for justice in Jena—and for media respect. "I make a final plea to the American media," wrote black blogger Shawn Williams on the day of Blogging for Justice, created by dozens of black bloggers who latched on to the Jena movement. "I'd ask that you raise your right hand and admit under oath that you just don't give a damn about black people. Your non-coverage of missing black women and children, your demonization of hip hop culture, your initial labeling of Katrina survivors as 'refugees' and your daily lynching of black athletes called sports talk radio is evidence of this fact. The Jena Six deserve justice." (dallassouthblog.com/2007/08/30/jena-six-deserve-justice/)

Wrote D. Yobachi Boswell on The Black Perspective: "The Afrosphere Jena 6 Coalition 'ask that the mainstream traditional media step forward and discharge their duty to provide coverage of this vitally important event to their viewers and readers and act as "the fourth institution" of governmental "checks and balance" that constitutional framers intended the press to be.'" (blackperspective.net/index.php/day-of-blogging-for-justice-jena-6/)

Says Wayne Bennett, who wrote about the lack of national media coverage on his blog The Field Negro: "I don't think it was a sexy story. Stuff like that happens all the time, especially in Southern towns. That's not something the mainstream media would chase. . . . They got on the story because Jesse Jackson and Al Sharpton got involved, then the big march, then it became sexier." (field-negro.blogspot.com/)

"I think it goes back to the difference of how the general media feels about an issue and how African Americans might feel," says Williams, author of Dallas South Blog. "It's because the media is made up of non-African Americans in general, and because of that they cover the stories from their personal point of view and that point of view is not shared by everyone. That's why I've really enjoyed what's happened lately with the blooming of bloggers. People can use their own spin to report what happens and how they feel about it."

After the bloggers were well into their crusade, in late summer, Jackson and Sharpton visited Jena. The Washington Post's first story came shortly after they announced their plans for demonstrations; others gradually trickled in. Coverage boomed the week of the September marches, held steady in some papers in October and decreased markedly in November.

Many bloggers credit themselves with bringing the events in Jena into the national spotlight.

Bennett wrote on September 20, the day of the marches: "For those of us black activists who use the web as a tool for change, we have been e-mailing each other, blogging about Jena, calling each other, and organizing on the web for months about this travesty of justice down in Bayou country. Now, finally, the rest of America has caught on. This is now national news, and the Jena 6 has springboarded into our national conscience. It also reinforces my belief that the Internet and the world wide web can also be used as a tremendous tool for activism and organizing for social change."

With so much percolating in the blogosphere, why did it take so long for the national media to jump on the Jena story?

"I certainly didn't become aware of it during much of that time," says Washington Post Executive Editor Leonard Downie Jr. "Apparently there was a growing communication about it on the Web and on radio, but it didn't reach our attention until later. Then when it did reach our attention . . . it took a while to nail it down." Says Darryl Fears, who covered Jena for the Post, "I found out about it the same way marchers did, through e-mail blasts. I didn't read any of the blogs, but there were these e-mails about a story of injustice in Jena. . . . Then my editor said, 'Hey, have you heard about this thing in Jena? Maybe we should go down there.'"

The Chicago Tribune's Witt says he "didn't know anything about [Jena] until April," when he got an e-mail from Alan Bean.

Keith Woods, dean of faculty at the Poynter Institute, says that the problem wasn't that journalists didn't know about Jena, but that they failed to see the deep implications of the case in terms of race relations and the black community, which has doubted the fairness of the criminal justice system for years. At last, a flesh-and-blood example, and nobody caught it.

"What's at work here, I believe, is a journalistic news judgment process that remains invisible even within news organizations, but certainly invisible to the public, that somebody is deciding the guilt or innocence of these young men or the level of their guilt or innocence or the level of justice they deserve before they tell the first story—and that dictates whether they send a reporter to answer the first questions or not," Woods says.

Catherine J. Mathis, senior vice president of corporate communications for the New York Times Co., said Times editors declined to be interviewed for this article. James O'Shea, who was ousted in January as editor of the Los Angeles Times, did not return phone calls.

At a panel titled "News Coverage of Hate Crimes" at the University of Maryland in November, participants agreed the media's slow response to the developments in Jena can be attributed to the death of the race beat—and the death of sensitivity to small stories with deeper meanings.

"I wish we still had race beats in this country now, because we miss the continuity of coverage we used to have," Gene Roberts said. "The people I wrote about [in 'The Race Beat'] would have been right in the middle of it."

"I think that we do need a race beat," said University of Maryland journalism professor and former Washington Post journalist Alice Bonner during the discussion. "We get caught up in episode and event coverage because we fail to take them up routinely. We need to cover race because it's a live, active, dynamic part of society. If we covered it routinely we wouldn't have to be so frenzied when something like this happens."

A race beat won't solve anything, Bonner said, if hiring patterns don't change. "The biggest problem with journalism," Bonner continued, "is journalism is still too white. . . . It's too white for a society that is increasingly brown. . . . It is too white for its own good."

But diversifying hiring won't help, the panelists said, if cultural sensitivity isn't instilled in reporters and news gatekeepers. "I don't want us to think racial hiring is the answer. Having two, five, 10 people of color is not even going to make a dent," Bonner said. "The way you stay there is you conform. And conformity is staying with the status quo."

At the Post, Fears is the only reporter specifically assigned to cover race, Executive Editor Downie says. But he says other beats, such as politics, regularly touch on racial issues, like immigration.

And the Post is trying to diversify. "Our staff is around 25 percent journalists of color, and we do have targets for our hiring, and diversity is a very important priority for us," he says. "But diversity is large territory. . . . You have gay readers, readers of different backgrounds. We're trying to match the diversity of the [Metro] area, which we're a long way away from, like most newsrooms, because this area is more diverse all the time."

Has any of this hindered the Post's Jena coverage?

"For our readership," Downie says, "our coverage [of Jena] has been relatively thorough."

On August 24, 2007, a LaSalle Parish judge made one of the heaviest decisions in the Jena 6 case: Mychal Bell would not be granted bail. The 17-year-old would stay behind bars until the end of his then-undetermined sentence—until, we know now, September 27, for more than nine months, longer than any other member of the Jena 6.

Only two local reporters showed up to witness the proceedings. One of them was Abbey Brown, 26, of Alexandria, Louisiana's Town Talk newspaper. And at the hearing, she learned more than Bell's fate: She learned he had a prior criminal record.

Her story the following day said that record included four previous violent crimes, including two Bell committed "while on probation for a Christmas Day battery in 2005, according to testimony." He was adjudicated—the juvenile equivalent of conviction—for three of the crimes, the story says. It goes on to explain why Judge J.P. Mauffray Jr. decided to hold Bell without bail; the reasons included Bell's criminal record.

But no major papers reported this fact, Brown says—not that day, not that week, not for months, not, in some cases, ever. "A reporter for the Jena Times and I were the only two people at that hearing," Brown says. "I know that we thought it was important to go to every single hearing that we heard about, but even after we reported it, it wasn't something the other media were picking up."

The two local papers that have covered the case vigorously from the beginning insist mainstream news organizations are misrepresenting pertinent facts and unjustly skewing a story about justice.

The Town Talk, a 32,000-circulation daily that routinely covers Jena as well as a number of other small towns, published its first story on the Jena 6 case on September 6, 2006, a short piece about the hanging of the nooses at Jena High School.

As of last November 15, the paper, based 37 miles from Jena, had published more than 140 additional stories on the episode, all easily accessible from its homepage (thetowntalk.com). A click on a sizable black, yellow and white box with JENA SIX takes you to the paper's Jena Web page, with links not just to all its coverage of the case but also to 21 photo albums, downloads of videos and court filings, a Jena map, a Jena timeline, a message board and a list of frequently asked questions about Jena and its coverage.

Paul Carty, the Town Talk's executive editor, has his own list of gripes, gripes that have positioned him as the enemy of those who insist coverage of the Jena saga has been just and groundbreaking:

- The national media routinely refer to the jury that prosecuted Mychal Bell as "all white" without explaining why it was so. Carty says that explanation is simple—as well as enlightening. A Town Talk story on June 27 said that, according to court officials, the court summoned 150 people for the jury pool, but only 50 showed up, and those 50 were white. According to the story, Bell's attorney, Blane Williams, said some of the 100 who didn't show up were black—which is important to consider in such a racially charged case, Carty says. "I think there's an obligation there that if you say there's an all-white jury, that should raise some concerns as a writer, because talking about an all-white jury in the Deep South in a case that has to do with race, that's fairly inflammatory writing, unless you provide context."

- The labeling of the tree a black student asked to sit under, and the nooses were subsequently strung from, as the "white tree" is "unfair and unsupported." "We've never referred to it as the 'white tree' because it's not an official name for the tree, and it's kind of like one side says white kids just sat under, others say black and white sat under it . . . so we've left it alone," Brown says. "I'm kind of a purist as far as sourcing things, and people have shown me pictures of white students sitting under the tree, of white and black students sitting under the tree. . . . We've kind of left it as [the] tree where nooses were hung."

- Jena has been unfairly portrayed by the media as a racist town. "One thing that just about knocked me out of my chair was when a TV reporter did a live shot in September, the day of the demonstration, and he asks a member of the community, 'How long has Jena been a racist town?' That's not to say that Jena doesn't have some racial problems, but Jena has the same kind of racial problems that every other community in this country has," Carty says. He declines to name the reporter or the news outlet.

- Feeding this portrayal is the fact that reporters are not talking to sources on all sides of the story. They either talk to the Jena 6, their parents or civil rights activists, Carty says. What about the residents of Jena? The judges? Justin Barker?

- Poor descriptions of Barker's condition. Brown reported on June 11 that Barker's initial medical bills totaled $5,467 and that students described the fight in statements with phrases like "stomped him badly," "stepped on his face," "knocked out cold on the ground," and "slammed his head on the concrete beam." "I've seen pictures that were taken of him and I've got to tell you this, this was no normal schoolyard brawl, this was a kid with blood coming out of his ears," Carty says. "Where it gets reported that he was treated at a local hospital and released, that's true, but I can tell you right now that he's sitting at home with internal injuries."

Carty is not the only one who believes Jena coverage has been inadequate. Similar charges have been brought by Craig Franklin, assistant editor of the Jena Times, a small weekly that has covered the town since 1905 and the Jena 6 case since the nooses appeared. In an October 24 column in the Christian Science Monitor titled "Media Myths About the Jena 6," Franklin, the paper's sole reporter on the case and a 20-year Jena resident, lists 12 of the fundamental things the national media got wrong about the Jena 6. Some echo Carty's critique.

Franklin says the plethora of errors has led Jena residents to stop speaking to national reporters. And if the media continue to get it wrong, such boycotts will become commonplace, he says.

"What I'm fearful of is the more that these types of cases are exposed in the public's view"—such as the Duke lacrosse case (see "Justice Delayed," August/September)—"and the national media does not do its job and report its facts and not just go with the person who cries the loudest or gives the best headline, I think we're going to lose our purpose. Right here in Jena, Louisiana, you can walk down the street and pick out any person and ask them, 'Do you trust the national media?' And they'll say, 'No.'"

An independent assessment of the critics' main arguments shows many of them to be largely true.

An analysis of all news stories and briefs about Jena in four major newspapers—the Washington Post, the New York Times, the Los Angeles Times and the Chicago Tribune—from the beginning of their coverage until November 15, found the following. Out of 57 stories:

- Only eight stories allude to Mychal Bell's prior criminal record, and only three—two October stories in the Chicago Tribune and one short, late-September story in the New York Times—mention the specifics. The Washington Post's first major story on Jena incorrectly says "Bell had no prior criminal record." On October 17, it mentions that Bell "was recently re-incarcerated on a probation violation" but gives no hint that his record included violent acts.
- Ten stories use the phrase "all white" to describe the jury that found Mychal Bell guilty of aggravated second-degree battery and conspiracy to commit aggravated second-degree battery. None explains why the jury was all white, though the Town Talk laid it out in June. Only the New York Times does not use the description.
- Multiple stories describe the tree the nooses were found on as a "white tree," either directly calling it a "white tree" or using a more rounded term: "tree that was a traditional gathering place for whites" or tree "on the side of the campus that, by long-standing tradition, had always been claimed by white students." No stories question if the description is correct, and none asks students about the tree. Only the L.A. Times does not describe the tree as "white."
- Descriptions of white student Justin Barker's medical condition vary from paper to paper and from story to story. The first Post story to discuss Barker's injuries says he had "two hours of treatment for a concussion and an eye that was swollen shut." The concussion is never mentioned again, and subsequent Post stories simply say he was knocked unconscious and released from the hospital. The first New York Times story to mention Barker's injuries says he was "treated at a local hospital and released." The next says he was knocked unconscious and kicked. The last just says he was "knocked unconscious." The L.A. Times' first story says Barker was "kicked in the head and knocked unconscious" and "taken to the hospital and treated for injuries to the ears, face and eye." The next mention simply says he was "beaten and knocked briefly unconscious." The Chicago Tribune's first story mentioning Barker's condition says he "spent only a few hours at the hospital." The next story says he was knocked unconscious and did not require hospitalization.
- The Washington Post, the L.A. Times and the Chicago Tribune never, in months of coverage, mention Barker's medical bills. The New York Times mentions them in only two stories, the first on September 22, more than three months after the Town Talk reported them in June.
- The phrase "schoolyard brawl" or "schoolyard fight" is used multiple times to describe the December 4 beating. Many times, it is the only description.
- All four papers link the events in Jena multiple times, without ever explaining why they're linked. The Washington Post calls them a "chain of events." The New York Times says the nooses "set off a series of events."
- Thirty stories quote civil rights activists, organizations or advocates. Eight stories quote Jesse Jackson; twelve quote Al Sharpton; others quote the ACLU, the Southern Poverty Law Center and the NAACP. Six quote Alan Bean of Friends of Justice—five of them in the Chicago Tribune. Many times these are the only people quoted.
- District Attorney Reed Walters is quoted in only five stories. Many of the quotes are paraphrased. The New York Times is a notable exception here—it printed a column by Walters on September 26. Only six stories quote the parents of the Jena 6.
- A point not raised by other critics: The L.A. Times, the Washington Post, the New York Times and the Chicago Tribune repeatedly say the white students accused of hanging the nooses were "suspended for three days" or "were suspended from school" or "received brief suspensions." None addresses additional facts, like these, reported in an October 8 correction by the Atlanta-Journal Constitution: "The students [who hung the nooses] were disciplined with nine days of alternative school, two weeks of in-school suspension, Saturday detentions, attendance in discipline court, evaluation before returning to school and participation in a state intervention program for families."

Part of the problem with the coverage, says Kansas City Star columnist Jason Whitlock, is that the national media relied too heavily on Jena According to Alan Bean. In a piece titled "How One Man Fired Up Jena 6 Case," Whitlock wrote that the media blindly accepted Bean's story—to the detriment of the truth. Why? Because it was easy, he says.

"If you're part of the mainstream media, I think that you see the story as something that should win you a lot of acclaim," Whitlock says. "The media is so lost right now. In the '60s, we were very important . . . and we don't know how to be important anymore. So if we can hop on some explosive case and appear like we're championing the right cause and protecting the defenseless or whatever, we will."

"He called attention to Jena with his agenda as a point of entry," Carty, the Town Talk editor, says of Bean. "He was spoon-feeding to the media what the story was all about. His perspective on the story is a partisan perspective; he thinks an injustice has been done, and that's his starting point, and it's picked up in the mainstream."

Jena Times Assistant Editor Franklin wrote in a column: "First, because local officials did not speak publicly early on about the true events of the past year, the media simply formed their stories based on one side's statements—the Jena 6. Second, the media were downright lazy in their efforts to find the truth. Often, they simply reported what they'd read on blogs, which expressed only one side of the issue."

Bean knew the media would bite. They did in 1999, when he told them about incidents in his hometown of Tulia, Texas. He exposed a corrupt cop and helped overturn more than a dozen drug convictions against minorities. Tulia was quickly labeled a racist town.

"I knew that it was probably the kind of case the media could be talked into covering because it had so many spectacular features: The fire—something that was terribly significant that nobody was picking up—the nooses and the racial tension. I thought that if the story was framed properly and people could see the connective tissue they could see how one thing led to another," Bean says.

While he is critical of the coverage, Whitlock doesn't cast Bean as the villain. "I'm not saying it's Bean's fault—that's unfair to him. If there's any bad guys in the Jena 6 story it's the media. We blew this."

The Chicago Tribune's Witt defends his coverage of Jena and says Bean was a reliable source. The reporter says he found factual problems with one story promoted by Bean, "and there's certain aspects of it that he was certainly trying to push one way or another, but, for me, that's no different from what other sources do. And the job of journalists is to listen, to try to find the good story in there, but not to be led by the nose with a particular spin. But by and large . . . he was a credible source."

As for his own work on Jena, says Witt, "I don't see where I've been inaccurate in anything I've described."

He acknowledges that he did not mention Barker's medical bills but stands by his description of Barker's condition: "I don't know what his medical bills are; I've seen some claims from his family that he had medical bills. But he was knocked unconscious, and he was in hospital I believe for three or four hours. That's all true."

He says his description of the punishment for the students who hung the nooses as a "three-day suspension" is incomplete, but says it is the fault of the school superintendent, who did not explain the depth of the students' punishment. The superintendent "did not reveal any of the other details about this other type of discipline," Witt says. "I know that subsequently when people started focusing on the story he gave a press conference in which he did detail the other dimensions of that discipline . . . but if he had chosen to tell me about the rest of discipline, I would have reported that, too."

What about the all white jury? Readers don't need an explanation of why it was all white, Witt says. "I guess that's a salient detail, but I'm not sure in the scheme of things it makes that much of a difference."

Shortly after his interview, Witt sent AJR an e-mail, with "a couple of additional points." Part of it: "It's also inaccurate to intimate that I was somehow partisan in my reporting of this story. I have accurately reported all sides of this ongoing saga. You should note, for example, that last month I wrote a highly critical story about questions surrounding the fundraising for the Jena 6 families and how those funds were being accounted for. . . . I can assure you that story won me no fans among the Jena 6 families and their supporters, who believe that by writing that story I damaged their cause, even as it elated many right-wing bloggers and commentators. [Bill] O'Reilly invited me onto his Fox News show to talk about it. As a journalist, my role is not to support any particular cause but to report all the significant developments in the story without fear or favor."

In late October, Witt's Tribune, along with several other major news organizations, sued to force the courts to give the media access to all legal proceedings involving Mychal Bell, "whose prosecution had been shrouded in secrecy on orders of the trial judge," he wrote. The media won.

Post reporter Fears defends his reportage on grounds similar to Witt's. Why didn't he clarify the punishment for the students who hung the nooses? Because the suspension is the only part that matters, he says. "We weren't going to get into any long litany of things these students had to undergo. We wanted to look at one, the three-day suspension being out of school, versus what the parents [of other students] wanted, which was their expulsion."

Why didn't he correct his statement that Bell had no prior criminal record? "There was no correction because . . . I made several attempts to verify it. One, I flew to Jena and looked at Bell's court jacket, and it wasn't in there. And the prosecutor [Reed Walters] was not talking to the press. He didn't talk to press before the march. . . . That rests squarely on his shoulders.

"It's interesting to me that these explanations were out after Jena came squarely in public eye, after these marches. They could have come very early on but they didn't. . . . Someone needs to ask, 'Why is that happening just now? Why didn't you explain that before?'"

New information is coming out now. There are conflicting reports. Why doesn't Fears report on it? Why hasn't he investigated what really happened with the Jena 6?

"For a national newspaper, you don't generally go back and try and follow all of that out," he says. "I do think the Jena story was a very interesting story, but to go back and investigate in Jena based on this flashpoint incident. . . . It just didn't rise to that type of story. It wasn't Hurricane Katrina. It wasn't so many things. It just wasn't the biggest story that a newspaper like the Washington Post or even the New York Times or the Boston Globe would do."

Carty admits the story was easier for the Town Talk because of its proximity to Jena and its familiarity with the town. But it was far from a breeze. At times, the small paper had a dozen reporters—a good part of its staff—working on the story, limiting its ability to cover other things.

And at times, people were very unsatisfied with its coverage. Lead Jena reporter Abbey Brown has received threatening phone calls and e-mails. But Brown stayed on the story—if anything, because the efforts of the national media left her disenchanted. "I guess it just kind of disappointed me a little. I'm a young journalist, and I've always been sort of an idealist," Brown says.

"I know our goal as journalists is to be fair, and I've seen some things that I kind of thought weren't so fair," she continues. "I don't think it was malicious, but there was just not enough effort. I had to talk to more than 30 people to get five people to go on record, but if that's what it takes then that's what it takes. At least that's how we feel."

Sometimes, the facts came quite easily.

"We just walked into the courthouse and said, 'Can we see the court documents?'" Brown says. "I've got countless calls from people saying, 'Who's a good person to talk to for this and that' and I've directed each of them to go into the courthouse and ask for the documents. . . . There's a wealth of information for both sides; if one side isn't talking it doesn't mean that's the end of it."

Gene Roberts recalls the sit-in movement of the 1960s and the Montgomery bus boycott. Like Jena, they were initially brushed off, and early reporting was hearsay, Roberts says. But they ended up being turning points of the civil rights movement.

"As journalists, you have to get up and use shoe leather and talk to people and do the story in all its roundness. Constantly people of authority, no matter what race they are, will give you the established line of what's going on, and you have to dig beneath that. . . . It's just not one side said this, one side said that. . . . You have to dig beneath and see what's right. The truth doesn't always lie between them."

At a "Covering Immigration and Race" discussion at the Poynter Institute, dean of faculty Keith Woods wanted to focus on Jena. So he spoke to the Town Talk's Carty and Williams from Dallas South Blog. What he found was a serious disconnect—two very different perceptions of the Jena story.

"The most profound realization coming out of those two conversations was how utterly differently two people could see the same story," Woods says. "To essentially paint it as the participants did, in the case of Paul [Carty], a story about overblown and incorrect media coverage, as much as it was about Jena, and to Shawn [Williams], it was a story about injustice."

Which is it about? The media should tell us, he says.

"First, I do think that the national media—and this is a phenomenon of the national media, not specific to Jena—tends to come in and sweep broadly in its reporting. And I would say it's subject to cast things inaccurately by not delving down deeply enough into individual details of the story," Woods says. "We wind up with bickering over whether there were three nooses in the tree or two, whether white people alone sat under the tree or whether there was a period when black and white people sat under the tree, and that's because national media doesn't climb down and check on those facts itself. It tends to rely on previous reporting. In this conversation, those inaccuracies have become the implicit argument against national coverage or a more just treatment of the young men in the story, and I think both of those are illogical conclusions.

"But here is the thing: If we are a nation of paranoid people, we need to know that. And so if it is pure paranoia that's driving the busloads of people that drive down to Jena, some of us need to report that, and if we believe it's paranoia, our belief needs to be taken to the journalistic test of reporting, and not simply dismissed, while we go off and cover O.J. And if it's not paranoia, who but journalists to help us understand it and see the injustice? Either argument deserves national attention before [the first story appeared] May 20."

RAQUEL CHRISTIE (raquelchristie@gmail.com) wrote about coverage of onetime professional football player Pat Tillman's death in Afghanistan in *AJR*'s October/November issue.

Article 20

Wonderful Weeklies

Far away from the high-pressure, profit-margin-obsessed world of corporate journalism, four Mississippi weeklies provide their readers with first-rate local coverage. Despite their tiny staffs, they manage to find time for investigative reporting. And their hard-hitting editorials often have significant impact on public policy.

JULIA CASS

Ray Mosby runs the Deer Creek Pilot from his mother-in-law's former house in tiny Rolling Fork, Mississippi. In what had been the bedroom, Mosby writes take-no-prisoners editorials, in one directing a strongly worded lesson on the First Amendment to a crooked judge who said that the Pilot better not write about him again. It was titled "And what if we do, Judge?"

Waid Prather gets involved in a way an urban editor never would. When a storm downs trees and power lines, he doesn't leave after taking a photograph and gathering information for the Carthaginian in Carthage, Mississippi. He pulls out his chain saw and helps clear the road.

Jim Abbott lost friends and was publicly embarrassed at the Rotary Club when powerful white leaders objected to the Enterprise-Tocsin's balanced coverage of a racial controversy and boycott in Indianola.

Stanley Dearman and James Prince III, successive owners of the Neshoba Democrat in Philadelphia, where three civil rights workers were murdered in 1964, similarly braved anger and rejection from people they go to church with for their leadership in acknowledging the wrong and calling for justice.

I visited these newspapers last summer after a conversation with a University of Mississippi journalism professor about four Mississippi weeklies he and other experts on the state's media consider exceptionally good. I thought that these small, individually owned community papers might be a refreshing antidote to all the discouraging news about journalism—plagiarism and fabrication, uncaring chain ownership, bottom-line mentality, staff cutbacks, bland product, falling circulation. And, indeed, these weekly newspapers in rural Mississippi reveal that good, enterprising journalism still goes on in the hinterlands even in the poorest state in the nation.

Mississippi has a relatively large number of weekly newspapers. The Mississippi Press Association membership includes 86 of them compared with 24 dailies, and 56 of them are individually owned, according to Carolyn Wilson, the association's executive director. The Deer Creek Pilot, Carthaginian, Enterprise-Tocsin and Neshoba Democrat, all owned and run by native Mississippians, maintain independent voices solidly rooted in a particular place.

Despite their newspapers' small size—ranging from two employees and a circulation of 1,500 at the Deer Creek Pilot to 12 employees and a circulation of 7,800 at the Neshoba Democrat—these owner-editors regularly hold their local officials' feet to the fire; publish investigative stories, even series; write hard-hitting editorials; demand public records; shape public policy and provide leadership during the wrenching transitions that have followed the civil rights movement.

They have more in common with the crusty old small-town newspaper publishers of days gone by, who wrote what they had to say and stuck their necks out when necessary, than with the contemporary corporate model of reflecting the community rather than leading it.

Unlike many urban newspapers, rural weeklies in Mississippi are not losing circulation—primarily because they are the only source of local news in their counties. Web sites and blogs don't cover events or personalities in, say, Panther Burn or Kosciusko, and the statewide media, such as the Clarion-Ledger in Jackson and a few television stations, come to rural communities only for the big stories.

As Ray Mosby puts it, "We are the only media outlet in the world that gives a damn about Sharkey and Issaquena counties."

My first stop, Rolling Fork (population 2,486), the seat of Sharkey County, was heralded by two agricultural implement companies, a building supply business, a gas station and convenience store, a tire and auto repair shop, and a few small motels and cafés. The downtown contains a courthouse ringed by retail businesses, about a quarter of them unoccupied.

Ray Mosby, 54, greeted me in what had been the living room of his mother-in-law's former house two blocks from the courthouse square. (She has Alzheimer's disease and lives with Mosby and his wife in the house next door.) From his strong voice on the

> My trip began in the Delta, the tabletop-flat, cotton-producing, former slave-holding area of Mississippi that stretches from Memphis to Vicksburg on the western side of the state. Two of the newspapers, the Deer Creek Pilot in Rolling Fork and the Enterprise-Tocsin in Indianola, are located in this region, which has a predominately black population and is the poorest part of the state. From there, I drove southeast to Carthage and Philadelphia. These two towns, in a timber-producing area that has attracted some light industry, are more prosperous and are gaining rather than losing population.

telephone, I'd expected a large man, but he's a featherweight—six feet tall and a mere 130 pounds—with graying hair and a short beard. He wore trousers and a shirt and tie and held a pipe in his hand.

The Deer Creek Pilot is the newspaper of record for both Sharkey and Issaquena counties, which have a combined population of fewer than 9,000. That morning, Mosby was about to go to the courthouse for the bimonthly meeting of the Sharkey County Board of Supervisors. Natalie Perkins, his sole employee, had already left to go to the supervisors' meeting in Issaquena County.

The two divide all the work of putting out the paper. Mosby is publisher/editor/reporter/editorial writer/columnist/photographer and ad salesman. Perkins reports and takes photographs, does the layout and handles circulation and billing. They both deliver the Pilot to the racks, boxes and post office on Thursdays, when the paper comes out.

"I'm afraid this is gonna to be as excitin' as watchin' paint dry," Mosby warned me as we entered the meeting room in the courthouse. Sitting around a table in the small room, the supervisors—three black men and two white men—listened to announcements (seven trappers cut from beaver control), opened sealed bids for gravel and divided up the delinquent garbage bills for collection. The real news came in an announcement by the tax assessor that the state's valuation of the county's property had dropped by 10 percent, meaning that county taxes will have to go up next year if expenditures remain the same.

Before the meeting ended, one supervisor said he'd been talking with a guy about buying a truck for road-building that the county could sell back after a year for more money than it cost—and finance it without paying interest that year. Mosby thought that sounded fishy; he leaned over to me and whispered, "Between me and the lawyer, that *ain't gonna happen*."

Later, Mosby said he doesn't often intrude in government decision-making outside of his articles and editorials. "But sometimes it's useful. If I see a public body fixin' to walk down a road where I can see a land mine, I think I should tell them, 'You don't want to go there,' instead of sayin' nothing and when it blows up, report it. I'd rather prevent a problem than write about it."

Mosby learned this approach from his mentor, the late Joe Ellis, the former owner of the daily Press Register in Clarksdale, further north in the Delta. He did a lot face-to-face with people, saying: "This is *not* going to happen here." Mosby grew up on a farm near Clarksdale. When he started work at the Press Register, he had just graduated from the University of Mississippi, where he majored in English.

The Pilot has won 42 first place awards in the Mississippi Press Association's annual competition since 1993, when Mosby bought the newspaper. (The paper competes with 35 other weeklies with circulations of less than 2,500.) Many prizes were for investigative stories or projects.

The most ambitious was the four-part series on a multimillion-dollar flood control project called the Yazoo Backwater Pump Project. For the 2003 series, Mosby and Perkins studied documents, reports, elevation maps and land records. Their research discredited claims by proponents, including Mississippi Republican Sens. Trent Lott and Thad Cochran, that homes in the area were being routinely flooded, and demonstrated that the primary benefit of the project would be to allow large landowners to increase agricultural production on marginal land.

> "We just started reporting what was going on," Mosby says—a popular and well-connected tax assessor who was double-dipping and charging the county more than he should have, for example, and elected officials steering business to friends instead of using sealed bids. County and city government then were run by a group of white men—"good-old-boy network," Mosby calls them—and his reporting caused "much gnashing of teeth."

The series was a huge undertaking for a small paper like the Pilot. Mosby decided to commit the time, he says, because "when it got to the point where Congress was appropriating money on a premise I knew was untrue for something in my backyard, I felt I had an obligation to look into it." He knew, he says, that people weren't being flooded, because "if they were, we would be called to take pictures, and there would be people coming to the newspaper to donate money to help them. The whole thing smelled fishy." The pump project, however, is alive and well. "My gun is too small," Mosby says.

Mosby is even better known for his editorials; his 1999 piece on the judge won the press association's special award for best editorial in the state that year. My favorite is "Do you feel lucky?" directed at the Issaquena County Board of Supervisors' 2003 plan to buy a bankrupt cotton gin in which one supervisor had an ownership interest.

Metaphorical guns blazing, Mosby called the plan a "purely pernicious act of public policy which from more than one angle looks to be as crooked as a one-eyed, spastic snow snake." If the supervisors, he wrote, "conspire, meet illegally or otherwise grease the wheels of bureaucracy" to buy the gin "in spite of the ethical fungus so obviously growing on it . . . somebody is going to the penitentiary, or somebody is going to pay back lots of money, or both. . . . So what's it gonna be? Are you feeling lucky?" The supervisors didn't buy the gin.

Mosby is pleased with the many awards he's won but says that stories he wrote when he first came to Rolling Fork didn't take much effort, because years had gone by with no one covering City Hall and the Sharkey and Issaquena county governments.

"We just started reporting what was going on," Mosby says—a popular and well-connected tax assessor who was double-dipping and charging the county more than he should have, for example, and elected officials steering business to friends instead of using sealed bids. County and city government then were run by a group of white men—"a good-old-boy network," Mosby calls them—and his reporting caused "much gnashing of teeth."

Occasionally, readers have cancelled subscriptions and businesses have pulled advertisements when angered by something Mosby has written, although generally they return after a while. The other editors reported the same phenomenon. Mosby said he considers the potential financial impact when he knows he is about to do something that will be controversial. "At the same time, I absolutely believe you cannot do this running scared. I have agonized over the choice between the financial and the editorial, but I can't remember coming down on any side but the editorial."

By now, judging from interviews with officials and residents, Mosby seems to have become a valued community member. Lynne Moses, a lifelong resident of Sharkey County involved in many civic affairs, says that when Mosby began reporting on government meetings and wrongdoing, people "thought he made that stuff up" because such revelations hadn't been reported before. She thinks the Pilot has "made people more aware. It hasn't made our politicians any smarter but I think more cautious."

Mosby agrees that county government now is cleaner. "I don't care if you're a bad newspaper. The fact that you're a newspaper and cover a board meeting and write what happens has a Lysol effect. It's gonna kill some germs whether you're sprayin' real good or not."

The county's newspaper, the Enterprise-Tocsin, supported the council's goals and printed the addresses and phone numbers of the parents of young "outside agitators"—students who came to Sunflower County during "Freedom Summer" of 1964.

Jim Abbott is of the same generation as those "agitators." That summer, after his sophomore year at the University of Mississippi, he was in Greenwood, his hometown 27 miles from Indianola, helping his civil engineer father prepare a county map. At the courthouse, he saw some of the students bringing black people in to register to vote. When Abbott graduated, he joined the Army Reserves and served in Vietnam. There, he says, a three-week stint on night guard duty with a black soldier from a Chicago ghetto altered his racial consciousness. "He told me about sleeping in one bed with his nine siblings and how they arranged themselves so as not to cut off the circulation of the younger ones. It was so sad. One night he said something that seared into me: 'You'll go back to Mississippi, get a good job, join the country club, have a good life. Not me. I'm just going back to the ghetto.'"

When he returned to Mississippi, he went back to the University of Mississippi for a second undergraduate degree, this one in journalism. In 1970, at age 26, he got his first job—editor of the Enterprise-Tocsin, which had been purchased by a group of Indianola businessmen.

In describing the Enterprise-Tocsin as one of the state's exceptional weeklies, Ralph Braseth, assistant journalism

> Forty miles north and east of Rolling Fork, Indianola, the seat of Sunflower County, lies in the heart of the Delta and was a fountainhead of Southern opposition to integration and black empowerment. The White Citizens Council was formed here in 1954, the beginning of a movement of "massive resistance" to school desegregation that spread throughout the South. Sunflower County is also where Fannie Lou Hamer sharecropped until she was kicked off the land for trying to register to vote and where Emmett Till was brought to be killed after whistling at a white female store clerk in a neighboring county.

professor and director of student media at the University of Mississippi, said that Abbott "has to walk a lot of tightropes" as the white owner of a newspaper in a majority black county (70 percent) with a repressive racial history. "I don't know how he does it, but he has developed credibility with both races," says Braseth, who has visited the newsrooms of almost every newspaper in the state.

"I guess I've been pushing the envelope from day one," says Abbott, who is now 61, with a full head of thick gray hair. We spoke in the newspaper's office in a storefront building in downtown Indianola (population 12,066). On one wall are the plaques for the Mississippi Press Association public service awards the Enterprise-Tocsin won in 2002 for a series on conditions at the local jail and in 2003 for stories about illegal video slot machines that were gouging the poor. The sheriff either was overlooking the machines—or worse.

I'd been greeted at the door by Abbott's wife, Cynthia, who runs the office. "Oh, and I vacuumed this morning and swept up outside," she told me. Another woman helps with the ads and handles circulation (about 6,000) and billing. The paper's news reporter, David Rushing, is an Indianola native who has worked for the paper off and on for 33 years. A stringer does feature stories for the second section.

I arrived at the Enterprise-Tocsin on a Thursday, the day the paper came out, and Abbott and Rushing had time to talk. "Don't come on a Tuesday or Wednesday," Abbott warned. All the papers I visited have a similar weekly rhythm. Although news is unpredictable, Mondays are the meetings days for county and city government. Tuesday is usually a writing day and the day the feature section is prepared. Wednesday is the deadline—the final production day before the paginated pages are uploaded to the various daily newspapers that print them. On Thursday, delivery day, and Friday, the editors and writers work on longer enterprise or investigative pieces, in addition to routine newsgathering and photography. Taking photos of awards ceremonies and other festivities produces goodwill that is an important counterbalance to the unpopular stands these weeklies sometimes take.

Interestingly, the first racial controversy Abbott created involved a photograph. Three weeks after he started work at the Enterprise-Tocsin, he took a photo of the cheerleaders at the all-white private school, created when school desegregation became inevitable, and ran it on the front page. The next week, he ran a similar photograph of the cheerleaders at the virtually all-black public high school. "They were so thrilled about being in the paper, they'd rehearsed 10 poses," he says. The day the paper came out, he went to a steak supper for auxiliary lawmen at the invitation of a family friend and member of his church. Behind the building he was surrounded by a group of men who told him, " 'We don't want niggers on our front page, do you understand?' More men came up and said, 'Yeah!' I was exactly 12 months back from Vietnam and I wasn't that scared." On the way home, he told his host what had happened. "He said, 'Stick to your guns. Don't let them run you off.' " They didn't. Ten years later, in 1980, Abbott and John Emmerich, the owner of the daily Greenwood Commonwealth, bought the Enterprise-Tocsin, each with a 50 percent interest.

The racial battle lines have changed over the years, and Abbott has kept up with them. In 1984, he and his wife and three other couples sponsored a landmark Indianola social event: a biracial garden party in honor of native son B.B. King.

In 1986 came what Abbott called "the most painful story we ever covered."

In 1986 came what Abbott called "the most painful story we ever covered." After we toured the county's racial history monuments—the site of a firebombed "freedom school"; the small, brown, wood home, now for sale, where the Citizens Council held its first meeting; the old barn where Emmett Till is said to have been beaten to death—Abbott and Rushing talked about the two-month period in 1986 when black supporters of a black candidate for school superintendent organized a boycott of the town's businesses. They were protesting the majority white school board's appointment of a white superintendent to serve as head of a school district with 93 percent black enrollment.

"It was the last gasp of the old guard," Abbott says. In his view, the wealthy planters who'd dominated the school board wanted a superintendent they could control even in a virtually all-black system because the district includes land surrounding the city, and the school system has the power to tax it. "Then, too, they were accustomed to control and didn't want to give it up."

The boycott of businesses was very effective, and "nerves were frayed to the nth degree," Abbott says. He and Rushing wanted to write fairly and give both sides their due. They attended meetings of the Concerned Citizens group that led the boycott and quoted the statements of its leadership. Abbott wrote editorials urging communication and a biracial resolution to the crisis rather than "fighting '60s battles again."

Reporting both sides may sound routine, but historically the Enterprise-Tocsin and many other Southern newspapers did not present the experiences and points of view of the Fannie Lou Hamers or of the students, ministers and others who came south during the 1960s.

"I was bumping heads with folks I've known all my life and loved," says Rushing. "People who were close to my grandparents told me, 'They'd be ashamed of you if they were alive.' " Abbott says he lost friends and a few advertisers, got angry phone calls in the middle of the night and was publicly embarrassed by a speaker at the Rotary Club.

As I listened to Rushing and Abbott describe the personal fall-out from their coverage, it struck me that the editor-publishers of these small-town weeklies face ethical decisions at least as difficult and perhaps more emotionally wrenching than those faced by editors at big-city dailies. Probably the major difference between editing a weekly in a small-town compared with a daily in a city is intimacy. You know or know someone who knows or is related to the people you write about, including those in the police blotter. And if the same person is the ad salesman and the editor, there is no institutional wall between the business and editorial sides. When the publisher and editor are one and the same, the "publisher" belongs to the Chamber of Commerce and Rotary Club whose actions the "editor" may need to criticize.

Juggling hats and balancing involvement with objectivity take decisiveness, ethical surefootedness and a thick skin. Like Mosby, Abbott says he'd be "less than honest" if he didn't admit to worrying about retribution for some of the paper's stories. "But because we're dedicated to accept the challenge of controversy and publish a newspaper that's trusted by all in our community, we won't hold back due to economic threats or petty things like getting the cold shoulder from people." Anyway, he adds, "I think most people here are proud of their newspaper and understand that we strive to promote the well-being of Sunflower County."

He takes great satisfaction in the way the school controversy turned out. Without bloodshed, the school board bought out the contract of the new white superintendent and appointed the black candidate, Robert Merritt, who turned out to be an excellent superintendent, Abbott says.

In a 1996 article in the Western Journal of Black Studies, three journalism professors, who'd conducted interviews and analyzed the Enterprise-Tocsin's coverage of the crisis, praised Abbott for his courage in aggressively covering the conflict and not yielding to pressure. They credited him with helping lead public opinion toward a positive resolution. "The case deserves to be studied by all newspapers as a shining example of racial tolerance and sensitivity that can be given impetus by our country's community press," the article said.

Today, more African Americans hold public office in Sunflower County, and the Enterprise-Tocsin has just as aggressively held them accountable in cases of wrongdoing as they have done with white officials. An ongoing story over the past two years involves the first black woman elected to a countywide public office—as tax assessor/collector—who embezzled more than $100,000. "Some people in the black community told us we were writing too much about her, said that since she was the first, it made them look bad," Abbott says. "But the main thing is, people trust the newspaper."

Inside a paneled meeting room, law enforcement people and representatives of the county's volunteer fire departments and ambulance services coordinated plans for their activities should Dennis' overland path cross their county in east-central Mississippi. Prather took notes and photographs. He knew everyone there—and not only because this is a small community. Prather, 52, a friendly, energetic man who sports a handlebar mustache, has made it his business to try to get to every fire, accident scene and other emergency to take pictures and write a story—and help out if need be.

> Sunday afternoon, just as Hurricane Dennis was making landfall in July on the Mississippi Gulf Coast, Waid Prather, editor and associate publisher of the Carthaginian, headed to a meeting at the Leake County emergency management office across the courthouse square from the newspaper in downtown Carthage (population 4,600). Already rain was coming down and the wind was beginning to pick up. Prather wore a rain jacket over his shirt and jeans and L.L. Bean boots.

In the course of his journalistic work, Prather helped search for a missing child in the Pearl River swamp and went to so many fires one summer during a bad drought that the firemen got together and gave him a fire retardant suit. On an accident scene one night, he says, he learned that a MultiTool (a collapsible pair of pliers with screwdrivers, knife and saw blades, files, wire cutters and other tools folded inside the handles) is a good journalistic tool.

"The guys were in tight quarters trying to pull a local woman's body out of her mangled car. The windshield wipers were going and music playing on the radio and I could tell it was bothering them. I popped out the MultiTool, which I bought to use in my yard, reached under the hood and cut the battery cable." On another occasion, he used the tool to crimp the gas line of a wrecked car that was fueling a fire on the median strip.

That Sunday when I left, Prather had his scanner on and his camera and chain saw in his truck, expecting downed trees and power lines. Not much happened; Dennis took a more easterly path across Alabama. (Hurricane Katrina, though, struck Mississippi six weeks later, and Prather put his camera and chain saw to good use. Trees were down on virtually every road in the county and no one had power for several days. The Carthaginian used a generator to power a few computers and managed to get copy to the printer in Hattiesburg, which then also lost power and had to send the pages to another printer in a town with electricity. The paper came out on Thursday, as usual, though it was "bad late," Prather says. The office of the Neshoba Democrat, in neighboring Philadelphia, did not lose power; Prince, the owner, opened its doors and phone lines to two other area papers so they could publish that week.)

I wrote that we should make sure [the guardsmen] knew they would be missed. The community responded far beyond anything I could imagine"—with a prayer service, a huge ceremony, speeches and people lining the roads all the way to the county line, carrying signs saying, "We love you," as the buses passed by.

The next morning of my visit, Prather was at his desk early, planning the week's edition. Prather, whose father was a milkman in Jackson, got hooked on journalism at Hinds Junior College in Raymond, Mississippi. He went on to become a reporter and then editor of a number of Mississippi newspapers, most of them weeklies. A short stint as publisher of a chain-owned Texas newspaper made him eager to return to Mississippi and to individual ownership.

The Carthaginian (circulation 5,300) is owned by John Keith, 41, the third generation of the Keith family to own the paper going back to 1907. He handles the business side of the paper and happily delegates editorial matters to Prather, backing him against all critics. When he came into Prather's office to say good morning, Prather told the story of a man who came into the newspaper threatening to whip Prather's behind for writing about him. "John told him, 'If you're gonna whip somebody's tail here, you'll have to start with mine.'"

"This guy felt he was above everybody else," Keith says. According to the owners of the papers I visited, some people insist that because their families are important, the paper should not print anything negative about them, particularly arrests of their children. All said they make no exceptions, but Keith has the best response. "I tell 'em my daddy put my brother, his own son, on the front page when he broke into a drug store."

Keith hired Prather 11 years ago when Mildred Dearman, the managing editor, broke her hip. A wisp of a woman, Dearman, 82, now comes into the paper three days a week to write editorials and handle community news. While smoking a cigarette on the loading dock at the back of the building, she described doing every job on the newspaper—ladies' club news, taking photographs, ad sales and layout, news reporting—since she started in 1960. "She has a job here as long as she wants it," Keith says. The Carthaginian has three employees, including Dearman and Prather, on the editorial side, two in advertising, one-and-a-half in production and a bookkeeper.

According to Prather, his mentor, W. C. "Dub" Shoemaker, former owner of the Star-Herald in Kosciusko, liked to say, "When you run a newspaper, you own the community. I don't care who the sheriff or board of supervisors are. It's yours to take care of. You defend it, you criticize it, you do what needs to be done."

Prather uses the personal pronoun in speaking of Leake County and its institutions. Describing the upcoming week's paper, he says, "I've got a big story this week about my hospital. It got out from under a huge million-dollar liability. The hospital might make it yet, and I need a hospital if I expect my county to grow." Asked about city and county government, he says, "I worry about my county board of supervisors not so much for larceny as for being concerned with the roads in their own districts and to heck with the rest of the county. In the city, I worry more about the aldermen getting caught up in personal and petty politics than dipping into the till."

He sometimes uses his weekly column to criticize officials—and occasionally the citizenry—for what he considers their wrongheadedness, shortsightedness or small-mindedness. Other times he uses it to praise people or institutions for actions benefiting the community.

Prather's strongest recent campaign has been on behalf of Company A of the Mississippi Army National Guard, which is based in Carthage. When it was called up in 2004 to go to Iraq, he says, "I saw it as an opportunity for our community to do something together. These were our guys. I wrote that we should make sure they knew they would be missed. The community responded far beyond anything I could imagine"—with a prayer service, a huge ceremony, speeches and people lining the roads all the way to the county line, carrying signs saying, "We love you," as the buses passed by.

When the unit left for training in the Mojave Desert in California, Prather persuaded Keith to finance a trip to join it for five days. He wrote a series of stories on what the guardsmen experienced. Prather wanted to follow them to Iraq but says he couldn't spend that much money or time away from the paper. Now, he runs the Baghdad weather below the masthead each week. (Soldiers and Guard units in Iraq are big stories in the other weeklies as well; Mosby's editorial criticizing the white community in his counties for not attending a sendoff party for the mostly black Guard unit prodded a number into lining the road to wave goodbye when the guardsmen actually left.)

Unlike the Pilot and Enterprise-Tocsin, whose social news correspondents have died off and not been replaced, the Carthaginian still runs short columns sent in by a dozen correspondents Prather calls "country cousins," who are paid with a ham every Christmas. I read aloud an item in a column from the tiny community of Morris Hill relating that R.D. Rivers had gone to a hospital in Jackson to get a stent in his heart.

"I know," Prather says. "It's riveting. But it beats the stew out of who Madonna is sleeping with today. Nobody around here cares. But the guy with the stent in his heart, folks know him, and they're worried about his health. They'll read this and think, 'Oh, he got a stent. Maybe he'll be okay.'"

The dateline was Philadelphia, Mississippi, seat of Neshoba County, where James Earl Chaney, Andrew Goodman and Michael Schwerner were killed by Klansmen with the complicity of law enforcement and the support or silence of the citizenry. The story has been told many times by the national media and by Hollywood in the movie "Mississippi Burning," a fictionalized account of the infamous crime that put the mark of Cain on this town.

Less known is the story of the role of two owner-editors of the Neshoba Democrat—Stanley Dearman from 1966 to 2000 and James E. Prince III from 2000 on—in leading residents of the community to an acknowledgment of the wrong and a call for justice. Especially in small towns with a single local media organization, the publisher of the newspaper can be a powerful force, part of the unelected leadership that often includes the banker, school superintendent, owners of the largest industries and businesses, ministers of the leading churches and heads of the important families. In Dearman's view, a newspaper owner is the most independent of all.

Nobody in Philadelphia gave a damn what the New York Times had to say, but when the local newspaper started pushing for a grand jury, that had impact.

"I put the Neshoba Democrat in the heroic category," says Sid Salter, a longtime Mississippi newspaperman who writes a column for the Clarion Ledger. "Stan and Jim carried the torch to get the case reopened, which was not a popular stand. Nobody in Philadelphia gave a damn what the New York Times had to say, but when the local newspaper started pushing for a grand jury, that had impact."

> The New York Times' curtain-raiser for last summer's trial of an aged Klansman for the June 1964 murders of three civil rights workers began: "It is just a fork in a country road, with nothing to mark it but a retired newspaper editor named Stanley Dearman, standing there with a slight tremor in his stout frame, saying, 'This is where it happened.'"

Former owner Dearman, 73, lives in a pleasant, sunny house on the outskirts of Philadelphia (population 7,303), 25 miles east of Carthage. We sat and talked in a kitchen filled with jars of blueberry preserves his wife had just made. He says he has lost count of how many reporters from around the world he has led to that fork in the country road over the years. This was part of his effort to keep the story alive during the many years local residents did not talk about what happened.

A native of Meridian, an hour away, Dearman worked at the newspaper there after graduating from the University of Mississippi. He says that when he began running the Democrat in 1966, two years before he bought it, he didn't want to have anything to do with the civil rights case. "It happened before I got here, and I had other things to do." Still, the more he talked with people and asked questions and thought about it, "It sort of took possession of me in a way that's hard to explain."

In 1989, when the 25th anniversary was coming up, Dearman decided that the community should have a memorial service. The standard attitude in town was: Why bring all that up again? He wrote an editorial saying that the media would be in town regardless and the community could let outsiders define them, or they could define themselves. Dearman talked to then-Mississippi Secretary of State Dick Molpus, who contacted other state leaders, and Dearman initiated a coalition of local people who "wanted to show another face of this community, not the brutal, ugly face of 1964."

In an effort to learn more about the victims, Dearman interviewed Carolyn Goodman, Andrew's mother. "The only thing we knew about them was their names. I wanted to find out what they were like," he says. Dearman thought Goodman expressed herself so beautifully that he ran the entire interview in transcript form. The newspaper in 1964 had published no personal information about the three. They were "so-called civil rights workers" or "civil righters"—usually in quotation marks.

In 1989, the current owner, Prince, was working at a newspaper in Alabama when his Neshoba Democrat arrived in the mail. Prince, who was born in Philadelphia three months before the murders, had worked at the Democrat during high school and edited the school paper at Mississippi State University. The image he had of the three civil rights workers was that "they were agitators who had no business coming here," he said in an interview in his office at the newspaper, a former funeral parlor a few blocks from the courthouse square.

Dearman's interview with Goodman "put a face on them for me. I wasn't much older than Andy at the time I was reading the article. I was moved by the way his mother described him. He was athletic. He loved dramatic arts. He was a peaceful person who cared about people. That was a turning point for me, and I decided I had to be in Philadelphia for the memorial service." He left Alabama and worked at the Democrat over the summer.

The memorial service was "a profoundly changing experience for me," Prince says, especially when Molpus, the secretary of state, apologized to the family members. Dearman says he was disappointed at the local turnout; he'd hoped for a thousand but instead there were about 200. "But it got things moving. It got people thinking."

Over more than 30 years, Dearman covered everything from corruption on the county hospital board to each year's biggest tomato to the remarkable development of industries, casinos, hotels and golf courses by the Mississippi Band of Choctaw Indians. In the late 1990s, he began to think about selling the newspaper. He was contacted by a chain but would not even consider an offer.

"From what I've seen happen in other places, they try to squeeze out every cent they can and rotate publishers and editors in and out whose primary concern is their own upward mobility. They don't take a heart-and-soul interest in a town." Prince, who by then owned a newspaper in suburban Jackson, "was dedicated to the profession and the town," and Dearman sold him the paper in 2000.

For the 40th anniversary of the civil rights workers' deaths, in 2004, Prince got together with Leroy Clemens, the local NAACP chapter president who had worked with him at the Democrat. They formed another coalition to plan an event. This time, almost all of the town's leaders signed on. There was no organized opposition, Prince says, although there were people who grumbled and disapproved. Meetings were cathartic and led to a formal call for justice by the group. "We thought, 'How can we move on when we haven't dealt with the past?'" Clemens says. "A ceremony would be empty without a call for justice."

In January, a grand jury indicted Edgar Ray Killen, 80, a Klansman, for directing the killings. After a trial in the Neshoba County Courthouse in June, Killen was convicted of three counts of manslaughter and sentenced to 60 years in prison. Prince brought in extra help for the trial coverage. The paper ran day-by-day coverage of the trial on its Web site (neshobademocrat.com).

"The trial was televised, but I wanted our readers to know exactly what happened in the courtroom and what the evidence was," Prince says. "We had a former mayor who said on the stand that the Klan was a good thing. People needed to know that. They needed to read about it in our paper." He says he was surprised by the fear people, especially the elderly and potential jurors, felt as the trial began. He believes the conviction "is finally lifting the cloud of fear from our community."

Dearman says his stance on the murders cost him some readers and advertisers, but "I have felt so strongly about certain issues I didn't give a damn if I lost every subscription I had." The flip side of editors personally knowing the people in their stories is that the people in the community know the editors. Those who disagreed with Dearman knew him as an individual. He couldn't be stereotyped or dismissed as readily as the remote editor of the "liberal" New York Times or the editor of the "conservative" Washington Times.

Dearman's retirement party, held at the local library, was crowded with people who celebrated his service to the community.

"It was the whole town," Prince says. "All the leaders were there, plus people in work clothes who'd obviously come from the factories and lumber mill." Among those who came and spoke was Carolyn Goodman.

The weeklies I visited make most of their money from display and classified advertising, with the remainder coming from circulation and the legal advertising they receive as their counties' newspapers of record.

None of the publishers insists on a particular profit margin. The Carthaginian earns about a 15 percent profit, Keith says. Prince says the Neshoba Democrat's margin is "higher than the national average." The average for weekly newspapers is 17.09 percent, according to a 2004 survey conducted by the Inland Press Association.

In Indianola, which has lost population and businesses, Abbott is concerned about the financial impact of a Wal-Mart Superstore, with a grocery section, scheduled to open soon. "We've already seen the loss of a supermarket ad we've had for years. Of course, we now have cellular phone ads we didn't have before." The Enterprise-Tocsin profit margin exceeds the national average primarily, Abbott says, because he and his wife do much of the work.

Rolling Fork, which also has experienced decline, is far enough away from the larger towns of Greenville and Yazoo City to maintain a fair number of local businesses. At the same time, some stores in Greenville and Yazoo City advertise in the Pilot in hopes of persuading Sharkey and Issaquena county people to come shop there. Fred Miller, president of the Bank of Anguilla, says that the bank and some other local businesses advertise in the Pilot in part because "we think it's important for the community to have a local newspaper."

Mosby laughed when asked about his profit margin. "Knock on wood, we are able to make a few dollars, more each year over the previous one. I honestly don't know what the margin is. We don't have a resident bean counter. If I get the bills paid and have some money left over, I'm tickled." If the paper had more revenue, he went on, he could hire more people and produce a better product. He'd love to have another staffer to ride around and take photographs and to write features and cover sports.

We were sitting at the large table in his mother-in-law's former dining room. Mosby took a puff on his pipe and added, "Hell, we do the best we can with what we got. We're not tryin' to win a Pulitzer Prize. We're just tryin' to put out the best country newspaper we can. I think that's elevated enough."

JULIA CASS first came to know Mississippi when she served as the Southern bureau chief for the *Philadelphia Inquirer* from 1982 to 1985. Following her 19 years with the *Inquirer*, she was executive editor of the Buenos Aires *Herald* in Argentina and managing editor of the now-defunct Sunday magazine of the San Jose *Mercury News*. She is a freelance writer and journalism trainer.

From *American Journalism Review*, December 2005/January 2006. Copyright © 2005 by the Philip Merrill College of Journalism at the University of Maryland, College Park, MD 20742-7111. Reprinted with permission.

Article 21

Beyond News

Journalists worry about how the Web threatens the way they distribute their product. They are slower to see how it threatens the product itself.

MITCHELL STEPHENS

Call it the morning letdown. Your muffin may be fresh, but the newspaper beside it is decidedly stale. *Chavez bashes Bush on Un stage* reads the headline, to pick one morning's example, on the lead story of *The Miami Herald*. That was a Thursday in September. But Yahoo, AOL, and just about every major news Web site in the country had been displaying that story—President Hugo Chavez of Venezuela had called President Bush "the devil"—since around noon on Wednesday. The news had been all over the radio, all over cable, too: Fox News had carried, with gleeful indignation, twenty-three minutes of the speech live. Indeed, when Katie Couric introduced the Chavez story on the *CBS Evening News*, at 6:30 Wednesday, her audience may have experienced an evening letdown. By then—half a day before Chavez's name would appear in newsprint in Miami—his entry on Wikipedia, the online encyclopedia, had been updated to include an account of the speech in the United Nations.

Editors and news directors today fret about the Internet, as their predecessors worried about radio and TV, and all now see the huge threat the Web represents to the way they distribute their product. They have been slower to see the threat it represents to the product itself. In a day when information pours out of digital spigots, stories that package painstakingly gathered facts on current events—what happened, who said what, when—have lost much of their value. News now not only arrives astoundingly fast from an astounding number of directions, it arrives free of charge. Selling what is elsewhere available free is difficult, even if it isn't nineteen hours stale. Just ask an encyclopedia salesman, if you can find one.

Mainstream journalists can, of course, try to keep retailing somewhat stale morning-print or evening-television roundups to people who manage to get through the day without any contact with Matt Drudge, Wolf Blitzer, or Robert Siegel. They can continue to attempt to establish themselves online as a kind of après AP—selling news that's a little slower but a little smarter than what Yahoo displays, which is essentially what *The Washington Post* and *The New York Times* were up to when, about four or five hours after Chavez had left the UN podium, they published, online, their own accounts of his speech.

But another, more ambitious option is available to journalists: they could try to sell something besides news.

The notion that journalists might be in a business other than the collection, ordering, and distribution of facts isn't new. In the days when the latest news was available to more or less anyone who visited the market or chatted in the street, weekly newspapers (at the time, the only newspapers) provided mostly analysis or opinion—something extra. The growth of cities, the arrival of dailies, and the invention of swift fact-transmitting and fact-distributing machines (the telegraph and the steam press) encouraged the development of companies devoted to the mass production and sale of news. Their day lasted more than a hundred years. But the sun is setting.

Information is once again widely available to more or less everyone, and journalists, once again, are having difficulty selling news—at least to people under the age of fifty-five. If news organizations, large and small, remain in the business of routine newsgathering—even if they remain in the business of routine newsgathering for dissemination online—the dismal prophesy currently being proclaimed by their circulation and demographic charts may very well be fulfilled.

"If we don't do the basic reporting, who will?" journalists counter. Here's John S. Carroll, former editor of the *Los Angeles Times*, presenting, to the American Society of Newspaper Editors, this notion of mainstream journalists as the indispensable Prime Movers: "Newspapers dig up the news. Others repackage it." But the widely held belief that the Web is a parasite that lives off the metro desks and foreign bureaus of beleaguered yet civic-minded newspapers and broadcast news organizations is a bit facile.

For much of their breaking news, Yahoo and AOL often tap the same source as Drudge and *WashingtonPost.com:* The Associated Press, with Reuters, AFP, and a few others also playing a role. (Most of the early online Chavez reports linked to an AP story.) Nothing said here is meant to imply that the wire services, and whatever cousins of theirs may materialize on the Web, should stop gathering and wholesaling news in bulk.

However, the Web increasingly has other places to turn for raw materials: more and more cameras are being aimed at news events, and transcripts, reports, and budgets are regularly being placed on the Web, either by organizations themselves or by citizens trying to hold those organizations to account. We are still very early in the evolution of the form, but surely industrious bloggers won't always need reporters to package such materials before they commence picking them apart. Mainstream journalists are making a mistake if they believe their ability to collect and organize facts will continue to make them indispensable.

There will continue to be room, of course, for some kinds of traditional, thoroughly sourced reporting: exclusives, certainly. Investigations, certainly. That's something extra. Yahoo isn't in a position to muckrake.

But the extra value our quality news organizations can and must regularly add is analysis: thoughtful, incisive attempts to divine the significance of events—insights, not just information. What is required—if journalism is to move beyond selling cheap, widely available, staler-than-your-muffin news—is, to choose a not very journalistic-sounding word, wisdom.

Here's more historical precedent: In the days when dailies monopolized breaking news, slower journals—weeklies like *The Nation, The New Republic, Time*—stepped back from breaking news and sold smart analysis. Now it is the dailies, and even the evening news shows, that are slow. Now it is time for them to take that step back.

Insights into the significance of news events certainly do appear on one page or another in our dailies, in one segment or another on our evening newscasts; but a reader or viewer has no reason to believe that they will be there on any particular story on any particular day. It's hit or miss. And outside of the small patch of the paper that has been roped off for opinion, the chances of coming upon something that might qualify as wisdom are not great. Most reporters have spent too long pursuing and writing "just the facts" to move easily into drawing conclusions based on facts. Their editors have spent too long resisting the encroachment of anything that is not carefully sourced, that might be perceived as less than objective, to easily welcome such analyses now.

So you sometimes get, under a "news analysis" slug or not, pieces that construct their insights out of the unobjectionably obvious—proclaiming that "some" have "voiced concerns," that "developments" may have "profound ramifications," but "on the other hand" "it is too soon to tell." And you find situations as odd as this: In a column in June 2006, David Brooks of *The New York Times* introduced his "War Council"—the "twenty or thirty people" who, because of the soundness of their "judgments" and "analysis," he turns to for wisdom about Iraq. One of those people works at Brooks's own paper: the "übercorrespondent"—currently Baghdad bureau chief—John F. Burns. Brooks included two quotes from Burns about Iraq in his column, including: "I'd have to say the odds are against success, but they are better now than they were three months ago, that's for sure." However, neither of those quotes was taken from the newspaper that employs Burns, where he ventures beyond the facts only rarely and very cautiously. Instead they were comments Burns made on the PBS program *Charlie Rose*.

"We would be of little value in our television appearances," Burns acknowledges, "if we offered no more than a bare-bones recitation of events, without any attempt to place them in a wider context, and to analyze what they mean." But shouldn't the same standard of "value" apply to Burns's appearances in his newspaper? He denies that *Times* reporters "are muzzled in conveying the full range of our experience and impressions" under the proper rubrics in the paper. Nonetheless, the "impressions" from this *Times* correspondent that most interested a *Times* columnist had not originally appeared in the *Times* itself.

The Wall Street Journal got a taste of this the-best-stuff-doesn't-make-the-paper problem two years ago when an e-mail found its way onto the Web from one of its reporters in Iraq, Farnaz Fassihi. It proved not only more controversial but arguably more interesting than the stories Fassihi had been filing from that country. For in this e-mail, intended to be private, Fassihi wrote in the first person and she noted what things looked like to her: "For those of us on the ground," she said, "it's hard to imagine what if anything could salvage [Iraq] from its violent downward spiral."

Outside the strictures of mainstream journalism, Fassihi, in other words, did not have to attempt the magic trick American reporters have been attempting for a hundred years now: making themselves and their conclusions disappear.

The switch to a new product line is moving forward at a pretty good pace on the pages of at least two newspapers—one large and foreign, one small and local.

The *Independent* is a serious English national daily in a market with three other serious national dailies. So the *Independent*, looking for an edge, has begun devoting most of its front page, weeklylike, to a single story—a story covered with considerable perspective and depth, a story in which the paper is not shy about exhibiting a point of view. The *Independent* weighed in recently, for example, on the debate on global warming with this headline, and a picture of a large wave, dominating its front page: TSUNAMI HITS BRITAIN: 5 NOVEMBER 2060.

Simon Kelner, the paper's editor in chief, explains that his understanding of the situation of the daily newspaper "crystallized" during coverage in England of the American presidential election in 2004. The *Independent* reported and interpreted the results along with the other papers. "It was a really expensive, exhaustive exercise for us all," Kelner recalls. Yet the next morning newsstand circulation actually fell. For up-to-the-minute results people had turned instead to the radio, television, and the Internet. However, he explains, "The next day *The Independent* published twenty-one pages of analysis and interpretation of the election—and we put on fifteen percent in sales."

Kelner got the message. "The idea that a newspaper is going to be peoples' first port of call to find out what's going on in the world is simply no longer valid. So you have to add another layer: analysis, interpretation, point of view." Kelner now dubs his daily a "viewspaper."

Compare the *Independent*'s response to a visit by Secretary of State Condoleezza Rice to the Middle East with that of *The Washington Post*. The *Post* reported on a joint press conference she held with the Palestinian Authority's president, Mahmoud Abbas, on page A26 under this headline: RICE CITES CONCERN FOR PALESTINIANS, BUT LOW EXPECTATIONS MARK VISIT. The *Independent,* that same morning, emblazoned this headline on its front page: THE ROAD MAP TO NOWHERE: FOUR YEARS AFTER GEORGE BUSH UNVEILED HIS MIDDLE EAST PLAN, CONDOLEEZZA RICE ARRIVED TO FIND PEACE AS FAR AWAY AS EVER.

It is not that shocking, by European standards, that *The Independent* has been saying what it thinks; what is fresh and vital is the magazine-like boldness and focus (think *The Economist*) with which it is saying it. Beneath the ROAD MAP TO NOWHERE headline on its front page, the *Independent* displayed a map of Jerusalem. Around the map were arranged five short items—each divided into THE PROMISE (headlined in red) and WHAT HAPPENED—in which the paper compared what the Bush administration had claimed for its "road map for peace" with the little, nothing, or worse (the Lebanon war was mentioned), it has achieved. Inside the paper, an article combined the history of the Bush Middle East plan with a report on Secretary Rice's current, seemingly futile visit to the region. Such a mix of graphic, list, and article—of news event, wider focus, and point of view—is now typical for the *Independent*.

Producing such a paper certainly makes for an interesting newsroom. "Our competitors each select the best news story of the day," notes John Mullin, the *Independent*'s executive editor for news. "What we try to do is something much more holistic. We try to capture the entire feel of something. It makes life much more—some would say difficult, some would say rewarding." Mullin adds that the effort to present a big chunk of news with a coherent viewpoint can be particularly "challenging" for journalists who are "used to thinking in the time-honored fashion: who, what, when and where."

Nowhere in the world has that fashion been as honored, and for such a long time, as it has been in the United States. Mainstream journalists in America today live in fear of the charge of bias. To achieve more vigorous analysis, they may have to get over that fear. After all, opinions—from "these are the times that try men's souls" to FORD TO CITY: DROP DEAD—have, historically, managed to hold their own with facts as ways of understanding the world. And it's not as if there aren't things besides the effort to be balanced for which journalists might stand. Old-fashioned reason might, for example, do, too.

Journalists also might stand for honesty. Sure, the analytic journalist can prove wrong: Burns, on *Charlie Rose,* had one take on the situation in Iraq; in her e-mail Fassihi, writing at a different time, had another. But there is something to be said for being openly right or wrong rather than hiding an assessment behind the carefully choreographed quotes of various named and unnamed sources.

No one is suggesting that reporters pontificate, spout, hazard a guess, or "tell" when it is indeed "too soon to tell." No one is suggesting that they indulge in unsupported, shoot-from-the-hip tirades. "It's not like talk radio," explains one of the champions of analytic journalism, Mike Levine, executive editor of the *Times Herald-Record* in Middletown, New York. But it's not traditional American journalism either. Levine, a former columnist, had noticed that the analyses reporters unburdened themselves of in conversations in the newsroom were often much more interesting than what ended up in the paper. Some of that conversation is mere loose talk and speculation, of course. Yet "walk into any newsroom in America," Levine says, "turn the reporters upside down, and a hundred stories will come falling out. They know so much about the communities they cover, but they don't get it in the newspaper."

When he took over the *Times Herald-Record* in 1999, Levine was determined to change that. "We simply asked reporters to give the readers the benefit of their intelligent analysis," he explains. This means paying less attention to the mere fact that a hospital administrator resigned in nearby Sullivan County. It may even mean leaving the account of the resignation to the paper's Web site. It definitely means more attention, in the paper, to what that resignation might signify.

"We're not the infantry anymore," Levine explains. "We don't just go out to board meetings and take dictation. That's not really much of a contribution to the community. What are needed are journalists who can connect the dots." Levine, in other words, is not afraid of letting his reporters—after they've done the reporting, when they know as much about a subject as most of their sources—find meaning in the dots.

Accomplishing this at a newspaper that may not be at the top of the hiring ladder has required, in Levine's words, relying on "some experienced people devoted to community journalism"; it has required finding and hiring some young reporters who are "curious" enough not to "shut down inquiry" and surrender to what Levine calls "a stale, petrified 'objectivity.'" But Levine adds, "not every reporter on staff does this kind of reporting. We're evolving into it."

Here is an example of what happens when journalists do Levine's kind of reporting, from a multipart *Times Herald-Record* series by the reporters Tim Logan and John Doherty, on a renaissance in the city of Newburgh:

> The city is shaking off three decades of inertia. It's an exciting time. The real-estate market is hot. City politics are more harmonious. And there are plans galore. Plans for a community college on lower Broadway, plans for the long-empty stretch of land on Water Street, a master plan under way for the city as a whole.
>
> But there's no plan for the city's poor. . . . If this city is truly going to rebuild, if it will ever fill the void at its heart, if it can transform itself from a drain on the rest of Orange County into the thriving hub the county desperately needs, Newburgh can no longer ignore its poverty.

Note: That's not, "Some observers suggest Newburgh can no longer ignore its poverty." Nor is that an editorial or a column. The point is being made in news pages, at a small, local newspaper, by journalists—based on what they have learned on their beats (the *Times Herald-Record* employs a traditional, geography-based beat structure), and based on their own reasoned and informed appraisal of the situation.

Burned-out reporters can be forgiven for dreaming that the coming of this analyzing and appraising will lead to a life of leisurely speculation. But, alas, more industrious reporting, not less, will be required. You'd better know an awful lot about plans for rebuilding Newburgh before you contemplate criticizing those plans. Getting at the meaning of events will demand looking beyond press conferences, escaping the pack, tracking down more knowledgeable sources, spending more time with those who have been affected, even seeking out those whom Levine of the *Times Herald-Record* calls "the invisible people—people who are not at board meetings who may not even show up at the voting booth." When Levine took over, his paper began a "sourcing project," designed to force reporters to avoid "going to the same three or four sources [for] every story." More and more diverse sources, the theory goes, should improve story ideas and stories, and help reporters know more when they say what they know.

Strategies developed at the *Times Herald-Record* might be of use at larger papers, too. As a source of timely and important analysis, our journalistic heavyweights are simply not—on a day-to-day, story-to-story basis—reliable. We will know that they have grasped their role in this staler-than-your-muffin news world only when they realize that being fast with the analysis is as important today as being fast with the news has been for the last hundred years.

For that to happen, our major news organizations—we need to begin thinking of them as "news-analysis organizations"—will have to develop a stable of knowledgeable analysts whom they can assign each day to the major stories—as they currently assign reporters. Some of these "wisdom journalists" might be obtained through raids on think tanks and weeklies. Smaller papers, less able to filch an expert on urban issues from the Brookings Institution, might regularly borrow some analytic talent from the less jargon-infested corners of local universities.

But daily news-analysis organizations must also develop their own career path for analysts.

Working your way up through the metro desk, the Washington bureau, and a few overseas beats certainly has its value, but it does not necessarily qualify you for untangling the underlying causes of fundamentalist Islamic terrorism. Some extensive university training might. News-analysis organizations will have no more room for the sort of scholars who never leave the library or their laptops than they'll have room for the sort who stuff sixty words, two of them unfamiliar, into a sentence. "I have a degree in East-Asian studies," Susan Chira, foreign editor of *The New York Times,* states. "But when I went to Asia myself and lived there, I found out a lot of things my teachers didn't know." We will continue—in journalism, not academic journals—to need theory to be tested and illuminated by experience, including on-the-street, eyes-open, with-the-victims experience. But an ability to go and get is simply no longer sufficient. The best journalistic organizations are going to be selling the best thinking on current events—and that often is furthered by deep, directed study.

The old saying is that reporters are only as good as their sources. We will require many more journalists who, when occasion demands, are better than their sources, journalists who are impeccably *informed*. Let's call this one of the five I's—a guide to what journalists need to be, now that at least four of the old five W's are more widely and easily available. *Intelligent* would be another, along with *interesting* and a holdover from the previous ethos: *industrious*. But the crucial quality is probably *insightful*.

It is significant how many of the most respected names in the history of journalism—from Joseph Addison to Dorothy Thompson and Tom Wolfe, from Charles Dickens to Ernie Pyle and I.F. Stone—were, indeed, known for stories that were exhaustively reported, marvelously written, and often startlingly insightful. The disruptions caused by the new news technologies will prove a blessing if they allow journalists to stop romanticizing the mere gathering and organization of facts and once again aspire to those qualities.

MITCHELL STEPHENS, a professor of journalism at New York University, is the author of *A History of News*.

Reprinted from *Columbia Journalism Review*, January/February 2007, pp. 34–39. Copyright © 2007 by Columbia Journalism Review, Columbia University.

Rocketboom!

Episodes of a fast-growing, low-budget online newscast emanating from a cramped Manhattan apartment are viewed more than 300,000 times. Do Rocketboom and similar videoblogs pose a threat to the future of television news?

PAUL FARHI

Amanda Congdon isn't ready for her close-up. The Internet's most popular news presenter is cooling her heels while Andrew Baron—her director, cameraman, cue-card guy, cowriter and business partner—drapes pillows and a white down comforter around her tiny anchor desk. Baron is trying to deaden the echo on the news set, which happens to double as his apartment. As Congdon idly applies her makeup, Baron fiddles with the lights and a tripod holding a digital video camera. He also tapes strips of the day's script on the makeshift teleprompter, a music stand set just beneath the camera's lens.

"Ready?" he asks Congdon finally.

Congdon brightens and settles herself as Baron hits "record" on the camera.

"Hello and good Monday, March 27th, 2006," she says. "I'm Amanda Congdon, and this is Rocketboom!

With a mischievous smile and several flips of her blond hair, Congdon breezes through a series of offbeat and esoteric stories, introducing video clips by tapping a mock control console in front of her. First up is a short bit about a Scottish street puppeteer whose rock-star marionettes play little guitars to a thrash-metal soundtrack. Next, there's footage of a fellow in Tokyo dancing wildly in front of an arcade game. This is followed by stories about an odd, tank-like vehicle that's for sale on Amazon.com and a device that deadens the noise of multiple telephone conversations in busy offices. Congdon winds up a story about the man who designed the modern office cubicle by quipping, "Millions of people across the world are trapped in tiny boxes, and many of them may never get out."

No, it isn't the "CBS Evening News" or CNN. Actually, it isn't even television. Rocketboom.com is a videoblog, or vlog, produced every weekday in Baron's shoe-box-size apartment on Manhattan's Upper West Side. Baron then uploads the episode to an Internet server downtown. The three- to five-minute show, with its sub-amateur trappings and oddball sensibility, might easily be dismissed as an amusing piffle, except for one thing: on average, episodes of Rocketboom are viewed more than 300,000 times, according to Baron and the site's logs.

Let's run that number again—300,000—because it's a significant, potentially even ruinous figure for TV news professionals. Congdon and Baron, and a staff of four, produce a daily information program that reaches more people than almost any single local newscast in America. And Rocketboom is growing like a tulip in early spring. Between January and March of this year, its worldwide audience more than doubled, according to Baron, who has the server logs and hit counts to back up his figures. At its current growth rate, Rocketboom's audience will soon rival that of most national cable news programs.

What's revolutionary isn't just Rocketboom's popularity; it's also how the site achieved it. The short answer is, with almost nothing but some imagination and a little computer power. Congdon and Baron own no satellite trucks, command no camera crews, have spent zip on advertising and promotion. Their videography equipment is no more sophisticated than what's available at Circuit City or Best Buy. About the only things they invested upfront were their time and brain cells. What's more, almost all of the material they present each day—the clips of Scottish puppeteers and dancing arcade guys—comes gratis, much of it scooped from the bountiful pool of public-domain video available on the Internet.

Rocketboom could be a harbinger. What blogs have done to newspapers, vlogs may someday do to the nightly news—that is, offer a competing source of commentary and information, fulfill a lively watchdog role and, not incidentally, steal viewers and advertisers from traditional newscasts.

With bandwidth costs plummeting and video cell phones and cameras widely available (and human exhibitionism a constant), the Internet is awash with the sort of video that Baron, 36, and Congdon, 24, cobble together to make Rocketboom. While much of this raw material is hardly journalistic (and is indeed raw), some of it is as compelling, and as newsworthy, as what professionals produce. Many people got their first glimpse of the devastating South Asian tsunami from homemade videos on the Web. Ditto the London subway bombings, whose immediate aftermath was documented not by news photographers but by passengers and eyewitnesses. Sites like YouTube, Revver, Vimeo and Google Video, which enable anyone to upload video and share it with the world, give some sense of the endless sea of newsy material, from Hurricane Katrina footage to exploding roadside bombs in Iraq to brawls at the local schoolyard. The Web has also turned professional TV news clips into Internet staples; Jon Stewart's excoriation of the hosts of "Crossfire" in 2004 was an early landmark. It was passed around the Web and seen by far more people online than on CNN.

"The old model was that a TV station would put one or two cameras at a major event. Now the same event can be captured by a thousand or more cameras," says Craig Allen, coordinator of broadcast news at Arizona State University's Walter Cronkite School of Journalism and Mass Communication and the author of "News Is People," a history of the local TV news business. "Back when, a [bystander's] camera would often capture an event by luck. We're at a stage now where you'd have the Zapruder film [the home movie of John F. Kennedy's assassination] a thousand times over. Only now, no one would be able to conceal it for 15 years."

By cherry-picking some of these video goodies and adding a gloss of wit and cool, Baron, Congdon and Rocketboom are showing that a do-it-yourself newscast, stripped of expensive infrastructure and available free any time of the day, is not only possible but can be wildly successful. "Rocketboom basically shows that news is in the hands of people, not just the pros," says Jeff Jarvis, a blogger (buzzmachine.com), consultant and new-media evangelist. "With the Internet, we all have printing presses and broadcast towers. No one has to beg anyone for access anymore."

A typical Rocketboom episode might include ephemera like a report on a giant pillow fight in New York's Union Square. Or it might feature more substantial fare, such as stories on new technologies or on how the Internet may affect the 2008 election. Or both.

Not only is much of this raw material, this video flotsam, free for the taking, but a variety of inexpensive tools make the Rocketbooms of the world look almost as good as the pros. Near-broadcast-quality digital cameras can sell for a few hundred dollars (Baron uses a $1,500 model). Off-the-shelf digital editing programs are even cheaper; an audio editing tool called Audacity is free. Even so, no one really demands spiffy production values on the Internet. Jarvis says that conventional TV news often looks hopelessly slick and old school when compared with the more "authentic-looking" material found online. This is where Rocketboom has made a virtue out of what initially appears to be a drawback. Congdon's wardrobe (sometimes featuring a T-shirt provided by fans) and Rocketboom's cheesy, no-rent set (a small desk with a paper map of the world tacked behind it) subtly signal to viewers that this isn't your Grandpa's daily news feed.

"One thing we've learned is that the public's definition of quality is not the same as the professionals'," Jarvis says. "If the Iraq war proved one thing, it's that the public doesn't mind low-quality video of [a correspondent] talking on a camera phone if what he's saying is exciting enough. . . . Professionals are so hung up about being professional. They're hung up on style over substance."

But, in an odd reversal, pros are learning to play the amateur game, too. Many Web sites of mainstream news organizations now invite viewer and reader accounts of events, including those the news outlet itself has covered. MSNBC.com, which is among the most popular news sites on the Web, entreats visitors to "be a citizen journalist" and e-mail moving or still pictures for posting. In an experiment started last year, Nashville's WKRN-TV and San Francisco's KRON-TV, both owned by Young Broadcasting, handed out 3-pound Sony HD cameras to reporters, photographers and editors to create one-person video journalists. WKRN also trained about 20 local bloggers as stringers. While reviews have not been kind (SF Weekly recently described the work of some of KRON's video journalists as "distractingly bad"), it's still early. "There's no question," says Barbara Cochran, president of the Radio-Television News Directors Association, "that stations and networks are aware of [new sources of video] and are paying close attention."

Yet Cochran and others express a couple of obvious concerns about amateur news video: How much of it is really news? And how much of it can be trusted? "With more and more of this stuff available, I keep hearing that it's like trying to drink from a fire hose," she says. "There's so much material coming in from so many sources. How do you see everything that's worthwhile? How do you monitor it, assess it, verify it?—all the things that professional journalists are supposed to do."

CBS News has used amateur video but hasn't encouraged contributions, either on-air or online, says Larry Kramer, who heads the company's digital division, which includes CBSNews.com. "We have to keep a separation between journalists and user-generated content," he says. "We've always relied on the public in our reporting, but we filter it. You just have to be careful." Technology, he says, enables ordinary people to distribute content quickly after news breaks. But it also allows them to alter it or manipulate it without a news organization knowing. "We know when our own people do something, it adheres to the rules," Kramer says. "We vet our material. There's no expectation that Yahoo! or Google or YouTube will vet anything."

Or as Samuel G. Freedman, a journalism professor at Columbia, put it in a commentary on CBSNews.com in late March: "To its proponents, citizen journalism represents a democratization of the media, a shattering of the power of the unelected elite. . . . However wrapped in idealism, citizen journalism forms part of a larger attempt to degrade, even to disenfranchise journalism as practiced by trained professionals. . . . I appreciate the access that citizen journalism provides to first-hand accounts of major events. Yet I recognize those accounts are less journalism than the raw material, generated by amateurs, that a trained, skilled journalist should know how to weigh, analyze, describe and explain."

Congdon and Baron certainly have no pretensions about being journalists. Both freely admit they aren't, nor do they aspire to be, despite the nature of their enterprise. Indeed, they're not shy about working personal opinions into their Webcast. They'll often gin up little skits to comment on an issue or a thread in popular culture. In fact, there's a little gentle attitude—both are Democrats—in almost every show. In one memorable episode last September, Congdon donned a pearl necklace and a white dress to portray a stereotypical wealthy matron, observing blithely, "Oil at $70 a barrel? Make it an even $100. Then nobody can be on the road except me and my friends!" Congdon has interviewed former U.S. Sen. John Edwards twice on the show (Baron cooked up Rocketboom while he was a volunteer in Edwards' 2004 presidential campaign). Some of Congdon's interview in February was frivolous—she talked Edwards into drawing a picture of himself with facial hair—but it also elicited the North Carolina Democrat's assertion that energy conservation must become "mandatory" in the next 20 years.

"There's so much riding on [professional reporters] to be fair and balanced," Congdon says. "You can never tell what you actually think. We do say what we think. It's refreshing to hear, because it's honest."

"This is citizen journalism, but it really describes a style more than a professional obligation" or set of standards, adds Baron. "We're really saying, 'Don't bank on us.'"

Adds Congdon, "We're not trying to please everyone."

The duo make an unlikely pair of collaborators and business partners. Baron is short and intense. With a squeaky voice and an Apple-logo baseball cap pulled down over his brow, he suggests a nerdier version of James Spader's videographer character in the movie "sex, lies, and videotape." Congdon is the more outgoing one, a gangly beauty.

Baron was teaching at the Parsons School of Design in Manhattan when he came up with the idea for Rocketboom (the name has no special meaning; it just sounded good when Baron dreamed it up). His background is in computer-aided design. Figuring that he never would be the face or voice of his brainchild, he recruited the telegenic Congdon through a help-wanted ad on craigslist.com. At the time, she was working as an actress and model after graduating from Northwestern University.

Part of Rocketboom's charm is that it plays off the conventions of TV newscasts, much as "Saturday Night Live" and "The Daily Show" do. Congdon often rolls her eyes or throws up her hands over particularly absurd stories, and does hilariously exaggerated camera turns in between them, swinging her head from one angle to the next. She frequently breaks her newscaster character, commenting directly to the camera. On "Casual Fridays," the site dispenses with the newscast altogether and presents quirky commentaries or travelogues, many now produced by Congdon's boyfriend, Mario Librandi. Congdon's wealthy matron character was a popular Casual Friday entry.

Still, Baron and Congdon do some of the things regular TV journalists do. There are story conferences and story budgets, daily scriptwriting sessions and all-night editing benders (now handled by a hired editor). Both are equals when it comes to what gets on the show, although Baron is principally involved in scouring the Internet for material. (He's also the majority owner of Rocketboom, holding just a percent or two more than Congdon.) About a quarter of the story ideas and clips come from Rocketboom's tech-savvy viewers. Other stories are shot and produced by the site's 10 "field correspondents," nonjournalists who live in Los Angeles, Minneapolis, Boston and elsewhere.

Rocketboom's success has inspired some imitators. A German site called Ehrensef (www.ehrensenf.de) apes Rocketboom's single-anchor style, presentation and breezy attitude. The Public Eye (www.thepubliceye.tv), a daily video program out of Vancouver, Washington, is a little clunkier but uses the same news-from-everywhere approach of its fellow vlogs.

The growing audience of hipsters for the original, meanwhile, has helped Rocketboom attract plenty of attention from would-be buyers and investors. Baron says he's gotten offers from two "mainstream networks" (he won't identify them), but neither he nor Congdon is interested in selling right now. Nor are they returning calls from venture capitalists who want to put money into their hands. "We decided we can skip that step," Baron says. "Other than investing our own time, we haven't really needed any money to keep us going."

But the money is coming anyway. Earlier this year, Rocketboom accepted its first advertising, and in a typically unusual way. Rather than opening the site to any advertiser who cared to pay the freight, Congdon and Baron put a single advertising position up for auction on eBay. After nearly 100 bids, the winner was TRM Corp., a marketer of automatic-teller machines. The price: $40,000 for a week of ads, which Baron and Congdon insisted could only run after each episode. "We could have gotten three times the money if we had given away control," Congdon says. The site has subsequently attracted a second advertiser, the Internet service provider EarthLink, at a similar price. And since that deal closed, Rocketboom's audience has grown substantially.

Before the advent of ads, Rocketboom's revenue sources were licensing fees (to cell phones, TiVo, other online platforms) and merchandising. Congdon says she and her full-time fellow staffers now have salaries that enable them to live comfortably in Manhattan.

Still more mainstream acceptance came in February, when Rocketboom was featured in an episode of "CSI: Crime Scene Investigation," TV's most popular drama series. Congdon briefly played herself reporting on a lurid crime. Baron shot the segment with his own equipment and on Rocketboom's homemade set, proving perhaps that it doesn't take Hollywood's overhead to produce Hollywood-quality video.

All this has inspired the Rocketboomers to think bigger. Congdon says the pair has "20 ideas" for new vlogs. There are also talks with a number of possible partners. "We have the potential to grow this into a billion-dollar business," Baron says.

Arizona State's Craig Allen doesn't doubt that Rocketboom, and more serious versions to come, will have their own niche. But he doubts it will ever be big enough to displace conventional TV news. The majority of the population, he points out, are working-class people who don't sit behind computers during the day, when most people consume online news. "You'll certainly have some providers who are going to reach 300,000 people on a regular basis [online], but the impact on the broader society, I think, is going to be small."

Jeff Jarvis says that he misses the trees in a very large forest. Rocketboom alone won't kill the mainstream TV news, he says—but a thousand Rocketbooms just might.

Paul Farhi (farhip@washpost.com), a *Washington Post* reporter, writes frequently about the media. He explored the future of the newspaper business in *AJR*'s February/March issue.

Article 23

Epidemic

TRUDY LIEBERMAN

When 19 thousand viewers tuned in to the 7 A.M. news on KTBC-TV, the local Fox channel in Austin, Texas, in mid-January, they heard the anchor, Joe Bickett, introduce a story about a new electronic rehabilitation system for injured kids. "Sharon Dennis has more on that," Bickett said. Dennis then described how a lively fifteen-year-old named Merrill, who had sprained her ankle, was getting better thanks to the computer-guided rehab program that Cleveland Clinic researchers are calling "the world's first virtual-only gym."

The professional-looking story had that gee-whiz feel so typical of TV health news, explaining how the technology was making it easier for patients to get back to normal. It ended with "Sharon Dennis reporting."

Viewers could be forgiven if they thought they were seeing real news reported by one of the station's reporters. But Sharon Dennis does not work for KTBC. The story had been fed to the station by the Cleveland Clinic, the health care behemoth. Dennis, who earned her broadcasting bona fides at ABC News and at KOMO-TV in Seattle, works in Cleveland as the executive producer of the Cleveland Clinic News Service, in a windowless office on the fourth floor of the Intercontinental Hotel on the clinic's sprawling 140-acre campus. There the clinic has constructed broadcast facilities for Dennis and her four-person staff, complete with three cameras, a background set, and an ON AIR sign purchased at Target. Every day, Dennis sends out prepackaged stories to, among others, Fox News Edge, a service for Fox affiliates that in turn distributes the pieces to 140 Fox stations. What Texas viewers heard that January morning was a script written at the Intercontinental Hotel.

In essence, the story was a hybrid of news and marketing, the likes of which has spread to local TV newsrooms all across the country in a variety of forms, almost like an epidemic. It's the product of a marriage of the hospitals' desperate need to compete for lucrative lines of business in our current health system and of TV's hunger for cheap and easy stories. In some cases the hospitals pay for airtime, a sponsorship, and in others, they don't but still provide expertise and story ideas. Either way, the result is that too often the hospitals control the story. Viewers who think they are getting news are really getting a form of advertising. And critical stories—hospital infection rates, for example, or medical mistakes or poor care—tend not to be covered in such a cozy atmosphere. The public, which could use real health reporting these days, gets something far less than quality, arms-length journalism.

The story about the virtual gym—which ran on twenty-one other stations, too—ended with Bickett saying that its developers hope to have the technology available in hospitals around the U.S. by the end of the year. Though he didn't mention which hospitals, viewers could easily conclude that the Cleveland Clinic was one of them. Indeed that is what the clinic hopes, Cleveland Clinic News Service stories almost always feature Cleveland Clinic doctors and patients touting some new surgical technique or medical breakthrough, like antiaging proteins or a new sensor to measure spinal disc damage, or sometimes offering basic health tips, like flu shots or exercise. Stories occasionally mention research from another institution or a medical journal, but never a doctor from a rival hospital in Cleveland. That would hardly further the underlying goal of the news service: public awareness of the Cleveland Clinic brand.

The Cleveland Clinic News Service is just one variation on the new alliance between hospitals and local TV news. Most of these arrangements are between a single health institution and a single TV station. They take different forms in different cities, but the deals all too frequently slide across the ad-edit wall. The partnerships may involve traditional commercials, but they often include a promise of some kind of "news" stories, too, involving reporters or news anchors. These can take the form of "ask the expert" programs, quick helpings of medical advice, short stories inserted into the newscasts, or longer, news-like specials that may be hosted by a news anchor or health reporter. In the worst cases, hospitals create the storyline, supplying both the experts and the patients. Some partnerships include a Web component; viewers are sent to the TV station Web site, where they find links to hospital Web sites that provide referrals to doctors or hospital services, and it becomes nearly impossible to separate news and marketing.

Rick Wade, senior vice president for strategic communications at the American Hospital Association, says that the TV/hospital partnerships are an unwelcome result of fierce marketplace competition in health care. "There's a lot of it going on," says Wade. "It happens in major media markets where TV stations are starving and hospitals are under competitive pressure." In response to cost-cutting by managed-care firms over the last decade, hospitals have glued themselves into large systems to fight back. Branding and marketing have become the weapons of choice. Ultimately the goal is to attract patients.

The hospitals don't want just any patient, though—only those with good insurance to pay for the big-ticket procedures that bring in the big bucks. One result of the epidemic is that the health stories that dominate local TV news tend to push expensive specialties and procedures—like bariatric surgery for obesity, which can cost upwards of $20,000, or expensive gamma knife surgery for brain cancer, with a price tag of $10,000 or more. Stories about less profitable diagnoses, like AIDS or pneumonia, are rare, let alone pieces about care for the uninsured. The bland stories almost always discuss non-controversial topics, such as new technology, a hospital's special services, or health and nutrition tips.

Worse, since TV news operations are finding that they can get this kind of health "news" supplied to them—and might even make money on the deal—they are tempted not to invest in a legitimate health reporter who would ask harder questions and look at the larger picture in health care. "I don't feel we need a full-time health reporter," says Regent Ducas, news director at KCTV in Kansas City, which had a lucrative partnership with the HCA hospital system until the end of 2006. When it lost the HCA partnership, KCTV moved quickly to look for a new one. Not all TV stations, of course, strike such deals. Sam Rosenwasser, president and general manager of WTSP-TV in St. Petersburg, Florida, says his station just hasn't pursued one, but said he would "entertain anything if it makes sense." It would make sense, he said, "as long as you let people know you have some partnership." But too often the full nature of the arrangements is not disclosed, or inadequately disclosed, leaving the viewer without any understanding of what it means when the hospital gets involved in the content of news.

Good reporters are often afraid to talk on the record about the partnerships, but it's clear that they don't like them. "How are you as a journalist supposed to impart a sense of trust if the story is essentially directed and produced by a company not related to your news department?" asks one TV health reporter whose news director would not let her speak for attribution.

"I have to do these. I'm not given a choice," said another reporter who asked for anonymity. "I kick, scream, and fight, and make them as journalistically ethical as possible. It makes me sick."

The Cleveland Clinic started its news service nearly four years ago with a pilot sent to NBC affiliates that signed up and a handshake agreement with Fox News. The service acts as "a customer service arm for reporters," says the Cleveland Clinic's media relations specialist, Raquel Santiago.

At one end of the customer-service spectrum, NBC seems to use the Cleveland Clinic material as a kind of story-idea service. Helen Chickering, a medical reporter for NBC News Channel, which sends stories to NBC affiliates, says the network cannot use prepackaged Video News Releases, known as VNRS, in stories, but will make its own interview requests based on them. "The only way we can connect is with an interview request," she says of the rules about dealing with VNR providers. One story in a special series called Modern Medical Miracles, which aired on NBC'S *Today* at the end of November, demonstrates how the network uses the clinic's material. In October, the Cleveland Clinic sent out a story called "Racing Hearts," which showed how race-car drivers are testing a new heart-monitoring device, and featured a Cleveland Clinic doctor. *Today* then created its own story featuring the Cleveland Clinic doctor; the medical affairs director for the Champ Car World Series, an international car race; and NBC'S chief medical editor, Dr. Nancy Snyderman, who called the device a "very cool breakthrough." The segment discussed other kinds of heart devices and did note that the one tested on race-car drivers was not yet on the market.

Toward the other end of the spectrum is Fox. As Cleveland Clinic's Sharon Dennis sees it, "We act as a news bureau for Fox." A CJR analysis shows just how true that is. We traced the use of eight stories the clinic sent out last fall and found that twenty-six stations—all Fox except three—used them almost verbatim. Dave Winstrom, the director of Fox News Edge, says Fox approves the scripts before the packages are sent to the stations, and adds that the stations may choose how to use them. "Some may use them verbatim, or cut them down, or not use them at all." What's sent to the stations, he says, is identified as being from the Cleveland Clinic, but "it's up to them how they present the story." (The piece about the virtual gym that ran in Austin did not tell viewers the source of the story.)

Marketing like that can produce a big return on a hospital's investment. The Mayo Clinic, which started its own news service in 2000, sends its weekly Medical Edge stories to 130 TV stations in the U.S. and Canada. No other station in those markets can use Mayo's Medical Edge offerings. Stations using the material must agree to say that the featured physician belongs to the Mayo Clinic and provide a link from the station Web site to Mayo's.

How well does that work? CJR obtained a PowerPoint presentation given in 2004 to hospital marketers by the Mayo Clinic's media relations manager, Lee Aase. It showed that brand preference for Mayo for serious medical conditions had increased 59 percent three years after the service began, and brought in new patients to boot. One story, called "Same-Day Teeth," which told of a quicker way of doing lower-jaw dental implants, generated more than 175 calls, Aase's report said. It resulted in twenty-three scheduled appointments and downstream revenue—money from patients who eventually had the procedure—estimated at $345,000. The presentation noted that 8.6 million people had seen the December 2001 Medical Edge stories. The value, said Mayo, was greater than ten times the cost of producing the shows.

Sharon O'Brien, the marketing director for University Health System in San Antonio, says she is moving away from paid advertising in favor of such media partnerships. "The hallmark of these packages is that they don't look like paid advertising," she says.

Marketing like this is so powerful, in fact, that some TV stations have found that they can charge serious money for "news." Their sales departments aggressively pitch business proposals to health institutions, laid out in thick spiral binders that look like a prospectus, according to L. G. Blanchard, media relations manager for the University of Alabama Health System, who has seen many of them. Most hospital officials that CJR interviewed would not talk about their financial arrangements with TV stations, but the few who did offered a glimpse into how profitable the deals can be to those stations willing to charge for them.

Leni Kirkman, the executive director of corporate communications at University Health System in San Antonio, said her hospital paid about $90,000 in 2002 to KENS-TV for a year-long sponsorship that involved thirty-second promotions, prominent placement of the hospital's logo—and a monthly feature called "Family First" that was narrated by the station's news anchor but written by the hospital's p.r. staff. Kirkman says the hospital has also had a deal with Univision, in which no money changed hands. In that partnership, she says, the hospital provides a tape with B-roll footage and interviews for a show called "A Su Salud (To Your Health)," which features the hospital's experts and patients. "We get to have our experts interviewed, so we get the PR value." But there's a bonus: "When we want them to cover something else," Kirkman adds, "they are extremely receptive."

Rob Dyer, a vice president for marketing and public relations at HCA hospitals in Kansas City, said his organization paid KCTV $1.5 million over the three years of their partnership, which ended in December. That deal involved advertising spots, promotion on the station's Web site, four Doctor on Call specials each year with the station's morning anchor and hospital medical personnel.

In 2002, the Radio-Television News Directors Association (RTNDA) established voluntary guidelines for balancing business pressures and journalism values. One RTNDA standard says advertisers should have no influence over news content. Yet in many of these TV partnerships, hospital p.r. people decide the story and may even write or edit the script.

Another standard says that a news operation's online product should clearly separate commercial and editorial content. But such clarity is often lacking. For example, WIS-TV in Columbia, South Carolina, featured one of its former reporters in a Web story as she had her risk for heart disease assessed by a local hospital heart center; the story blended so smoothly on the site with the hospital's ads it was difficult to tell the difference.

For the most part, TV stations and hospitals see little wrong with their partnerships. Hospital p.r. officials often believe it is simply another way to inform consumers about health care. Chad Dillard, a former hospital marketing vice president for Good Samaritan Hospital in Baltimore, said he didn't think the partnerships crossed the line. "I never honestly thought it was anything more than getting a good story out to the consumer." For his part, Regent Ducas of Kansas City's KCTV concedes that his station's Doctor on Call programs are not news, but are more like "a Billy Graham special." But, says Barbara Cochran, the president of the RTNDA: "If your viewers and listeners start to think your news content is for sale, you'll lose credibility and the value that advertisers want will be damaged."

TV anchors and health reporters lend credibility to stories resulting from partnerships. In Seattle, the popular KING-TV anchor Jean Enersen starred in a package on lung cancer that ran last October and was promoted as a "KING 5 Cancer Free Washington Special." Although the program reported on patients in lung cancer support groups and smokers trying to kick the habit, it was also unquestionably a plug for the work of three hospitals that formed the Seattle Cancer Care Alliance, which partners with KING. Enersen has hosted eight hour-long shows on cancer over the last two years, as well as shorter "health link" pieces that run during the primetime news once a week. Sometimes anchors also appear in commercials for the hospitals, giving the ads the patina of news. Wayne Dawson, a news anchor at Cleveland's Fox station WJW, for example, does spots promoting MetroHealth's help line. The spots run during WJW's news and entertainment programming, earmarked as commercials.

In its 2003 annual report, Meredith Corporation, which owns fourteen TV stations, noted, "Now everyone at each station, including news anchors and other on-air personalities, is playing a role in generating advertising revenues or supporting sales operations." Thus it was only natural that Meredith's station in Kansas City, KCTV, would agree that, as part of its deal with HCA, one of the station's anchors would host the Doctor on Call specials that featured HCA doctors and nurses answering viewer questions. HCA'S Dyer says the station wanted a representative to host the shows and "we didn't mind that."

The larger problem with TV-hospital partnerships is that in many of them the hospitals effectively co-opt the station's journalistic duties. How much control the hospitals get varies from partnership to partnership, but they often select the topics, choose the patients and doctors, and sometimes write or edit the script. Shawnee Mission Medical Center just outside Kansas City, Kansas, for example, has a sponsorship deal with an ABC affiliate, KMBC, owned by Hearst-Argyle, to air stories called Health Watch for Women, which airs every Wednesday and Sunday, featuring only the health system's medical experts. Shannon Cates, a hospital media relations specialist, says the stories, which discuss such subjects as osteoperosis, progesterone, and bladder control, are "definitely" news. "I develop the story ideas and arrange for the physicians and patients to speak on the air," she says. "Channel 9 comes to do the interview for the segment. It's like any other news story they would do." The partnership goes deeper. "Working on a regular basis we've come to trust each other. They feel comfortable with me developing story ideas, and I trust them to put the story together that represents the hospital well."

Thomas McCormally, a public information officer at rival Children's Mercy Hospitals, based in Kansas City, Missouri, says this about the women's health stories: "As a consumer you wouldn't know they are advertising."

He should know. His hospital has its own unpaid arrangement with KMBC and with the same reporter, Kelly Eckerman, who also anchors the evening news. Every other Wednesday between 12 P.M. and 2 P.M., Eckerman and a camera crew arrive at the hospital, where McCormally has lined up doctors, a family, and a child for interviews and B-roll shots on a topic the hospital has suggested. McCormally describes the hospital as a "quasi producer," though it doesn't write the script. At each session the station gets two packages—four in total for the month—which run on Thursday's 5 P.M. broadcast. "Kelly gets a ready-made story. We're getting what we want," McCormally says. What he wants is visibility, in order to recruit physicians and to "plant seeds in the minds of donors we're working hard to take care of children." The easier you make things for a TV news operation, he says, the easier it is to get your message out.

Another seed that gets planted is that the doctor or hospital featured on TV is the best around, whether true or not. KOCO-TV in Oklahoma City devotes airtime to health care providers—a Lasik eye specialist, plastic surgeons affiliated with a hospital that is one of the program sponsors, and a dentist specializing in cosmetic procedures—to perform what the station brands "Oklahoma's Ultimate Makeover." Two people are chosen from the community to have a complete make-over with some aspects of their transformation woven into a one-hour TV special. Dominique Homsey Gross, the station's sales marketing manager, says the makeover is a source of "nontraditional revenue." Viewers might easily assume that because the doctors were picked to "perform" on camera, they must be top-notch. But the actual requirement seems to be that, as Gross put it, "these people partner with the TV station to show what they do."

Such branding partnerships can even obscure problems at a hospital. The CBS station KYW-TV in Philadelphia has a partnership with Temple University Hospital. Stories resulting from the partnership, called Temple LifeLines specials, won two mid-Atlantic regional Emmys—one in 2004 for a story about the hospital's heart transplant program and one last September for a story on bone marrow transplants. According to a hospital press release, the transplant program profiled "some of the wonderful patients who have benefited from their quality-care experiences at Temple." The hospital pays for the airtime and, although the station's medical reporter, Stephanie Stahl, hosts the half-hour show, hospital officials are very much a part of the creative process. Charles Soltoff, associate vice president for marketing at Temple, says the hospital presents ideas to the station—what's interesting, where the hospital has opportunities for new business development, advances in treatment options. "We tell them what's valuable," Soltoff says. The decision on topics is "shared," he says, but a hospital official who talked to CJR on the condition of anonymity said: "Ultimately it's Temple's decision about what to feature," further explaining that "the writer does the script and submits a draft to us. We edit the script." Soltoff says, "We edit it down from various perspectives."

But there have been problems with Temple's transplant services. In a 2006 series on organ transplants, the *Los Angeles Times* reported that Temple had found a way to move prospective heart recipients ahead in the queue by saying they were sicker than they actually were, a practice that's unfair to those lower on the list, but one that might boost volume and thus revenue— and, of course, help Temple's own patients. The *Times* also reported that Temple's story has "never been publicly disclosed." The public did not know that the United Network for Organ Sharing (UNOS), a private, non-profit group that has a federal contract to ensure safety and equity in the nation's transplant system, had disciplined the hospital. In 2002, UNOS found more evidence that the hospital was inflating its patients' conditions, and in November of that year placed the hospital on "confidential probation." The probation ended in January 2006, which means that it spanned the time that Temple and KYW were producing and airing their award-winning specials promoting the hospital's transplant services.

Another example: the Alta Bates Summit Medical Center, with campuses in Oakland and Berkeley, California, part of the Sutter Health Network, got into trouble in early 2005. The Joint Commission on the Accreditation of Health Care Organizations (JCAHO) gave a preliminary accreditation denial to Alta Bates. In 2004 JCAHO had issued only twelve preliminary denials out of about 1,500 hospitals it surveyed. Later JCAHO changed its rating to a conditional accreditation, indicating the hospital still had to prove it had corrected deficiencies that inspectors had found. The *San Francisco Chronicle* and the *Contra Costa Times* both covered the problems at Alta Bates. But a search of the video library of KPIX-TV, which partners with Sutter Health, turned up no stories about Alta Bates and JCAHO. The station's communications director, Akilah Monifa, confirmed that no such stories had run on the newscast. As part of its advertising deal with Sutter Health, KPIX receives a fully produced program called "Your Health," which it runs twice a month. The annual cost of the program, according to Tracy Murphy, a marketing vice president at Sutter Health, is about $350,000.

The clever packaging and convergent marketing that come with TV-hospital partnerships fly in the face or a consumer empowerment movement for transparency in health care, pushed by some academics, employers, and patient advocacy groups, that is beginning to take root in the U.S. The movement envisions that educated patients will take responsibility for choosing the best care by using scientific and objective data—if data are available. But when patients get the impression through branding activities with local news stations that hospital A is superior, data that show hospital B is really better may have little meaning. In fact, such data may be overlooked entirely by TV news departments as well as patients. The tremendous investment being made to devise fair and useful health care metrics may well be wasted because television's complicity in hospital branding activities will ultimately overwhelm those efforts.

The partnerships also contribute to the dysfunction of the U.S. health care system. Hospitals understandably want high revenue from high-cost services to help subsidize the uncompensated care they provide to the uninsured who can't pay on their own, a practice that might be eliminated with a more rational payment system. But stories about profitable, high-tech, yet often unproven procedures stimulate demand for them, fueling ever-rising health care costs.

Local TV health journalism doesn't often discuss those big issues, or even often take on the smaller stories that together weave a tale of a health care system in trouble. And marketing partnerships with local hospitals almost mandate that it will be so, substituting lazy journalism and gee-whiz technology stories for the real thing.

It's hard to see that the TV-hospital partnerships do much for the public interest. Citizens groups have challenged the licenses of stations in Illinois, Wisconsin, and Oregon for offering scant local election coverage. Perhaps fake health news should be their next target.

Last October at a reunion of fellows from the Joan Shorenstein Center on the Press, Politics, and Public Policy, Vartan Gregorian, president of the Carnegie Corporation, spoke of a problem with choice in America. "Choice can be manipulated," Gregorian said. "Choice without knowledge is no choice at all." That's what local TV news is in danger of giving us when it comes to health care.

UNIT 3
Players and Guides

Unit Selections

24. **Break Up This Band!,** Ted Turner
25. **Into the Great Wide Open,** Jesse Sunenblick
26. **Why Journalists Are Not Above the Law,** Gabriel Schoenfeld
27. **Copyright Jungle,** Siva Vaidhyanathan
28. **Distorted Picture,** Sherry Ricchiardi
29. **What Would You Do?,** Daniel Weiss
30. **Naming Names: Credibility vs. Deportation,** Lucy Hood
31. **The Lives of Others,** Julia Dahl
32. **The Shame Game,** Douglas McCollam

Key Points to Consider

- What are the arguments for deregulation of media ownership? Against deregulation? Which do you think is stronger? Why?

- It has been argued that spectrum scarcity, the driving force behind FCC regulation of electronic media, is no longer an issue. Is there a need for the regulation of the collective reach of media that one organization can acquire? And what about Internet access and content? Why or why not?

- What kinds of media content do you advocate government regulation? And for what do you advocate industry regulation? Sex? Violence? Portrayals of minority groups? Anti-American messages? Liberal versus conservative viewpoints? Evangelical Christian messages? Atheist messages? How should the rules regarding objectionable content be enforced?

- How would you define the rules of "ethical practice?" Who, besides the subject of a news story, is affected by such judgments?

Student Web Site
www.mhcls.com

Internet References

The Electronic Journalist
http://spj.org

Federal Communications Commission (FCC)
http://www.fcc.gov

Index on Censorship
http://www.indexonline.org

Internet Law Library
http://www.phillylawyer.com

Michigan Press Photographers Association (MPPA)
http://www.mppa.org

Poynter Online: Research Center
http://www.poynter.org

World Intellectual Property Organization (WIPO)
http://www.wipo.org

The freedom of speech and of the press are regarded as fundamental American rights, protected under the U.S. Constitution. These freedoms, however, are not without any restrictions; the media are held accountable to legal and regulatory authorities, whose involvement reflects a belief that the public sometimes requires protection.

Regulatory agencies, such as the Federal Communications Commission (FCC), exert influence over media access and content through their power to grant, regulate, and revoke licenses to operate. They are primarily concerned with the electronic media because of the historically limited number of broadcast bands available in any community (called spectrum scarcity). The first two articles in this section contribute differing perspectives on ownership and access—the "players" of the unit's title. "Break Up This Band!" offers Ted Turner's view of loosening the FCC ownership rules and its effect on independent media companies: "We just shouldn't have those rules. They make sense for a corporation. But for a society, it's like over-fishing the oceans. When the independent businesses are gone, where will the new ideas come from?" "Into the Great Wide Open" looks at the challenges and potential of spread spectrum technology, which could allow unrestricted access for just about anyone to broadcast over long distances, removing the functional need for FCC licensing that is based on spectrum scarcity.

The courts exert influence over media practice through hearing cases of alleged violation of legal principles such as the protection from libel and the right to privacy. Shield laws grant reporters the right to promise informants confidentiality, and are the topic of debate in "Why Journalists Are Not Above the Law." "Copyright Jungle" describes similar tension in interpretation of copyright law: "Copyright provides the incentive to bring work to market. . . Yet, Copyright has the potential of locking up knowledge, insight, information, and wisdom from the rest of the world. So it is also fundamentally a *conditional* restriction on speech and print."

The courts have heard cases based on product liability law, in which plaintiffs have—sometimes successfully and sometimes not—sued media companies for harmful acts attributed to the perpetrator's exposure to violent media content. Antitrust law has been summoned in an attempt to break up media monopolies. The Federal Trade Commission (FTC) and the U.S. Food and the Drug Administration (FDA) have regulatory controls that affect advertising.

There is, however, a wide grey zone between an actionable offense and an error in judgment. For example, while legal precedence makes it difficult for public figures to prevail in either libel or invasion-of-privacy cases, it is not necessarily right to print information that might be hurtful to them. Nor is it necessarily wrong to do so. Sometimes a "good business decision" from one player's perspective impedes another's success.

© Photodisc/Alamy

Sometimes being "truthful" is insensitive. Sometimes being "interesting" means being exploitive. Some media organizations seem to have a greater concern for ethical policy than do others; however, even with the best intentions, drawing the line is not always simple.

The last five articles in this unit raise questions of ethical practice. "Distorted Picture" addresses the ethics of altering photographs. Technology such as Photoshop makes it easy, and often, photo editing is done for aesthetic reasons rather than with an intent to deceive. What are the limits of acceptable practice? "What Would You Do?" ponders the ethics of investigative experimenters, who "step out of their customary role as observers and play with reality to see what will happen." "Naming Names: Credibility vs. Deportation" reflects on the implications of identifying sources. "The Lives of Others" is about gatekeeping. "The Shame Game" addresses reality TV sting operations, such as the "To Catch a Predator" series on *Dateline NBC*.

What rules of practice should be applied in balancing the public's right to know against potential effects on individuals and society at large? Which great photograph shouldn't run? Which facts shouldn't be printed? Who owns media channels and makes these decisions? Is it ethical for journalists to cover stories on issues about which they have strong personal views, or does such practice compromise objectivity? Is it fair to become a "friend" to win trust, then write a story that is not flattering, or does not support the source's views or actions? Should the paparazzi be held legally responsible for causing harm to those they stalk, or should that responsibility be borne by consumers who buy their products? What about the well-intentioned story that attempts to right a social wrong, but hurts people in the process?

These are not easy questions, and they do not have easy answers. Media in the United States are grounded in a legacy of fiercely protected First Amendment rights, and shaped by a code for conducting business with a strong sense of moral obligation to society. But no laws or codes of conduct can prescribe an appropriate behavior for every possible situation. When people tell us something in face-to-face communication, we are often quick to "consider the source" to evaluate the message. Media-literate consumers do the same in evaluate media messages.

# Article 24

Break Up This Band!

How government protects big media—and shuts out upstarts like me.

TED TURNER

In the late 1960s, when Turner Communications was a business of billboards and radio stations and I was spending much of my energy ocean racing, a UHF-TV station came up for sale in Atlanta. It was losing $50,000 a month and its programs were viewed by fewer than 5 percent of the market.

I acquired it.

When I moved to buy a second station in Charlotte—this one worse than the first—my accountant quit in protest, and the company's board vetoed the deal. So I mortgaged my house and bought it myself. The Atlanta purchase turned into the Superstation; the Charlotte purchase—when I sold it 10 years later—gave me the capital to launch CNN.

Both purchases played a role in revolutionizing television. Both required a streak of independence and a taste for risk. And neither could happen today. In the current climate of consolidation, independent broadcasters simply don't survive for long. That's why we haven't seen a new generation of people like me or even Rupert Murdoch—independent television upstarts who challenge the big boys and force the whole industry to compete and change.

It's not that there aren't entrepreneurs eager to make their names and fortunes in broadcasting if given the chance. If nothing else, the 1990s dot-com boom showed that the spirit of entrepreneurship is alive and well in America, with plenty of investors willing to put real money into new media ventures. The difference is that Washington has changed the rules of the game. When I was getting into the television business, lawmakers and the Federal Communications Commission (FCC) took seriously the commission's mandate to promote diversity, localism, and competition in the media marketplace. They wanted to make sure that the big, established networks—CBS, ABC, NBC—wouldn't forever dominate what the American public could watch on TV. They wanted independent producers to thrive. They wanted more people to be able to own TV stations. They believed in the value of competition.

So when the FCC received a glut of applications for new television stations after World War II, the agency set aside dozens of channels on the new UHF spectrum so independents could get a foothold in television. That helped me get my start 35 years ago. Congress also passed a law in 1962 requiring that TVs be equipped to receive both UHF and VHF channels. That's how I was able to compete as a UHF station, although it was never easy. (I used to tell potential advertisers that our UHF viewers were smarter than the rest, because you had to be a genius just to figure out how to tune us in.) And in 1972, the FCC ruled that cable TV operators could import distant signals. That's how we were able to beam our Atlanta station to homes throughout the South. Five years later, with the help of an RCA satellite, we were sending our signal across the nation, and the Superstation was born. That was then. Today, media companies are more concentrated than at any time over the past 40 years, thanks to a continual loosening of ownership rules by Washington. The media giants now own not only broadcast networks and local stations; they also own the cable companies that pipe in the signals of their competitors and the studios that produce most of the programming. To get a flavor of how consolidated the industry has become, consider this: In 1990, the major broadcast networks—ABC, CBS, NBC, and Fox—fully or partially owned just 12.5 percent of the new series they aired. By 2000, it was 56.3 percent. Just two years later, it had surged to 77.5 percent.

In this environment, most independent media firms either get gobbled up by one of the big companies or driven out of business altogether. Yet instead of balancing the rules to give independent broadcasters a fair chance in the market, Washington continues to tilt the playing field to favor the biggest players. Last summer, the FCC passed another round of sweeping pro-consolidation rules that, among other things, further raised the cap on the number of TV stations a company can own.

In the media, as in any industry, big corporations play a vital role, but so do small, emerging ones. When you lose small businesses, you lose big ideas. People who own their own businesses are their own bosses. They are independent thinkers. They know they can't compete by imitating the big guys—they have to innovate, so they're less obsessed with earnings than they are with ideas. They are quicker to seize on new technologies and new product ideas. They steal market share from the big companies, spurring them to adopt new approaches. This process promotes competition, which leads to higher product and service quality, more jobs, and greater wealth. It's called capitalism.

But without the proper rules, healthy capitalist markets turn into sluggish oligopolies, and that is what's happening in media today. Large corporations are more profit-focused and risk-averse. They often kill local programming because it's expensive, and they push national programming because it's cheap—even if their decisions run counter to local interests and community values. Their managers are more averse to innovation because they're afraid of being fired for an idea that fails. They prefer to sit on the sidelines, waiting to buy the businesses of the risk-takers who succeed.

Unless we have a climate that will allow more independent media companies to survive, a dangerously high percentage of what we see—and what we don't see—will be shaped by the profit motives and political interests of large, publicly traded conglomerates. The economy will suffer, and so will the quality of our public life.

Let me be clear: As a business proposition, consolidation makes sense. The moguls behind the mergers are acting in their corporate interests and playing by the rules. We just shouldn't have those rules. They make sense for a corporation. But for a society, it's like over-fishing the oceans. When the independent businesses are gone, where will the new ideas come from? We have to do more than keep media giants from growing larger; they're already too big. We need a new set of rules that will break these huge companies to pieces.

The Big Squeeze

In the 1970s, I became convinced that a 24-hour all-news network could make money, and perhaps even change the world. But when I invited two large media corporations to invest in the launch of CNN, they turned me down. I couldn't believe it. Together we could have launched the network for a fraction of what it would have taken me alone; they had all the infrastructure, contacts, experience, knowledge. When no one would go in with me, I risked my personal wealth to start CNN.

Soon after our launch in 1980, our expenses were twice what we had expected and revenues half what we had projected. Our losses were so high that our loans were called in. I refinanced at 18 percent interest, up from 9, and stayed just a step ahead of the bankers. Eventually, we not only became profitable, but also changed the nature of news—from watching something that happened to watching it as it happened.

But even as CNN was getting its start, the climate for independent broadcasting was turning hostile. This trend began in 1984, when the FCC raised the number of stations a single entity could own from seven—where it had been capped since the 1950s—to 12. A year later, it revised its rule again, adding a national audience-reach cap of 25 percent to the 12 station limit—meaning media companies were prohibited from owning TV stations that together reached more than 25 percent of the national audience. In 1996, the FCC did away with numerical caps altogether and raised the audience-reach cap to 35 percent. This wasn't necessarily bad for Turner Broadcasting; we had already achieved scale. But seeing these rules changed was like watching someone knock down the ladder I had already climbed.

Without the proper rules, healthy capitalist markets turn into sluggish oligopolies, and that is what's happening in media today. When the independent businesses are gone, where will the new ideas come from?

Meanwhile, the forces of consolidation focused their attention on another rule, one that restricted ownership of content. Throughout the 1980s, network lobbyists worked to overturn the so-called Financial Interest and Syndication Rules, or fin-syn, which had been put in place in 1970, after federal officials became alarmed at the networks' growing control over programming. As the FCC wrote in the fin-syn decision: "The power to determine form and content rests only in the three networks and is exercised extensively and exclusively by them, hourly and daily." In 1957, the commission pointed out, independent companies had produced a third of all net work shows; by 1968, that number had dropped to 4 percent. The rules essentially forbade networks from profiting from reselling programs that they had already aired.

This had the result of forcing networks to sell off their syndication arms, as CBS did with Viacom in 1973. Once networks no longer produced their own content, new competition was launched, creating fresh opportunities for independents.

For a time, Hollywood and its production studios were politically strong enough to keep the fin-syn rules in place. But by the early 1990s, the networks began arguing that their dominance had been undercut by the rise of independent broadcasters, cable networks, and even videocassettes, which they claimed gave viewers enough choice to make fin-syn unnecessary. The FCC ultimately agreed—and suddenly the broadcast networks could tell independent production studios, "We won't air it unless we own it." The networks then bought up the weakened studios or were bought out by their own syndication arms, the way Viacom turned the tables on CBS, buying the network in 2000. This silenced the major political opponents of consolidation.

Even before the repeal of fin-syn, I could see that the trend toward consolidation spelled trouble for independents like me. In a climate of consolidation, there would be only one sure way to win: bring a broadcast network, production studios, and cable and satellite systems under one roof. If you didn't have it inside, you'd have to get it outside—and that meant, increasingly, from a large corporation that was competing with you. It's difficult to survive when your suppliers are owned by your competitors. I had tried and failed to buy a major broadcast network, but the repeal of fin-syn turned up the pressure. Since I couldn't buy a network, I bought MGM to bring more content in-house, and I kept looking for other ways to gain scale. In the end, I found the only way to stay competitive was to merge with Time Warner and relinquish control of my companies.

Today, the only way for media companies to survive is to own everything up and down the media chain—from broadcast and cable networks to the sitcoms, movies, and news broadcasts you see on those stations; to the production studios that make them; to the cable, satellite, and broadcast systems that bring the programs to your television set; to the Web sites you visit to read about those programs; to the way you log on to the Internet to view those pages. Big media today wants to own the faucet, pipeline, water, and the reservoir. The rain clouds come next.

Supersizing Networks

Throughout the 1990s, media mergers were celebrated in the press and otherwise seemingly ignored by the American public. So, it was easy to assume that media consolidation was neither controversial nor problematic. But then a funny thing happened.

In the summer of 2003, the FCC raised the national audience-reach cap from 35 percent to 45 percent. The FCC also allowed corporations to own a newspaper and a TV station in the same market and permitted corporations to own three TV stations in the largest markets, up from two, and two stations in medium-sized markets, up from one. Unexpectedly, the public rebelled. Hundreds of thousands of citizens complained to the FCC. Groups from the National Organization for Women to the National Rifle Association demanded that Congress reverse the ruling. And likeminded lawmakers, including many long-time opponents of media consolidation, took action, pushing the cap back down to 35, until—under strong White House pressure—it was revised back up to 39 percent. This June, the U.S. Court of Appeals for the Third Circuit threw out the rules that would have allowed corporations to own more television and radio stations in a single market, let stand the higher 39 percent cap, and also upheld the rule permitting a corporation to own a TV station and a newspaper in the same market; then, it sent the issues back to the same FCC that had pushed through the pro-consolidation rules in the first place.

In reaching its 2003 decision, the FCC did not argue that its policies would advance its core objectives of diversity, competition, and localism. Instead, it justified its decision by saying that there was already a lot of diversity, competition, and localism in the media—so it wouldn't hurt if the rules were changed to allow more consolidation.

Their decision reads: "Our current rules inadequately account for the competitive presence of cable, ignore the diversity-enhancing value of the Internet, and lack any sound bases for a national audience-reach cap." Let's pick that assertion apart.

We have to do more than keep media giants from growing larger—they're already too big. We need a new set of rules that will break these huge companies to pieces.

First, the "competitive presence of cable" is a mirage. Broadcast networks have for years pointed to their loss of prime-time viewers to cable networks—but they are losing viewers to cable networks that they themselves own. Ninety percent of the top 50 cable TV stations are owned by the same parent companies that own the broadcast networks. Yes, Disney's ABC network has lost viewers to cable networks. But it's losing viewers to cable networks like Disney's ESPN, Disney's ESPN2, and Disney's Disney Channel. The media giants are getting a deal from Congress and the FCC because their broadcast networks are losing share to their own cable networks. It's a scam.

Second, the decision cites the "diversity-enhancing value of the Internet." The FCC is confusing diversity with variety. The top 20 Internet news sites are owned by the same media conglomerates that control the broadcast and cable networks. Sure, a hundred-person choir gives you a choice of voices, but they're all singing the same song.

The FCC says that we have more media choices than ever before. But only a few corporations decide what we can choose. That is not choice. That's like a dictator deciding what candidates are allowed to stand for parliamentary elections, and then claiming that the people choose their leaders. Different voices do not mean different viewpoints, and these huge corporations all have the same viewpoint—they want to shape government policy in a way that helps them maximize profits, drive out competition, and keep getting bigger.

Because the new technologies have not fundamentally changed the market, it's wrong for the FCC to say that there are no "sound bases for a national audience-reach cap." The rationale for such a cap is the same as it has always been. If there is a limit to the number of TV stations a corporation can own, then the chance exists that after all the corporations have reached this limit, there may still be some stations left over to be bought and run by independents. A lower limit would encourage the entry of independents and promote competition. A higher limit does the opposite.

Triple Blight

The loss of independent operators hurts both the media business and its citizen-customers. When the ownership of these firms passes to people under pressure to show quick financial results in order to justify the purchase, the corporate emphasis instantly shifts from taking risks to taking profits. When that happens, quality suffers, localism suffers, and democracy itself suffers.

Loss of Quality

The Forbes list of the 400 richest Americans exerts a negative influence on society, because it discourages people who want to climb up the list from giving more money to charity. The Nielsen ratings are dangerous in a similar way—because they scare companies away from good shows that don't produce immediate blockbuster ratings. The producer Norman Lear once asked, "You know what ruined television?" His answer: when *The New York Times* began publishing the Nielsen ratings. "That list every week became all anyone cared about."

When all companies are quarterly earnings-obsessed, the market starts punishing companies that aren't yielding an instant return. This not only creates a big incentive for bogus accounting, but also it inhibits the kind of investment that builds economic value. America used to know this. We used to be a nation of farmers. You can't plant something today and harvest tomorrow. Had Turner Communications been required to show earnings growth every quarter, we never would have purchased those first two TV stations.

When CNN reported to me, if we needed more money for Kosovo or Baghdad, we'd find it. If we had to bust the budget, we busted the budget. We put journalism first, and that's how we built CNN into something the world wanted to watch. I had the power to make these budget decisions because they were my companies. I was an independent entrepreneur who controlled the majority of the votes and could run my company for the long term. Top managers in these huge media conglomerates run their companies for the short term. After we sold Turner Broadcasting to Time Warner, we came under such earnings pressure that we had to cut our promotion budget every year at CNN to make our numbers. Media mega-mergers inevitably lead to an overemphasis on short-term earnings.

You can see this overemphasis in the spread of reality television. Shows like "Fear Factor" cost little to produce—there are no actors to pay and no sets to maintain—and they get big ratings. Thus, American television has moved away from expensive sitcoms and on to cheap thrills. We've gone from "Father Knows Best" to "Who Wants to Marry My Dad?", and from "My Three Sons" to "My Big Fat Obnoxious Fiance."

The story of Grant Tinker and Mary Tyler Moore's production studio, MTM, helps illustrate the point. When the company was founded in 1969, Tinker and Moore hired the best writers they could find and then left them alone—and were rewarded with some of the best shows of the 1970s. But eventually, MTM was bought by a company that imposed budget ceilings and laid off employees. That company was later purchased by Rev. Pat Robertson; then, he was bought out by Fox. Exit "The Mary Tyler Moore Show." Enter "The Littlest Groom."

Loss of Localism

Consolidation has also meant a decline in the local focus of both news and programming. After analyzing 23,000 stories on 172 news programs over five years, the Project for Excellence in Journalism found that big media news organizations relied more on syndicated feeds and were more likely to air national stories with no local connection.

That's not surprising. Local coverage is expensive, and thus will tend be a casualty in the quest for short-term earnings. In 2002, Fox Television bought Chicago's Channel 50 and eliminated all of the station's locally produced shows. One of the cancelled programs (which targeted pre-teens) had scored a perfect rating for educational content in a 1999 University of Pennsylvania study, according to *The Chicago Tribune*. That accolade wasn't enough to save the program. Once the station's ownership changed, so did its mission and programming.

Loss of localism also undercuts the public-service mission of the media, and this can have dangerous consequences. In early 2002, when a freight train derailed near Minot, N.D., releasing a cloud of anhydrous ammonia over the town, police tried to call local radio stations, six of which are owned by radio mammoth Clear Channel Communications. According to news reports, it took them over an hour to reach anyone—no one was answering the Clear Channel phone. By the next day, 300 people had been hospitalized, many partially blinded by the ammonia. Pets and livestock died. And Clear Channel continued beaming its signal from headquarters in San Antonio, Texas—some 1,600 miles away.

Loss of Democratic Debate

When media companies dominate their markets, it undercuts our democracy. Justice Hugo Black, in a landmark media-ownership case in 1945, wrote: "The First Amendment rests on the assumption that the widest possible dissemination of information from diverse and antagonistic sources is essential to the welfare of the public."

These big companies are not antagonistic; they do billions of dollars in business with each other. They don't compete; they cooperate to inhibit competition. You and I have both felt the impact. I felt it in 1981, when CBS, NBC, and ABC all came together to try to keep CNN from covering the White House. You've felt the impact over the past two years, as you saw little news from ABC, CBS, NBC, MSNBC, Fox, or CNN on the FCC's actions. In early 2003, the Pew Research Center found that 72 percent of Americans had heard "nothing at all" about the proposed FCC rule changes. Why? One never knows for sure, but it must have been clear to news directors that the more they covered this issue, the harder it would be for their corporate bosses to get the policy result they wanted.

A few media conglomerates now exercise a near-monopoly over television news. There is always a risk that news organizations can emphasize or ignore stories to serve their corporate purpose. But the risk is far greater when there are no independent competitors to air the side of the story the corporation wants to ignore.

More consolidation has often meant more news-sharing. But closing bureaus and downsizing staff have more than economic consequences. A smaller press is less capable of holding our leaders accountable. When Viacom merged two news stations it owned in Los Angeles, reports *The American Journalism Review*, "field reporters began carrying microphones labeled KCBS on one side and KCAL on the other." This was no accident. As the Viacom executive in charge told *The Los Angeles Business Journal*: "In this duopoly, we should be able to control the news in the marketplace."

This ability to control the news is especially worrisome when a large media organization is itself the subject of a news story. Disney's boss, after buying ABC in 1995, was quoted in *LA Weekly* as saying, "I would prefer ABC not cover Disney." A few days later, ABC killed a "20/20" story critical of the parent company.

But networks have also been compromised when it comes to non-news programs which involve their corporate parent's business interests. General Electric subsidiary NBC Sports raised eyebrows by apologizing to the Chinese government for Bob Costas's reference to Chinas "problems with human rights" during a telecast of the Atlanta Olympic Games. China, of course, is a huge market for GE products.

Consolidation has given big media companies new Power over what is said not just on the air, but off it as well. Cumulus Media banned the Dixie Chicks on its 42 country music stations for 30 days after lead singer Natalie Maines criticized President Bush for the war in Iraq. It's hard to imagine Cumulus would have been so bold if its listeners had more of a choice in country music stations. And Disney recently provoked an uproar when it prevented its subsidiary Miramax from distributing Michael Moore's film *Fahrenheit 9/11*. As a senior Disney executive told *The New York Times*: "It's not in the interest of any major corporation to be dragged into a highly charged partisan political battle." Follow the logic, and you can see what lies ahead: If the only media companies are major corporations, controversial and dissenting views may not be aired at all.

Naturally, corporations say they would never suppress speech. But it's not their intentions that matter; it's their capabilities. Consolidation gives them more power to tilt the news and cut important ideas out of the public debate. And it's precisely that power that the rules should prevent.

Independents' Day

This is a fight about freedom—the freedom of independent entrepreneurs to start and run a media business, and the freedom of citizens to get news, information, and entertainment from a wide variety of sources, at least some of which are truly independent and not run by people facing the pressure of quarterly earnings reports.

No one should underestimate the danger. Big media companies want to eliminate all ownership limits. With the removal of these limits, immense media power will pass into the hands of a very few corporations and individuals.

What will programming be like when it's produced for no other purpose than profit? What will news be like when there are no independent news organizations to go after stories the big corporations avoid? Who really wants to find out?

Safeguarding the welfare of the public cannot be the first concern of a large publicly traded media company. Its job is to seek profits. But if the government writes the rules in a way that encourages the entry into the market of entrepreneurs—men and women with big dreams, new ideas, and a willingness to take long-term risks the economy will be stronger, and the country will be better off.

I freely admit: When I was in the media business, especially after the federal government changed the rules to favor large companies, I tried to sweep the board, and I came within one move of owning every link up and down the media chain. Yet I felt then, as I do now, that the government was not doing its job. The role of the government ought to be like the role of a referee in boxing, keeping the big guys from killing the little guys. If the little guy gets knocked down, the referee should send the big guy to his corner, count the little guy out, and then help him back up. But today the government has cast down its duty, and media competition is less like boxing and more like professional wrestling: The wrestler and the referee are both kicking the guy on the canvas.

At this late stage, media companies have grown so large and powerful, and their dominance has become so detrimental to the survival of small, emerging companies, that there remains only one alternative: bust up the big conglomerates. We've done this before: to the railroad trusts in the first part of the 20th century, to Ma Bell more recently. Indeed, big media itself was cut down to size in the 1970s, and a period of staggering innovation and growth followed. Breaking up the reconstituted media conglomerates may seem like an impossible task when their grip on the policy-making process in Washington seems so sure. But the public's broad and bipartisan rebellion against the FCC's pro-consolidation decisions suggests something different. Politically, big media may again be on the wrong side of history—and up against a country unwilling to lose its independents.

TED TURNER is founder of CNN and chairman of Turner Enterprises.

From *Washington Monthly*, July/August 2004, pp. 30–36. Copyright © 2004 by Washington Monthly. Reprinted by permission.

Article 25

Into the Great Wide Open

New technology could radically transform broadcasting. The dreamers and players are already debating how far to go.

JESSE SUNENBLICK

In 1940, the Austrian-born actress Hedy Lamarr, considered by some the most beautiful woman in Hollywood, approached her neighbor there, the avant-garde composer George Antheil, and asked him a question about glands. Antheil, known for his propulsive film scores for multiple player pianos, had broad interests: in addition to his music he wrote a syndicated advice-to-the-lovelorn column and had even published a medical book, *Every Man His Own Detective: A Study of Glandular Endocrinology*. As the story goes, Lamarr—whose acting exploits (which include the first big-screen nude scene) and marriages (there were six husbands, most notably Fritz Mandl, an Austrian arms dealer with ties to Hitler and Mussolini) are too varied to discuss here except to say that she was a woman far ahead of her time—wanted to know how she might enlarge her breasts. Somehow, though, they ended up talking about radio-controlled torpedoes, and the future of communications was changed.

After years of living with Mandl, Lamarr was familiar with the problem of sending control signals to a torpedo after it was launched from a ship, especially radio signals, which the enemy could easily detect and jam. She had a notion of a radio transmission that, by changing its frequency many times a second, could allow an observation plane to covertly guide a torpedo over long distances. Combining Lamarr's knowledge of radio control with the model Antheil had used to coordinate sixteen pianos in his *Ballet Mécanique*, the pair invented the idea of "frequency hopping," and obtained a patent for a Secret Communications System. This was the first example of a single radio transmission using multiple frequencies across the radio spectrum—the range of electromagnetic frequencies that are useful for sending broadcast signals—without bumping into other transmissions and causing interference. Sixty-plus years later, frequency-hopping has evolved into a technology, called "spread spectrum," that proponents claim could put an end to most forms of radio interference, presaging a time when the airwaves (TV signals travel over the same spectrum), one of our most heavily regulated resources, could be opened up.

The technological reason that we have given in the past for why a system of licensing is constitutional no longer exists.

The implications of this idea are far-reaching for human communication, including journalism. If there is no longer a reason to tightly regulate the broadcast spectrum, then just about anyone would be allowed to broadcast. As technology continues its march toward miniaturization and higher speeds, we might soon have devices that fit in our pockets capable of sending voice, video, and other data over long distances. And if we could use such devices without causing interference, then today's bloggers, for example, confined by laptops, short-range wireless connections, and slow video feeds, could be tomorrow's roving band of telejournalists. Imagine lone-wolf Christiane Amanpours showing up on site, unencumbered by the demands and the strictures of our modern media monopolies, beaming reports live to whoever might care to watch; not just on television, but on a computer, on a cell phone, on the dashboard of a car.

As in the earliest days, broadcast pioneers are once again talking and dreaming about broadcast's potential to connect all corners of the earth. Of course, in the world of broadcasting what is possible is often undone by what is profitable—or politically expedient. The advent of spread spectrum has spawned a subterranean debate about how to manage the radio spectrum that has broadcasters arguing with technologists, economists arguing with media critics, and everybody arguing with the FCC about a radio revolution.

When you connect to the Internet at Starbucks, when you talk on your cell phone, or when you use many of the other radio technologies that constitute our current wireless craze, you are using spread spectrum. Spread spectrum works by contradicting the traditional rules of radio communication, in which a single signal is sent over a single frequency in the electromagnetic spectrum for which it has a license from the FCC. With spread spectrum, a transmission is disassembled and sent out over a variety of frequencies, without causing interference to whatever else might be operating within those frequencies, and is reassembled on the other end by a "smart" receiver. Licenses aren't necessary for spread-spectrum transmissions, but the devices currently aren't allowed to operate at more than a few watts of power. And since the early 1990s, when they were first available for use by consumers, they have been relegated to that portion of the radio spectrum known as the "junk band"—the uppermost usable frequencies that are home to gadgets like cordless phones, microwave ovens, and baby monitors, and which, because of shorter wavelengths, have trouble cutting through bad weather and obstacles like trees and buildings.

The FCC has issued licenses for frequencies since it was established in 1927, and the impetus to do so was an outgrowth of a decade of ethereal chaos in the 1920s, when the airwaves were overloaded with so many new broadcasters on so few available frequencies that it was impossible in many urban areas to receive a steady signal. Media critics like to point out how this licensing system has contributed to an oligarchy of the air, in which the Viacoms and Clear Channels of the world control access to most radio communication. But by 1990 it had contributed to something else: a dearth of available frequencies left to license. The spectrum, like an oil reserve, was nearly depleted.

Spread spectrum offers a far more efficient way of using the radio spectrum, and throughout the 1990s the FCC opened up license-free slivers for devices that employ spread-spectrum technology—first for gadgets like garage door openers and home alarm systems, and later for Wi-Fi, which has blossomed into a multibillion-dollar industry. Wi-Fi not only allows city dwellers to hook up to the Internet at Starbucks, but is pushing the Internet into rural locales not served by cable or DSL, and making possible public-safety networks for police and fire departments.

Now the FCC is considering a series of rule changes that would open up much more of the spectrum for unlicensed radio. The timetable on any commission decision on such rule changes is fluid, and depends, in part, on who replaces Michael Powell, a strong proponent of unlicensed radio technology, as FCC chairman. The most significant of the rule changes would allow unlicensed radio to operate with more power, over longer distances, and in portions of the spectrum currently occupied by heavyweight incumbents such as the television networks; they would also clear the path for the manufacture of smart radios, which can transmit selectively through little-trafficked frequencies, essentially dodging interference. The big broadcasters are engaged in a rigorous lobbying effort to discredit the science of spread spectrum, which they believe could undercut their competitive edge by allowing thousands of individuals to establish their own television or radio programming, or offer wireless Internet service on the cheap. To public-interest groups, however, the advent of unlicensed radio represents an opportunity for greater citizen access to the airwaves, and the possibility of a network of community radio or TV stations in every town in America.

"The rule changes represent the most important communications decision the FCC will face in the next ten years," says Harold Feld, associate director of the Media Access Project, a nonprofit, public-interest telecommunications law firm that hopes the FCC will expand the role of unlicensed radio. "If the commission can stand up to the most powerful industry lobbies in Washington and create new rules that reflect new technologies, the American people will see nothing short of miracles."

In my conversations with Feld, he kept repeating the phrase "cheap, ubiquitous Internet access"—which, in his opinion, is the crux of the debate—and emphasizing the importance of getting these spread-spectrum devices deployed with sufficient power, and with access to the lower frequency, "beachfront" sections of the radio spectrum dominated by the big broadcasters. That, he says, would create a plethora of journalistic opportunities, for media big and small. In addition to creating a nation of broadcasters, network news companies could bolster their Web offerings with live-action video feeds, using a one-person news crew, from anywhere with a Wi-Fi connection. A Wi-Fi media reader, meanwhile, could replace the bundle of newspapers and magazines that you carry to work or home every day. And ubiquitous mobile Internet connections would mean that reporters, who would have constant access to research tools, could improve the content of their stories. (Of course, someone would have to pay for all these technological goodies.)

Everyone, it seems, has a dog in this fight. Venture capitalists who stand to make a buck off more powerful versions of Wi-Fi. Technologists who want an arena for their futuristic ideas. Media activists who envision an unlimited radio dial with thousands, if not millions of noncommercial stations. Wireless Internet service providers who want to extend their reach. Economists who think that the best way to make use of new radio technology is to privatize the radio spectrum and let the instincts of capitalism take over. And of course lobbyists for powerful incumbents who want to preserve their exclusive licenses.

Out of this fray has come a distinctive vision of the spectrum as a public commons, in which an unlimited number of users share unlicensed portions of the radio spectrum, and—subject, of course, to power and usage restrictions—do with it what they want. The movement gained steam throughout the 1990s, as advancing spread-spectrum technologies called the FCC's licensing system into question. One of the movement's philosophical pillars is that unlicensed radio technology has the ability to democratize the media, much the same way that the Internet did through blogging, although on a profoundly grander scale. Eben Moglen, a Columbia University law professor and one of open spectrum's biggest supporters, has an idea about how open spectrum might accomplish this.

For the last eleven years, Moglen has served as general counsel (pro bono, of course) to the Free Software Foundation, a group that promotes the creation and distribution of, well, free software. He is also an unabashed Marxist. In his office, I told Moglen I was having trouble understanding how an "open" spectrum would differ from a "closed" spectrum, and could he please offer an analogy from the real world that would bring the otherworldliness of the radio spectrum into context?

He leaned back in his chair and spread his arms out wide, as though everything around us were part of the analogy he was about to give. Which was true. "Take the island of Manhattan," Moglen said. "The level of anonymity in Manhattan is subject to social regulation, like the radio spectrum is subject to political regulation. And it's variable: sometimes you go places where you have to identify yourself, sometimes not. And as the city imposes restrictions on movement, zoning, and behavior, the federal government places restrictions upon the radio spectrum.

"However," he went on, "the difference is in the number of restrictions. The essence of life in Manhattan is openness. It's all free, it's all here, you can get to it. You can walk from the West Side to the East Side, from Harlem to Chinatown. Or take a cab. But what would Manhattan look like if its social policies were on par with the current government policies concerning use of the radio spectrum? It would be unendurable. You'd have David Rockefeller owning Rockefeller Center. Rupert Murdoch would have a dominant say in everything that happens between the Battery and 23rd Street. Worse, you'd be sitting in Starbucks, having a conversation, and somebody would say, 'You, stop talking! You, talk about the weather!' You're allowed to have person-to-person conversations, but for the privilege of doing so in my neighborhood you have to pay six dollars a minute. And, because there's nothing resembling a Central Park on the radio spectrum, if you want to gather people and talk about the war in Iraq, tough luck! We need a Central Park for radio!"

Powell's Digital Migration would empower individuals, rather than institutions, to become central in the creation and dissemination of ideas.

If the government tried to license newspapers, Moglen says, the courts would block it on the ground that it violated the First Amendment. "The technological reason that we have given in the past for why a system of licensing—one that would be completely unconstitutional with respect to print—is constitutional in the spectrum, no longer exists! And when the broadcasting licensing system falls, as it inevitably must, American society will be transformed. Mr. Murdoch, Mr. Eisner, Mr. Gates—Will. Be. Poorer. We. Will. Be. Richer. And there will again be news in this society, which at the moment, there almost isn't."

Many media critics accuse the FCC, under Chairman Powell, of perpetuating communications policies that favor forces of media consolidation and the status quo. Yet interestingly, in the case of unlicensed wireless communication, Powell has been on the other side of the barricades from big media. To Powell, Wi-Fi is the prototype for the role that unlicensed radio will play in the future, an example of what he has described, in various speeches, as "the great Digital Migration," or "The Age of Personal Communications"—optimistic assessments of what he sees as a new information paradigm that lies just over the horizon. In terms of convenience, at least, we are certainly on the cusp of profound changes: we will soon talk over the Internet the way we talk today over telephones, but for less money, because Internet voice is a computer application, not a government-regulated telecom, and because providers don't need to build a multibillion-dollar infrastructure to offer it. This is likely to give rise to an Internet of Things, a state of über-connectivity. "The visionary sermons of technology futurists seem to have materialized," Powell said in a January 2004 speech at the National Press Club in Washington, an assessment of the transition from the world of analog to digital. "No longer the stuff of science fiction novels, crystal balls, and academic conferences, it is real. Technology is bringing more power to the people."

But a running theme in Powell's Washington speech is that the Digital Migration means far more to Americans than convenience—that the ubiquity of the Internet, combined with the miniaturization and higher power of radio technology, will empower individuals, rather than large institutions, to become central in the creation and dissemination of ideas. "Governments are almost always about geography, jurisdiction, and centralized control," Powell said in his Washington speech. "The Internet is unhindered by geography, dismissive of jurisdiction, and decentralizes control." The implication here is that technology, if given the chance, will level the playing field. Toward the end of his Washington speech the chairman laid out a multipronged strategy for accomplishing the "migration," much of it dependent on reforming the radio spectrum to allow the next generation of unlicensed radio to operate with more power and bandwidth—so that a wireless Internet network that can now reach a distance of 200 feet, for example, might some day spread across 200 miles, or perhaps the entire planet. Whoever gets Powell's job is unlikely to share his passion for unlicensed radio, but the debate isn't going away.

Dave Hughes, a retired Army colonel from Colorado Springs, knows better than most what a network like the one Powell described might look like. It was Hughes who told me the story of Hedy Lamarr, because it was Hughes who had resurrected her name from the dustbin of technological afterthoughts when he nominated her for an achievement award (which she ultimately won) from the Electronic Frontier Foundation, a watchdog for digital civil liberties, in 1997, when Lamarr, who died in 2000, was old and forgotten and living in Florida. ("It's about time," Lamarr is rumored to have said upon hearing of the award.) Colonel Hughes has been a lot of things in life—a hero of the wars in Korea and Vietnam, a professor of English at West Point, an inventor of America's first online computer bulletin board, and a pioneer of rural computer networking—but what he is most is a vociferous advocate of radio, and in particular of spread spectrum.

"My humble goal," Hughes likes to say, "is to see all six billion minds on the planet connected in all the ways our brains and ears and mouths and eyes can communicate. At least when you can communicate, you can reduce the areas of disagreement to real substance."

In 1991, Hughes bought two of the earliest spread-spectrum radios to hit the marketplace, units that produced a single watt of power. He connected them between his Internet-equipped office building and an early IBM version of a Web site on his home computer. The wireless link of that connection between the two radios cost him nothing; had U.S. West provided the connection, it would have cost $600 a month. Hughes thought: if it works between buildings, why not rural towns? In the mountains of southwest Colorado, Hughes perched a pair of spread-spectrum radios in such a way that a school district in the town of San Luis was connected wirelessly to an early version of the Internet, for a one-time cost of $3,000, as opposed to the $2,000 a month that U.S. West was asking at the time to run a forty-mile cable to Alamosa, where the closest Internet provider was. Then he thought, if we can connect towns here, why not in the most remote places on earth? He went to Mongolia with spread-spectrum radios, and now Ulan Bator is the Third World's most wirelessly connected city.

In 2003, Hughes used three Wi-Fi radios in his most ambitious project yet: constructing the world's highest Internet café at the base camp of Mount Everest. From his home in Colorado, Hughes collaborated with Tsering Gyaltsen, the grandson of the only surviving Sherpa to have accompanied Sir Edmund Hillary on his first ascent of the mountain, and designed a network in which Wi-Fi radios in the Café Tent beneath the Khumbu Ice Fall are linked to a satellite dish 1,500 feet away that sends data, via satellite, to an Internet service provider in Israel. Then, last year, Hughes helped another Nepalese entrepreneur add computers and a wireless link to his cybercafé in the Namche Bazaar, the trading center of the Everest region. He used three antenna relays (one hanging off the side of a monastery at 14,000 feet) to extend the network to a school in the nearby town of Thame, where ten Sherpa children are now taking English and computer classes over the Internet from a Nepalese-born, English-speaking Sherpa computer programmer who lives in Pittsburgh.

The computers the Nepalese children use rely on a free software program called Free World Dial Up, which allows them to speak to their teacher over computers, for a flat rate, the way most people do over telephones. To Hughes, when Nepalese children are talking to their teacher in Pittsburgh and handing in their lessons by computer, giving them, as he says, "half a fighting chance to succeed in this world," that represents more than a demonstration of the possibilities of technology. It is a paradigm shift, a revolution. "You have to understand the disruptive nature of this technology," he often says. "Who's getting robbed? Because of the technology, it's AT&T that's getting robbed. The technology is way out in front of the regulatory, legal, and economic communications systems of this country. There's going to be titanic battles. But ask yourself, What happens to the incumbents? Well, what happened to the horse and buggy? What happened to the printing press?" Of course, the revolution Hughes envisions can always be interrupted by the real world. On February 1, Nepal's King Gyanendra dissolved the government and shut down all telephone and Internet connections in the country. A Wi-Fi network—even a global one—could not stop a power grab in Nepal.

It is easy to be nostalgic for the earliest days of radio, when, before a licensing regime was put in place, tens of thousands of amateur operators shared the still-mysterious airwaves in a raw, often free-form haze of chatter, music, and news, much like the Internet today. There was something supernatural about radio then, and one line of thinking saw the medium as a force of social connectivity. An article from *Collier's Magazine* in 1922 entitled, "Radio Dreams That Can Come True," talks about radio "spreading mutual understanding to all the sections of the country, unifying our thoughts, ideas and purposes, making us a strong and well-knit people." There is an obvious utopian quality to such declarations, common in all periods of significant technological change. While one could certainly argue that first radio, and then television, did achieve the task of uniting us, it did not happen in a way that the Collier's writer could have imagined, and it did not happen in a way that had all that much to do with making us strong and well-knit.

By the mid-1920s radio was controlled by two national networks—NBC and CBS—and the coming years would witness the invention of advertising and the fine-tuning of capitalism on the radio dial. Does the same fate await spread spectrum and smart radios? In the mainstream press, techno-enthusiast feature stories appear regularly, touting the cutting edge of unlicensed wireless communications like Wi-Max, which is essentially a pumped-up version of Wi-Fi, with a networking reach of thirty miles; Zigbee, a tiny wireless sensor that can be placed on crops to track heat, moisture, and nutrients in the soil; and Ultrawideband, an emerging technology that can move huge amounts of data over short distances. The attendant prophecies sound transformative. "These technologies will usher in a new era for the wireless Web," *Business Week* declared last April. "They'll work with each other and with traditional telephone networks to let people and machines communicate like never before." Lost in such assumptions is a legitimate chance that even if unlicensed devices like smart radios become available to the public, regulators would compromise the potential of such equipment by, for example, imposing strict power limitations to avoid even the slightest chance of interference.

And then there are the economic realities. One of the groups fighting the hardest to open up the radio spectrum to unlicensed radios is the New America Foundation, a public-policy think tank in Washington. On its Web site, New America offers a mini-treatise on solutions to our current spectrum woes, and comes across as a voice of the people, advocating, among other things, "greater shared citizen access to the airwaves." Yet unlike many supporters of unlicensed radio, New America's vision contains a seed of economic prudence. Jim Snider, a research fellow there who specializes in spectrum issues, was quick to point out not only the "open" and "unmediated" nature of unlicensed radio, but also the rising tide of interest from the venture capital community, which over the last two years has produced over twenty well-financed startups and a variety of new products.

Snider advised me to visit the offices of Shared Spectrum Company, a venture capital firm in Virginia that builds prototype frequency-agile radio transmitters (which hop from channel to channel across wide swaths of the radio spectrum, looking for quiet places to transmit), and whose efforts New

America endorses. And so, on a stultifying day in late July, I took a ride on the Metro out to Tyson's Corner, Virginia, the East Coast's consummate "edge city"—those hybrid constellations of retail, office, and residential developments near highway interchanges and an older, central city, that are paragons of the new economy.

Shared Spectrum rented an office on the second floor of a building with tinted windows, across the hall from a travel agency called Vacation Station. When I arrived, its founder, Mark McHenry, accompanied by his lawyer, suggested we go to the roof so that he could show me what a vast, empty wasteland the supposedly crowded spectrum really is. On the roof, a young employee had set up an antenna and an expensive machine called a spectrum analyzer, a boxy device that sweeps through every radio frequency and displays, on a screen, how much signal strength, which McHenry referred to as "energy," is operating at each frequency. The four of us got down on hands and knees to watch the machine work. Zipping through swaths of spectrum, it immediately made clear why McHenry had such confidence in smart radios, and why the prospect of building them had enticed him to leave a cushy job as a program manager at the Defense Advanced Research Projects Agency, or DARPA, the furtive technology arm of the Pentagon widely credited with having invented the Internet.

We zoomed in on the aviation band, where there was little activity. Then the TV band, where there were gaps all over the place. The military band, eerily dead. "There's basically nothing here," McHenry said. He beamed. "Once you accept the idea of frequency-agile radios, anything becomes possible."

Back inside, I asked if he (like Michael Powell, Dave Hughes, and Eben Moglen) thought that smart radios would empower people to become active participants in the creation of knowledge. I had assumed that McHenry, like the folks at the New America Foundation, would see these gadgets as an egalitarian force. But his response—a slight shake of the head and a bewildered look—made me feel silly for asking.

Back in New York, I thought of something McHenry had told me about the U.S. military's plans to use spread-spectrum technology in warfare. I remembered his saying the word "robots," and so I did some research and found what seemed like a good window into the nexus between technology and corporate and military power. DARPA, the outfit McHenry used to work for, is in the process of developing what it calls Next Generation, or XG technology—the mother of all spectrum-sharing protocols—that will enable every unit on the battlefield to communicate by radio, over longer distances, and with more ease of use, than is currently possible. Using smart technology, XG radios will store the spectrum conditions for every country on earth on a microchip, and automatically conform to the conditions of its environment, avoiding the hassle of manually assigning frequencies to military radios during combat. Shared Spectrum is getting paid millions of dollars to help DARPA develop algorithms for XG radios. As I clicked further into the bowels of various military Web sites, I came across another organization, the Artificial Intelligence Center, which has a hand in several Army projects, including TEAMBOTICA—radio-controlled robots that the Army plans to use in reconnaissance and surveillance missions.

As I looked at pictures of the TEAMBOTICA robot on my computer, the words of Mark McHenry echoed in my ears: "Once you accept the idea of frequency-agile radios, anything becomes possible." Indeed. Eben Moglen and Dave Hughes had said essentially the same thing. With the exception of heavyweight spectrum incumbents like the broadcasters, who are unable or unwilling to concede the end of interference, most everyone who talks about unlicensed radio uses the same vocabulary, although to radically different ends. For Moglen it is about democracy. For Hughes it is about connectivity. And for McHenry it is about money. His frequency-agile radios have already entered the military-industrial complex; someday soon, this technology will likely enter the civilian realm and forge a path not unlike the Internet, making a few people very rich, producing devices that we might come to see as indispensable, but that in the end may or may not have much to do with freedom, personal or otherwise.

JESSE SUNENBLICK (jessesunenblick@fastmail.fm) is a Brooklyn-based writer. His last piece for the magazine was "Little Murders: The Death of Dangerous Art," in the January/February 2004 issue.

Reprinted from *Columbia Journalism Review*, March/April 2005, pp. 44–50. Copyright © 2005 by Columbia Journalism Review, Columbia University.

Article 26

Why Journalists Are Not Above the Law

GABRIEL SCHOENFELD

To hear some tell it, the fundamental freedom of the press promised by the First Amendment of the U.S. Constitution is in peril today as perhaps never before. In his four decades representing the media, says Floyd Abrams, one of the country's leading First Amendment lawyers, the work of reporting has "never been as seriously threatened as it is today." Norman Pearlstine, until recently the editor-in-chief of Time Inc., warns that today's situation "chills essential newsgathering and reporting." William Safire, the longtime columnist for the *New York Times,* says "the ability of journalists to gather the news" is "under attack." Nicholas Kristof, also a *Times* columnist, says "we're seeing a broad assault on freedom of the press that would appall us if it were happening in Kazakhstan."

The source of the problem, according to these and other concerned observers, is the American government, in the form of the White House and the Justice Department. Both are threatening to prevent journalists from doing their work by depriving them of the right to rely on confidential sources of information: the lifeblood of the journalistic profession and the prime avenue through which the public learns about impending shifts in policy, about official wrongdoing, and about much else besides.

Overstated or not, such worries reflect continuing reverberations from a number of recent cases. The most prominent involves Judith Miller, a reporter for the *New York Times* who had gathered information about the leak of an undercover CIA officer's name in possible violation of the Intelligence Identities Act. In his effort to uncover the leaker, the government's special counsel, Patrick Fitzgerald, brought Miller before a grand jury in 2005 to answer questions about what she had learned.

Declining to disgorge her confidential sources, and citing her First Amendment rights as a journalist, Miller refused to testify. In July 2005, the judge presiding over the process held her in contempt. She spent the next 85 days in the Alexandria City jail before finally naming her source: I. Lewis "Scooter" Libby, chief of staff to Vice President Dick Cheney.[1]

The spectacle of a reporter from our country's premier newspaper going to prison for almost three months was only the most visible example of the heavy hand of government. Another journalist, a video blogger by the name of Josh Wolf, is currently sitting in a California jail for declining to turn over to a grand jury video clips of an anarchist riot in San Francisco. And there are similar cases elsewhere that have stirred fears among reporters over the increasing legal hazards of their work—not to mention the alarm of those like Floyd Abrams who are convinced that the public's fundamental access to vital news is being impaired by an overreaching officialdom, bent on protecting itself from legitimate scrutiny.

With such apprehensions on the rise, Congress has come under increasing pressure to establish an official reporter's privilege—analogous to the attorney-client, the priest-penitent, and the husband-wife privilege that already exist in law—exempting a journalist from having to disclose his sources in any federal criminal investigation or trial. Today some 31 states have formally created such a "shield law," while everywhere else, with the exception of Wyoming, reporters enjoy a more qualified privilege as a matter of common law. Only the federal system remains without such a statute—a deficit that a coalition of news organizations and First Amendment activists now seeks to rectify in the new Congress.

A number of prominent Republicans, including Senators Arlen Specter and Richard Lugar, have long championed such a law. The new chairman of the Judiciary Committee, Patrick Leahy of Vermont, and a bevy of other Democrats including Charles Schumer of New York and Christopher Dodd of Connecticut, are also firmly behind it. With bipartisan support in place, and with the Democrats now in charge, the prospects for passage of such a bill are better than they have been for a generation.

In its modern form, the issue of a reporter's privilege is exceptionally nettlesome, and has been so ever since the Supreme Court ruling in *Branzburg v. Hayes* (1972). That ruling brought together a number of then-recent cases. Paul Branzburg, a reporter for the Louisville *Courier-Journal,* had witnessed people manufacturing and using illegal narcotics. More or less at the same time, two other journalists, a Massachusetts television reporter and a reporter for the *New York Times,* were also believed to have witnessed behavior that appeared to be illegal. All three were summoned to testify before grand juries. All three, citing the First Amendment, declined to answer questions about their confidential sources. All three were held in contempt.

Presenting the same set of legal issues, the three cases were combined and made their way up to the Supreme Court. Its majority decision, written by Justice Byron White, held that the First Amendment did not offer a privilege for journalists that "other citizens do not enjoy," and the Court emphatically declined to create one.

White's ruling was crystalline in its logic and seemingly absolute in its conclusion. But it did not put an end to controversy. For one thing, nothing in White's ruling barred Congress from establishing a reporter's privilege as an act of law. For another thing, the 5–4 decision of the Court was itself deeply muddied by a concurring opinion, written by Justice Lewis Powell, which even Powell's colleagues called "enigmatic."

While adding his name to White's decision, Powell undercut its central premise by suggesting that courts should operate on a case-by-case basis, the better to strike "a proper balance between freedom of the press and the obligation of all citizens to give relevant testimony with respect to criminal conduct." Leaving unspecified the ground rules for this balancing act, Powell's opinion had the effect of plunging lower courts into confusion. Today, five of the twelve circuits in the federal system have relied on *Branzburg* to compel journalists to provide confidential information; another four, basing themselves on Powell's inscrutable words, have granted journalists a qualified privilege.

This confusion has only added fuel to the latest push for a shield law. But is such a privilege warranted? And is it desirable?

In considering those questions, one might profitably turn to another case now before the courts. This one, too, involves Patrick Fitzgerald and Judith Miller, and centers on the disclosure of sensitive government material. In contrast to the Scooter Libby affair, this case is surprisingly low-profile; and again in contrast to the Scooter Libby affair, it is of exceptional national importance.

In December 2001, federal law-enforcement officers were preparing to raid the offices and seize the assets of the Holy Land Foundation and the Global Relief Foundation—two Chicago-based Islamic "charities," both of which were linked to terrorist organizations abroad. Evidently, on the eve of the raid, Miller and another *Times* reporter, Philip Shenon, acting on confidential information from a source inside a federal grand jury, telephoned officials of the two foundations and asked questions that had the effect of tipping them off to the impending operation, thereby potentially if not actually nullifying its value and imperiling the law officers carrying it out.

Given this breach of closely held information, Fitzgerald, acting in his capacity as U.S. attorney in Chicago, opened an investigation. Among other things, he issued a subpoena for the telephone records of the two *Times* reporters during the period in which the leak was thought to have occurred. The *Times* strenuously resisted, and for the last four or five years the matter has slowly moved through the courts. This past August, a three-judge federal panel ruled against the *Times*. "We see no danger to a free press" in so ruling, wrote one of the panel's members. "Learning of imminent law-enforcement-asset freezes/searches and informing targets of them is not an activity essential, or even common, to journalism." In December, the Supreme Court, declining to hear an appeal, let stand the decision of the three-judge panel.

The *Times*, for its part, has steadfastly insisted that no damage was done by its reporters' actions. According to an attorney for the paper, the pair were merely "conducting their journalistic duties by getting reaction to an ongoing story." The *Times* editorial page has blasted the Supreme Court's December action as "the latest legal blow to the diminishing right of journalists to shield informants." Citing the public interest in the "dissemination of information," it has seized the occasion to argue yet again that the "privilege granted to journalists to protect their sources needs to be bolstered with a strong federal shield law."

But the *Times* is wrong. For here is an instance, one of many in the recent past, where it is hardly clear that the public interest resides in promoting the "dissemination of information." To the contrary, where protecting the country from terrorism is at stake, the public interest may rather reside in *narrowing* access to information, and not in broadcasting it to terrorist fundraisers and to the public at large. Although the two reporters have not been charged with any crime, and although there is no evidence that either of them acted with malicious intent, a convincing argument can be made that in ferreting out secret information from a grand jury, and in placing telephone calls to criminal suspects on that basis, they endangered us all.

Considerations like these have, in fact, informed recent congressional debates over whether to enact a shield law. Thus, a bill considered by the Senate Judiciary Committee in 2005 made a point of excluding from any such privilege information that posed "imminent" harm to national security—a very narrow exclusion that was duly subjected to withering criticism by the Justice Department. The following year, a bill introduced by Lugar and Specter appeared to take Justice's concerns into account, broadening the array of unprotected categories to include, among other things, any information necessary to government in fulfilling its obligation to "prevent significant and actual harm" to national security.

A parade of Senators have pronounced themselves satisfied with this compromise, hailing it as a way of ensuring the flow of information to the public while also safeguarding genuine secrets. But a moment's reflection exposes the defect in this reasoning. For what exactly constitutes "significant and actual harm" to national security, and how would a court, of all institutions, go about determining it?

The military, diplomatic, and intelligence machinery of the U.S. government, acting under the authority of presidential executive orders and employing criminal sanctions enacted by Congress, classifies an immense volume of information. It also keeps a careful account of what it is doing—tabulating, for example, 14,206,773 "classification decisions" in fiscal year 2005 alone.[2] Three primary categories are in use—top-secret, secret, and confidential—of which the overwhelming share is "secret." According to official definitions, the disclosure of "top-secret" or "secret" material "could reasonably be expected" to cause either "exceptionally grave" or "serious" damage to the United States, while disclosure of "confidential" material "could reasonably be expected" to cause only "damage." By passing a shield law that requires prosecutors to demonstrate "significant and actual harm" before compelling a journalist to testify, Congress would effectively dismantle this entire classification system without erecting any safeguards in its place.

To begin with, while leaving statutes on the books that ostensibly criminalize leaks of *all* classified documents, the exception would almost automatically free journalists who come into possession of "confidential" information from the possibility of ever being subpoenaed—on its face, mere "damage" would not qualify as "significant" harm. But even "secret" and "top-secret" material might also not fall under the exception, since "actual" harm is virtually impossible to prove, hinging almost always on an evaluation of actions taken in secret by an adversary about which we may not ever learn. It is for this very reason that the rules of the classification system do not speak of actual harm, safeguarding instead information that could "reasonably be expected" to injure our national security.

A shield law, in other words, would effectively immunize one large category of leakers at a stroke, and perhaps immunize almost all leakers, dramatically intensifying the flow of even the most sensitive secrets into the public domain. Every bureaucrat with a private agenda would feel free to contact a Judith Miller or an even more prolific collector of leaks like the *New Yorker*'s Seymour Hersh to relay classified national-defense information without any apprehension of ever being arrested or prosecuted on the basis of something that might one day be disclosed by a reporter in a court proceeding.

Protecting national secrets is already a problematic venture. Some of the most notorious leaks of the past several years have been not of the confidential but of the secret and top-secret variety. Thus, in 2005, the *Washington Post* revealed a highly classified network of clandestine CIA prisons in Europe for al-Qaeda captives. That same year, the *New York Times* disclosed the existence of a highly classified National Security Agency program of government surveillance of al-Qaeda suspects.[3] In 2006, the *Times* revealed a highly classified program monitoring al-Qaeda financial transactions; most recently, it published the contents of a highly classified memo revealing administration misgivings about the prime minister of Iraq, a leak described by one government official as among the most damaging in recent memory. And this is not even to take account of leaks from the criminal-justice system like police and FBI investigative reports, surveillance tapes, and grand-jury transcripts (as in the Holy Land Foundation case) that are not marked with a classification stamp.

Such leaks have proliferated, even though *Branzburg* is on the books and the shadow of Judith Miller's imprisonment has supposedly given pause to informants considering whether they can trust a reporter. This hardly suggests that journalists are in desperate need of a shield law to induce leakers to impart information to them. On the contrary, such a law would only unleash a great tidal wave of leaks, to be followed inevitably by an equally destructive backwash of litigation.

In the case of each such contested leak, courts would be asked to weigh whether the disclosed information caused "significant and actual harm" to national security, which in every instance the press would deny, claiming (a) that the information at issue, even if secret or top secret, was improperly classified and (b) that disclosure of this information provided a vital service to the public weal. The main effect of a shield law would thus be to the draw the judicial branch into the very heart of foreign-policy decision making, requiring judges to evaluate matters that they lack either the expertise or the experience to assess. As a result, the confusion that now exists among the various federal circuit courts would not be cleared up; it would be deepened.

And even that is not the end of it. Any legislation in this area would ineluctably have to specify exactly who is worthy of being shielded. Anticipating this very problem, Justice White observed in *Branzburg* that, sooner or later, administering a constitutional privilege for reporters would necessitate defining "those categories of newsmen who qualified for the privilege." But such a procedure, he noted, would itself inevitably do violence to "the traditional doctrine that liberty of the press is the right of the lonely pamphleteer who uses carbon paper or a mimeograph just as much as of the large metropolitan publisher who utilizes the latest photocomposition methods."

The Lugar-Specter bill already does precisely this sort of violence. It defines the term "journalist" as a person who, "for financial gain or livelihood," is engaged in the news business "as a salaried employee of or independent contractor" to a news agency. This definition, with its emphasis on monetary compensation, no doubt applies to many journalists. But it excludes many more. And it takes a large first step toward erecting a system of federally recognized or federally licensed journalists.

In the Internet age, the functional equivalent of the lonely pamphleteer is the lonely blogger, working at home in front of his computer screen. Internet blogs have become a major force in the dissemination of news and opinion; one has only to recall the role played by the website PowerLine.com in unmasking the fraudulent documents employed by Dan Rather and CBS in their 2004 election-eve coverage of the military service of George W. Bush. In the Lugar-Specter version of a shield law, bloggers would be ineligible for membership in the new privileged caste.

Nor would they be alone. As Justice White stressed in *Branzburg,* freedom of the press is not a right "confined to newspapers and periodicals" but rather a "fundamental personal right" that attaches to all of us. Any effort to restrict this personal right to a few select professionals will collide with the reality that "[t]he informative function asserted by representatives of the organized press . . . is also performed by lecturers, political pollsters, novelists, academic researchers, and dramatists."

Herein, continued White, lies the difficulty in crafting a shield, for almost any author "may quite accurately assert that he is contributing to the flow of information to the public, that he relies on confidential sources of information, and that these sources will be silenced if he is forced to make disclosures before a grand jury."

The proposed shield legislation attempts to surmount this difficulty by excluding amateurs and many other categories of purveyors of information from its reach—thereby violating the spirit if not the letter of the First Amendment. Even worse, however, is that it would *include* under its protection all sorts of highly dubious *professional* journalists: American reporters in the employ of Al Jazeera, the pan-Arab broadcasting company, for example; American journalists working in, say, the Washington bureau of the Chinese Communist party's *People's Daily;* journalists for extremist domestic publications like the Nation of Islam's *The Call,* or the Liberty Lobby's avowedly racist *Spotlight,* or Lyndon LaRouche's crackpot *Executive Intelligence Review.* So long as they were drawing a salary, they too could receive immunity for any leaked confidential information they collected or published.

So where does that leave us? When all is said and done, do we really want to retain a system that on occasion can imprison journalists merely for going about their daily work? Is there perhaps some alternative, short of enacting a shield law, that would avoid that untoward result?

A better question is this: do we need such an alternative? Despite what newsmen and their lawyers incessantly tell us, our current laws governing confidential informants do not require journalists to go to prison *ever.* On the contrary, this is always a choice they make of their own free will. Like every journalist who has dealt with a confidential informant, Judith Miller made a series of such choices, each of her own volition, before she was led away to her cell. They are worth reviewing.

In the first place, as she went about gathering information about the leak of an (allegedly) undercover CIA officer, Miller was under no obligation to promise her contacts in or out of government that she was prepared to violate U.S. law to protect their identity. In seeking to gain their trust and cooperation, she might have chosen to promise something less—that, for example, she would never disclose their identity unless she herself were subpoenaed. Such a promise might well have sufficed to elicit the information she was pursuing while avoiding any suggestion that she was ready to go to prison to keep her word.

Many confidential informants would readily accept such terms, as Miller's own case eventually proved. For after she was hit with a contempt citation, I. Lewis Libby, the man who turned out to be her principal source, offered to sign letters freeing her of any obligation to observe promises of confidentiality she had made. What this suggests is that an absolute promise, one that holds the potential of dragging a reporter into conflict with the law, is likely to be necessary only under extraordinary circumstances.

Article 26. Why Journalists Are Not Above the Law

The Justice Department has its own highly restrictive internal guidelines that sharply limit the circumstances in which it will subpoena reporters. Historically, indeed, such subpoenas have been rare; the Justice Department has issued only 12 over the past 15 years.[4] Ours is thus not a hostile environment for journalists but a congenial one, assuring them that they need incur the risk of offering an absolute promise of confidentiality only when the information at stake is worth the highest price in terms of the public's right to know. There was certainly no information of such value in the Miller fiasco. Whatever she learned from Libby, she wrote about only in her notebook; neither she nor, evidently, her editors ever thought it sufficiently important to be printed in the pages of the *New York Times.*[5]

Confronted by a subpoena to a grand jury, and having failed to quash that subpoena, Miller still could have chosen to avoid jail merely by following the law of the land, fulfilling her obligation as a citizen to tell the grand jury what she knew about a possible crime. This she declined to do. But despite the plaudits she earned from many for keeping her promises, it is debatable whether this act of civil disobedience on her part was either honorable or wise. For what Miller was defying was the will not only of the special counsel or of the Supreme Court but of the highest power in a democracy, namely, the American people.

At the time Miller was incarcerated, the American people acting through their elected representatives had had decades to contemplate establishing a testimonial privilege for journalists. Up until then, and indeed up until this moment, they have declined to bestow such a privilege on a profession they do not hold in particularly high esteem. Successive Congresses have considered the idea of a shield law only to reject it; and as I have tried to show, they have had good reasons for rejecting it. It was proper that Miller should have been cited for contempt, for she was being contemptuous of a grand-jury process that is the cornerstone of our criminal laws.

Once again, Justice White cut to the essence. "[I]t is obvious," he wrote in *Branzburg,* "that agreements to conceal information relevant to commission of crime have very little to recommend them from the standpoint of public policy." Historically, White pointed out, citizens not only are forbidden to conceal a crime, they have a positive "duty to raise the 'hue and cry' and report felonies to the authorities." Concealment, even of a crime in which one is oneself not a participant, is itself a crime—misprision of a felony—punishable by a statute enacted by the very first Congress and still on the books. Covering up a crime, wrote White, "deserves no encomium, and we decline to afford it First Amendment protection by denigrating the duty of a citizen, whether reporter or informer, to respond to grand-jury subpoena and answer relevant questions put to him."

The claim that Miller, or any other journalist in similar circumstances, had no choice but to go jail is, therefore, specious in the extreme, a rationalization put forward by spokesmen of the establishment media in their own effort to gain and maintain their privileges and powers. These they require not in order to report the news but rather, it would appear, to ratify their self-proclaimed position as the arbiters and shapers of American opinion. In the performance of that role, they fancy, their exalted position should place them beyond the reach of American law.

A free press is a vital component of our democracy, but it is not the only component. The same preamble of the Constitution that speaks of securing "the blessings of liberty to ourselves and our posterity" also speaks of insuring "domestic tranquility" and providing "for the common defense." At a moment when the United States faces the present danger of assault by Islamic terrorists and is struggling to protect itself from falling victim to a second September 11, a murmuration of over-zealous, self-interested, and mistaken advocates is striving to shield the press's freedom of movement at the expense of many if not all of the competing imperatives of a system based upon the rule of law. By acquiescing in this hubristic folly, Congress would do a disservice both to the First Amendment and to the security of the American people.

Notes

1. Shortly thereafter, Libby was indicted, not for any violation of the Intelligence Identities Act but for allegedly lying to the FBI during the course of the investigation.
2. A "classification decision" is the bureaucracy's label for the creation of a classified fact. Of this gigantic number, only 258,633 were brand-new classified facts; the remainder were "derivative," that is, based upon a paraphrase or a restatement of an original decision to classify something. A widely recognized problem is that a significant fraction of what the government classifies or retains as classified is actually misclassified or over-classified. The solution has been an orderly and timely process to *de*classify records: in 2005, some 29,540,603 pages of historical records were declassified. A "record" is defined by law "as a book, paper, map, photograph, sound or video recording, machine-readable material, computerized, digitized, or electronic information, regardless of the medium on which it is stored, or other documentary material, regardless of its physical form or characteristics."
3. For a discussion of this case, and the broader framework of laws governing the publication of national-defense information, see my "Has the *New York Times* Violated the Espionage Act?" in the March 2006 COMMENTARY.
4. A different set of issues is presented by the fact that, in the aftermath of *Branzburg,* the press has been hit with a growing number of subpoenas for source material arising out of *civil* litigation, including in two high-profile cases. In 2004, five reporters were held in contempt by a federal judge for refusing to testify about their sources in a case brought by Wen Ho Lee, the Los Alamos atomic scientist who pleaded guilty to a charge of mishandling secret documents but then sued the government for violating his privacy rights. The case was dropped when the five news agencies involved agreed to contribute $750,000 to a settlement with Lee to avoid having their reporters testify. In a libel case brought against Nicholas Kristof by Stephen J. Hatfill, who had been named by Kristof as a suspect in the post-9/11 anthrax attacks, a federal magistrate judge ruled that the *Times* could not refuse to identify Kristof's confidential sources. That case is still moving through the courts.
5. As we now know, for its own partisan reasons the *Times* was wildly overstating the significance of the leak, which had its origins not (as the paper alleged) in a White House plot to discredit its critics but in the careless talk of a ranking official at the Department of State named Richard Armitage.

GABRIEL SCHOENFELD is the senior editor of *Commentary.* Correspondence on his "Dual Loyalty and the 'Israel Lobby' " (November 2006) appears on page 3.

Reprinted from *Commentary,* February 2007, pp. 40–45, by permission of Commentary and Gabriel Schoenfeld. Copyright © 2007 by Commentary, Inc. All rights reserved.

Copyright Jungle

Reporters seem lost in the realm of copyright, where a riot of new restrictions threaten creativity, research, and history. Here's a map.

SIVA VAIDHYANATHAN

Last May, Kevin Kelly, *Wired* magazine's "senior maverick," published in *The New York Times Magazine* his predictive account of flux within the book-publishing world. Kelly outlined what he claimed will happen (not might or could—*will*) to the practices of writing and reading under a new regime fostered by Google's plan to scan millions of books and offer searchable texts to Internet users.

"So what happens when all the books in the world become a single liquid fabric of interconnected words and ideas?" Kelly wrote. "First, works on the margins of popularity will find a small audience larger than the near-zero audience they usually have now. . . . Second, the universal library will deepen our grasp of history, as every original document in the course of civilization is scanned and cross-linked. Third, the universal library of all books will cultivate a new sense of authority. . . ."

Kelly saw the linkage of text to text, book to book, as the answer to the information gaps that have made the progress of knowledge such a hard climb. "If you can truly incorporate all texts—past and present, multilingual—on a particular subject," Kelly wrote, "then you can have a clearer sense of what we as a civilization, a species, do know and don't know. The white spaces of our collective ignorance are highlighted, while the golden peaks of our knowledge are drawn with completeness. This degree of authority is only rarely achieved in scholarship today, but it will become routine."

Such heady predictions of technological revolution have become so common, so accepted in our techno-fundamentalist culture, that even when John Updike criticized Kelly's vision in an essay published a month later in *The New York Times Book Review*, he did not so much doubt Kelly's vision of a universal digital library as lament it.

Reporters often fail to see the big picture in copyright stories: that what is at stake is the long-term health of our culture.

As it turns out, the move toward universal knowledge is not so easy. Google's project, if it survives court challenges, would probably have modest effects on writing, reading, and publishing. For one thing, Kelly's predictions depend on a part of the system he slights in his article: the copyright system. Copyright is not Kelly's friend. He mentions it as a nuisance on the edge of his dream. To acknowledge that a lawyer-built system might trump an engineer-built system would have run counter to Kelly's sermon.

Much of the press coverage of the Google project has missed some key facts: most libraries that are allowing Google to scan books are, so far, providing only books published before 1923 and thus already in the public domain, essentially missing most of the relevant and important books that scholars and researchers—not to mention casual readers—might want. Meanwhile, the current American copyright system will probably kill Google's plan to scan the collections of the University of Michigan and the University of California system—the only libraries willing to offer Google works currently covered by copyright. In his article, Kelly breezed past the fact that the copyrighted works will be presented in a useless format—"snippets" that allow readers only glimpses into how a term is used in the text. Google users will not be able to read, copy, or print copyrighted works via Google. Google accepted that arrangement to limit its copyright liability. But the more "copyright friendly" the Google system is, the less user-friendly, and useful, it is. And even so it still may not fly in court.

Google is exploiting the instability of the copyright system in a digital age. The company's struggle with publishers over its legal ability to pursue its project is the most interesting and perhaps most transformative conflict in the copyright wars. But there are many other battles—and many other significant stories—out in the copyright jungle. Yet reporters seem lost.

Copyright in recent years has certainly become too strong for its own good. It protects more content and outlaws more acts than ever before. It stifles individual creativity and hampers the discovery and sharing of culture and knowledge. To convey all this to readers, journalists need to understand the principles, paradoxes, licenses, and limits of the increasingly troubled copyright system. Copyright is not just an interesting story. As the most pervasive regulation of speech and culture, the copyright system will help determine the richness and strength of democracy in the twenty-first century.

The Copyright Wars

It's not that the press has ignored copyright. Recent fights have generated a remarkable amount of press. Since Napster broke into the news in 2000, journalists have been scrambling to keep up with the fast-moving and complicated stories of content protection, distribution, and revision that make up the wide array of copyright conflicts.

During this time of rapid change it's been all too easy for reporters to fall into the trap of false dichotomies: hackers versus movie studios; kids versus music companies; librarians versus publishers. The peer-to-peer and music-file-sharing story, for instance, has consistently been covered as a business story with the tone of the sports page: winners and losers, scores and stats. In fact, peer-to-peer file sharing was more about technological innovation and the ways we use music in our lives than any sort of threat to the commercial music industry. As it stands today, after dozens of court cases and congressional hearings, peer-to-peer file-sharing remains strong. So does the music industry. The sky did not fall, our expectations did.

The most recent headline-grabbing copyright battle involved *The Da Vinci Code*. Did Dan Brown recycle elements of a 1982 nonfiction book for his bestselling novel? The authors of the earlier book sued Brown's publisher, Random House U.K., in a London court in the spring of 2006 in an effort to prove that Brown lifted protected elements of their book, what they called "the architecture" of a speculative conspiracy theory about the life of Jesus. In the coverage of the trial, some reporters—even in publications like *The New York Times, The Washington Post*, and *The San Diego Union-Tribune*—used the word "plagiarism" as if it were a legal concept or cause of action. It isn't. Copyright infringement and plagiarism are different acts with some potential overlap. One may infringe upon a copyright without plagiarizing and one may plagiarize—use ideas without attribution—without breaking the law. Plagiarism is an ethical concept. Copyright is a legal one.

Perhaps most troubling, though, was the way in which the *Da Vinci Code* story was so often covered without a clear statement of the operative principle of copyright: one cannot protect facts and ideas, only specific expressions of ideas. Dan Brown and Random House U.K. prevailed in the London court because the judge clearly saw that the earlier authors were trying to protect ideas. Most people don't understand that important distinction. So it's no surprise that most reporters don't either.

Reporters often fail to see the big picture in copyright stories: that what is at stake is the long-term health of our culture. If the copyright system fails, huge industries could crumble. If it gets too strong, it could strangle future creativity and research. It is complex, and complexity can be a hard thing to render in journalistic prose.

The work situation of most reporters may also impede a thorough understanding of how copyright affects us all. Reporters labor for content companies, after all, and tend to view their role in the copyright system as one-dimensional. They are creators who get paid by copyright holders. So it's understandable for journalists to express a certain amount of anxiety about the ways digital technologies have allowed expensive content to flow around the world cheaply.

Yet reporters can't gather the raw material for their craft without a rich library of information in accessible form. When I was a reporter in the 1980s and 1990s, I could not write a good story without scouring the library and newspaper archives for other stories that added context. And like every reporter, I was constantly aware that my work was just one element in a cacophony of texts seeking readers and contributing to the aggregate understanding of our world. I was as much a copyright user as I was a copyright producer. Now that I write books, I am even more aware of my role as a taker and a giver. It takes a library, after all, to write a book.

The Right to Say No

We are constantly reminded that copyright law, as the Supreme Court once declared, is an "engine of free expression." But more often these days, it's instead an engine of corporate censorship.

Copyright is the right to say no. Copyright holders get to tell the rest of us that we can't build on, revise, copy, or distribute their work. That's a fair bargain most of the time. Copyright provides the incentive to bring work to market. It's impossible to imagine anyone anteing up $300 million for *Spider-Man 3* if we did not have a reasonable belief that copyright laws would limit its distribution to mostly legitimate and moneymaking channels.

Yet copyright has the potential of locking up knowledge, insight, information, and wisdom from the rest of the world. So it is also fundamentally a *conditional* restriction on speech and print. Copyright and the First Amendment are in constant and necessary tension. The law has for most of American history limited copyright—allowing it to fill its role as an incentive-maker for new creators yet curbing its censorious powers. For most of its 300-year history, the system has served us well, protecting the integrity of creative work while allowing the next generation of creators to build on the cultural foundations around them. These rights have helped fill our libraries with books, our walls with art, and our lives with song.

But something has gone terribly wrong. In recent years, large multinational media companies have captured the global copyright system and twisted it toward their own short-term interests. The people who are supposed to benefit most from a system that makes ideas available—readers, students, and citizens—have been excluded. No one in Congress wants to hear from college students or librarians.

More than ever, the law restricts what individuals can do with elements of their own culture. Generally the exercise of copyright protection is so extreme these days that even the most innocent use of images or song lyrics in scholarly work can generate a legal threat. Last year one of the brightest students in my department got an article accepted in the leading journal in the field. It was about advertising in the 1930s. The journal's lawyers and editors refused to let her use images from the ads in question without permission, even though it is impossible to find out who owns the ads or if they were ever covered by copyright in the first place. The chilling effect trumped any claim of scholarly "fair use" or even common sense.

What Has Changed

For most of the history of copyright in Europe and the United States, copying was hard and expensive, and the law punished those who made whole copies of others' material for profit. The principle was simple: legitimate publishers would make no money after investing so much in authors, editors, and printing presses if the same products were available on the street. The price in such a hypercompetitive market would drop to close to zero. So copyright created artificial scarcity.

But we live in an age of abundance. Millions of people have in their homes and offices powerful copying machines and communication devices: their personal computers. It's almost impossible to keep digital materials scarce once they are released to the public.

The industries that live by copyright—music, film, publishing, and software companies—continue to try. They encrypt video discs and compact discs so that consumers can't play them on computers or make personal copies. They monitor and sue consumers who allow others to share digital materials over the Internet. But none of these tactics seem to be working. In fact, they have been counterproductive. The bullying attitude has alienated consumers. That does not mean that copyright has failed or that it has no future. It just has a more complicated and nuanced existence.

Here is the paradox: media companies keep expanding across the globe, producing more products every year, yet repeatedly telling us they are in crisis.

Here is the fundamental paradox: media companies keep expanding across the globe. They produce more software, books, music, video games, and films every year. They charge more for those products every year. And those industries repeatedly tell us that they are in crisis. If we do not radically alter our laws, technologies, and habits, the media companies argue, the industries that copyright protects will wither and die.

Yet they are not dying. Strangely, the global copyright industries are still rich and powerful. Many of them are adapting, changing their containers and their content, but they keep growing, expanding across the globe. Revenues in the music business did drop steadily from 2000 to 2003—some years by up to 6.8 percent. Millions of people in Europe and North America use their high-speed Internet connections to download music files free. From Moscow to Mexico City to Manila, film and video piracy is rampant. For much of the world, teeming pirate bazaars serve as the chief (often only) source of those products. Yet the music industry has recovered from its early-decade lull rather well. Revenues for the major commercial labels in 2004 were 3.3 percent above 2003. Unit sales were up 4.4 percent. Revenues in 2004 were higher than in 1997 and comparable to those of 1998—then considered very healthy years for the recording industry. This while illegal downloading continued all over the world.

Yet despite their ability to thrive in a new global/digital environment, the companies push for ever more restrictive laws—laws that fail to recognize the realities of the global flows of people, culture, and technology.

Recent changes to copyright in North America, Europe, and Australia threaten to chill creativity at the ground level—among noncorporate, individual, and communal artists. As a result, the risk and price of reusing elements of copyrighted culture are higher than ever before. If you wanted to make a scholarly documentary film about the history of country music, for example, you might end up with one that slights the contribution of Hank Williams and Elvis Presley because their estates would deny you permission to use the archival material. Other archives and estates would charge you prohibitive fees. We are losing much of the history of the twentieth century because the copyright industries are more litigious than ever.

Yet copyright, like culture itself, is not zero-sum. In its first weekend of theatrical release, *Star Wars Episode III. Revenge of the Sith* made a record $158.5 million at the box office. At the same time, thousands of people downloaded high-quality pirated digital copies from the Internet. Just days after the blockbuster release of the movie, attorneys for 20th Century Fox sent thousands of "cease-and-desist" letters to those sharing copies of the film over the Internet. The practice continued unabated.

How could a film make so much money when it was competing against its free version? The key to understanding that seeming paradox—less control, more revenue—is to realize that every download does not equal a lost sale. As the Stanford law professor Lawrence Lessig has argued, during the time when music downloads were 2.6 times those of legitimate music sales, revenues dropped less than 7 percent. If every download replaced a sale, there would be no commercial music industry left. The relationship between the free version and the legitimate version is rather complex, like the relationship between a public library and a book publisher. Sometimes free stuff sells stuff.

Checks and Unbalances

Here's a primer for reporters who find themselves lost in the copyright jungle: American copyright law offers four basic democratic safeguards to the censorious power of copyright, a sort of bargain with the people. Each of these safeguards is currently at risk:

- First and foremost, copyrights eventually expire, thus placing works into the public domain for all to buy cheaply and use freely. That is the most important part of the copyright bargain: We the people grant copyright as a temporary monopoly over the reproduction and distribution of specific works, and eventually we get the material back for the sake of our common heritage and collective knowledge. The works of Melville and Twain once benefited their authors exclusively. Now they belong to all of us. But as Congress continues to extend the term of copyright protection for works created decades ago (as it did in 1998 by adding twenty years to all active copyrights) it robs the people of their legacy.

- Second, copyright restricts what consumers can do with the text of a book, but not the book itself; it governs the content, not the container. Thus people may sell and buy used books, and libraries may lend books freely, without permission from publishers. In the digital realm, however, copyright holders may install digital-rights-management schemes that limit the transportation of both the container and the content. So libraries may not lend out major portions of their materials if they are in digital form. As more works are digitized, libraries are shifting to the lighter, space-saving formats. As a result, libraries of the future could be less useful to citizens.

- Third, as we have seen, copyright governs specific expressions, but not the facts or ideas upon which the expressions are based. Copyright does not protect ideas. But that is one of the most widely misunderstood aspects of copyright. And even that basic principle is under attack in the new digital environment. In 1997, the National Basketball Association tried to get pager and Internet companies to refrain from distributing game scores without permission. And more recently, Major League Baseball has tried, but so far has failed, to license the use of player statistics to limit "free riding" firms that make money facilitating fantasy baseball leagues. Every Congressional session, database companies try to create a new form of intellectual property that protects facts and data, thus evading the basic democratic right that lets facts flow freely.

- Fourth, and not least, the copyright system has built into it an exception to the power of copyright: fair use. This significant loophole, too, is widely misunderstood, and deserves further discussion.

Generally, one may copy portions of another's copyrighted work (and sometimes the entire work) for private, noncommercial uses, for education, criticism, journalism, or parody. Fair use operates as a defense against an accusation of infringement and grants confidence to users that they most likely will not be sued for using works in a reasonable way.

On paper, fair use seems pretty healthy. In recent years, for example, courts have definitively stated that making a parody of a copyrighted work is considered "transformative" and thus fair. Another example: a major ruling in 2002 enabled image search engines such as Google to thrive and expand beyond simple Web text searching into images and video because "thumbnails" of digital photographs are considered to be fair uses. Thumbnails, the court ruled, do not replace the original in the marketplace.

But two factors have put fair use beyond the reach of many users, especially artists and authors. First and foremost, fair use does not help you if your publisher or distributor does not believe in it. Many publishers demand that every quote—no matter how short or for what purpose—be cleared with specific permission, which is extremely cumbersome and often costly.

And fair use is somewhat confusing. There is widespread misunderstanding about it. In public forums I have heard claims such as "you can take 20 percent" of a work before the use becomes unfair, or, "there is a forty-word rule" for long quotes of text. Neither rule exists. Fair use is intentionally vague. It is meant for judges to apply, case by case. Meanwhile, copyright holders are more aggressive than ever and publishers and distributors are more concerned about suits. So in the real world, fair use is less fair and less useful.

The Biggest Copy Machine

Fair use is designed for small ball. It's supposed to create some breathing room for individual critics or creators to do what they do. Under current law it's not appropriate for large-scale endeavors—like the Google library project. Fair use may be too rickety a structure to support both free speech and the vast dreams of Google.

Reporters need to understand the company's copyright ambitions. Google announced in December 2004 that it would begin scanning in millions of copyrighted books from the University of Michigan library, and in August 2006 the University of California system signed on. Predictably, some prominent publishers and authors have filed suit against the search-engine company.

The company's plan was to include those works in its "Google Book Search" service. Books from the library would supplement both the copyrighted books that Google has contracted to offer via its "partner" program with publishers and the uncopyrighted works scanned from other libraries, including libraries of Harvard, Oxford, and New York City. While it would offer readers full-text access to older works out of copyright, it would provide only "snippets" of the copyrighted works that it scans without the authors' permission from Michigan and California.

If the concept of fair use is in danger, then good journalism is also threatened. Every journalist relies on fair use every day.

Google says that because users will only experience "snippets" of copyrighted text, their use of such material should be considered a fair use. That argument will be tested in court. But whether those snippets constitute fair use is just one part of the issue. To generate the "snippets," Google is scanning the entire works and storing them on its servers. The plaintiffs argue that the initial scanning of the books itself—done to create the snippets from a vast database—constitutes copyright infringement, the very core of copyright. Courts will have to weigh whether the public is better served by a strict and clear conception of copyright law—that only the copyright holder has the right to give permission for any copy, regardless of the ultimate use or effect on the market—or a more flexible and pragmatic one in which the user experience matters more.

One of the least understood concepts of Google's business is that it copies everything. When we post our words and images on the Web, we are implicitly licensing Google, Yahoo, and other search engines to make copies of our content to store in their huge farms of Servers. Without such "cache" copies, search engines could not read and link to Web pages. In the Web world, massive copying is just business as usual.

But through the library project, Google is imposing the norms of the Web on authors and publishers who have not willingly digitized their works and thus have not licensed search engines to make cache copies. Publishers, at first, worried that the Google project would threaten book sales, but it soon became clear that project offers no risk to publishers' core markets and projects. If anything, it could serve as a marketing boon. Now publishers are most offended by the prospect of a wealthy upstart corporation's "free-riding" on their content to offer a commercial and potentially lucrative service without any regard for compensation or quality control. The publishers, in short, would like a piece of the revenue, and some say about the manner of display and search results.

Copyright has rarely been used as leverage to govern ancillary markets for goods that enhance the value or utility of the copyrighted works. Publishers have never, for instance, sued the makers of library catalogs, eyeglasses, or bookcases. But these are extreme times.

The mood of U.S. courts in recent years, especially the Supreme Court, has been to side with the copyright holder in this time of great technological flux. Google is an upstart facing off against some of the most powerful media companies in the world, including Viacom, News Corporation, and Disney—all of which have publishing wings. Courts will probably see this case as the existential showdown over the nature and future of copyright and rule to defend the status quo. Journalists should follow the case closely. The footnotes of any court decision could shape the future of journalism, publishing, libraries, and democracy.

Out of the Jungle

Google aside, in recent years—thanks to the ferocious mania to protect everything and the astounding political power of media companies—the basic, democratic checks and balances that ensured that copyright would not operate as an instrument of private censorship have been seriously eroded. The most endangered principle is fair use: the right to use others' copyrighted works in a reasonable way to promote important public functions such as criticism or education. And if fair use is in danger then good journalism is also threatened. Every journalist relies on fair use every day. So journalists have a self-interest in the copyright story.

And so does our society. Copyright was designed, as the Constitution declares, to "promote the progress" of knowledge and creativity. In the last thirty years we have seen this brilliant system corrupted and captured by the very industries that the old laws fostered. Yet the complexity and nuanced nature of copyright battles make it hard for nonexperts to grasp what's at stake.

So it's up to journalists to push deeper into stories in which copyright plays a part. Then the real challenge begins: explaining this messy system in clear language to a curious but confused audience.

SIVA VAIDHYANATHAN is an associate professor of culture and communication at New York University. He is the author of *Copyrights and Copywrongs: The Rise of Intellectual Property and How It Threatens Creativity* and *The Anarchist in the Library*. He blogs at Sivacracy.net.

Reprinted from *Columbia Journalism Review*, September/October 2006. Copyright © 2006 by Columbia Journalism Review, Columbia University.

Distorted Picture

Thanks to Photoshop, it's awfully easy to manipulate photographs, as a number of recent scandals make painfully clear. Misuse of the technology poses a serious threat to photojournalism's credibility.

SHERRY RICCHIARDI

If photo sleuths in Ohio hadn't noticed a pair of missing legs, Allan Detrich still would be cruising to assignments in his sleek blue truck, building his reputation as a photographer extraordinaire at the Toledo Blade. In April, the veteran shooter was forced out of the newsroom in disgrace, igniting a scandal that swept the photojournalism community. Coworkers were mystified about why a highly talented, hard worker who had garnered a slew of awards would cheat.

Detrich says that for a time, he felt like the most "reviled journalist in the country." Internet forums buzzed about his misdeeds, and photographers attacked him for sullying the profession. Some even sent hateful e-mail messages. "I wasn't the first to tamper with news photos and, unfortunately, I probably won't be the last," he says. "I screwed up. I got caught."

In his case, he says, he was seduced by software that made altering images so easy that "anyone can do it."

With new technology, faking or doctoring photographs has never been simpler, faster or more difficult to detect. Skilled operators truly are like magicians, except they use tools like Photoshop, the leading digital imaging software, to create their illusions.

Detrich, who had worked for the Blade since 1989, manipulated most of the images while alone in his truck, using a cell phone or WiFi for quick and easy transmission to the photo desk. There was little reason for him to return to the newsroom to process images. Until April 5, no one challenged the veracity of his photographs.

The photographer's downfall underscores a disturbing reality: With readily accessible, relatively inexpensive imaging tools (Photoshop sells for around $650) and a low learning curve, the axiom "seeing is believing" never has been more at risk. That has led to doomsday predictions about documentary photojournalism in this country.

"The public is losing faith in us. Without credibility, we have nothing; we cannot survive," says John Long, chairman of the ethics and standards committee of the National Press Photographers Association. Long pushes for stricter newsroom standards with missionary zeal and believes all journalists are tarnished when someone like Detrich falls from grace.

On June 2, Long, who built a distinguished career in photography at the Hartford Courant before retiring earlier this year, preached to an audience at NPPA's photo summit in Portland, Oregon. If the self-described purist had his way, news photographers would take a vow of abstinence in regard to photo altering; editors would enforce zero-tolerance policies. "The problem is far greater than we fear," Long told the group that afternoon.

There are no statistics on the number of rule-breakers, but indicators within the profession do not bode well for the cherished precept of visual accuracy.

During an NPPA ethics session in Portland, a group of some 50 photographers and photo managers were asked for a show of hands if they believed they had ever worked with peers who routinely crossed ethical boundaries. Nearly every arm flew into the air. "That was a scary thing to see," says Long, who was on the panel. Ethical breaches were the topic of conversation at coffee breaks and during presentations at the photo summit.

Many of the offending photos and illustrations discussed in Portland appear in a rogues' gallery posted by computer scientist Hany Farid (www.cs.dartmouth.edu/farid/research/tampering).

Among the dozens he highlights are Time and Newsweek covers, a Pulitzer Prize-winning photo, images in the Charlotte Observer and Newsday, and a famous portrait of Abraham Lincoln that was discovered to be less than accurate.

The Dartmouth College professor uses the term "digital forensics" to describe pioneering methods to detect image altering. Although not a cure-all, these tools could provide help in the future, says Farid. He predicts that scandals over photo forgeries are "absolutely going to get worse." That notion is underlined by the attention being paid to the problem by media organizations and at conferences.

In August, visual communications expert David Perlmutter will serve on a panel titled "Seeing is Not Believing: Representations and Misrepresentations" at the Association for Education in Journalism and Mass Communication gathering in Washington, D.C. Perlmutter poses the question: "Is the craft I love being murdered, committing suicide or both?"

Article 28. Distorted Picture

The Toledo Blade's descent into photo hell began with a telephone call.

On April 4, Ron Royhab, the paper's executive editor, returned home to find a message requesting he phone back, no matter how late. He punched in the number and listened in stunned silence to the voice on the other end. There were suspicions that a photographer had altered a news photo that had run prominently on the Blade's front page four days earlier. The caller was Donald R. Winslow, editor of News Photographer magazine, an NPPA publication.

"I was speechless; I couldn't collect my thoughts. I felt like someone had punched me in the stomach," recalls Royhab. "I got off the phone and thought, 'Not at my newspaper. It can't be!'"

By noon the next day, Detrich, 44, was being questioned in the newsroom. He admitted altering the photograph but said it was for his personal use, a copy he intended to hang on an office wall. He claimed he had mistakenly transmitted the wrong version on deadline. He told Photo District News, "that's not something I would do."

The paper's editors decided to review all of the photos that Detrich, twice named Ohio Photographer of the Year and a Pulitzer Prize finalist in 1998, had submitted for publication this year. They didn't like what they found. By April 7, he had resigned. If he had not, he would have been fired, says Royhab.

The episode began on March 30, when Bluffton University's baseball team played for the first time since five of its athletes had been killed in a bus accident earlier that month. Photographers jostled for position as players knelt in front of banners bearing the names and uniform numbers of the dead.

When similar photos appeared in Cleveland's Plain Dealer, the Dayton Daily News and Ohio's Lima News the following day, a pair of legs clad in blue jeans was visible from behind one of the banners hanging from a fence. In Detrich's version, there was only grass under the banner, although he shot from roughly the same angle. Ohio photographers brought the mysterious disappearance to Winslow's attention.

A review of Detrich's original digital files revealed that he had habitually erased unwanted elements in photos, including people, tree limbs, utility poles, electrical wires, light switches and cabinet knobs. In some instances, he added tree branches or shrubbery. In one sports shot he added a hockey puck; in another he inserted a basketball.

Detrich submitted 947 photographs for publication from January through March of 2007. Editors found that 79 clearly had been doctored. The paper apologized to readers and Detrich posted a mea culpa on his Web site (www.detrichpix.typepad.com/allandetrich_picturethis). The investigation found that Detrich had altered photos as far back as 2002. The Blade noted that no evidence of tampering was discovered on Detrich's award-winning photos, and there were no alterations in earlier years, when he was shooting on film and editing and processing in the newsroom.

In the May issue of News Photographer, Winslow ran a report on the situation at the Blade and labeled Detrich a "serial digital manipulator," the most prolific to surface in newspaper history.

As for the legs, it turned out they belonged to freelancer Madalyn Ruggiero, who was shooting in Bluffton for the Chicago Tribune and had positioned herself behind the fence in search of a different angle.

Brian Walski had covered war in the Balkans, famine in Africa and conflict in Kashmir before he made a fateful decision while on assignment in Iraq for the Los Angeles Times. The Chicago native was fired via satellite phone on April 1, 2003, after it was discovered he used his computer to combine two images, taken seconds apart, into a composite that ran on page one of the Times on March 31. The subject was a British soldier helping Iraqi civilians find cover outside Basra.

After the photos appeared, an employee at the Hartford Courant noticed that several Iraqis in the background appeared twice (see Drop Cap, May 2003). The Courant, which like the Times is owned by the Tribune Co., had also published the picture.

In an e-mail to the newspaper's photo staff, Walski, who had been with the Times since 1998 and had won Photographer of the Year honors in California, wrote: "This was after an extremely long, hot and stressful day but I offer no excuses here.... I have always maintained the highest ethical standards throughout my career and cannot truly explain my complete breakdown in judgment at this time. That will only come in the many sleepless nights that are ahead."

Colin Crawford, the L.A. Times' assistant managing editor for photography, calls Walski "incredibly experienced and talented" and says there was no hint of wrongdoing before the lapse. A review of his work found no other evidence of tampering.

"It's hard for me to get into the head of someone who is risking his life every day," says Crawford, who acknowledges the pressures Walski was under on the battlefield. Still, "I can't imagine in my wildest dreams why he would ever do it." After leaving the Times, Walski started Colorado Visions, a commercial photo business.

In another war-zone episode, Adnan Hajj, a Lebanese freelancer on assignment for Reuters, was fired for doctoring images during the August 2006 conflict between Israel and Hezbollah in Lebanon. In one photo, Hajj darkened and cloned plumes of smoke rising from buildings the Israelis bombed in Beirut, amplifying the devastation. In another, he altered the image of an Israeli F-16 fighter jet to make it appear that it was firing several missiles instead of a single flare, as the original photo of the plane shows.

This time, bloggers acted as sheriff. According to news reports, Charles Johnson, who runs a blog called Little Green Footballs (www.littlegreenfootballs.com/weblog) sounded the alarm about the Beirut photo. Another conservative political blog, The Java Report (www.mypetjawa.mu.nu), drew attention to the phony missiles.

Bloggers also played a role in uncovering a USA Today misstep. (Disclosure: My husband, Frank Folwell, is a deputy managing editor who oversees photography and graphics for USA Today.) On October 26, 2005, WorldNetDaily.com reported that the newspaper pulled a photograph of Condoleezza Rice from its Web site after a blog called The Pen (www.fromthepen.com)

Back in Action

In early May, the message board for SportsShooter.com lit up after the headline "Detrich Rises From the Dead" appeared. Photographer Allan Detrich, who resigned from the Toledo Blade in April after an investigation showed he had doctored more than 79 images, was back.

The avid storm chaser had covered a tornado that leveled Greensburg, Kansas, on May 4, killing 12. Several news outlets interviewed Detrich, including Fox News Channel and CNN, and his pictures were shown on the air. The president of Polaris Images, a New York photo agency, saw the broadcasts and offered to distribute the Greensburg photos.

Some on SportsShooter.com were outraged by the turn of luck for a photographer ostracized one month earlier. Others took a more practical view. "Sad but true, it seems like the only people upset about this are the photographers. [They] liken what he did to a deadly sin, while the average person sees it as a simple mistake that should be forgiven," said a respondent from Cedar Park, Texas. That is what Detrich is counting on.

After he left the newspaper, he found it difficult to go out of the house, "I felt everybody would be looking at me, saying, 'That's the guy.'" Now he has moved on.

"I have apologized and admitted I was wrong. I'm being up-front with people if they ask about it. I can't do more than that," Detrich says. "I'm not going to sit back and sulk for the rest of my life. I am going to let my images speak for themselves."

—S.R.

---

revealed it had been manipulated, giving the secretary of state a menacing stare. The blog used the original version of the Associated Press photo to show the image had been doctored.

The altered photo circulated on other blogs, drawing a firestorm of public protest. USA Today explained in an editor's note that "after sharpening the photo for clarity," a portion of Rice's face was brightened, "giving her eyes an unnatural appearance." The distortion violated the paper's editorial standards, the note said.

One of the most ballyhooed examples of photo manipulation was Time magazine's June 27, 1994, cover. Time darkened the skin and added a five o'clock shadow to a mug shot of O.J. Simpson, making him look more sinister. On its December 1, 1997, cover, Newsweek glamorized Bobbi McCaughey, the Iowa mother of septuplets, by straightening her teeth. The magazine superimposed Martha Stewart's head on a model's body for the March 7, 2005, cover, when Stewart was released from prison.

The credit explaining the super-imposed photo of Stewart appeared inside the magazine. Since then, Newsweek's attribution policy has changed. When a photo illustration runs on the front of the magazine, the credit also appears on the cover, says Simon Barnett, Newsweek's director of photography. That provides "an additional layer of information, so if anyone is in any doubt whatsoever, it's there to confirm what they see as being an illustration," he wrote in an e-mail interview.

As for news photos, "We do nothing beyond what has traditionally been done in the photographic darkroom," says Barnett, who took over as photo director in July 2003.

Barnett says the advent of Photoshop has increased the push to create flawless magazine covers. "As digital technology has evolved, art directors at major magazines have forgotten how and when to say 'enough.' This tweaking and buffing and polishing down to the last pixel has frequently had the consequence of changing the photograph into something that at a minimum is plastic, and at worst inaccurate," says Barnett, who counts himself among a minority that appreciates the natural imperfections that real photography brings. "It adds to authenticity," he says.

Time's readers are accustomed to finding the credit for covers on the table of contents, says spokesman Daniel Kile. If the photograph has been altered, the image is clearly labeled a "photo-illustration." That was the case on March 15, when Time illustrated a story, "How the Right Went Wrong," on the cover with a photo of Ronald Reagan crying. The inside credits noted: "Photograph by David Hume Kennerly. Tear by Tim O'Brien." (See "Finding a Niche," April/May.)

But no matter how pure the intention, NPPA's John Long doesn't buy attribution as a substitute for authenticity. "No amount of captioning can ever cover for a visual lie or distortion. If it looks real in a news context, then it better be real," says Long, who maintains there should be the same respect for visual accuracy that there is for the written word in journalism.

Long points out that some photos are doctored with the sole intent of doing harm. In February 2004, a photograph showing Democratic presidential candidate John Kerry with actress Jane Fonda at a 1971 anti-Vietnam war rally swept the Internet. Two photos, taken a year part, were merged into one and carried a phony AP credit line.

Ken Light, who took the original Kerry photograph sans Fonda, raised a key question in a March 11, 2004, New York Times article about faked images: "What if that photo had floated around two days before the general election and there wasn't time to say it's not true?" The story noted that image tampering did not begin in 1989, with John Knoll's creation of Photoshop.

On the cusp of the digital revolution in 1991, ethicist Paul Lester documented the history of forgeries in a book, "Photojournalism: An Ethical Approach." He noted that Hippolyte Bayard made the first known counterfeit photograph more than 160 years ago, and during the Civil War soldiers were instructed to play dead and corpses were moved for dramatic impact. In World War I, photos were forged for propaganda purposes, including one of Kaiser Wilhelm cutting off the hands of babies.

Lester included a classic example from 1982 often cited as the beginning of the steep challenge for photojournalism in the digital age. When National Geographic employed what was considered computer wizardry to squeeze together Egypt's pyramids of Giza for the perfect cover shot, tremors shot through the photo community. Many bemoaned the onset of an era when tampering with photos would be effortless.

In his book, Lester quoted Tom Kennedy, photo director at the Geographic from 1987 to 1997, who laid down new rules for the magazine. Technology no longer would be used to manipulate elements in a photo simply to achieve a more compelling graphic effect, Kennedy said. As for the pyramids, "We regarded that afterwards as a mistake, and we wouldn't repeat that mistake today."

Writing for the New York Times in 1990, acclaimed photo critic Andy Grundberg predicted, "In the future, readers of newspapers and magazines will probably view news pictures more as illustrations than as reportage, since they will be aware that they can no longer distinguish between a genuine image and one that has been manipulated." History has given weight to his prophecy as photo managers search for answers.

"Fundamentally, there is only so much you can do. You hope and pray and respect your staff. . . . You trust that they're not going to do this kind of thing," says the L.A. Times' Crawford, who, like many others interviewed for this story, sees setting clear, strict policies as critical for quality control. He believes that, despite the Walski incident, the Times has had a solid system in place. "You do the best you can, talking to your staff and making sure they understand what your ethics are," he says.

Since the Detrich episode, the Toledo Blade is spot-checking more photos and scheduling more one-on-one time with photographers to go over their work. "With the ability to send electronically, it is easy to feel isolated from the rest of the photo department, so we will try harder to establish a sense of team," says Luann Sharp, the Blade's assistant managing editor for administration.

Santiago Lyon, the AP's director of photography, oversees the wire service's vast army of 300 shooters plus 700 others operating on a freelance or contract basis. The AP handles about three-quarters of a million images a year, leaving ample potential for error.

Lyon has turned to the Poynter Institute, NPPA, the White House News Photographers Association and other media groups for guidance as he updates and fine-tunes the wire service's standards.

"We're looking at their ethical guidelines and our own and coming up with wordage and phraseology more in tune with the changing world out there," says Lyon, who attended Photoshop training sessions for about 200 AP photographers and photo editors throughout the U.S. in 2006. At each stop, he hammered home the guidelines for responsible use of imaging tools and repeatedly stressed that "credibility is the most important thing we have at the AP and journalism in general."

Lyon says a handful of photographers have been fired for tampering with pictures over the years. He views the core of experienced photo editors at AP's editing hubs around the globe as a first line of defense for detecting phony images.

There are certain clues photo monitors look for. According to experts, the most common signs are differences in color or shadows, variations in graininess or pixilation, blurred images or elements in the photo that are too bright or much sharper than the rest.

Dartmouth College professor Farid is developing computer algorithms, or mathematical formulas, that can detect altered images. Lyon and Farid have met to discuss possibilities for the future, and Lyon has had the professor analyze old photos the AP had on file and knew had been altered to test the reliability of the detection software. It worked in all but one case, Lyon says.

But for now, the method is too cumbersome, given that the AP receives between 2,000 and 3,000 pictures each day. "To work for us, that type of process would have to be instantaneous, or close to it," says Lyon.

Farid doesn't promote his detection software as a magic formula. "The technology is getting better and better. It's getting easier to manipulate, and it is affordable. Everybody has it. At least we might slow [the forger] down, make it more challenging, more difficult," says the computer scientist, who likens the scramble for improved safeguards to an arms race.

"I guarantee you there will be people out there developing anti-forgery detection software or software that makes better forgeries," says Farid.

Beyond stopping cheaters, there also is the thorny issue of defining the limits of what is and is not acceptable. Photo editors commonly say that the only appropriate techniques with Photoshop are those analogous to what was acceptable in the traditional darkroom. That might ring hollow to a generation of photographers who have always processed images on computers and transmitted them to the photo desk from the nearest Starbucks. Still, one rule is clear: Removing visual content from a photo or adding it crosses the divide.

Lyon warns that using words to describe visual nuances in guidelines is very complicated. "How do you define the correct use of tonal differences—lightening or darkening aspects of a picture in a way that accurately reflects what the photographer saw?"

In an attempt to clarify standards, Kenny F. Irby, the Poynter Institute's photo expert, confessed in a September 2003 report that he had "dodged" (to lighten) and "burned" (to darken) elements in his pictures throughout his career. He maintained there was nothing sinful about his actions because he did not take those techniques to extremes.

Irby listed notables such as Gordon Parks and W. Eugene Smith among the many great photojournalists who employed the same techniques. When, then, do photographers slip into the abyss?

On August 15, 2003, Patrick Schneider of the Charlotte Observer was suspended for three days without pay for excessive adjustments in Photoshop. The North Carolina Press Photographers Association stripped Schneider of the awards he had won for the photos in question. Its investigation found that details such as parking lots, fences and people had been removed from pictures.

At the time, Schneider told Irby, "I used the tools that for decades have been used in the darkroom, and now, in Photoshop, I do them with more precision. My goal is to bring more impact to my images, to stop the readers and draw their attention."

The award-winning photographer was fired in July 2006 for an image of a firefighter on a ladder, silhouetted against a vivid sunlit sky. The Observer explained in an editor's note that in the original, the sky was brownish-gray. Enhanced with photo-editing software, the sky became a deep red, and the sun took on a more distinct halo. In the judgment of his bosses, Schneider had violated the paper's rules.

While the photo establishment buzzes over scandals like those of Schneider and Detrich, others ask, "So what?"

The Toledo Blade's Royhab was surprised when some readers questioned the ruckus raised over Detrich's misdeeds and asked what was wrong with changing the content of a photograph in a newspaper. "The answer is simple: It is dishonest," Royhab wrote in an April 15 column.

On SportsShooter.com, a Web site run by USA Today photographer Robert Hanashiro, some attacked Detrich for his duplicity while others defended his right to stay in journalism. That did not sit well with Bob DeMay, chairman of the board of the Ohio News Photographers Association and an acquaintance of Detrich's.

"I find it very scary that some people didn't find fault at all," says DeMay, photo editor at the Akron Beacon Journal. "There used to be an old saying, 'Pictures don't lie.' Well, they do now. Once that seed of doubt is put in somebody's mind, it's frightening."

Like many others, DeMay sees the troubled state of newspapers playing into the equation. Pushed to the limits by layoffs and hiring freezes, many photo departments have fewer bodies to do more work. Three photo staffers at the Beacon Journal were laid off last year, taking a toll on quality, says DeMay. As travel budgets are slashed, there is more reliance on freelancers who file photos from a distance, without the backstop of newsroom accountability or ethics codes. And the competition for newspaper space has never been fiercer, increasing the pressure for dramatic images.

There also has been a cultural change in how photo departments operate. In the past, photographers often worked together in the darkroom; there was more collaboration and more oversight from photo desks. Today, it is common to transmit images from the field via laptop computers, with only occasional newsroom visits.

Opportunities for misdeeds are boundless, warns Larry Gross, coeditor of the book "Image Ethics in the Digital Age." Once photographers step over the line, there is very little they can't do, and, if they are skilled enough, they may leave little or no trace, says Gross. Years ago, editors could ask for the photo negative to make comparisons, but digital images can be changed so that there's no original left, no way to track back to an initial state. Adding to the angst of photo watchdogs, new and better versions of Photoshop are on the horizon, which is likely to widen the scope of fakeries.

NPPA's Winslow wonders if the ethics quandary in photojournalism is akin to the problem professional baseball has with steroids. "Are there lots of people doing what Detrich did without editors and managers realizing the extent of the problem?" he asked in his May article. "Or do they suspect, but do nothing about it?"

Not everyone sees a dim future. Author David Perlmutter believes that, by some standards, this is the golden age of photojournalistic ethics.

"If you are caught faking a picture today, you are fired. Fifty years ago, it was just part of the business. Now most people have gone to journalism school and learned ethics. Newsrooms are taking these things more seriously. Standards are higher than ever," Perlmutter says. "On the other hand, it has become so much easier to get away with the crime."

Senior contributing writer **SHERRY RICCHIARDI** (sricchia@iupui.edu) has written about coverage of the war in Iraq and the Virginia Tech massacre in recent issues of *AJR*.

From *American Journalism Review,* August/September 2007. Copyright © by the Philip Merrill College of Journalism at the University of Maryland, College Park, MD 20742-7111. Reprinted with permission.

Article 29

What Would You Do?
The Journalism That Tweaks Reality, Then Reports What Happens

DANIEL WEISS

On a Friday morning last January, a group of Washington, D.C., commuters played an unwitting role in an experiment. As they emerged from the L'Enfant Plaza metro station, they passed a man playing a violin. Dressed in a long-sleeved T-shirt, baseball cap, and jeans, an open case for donations at his feet, he looked like an ordinary busker. In reality, he was Joshua Bell, an internationally renowned musician. The idea was to gauge whether Bell's virtuosic playing would entice the rushing commuters to stop and listen.

The experiment's mastermind was *Washington Post* staff writer Gene Weingarten, who had dreamed it up after seeing a talented keyboardist be completely ignored as he played outside another metro station. "I bet Yo-Yo Ma himself, if he were in disguise, couldn't get through to these deadheads," Weingarten says he thought at the time. Ma wasn't available to test the hypothesis, but Bell was.

For three-quarters of an hour, Bell played six pieces, including some of the most difficult and celebrated in the classical canon. Of 1,097 passersby, twenty-seven made donations totaling just over $30. Seven stopped for more than a minute. The remaining 1,070 breezed by, barely aware of the supremely talented violinist in their midst.

When Weingarten's account of the experiment ran in the *Post's* magazine three months later, readers followed the narrative with rapt attention that contrasted starkly with the indifference of the commuters. The article was discussed on blogs and other forums devoted to classical music, pop culture, politics, and social science. Weingarten said he received more feedback from readers than he had for any other article he had written in his thirty-five-year career. Many were taken with the chutzpah of disguising Joshua Bell as a mendicant just to see what would happen. Others were shocked that people could ignore a world-class musician. Still others argued that the results were insignificant: rerun the experiment outdoors on a sunny day, they said, and Bell would draw a massive crowd.

I was one of those rapt readers, but I wasn't quite sure what to make of the piece's appeal. Was it just a clever gimmick or was there something more profound going on? At the same time, the story felt familiar. Indeed, Weingarten's experiment was a recent entry in a journalistic genre with deep, quirky roots.

Working on a hunch that begs to be tested or simply struck with an idea for a good story, journalistic "experimenters," for lack of a better term, step out of their customary role as observers and play with reality to see what will happen. At their worst, these experiments are little more than variations on reality-TV operations that traffic in voyeurism and shame. At their best, they manage to deliver discussion-worthy insights into contemporary society and human nature. The very best, perhaps, serve up a bit of both. In any case, the growing number of journalists and news operations who do this sort of thing are heirs to a brand of social psychology practiced from the postwar years through the early seventies. During this period, considered by some the golden age of the discipline, experiments were bold and elaborately designed and frequently produced startling results. Many were conducted outside the laboratory and often placed subjects in stressful or disturbing situations.

These experiments also have roots in forms of investigative, immersion, and stunt journalism that have been practiced for more than a century. In 1887, while working on an exposé of asylum conditions, muckraker Nellie Bly demonstrated that one could feign insanity to gain admission to a madhouse—and when she began to insist that she was in fact perfectly sane, doctors interpreted her claims as delusions. In so doing, Bly anticipated psychologist David Rosenhan's classic 1972 experiment in which "pseudopatients" claiming to hear voices were admitted to psychiatric hospitals and then kept for an average of several weeks despite reverting to sane behavior.

It's difficult to pinpoint when the genre shifted, but by 1974, when New York City's WNBC-TV asked its viewers to call in and pick the perpetrator of a staged purse snatching from a lineup of suspects, the journalistic experiment had attained its modern form. The station was flooded with calls and, after fielding over 2,100, cut the experiment short. The results: respondents picked the correct assailant no more frequently than they would have by guessing.

Over the last decade, as best-sellers such as *The Tipping Point* and *Freakonomics* have lent social science a sheen of counterintuitive hipness and reality television has tapped into a cultural fascination with how people behave in contrived situations, journalistic experimentation has become increasingly common. In addition to *The Washington Post Magazine,* it has been featured in *The New York Times, Harper's,* and *Reader's Digest.* Its most regular home, however, has been on network-television newsmagazines.

ABC's *Primetime* has staged a series of experiments in recent years under the rubric "What Would You Do?" which enact provocative scenarios while hidden cameras capture the reactions of the public. Chris Whipple, the producer who conceived the series, refers to it as a *"Candid Camera* of ethics." Starting with a nanny verbally abusing a child, the series has gone on to present similar scenarios: an eldercare attendant ruthlessly mocking an old man; a group of adolescents bullying a chubby kid; a man viciously berating his girlfriend, seeming on the verge of violence; etc.

The sequences tend to begin with the narrator pointing out that many pass right by the incident. Several witnesses are confronted and asked to explain why they didn't step in. One man, who gave the fighting couple a long look before continuing on his way, reveals that he is an off-duty cop and says he determined that no laws were being broken, so there was nothing for him to do. The focus shifts to those who did intervene, and the camera lingers over the confrontations, playing up the drama.

These experiments are, in a sense, the flip side of the reality-TV coin: rather than show how people act in manufactured situations when they *know* they're being watched, they show us how people act when they don't. And the experiments have clearly appealed to viewers. From the first minutes of its first hour, when its ratings doubled those of the previous week, "What Would You Do?" has been a success. After appearing periodically in 2005 and 2006, ABC ordered five new hours that were scheduled to air last November before the writers' strike put them on hold. It is, Whipple says, highly "watchable" television.

In the world of print, *Reader's Digest* has come closest to making such experiments a franchise. Over the last two years, the magazine has pitted cities around the world against each other in tests of helpfulness and courtesy, to determine which city is most hospitable. The first round used the following three gauges to separate the rude from the solicitous in thirty-five cities: the percentage of people who picked up papers dropped by an experimenter; the percentage who held the door for experimenters when entering buildings; and the percentage of clerks who said "Thank you" after a sale. When the scores were tallied, it was clear that *Reader's Digest* had hit the counterintuition jackpot: the winner was New York City. According to Simon Hemelryk, an editor with the UK edition of *Reader's Digest* who came up with the idea for the tests, the press response was "totally, totally mad." Hundreds of media outlets picked up the story. David Letterman presented a tongue-in-cheek, top-ten list of the "Signs New York City Is Becoming More Polite."

The notion that New Yorkers are more polite than commonly believed was also at the center of a 2004 experiment conducted by *The New York Times.* Reenacting an experiment originally performed by graduate students of social psychologist Stanley Milgram at the City University of New York in the early seventies, two *Times* reporters asked riders on crowded subway cars to relinquish their seats. Remarkably, thirteen of fifteen did so. But the reporters found that crossing the unspoken social boundaries of the subway came at a cost: once seated, they grew tense, unable to make eye contact with their fellow passengers. Jennifer Medina, one of the reporters, says that she and Anthony Ramirez, her partner on the story, found the assignment ludicrous at first. "It was like, 'What? Really? You want me to do what?'" she says. "We made so much fun of it while we were doing it, but we got so much feedback. It was one of those stories that people really talked about." And papers around the world took notice: within weeks, reporters in London, Glasgow, Dublin, and Melbourne had repeated the experiment.

In these journalistic experiments, the prank always lurks just beneath the surface and is clearly part of the genre's appeal. During ABC *Primetime's* experiments, there always comes the moment when host John Quiñones enters and, with a soothing voice and congenial smile, ends the ruse. *These people are actors. You have been part of an experiment.* And in that moment, no matter how serious the scenario, there is always the hint of a practical joke revealed, a touch of "Smile, you're on *Candid Camera!"*

Sometimes the experiment is overwhelmed by the prank. Last year, *Radar Magazine* sent a reporter to snort confectioner's sugar in various New York City locales. The idea was to test anecdotal evidence from a *New York Times* article that cocaine use was growing more publicly acceptable. (The results: public snorting was actively discouraged at the New York Public Library's main reading room, but not at a Starbucks or *Vanity Fair* editor Graydon Carter's Waverly Inn.) Carter's own *Spy Magazine* pulled a classic prank/experiment in the late eighties when it sent checks of dwindling value to moguls in an attempt to determine who was the cheapest millionaire. (Donald Trump reportedly cashed one for just thirteen cents.) Even *Borat* was, in a sense, an extended experiment in the extremes to which a Kazakh "journalist" could push pliant Americans, and was anticipated by one of *Primetime's* "What Would You Do?" episodes in which a taxi driver goes off on racist or homophobic rants, baiting riders either to defy him or join in.

If Medina, the *Times* reporter, was made uneasy by the whiff of "stunt" in the subway experiment, she is not the only one. Even Weingarten, whose Joshua Bell experiment was a monumental success, looks at the genre slightly askance. Asked whether he plans to conduct similar experiments in the future, he replies: "If I can think of one this good, there's no reason I'd quail at it. But, you know, you also don't want to go off and be the stunt writer. I would need to feel as though the next thing I'm doing was of equal sociological importance. And this wasn't just a lark. We had something we wanted to examine, and it was the nature of the perception of beauty."

The appeal of the best journalistic experiments, indeed, runs much deeper than their entertainment value. Medina came to see her role in the subway experiment as that of a "street anthropologist or something, which is essentially what [reporters] are supposed to be doing every day." And Weingarten received over one hundred messages from people who said that his piece on the Bell experiment made them cry. (One testimonial from an online chat Weingarten had with readers: "I cried because I find it scary and depressing to think of how obliviously most people go through daily life, even smart and otherwise attentive people. Who knows what beautiful things I've missed by just hurrying along lost in my thoughts?") In essence, many readers imagined themselves as actors in the story. Weingarten set out to chronicle an experiment; he ended up writing a deeply effective profile of his own readers. "What Would You Do?" asks *Primetime*—and that, on some level, is the question that all such journalistic experiments ask. Would you walk by the famous violinist? Would you give up your seat on the subway? Would you protect a woman from an abusive boyfriend?

In that quirky, postwar "golden age" of the discipline that informs today's journalistic experimenters, researchers captured the public imagination with bold, elaborately choreographed experiments that frequently drove subjects to extreme behavior or confronted them with seemingly life-or-death situations.

Stanley Milgram, the designer of the subway-seat experiment, was one of the most creative social psychologists of that era. His infamous obedience experiment, first performed in 1961, in which subjects were instructed to shock a man in a separate room every time he gave an incorrect answer on a memory test, showed that normal people were capable of great cruelty. Sixty-five percent of the subjects went to the maximum—450 volts—despite the test-taker's cries of pain and pleas to be released due to a heart condition. By the end, the test-taker no longer responded at all, having presumably passed out or died. (In reality, the test-taker was an actor and his protests tape-recorded.) Even more unsettling was Stanford professor Philip Zimbardo's 1971 prison experiment, in which college students randomly assigned to play the role of guards in a mock prison terrorized those playing inmates. Slated to run for two weeks, it was terminated after six days, during which several "prisoners" came close to nervous breakdown.

Given the dramatic nature of these experiments, it's little wonder they've provided such inspiration to journalists. Bill Wasik, an editor at *Harper's,* started the flash mobs trend in 2003 as an homage to Milgram, whom he considers as much performance artist as scientist. Flash mobs were spontaneous gatherings in which participants showed up at a given location for a brief period and did something absurd, such as drop to their knees en masse before a giant Tyrannosaurus Rex at Toys "R" Us. In a piece published in *Harper's,* Wasik explained that he saw the mobs as a Milgram-esque test of hipster conformity. Like a hot new indie band, he hypothesized, the mobs would rapidly gain popularity before being discarded as too mainstream and, ultimately, co-opted by marketers, which is more or less what happened.

Wasik argues that the popular resonance of experiments by Milgram and others of the golden age derives from the compelling narratives they created. "It's like a demonstration whose value is more in the extremes that you can push people to and the extremes of the story that you can get out of what people do or don't do," he says. "Milgram could have done an authority experiment in which he got people to do all sorts of strange things that didn't seem to be simulating the death of the participant." Many contemporary social psychologists credit researchers from this fertile era with cleverly demonstrating how frequently human behavior defies expectations. But others, such as Joachim Krueger of Brown University, argue that the experiments were designed in ways that guaranteed unflattering results. "You could call it a 'gotcha psychology,'" he says.

Due in part to the rise of ethical concerns, contemporary social psychologists rarely do experiments that take place outside the laboratory or that involve deception or stressful situations. This has left journalistic experimenters as a sort of lost tribe of devotees of the golden-age social psychologists. Unlike investigative journalism, these experiments have largely flown under the ethical radar. This may be because of the fact that, while some journalistic experiments may be frivolous, they are on balance innocuous. However, as experimenters increasingly tackle sensitive topics, they have begun to draw some heat. In 2006, conservative bloggers accused *Dateline* of trying to manufacture a racist incident by bringing a group of Arab-looking men to a NASCAR race. And, last November, these same bloggers ripped an experiment by *Primetime* in which same-sex couples engaged in public displays of affection in Birmingham, Alabama, for attempting to provoke homophobic reactions. (As of press time, the same-sex segment had not yet aired, but according to the Fox affiliate in Birmingham, which broke the story, Birmingham police received several complaints from people disgusted by the sight of two men kissing in public.)

But what of the oft-cited "rule" that journalists should report the news rather than make it? Michael Kinsley, who conducted a 1985 experiment while at *The New Republic* to determine whether the Washington, D.C., elite actually read the books they act like they have, rejects the premise. "If you've got no other way to get a good story," he says, "and you're not being dishonest in what you write and publish, what's wrong with it?" Kinsley's experiment involved slipping notes deep into fashionable political books at several D.C. bookstores, offering $5 to anyone who called an intern at the magazine. In five months, not a single person claimed the reward.

Journalistic experiments have been criticized far more consistently for their scientific, rather than ethical, shortcomings. Robert Cialdini, an Arizona State University social psychologist, believes strongly in the value of communicating psychological insights via the media, but he has found that journalists don't always value the same material that he does. For a 1997 *Dateline* segment on conformity, he conducted an experiment showing that the number of people who donated to a New York City subway musician multiplied eightfold when others donated before them. A fascinating result, but even more fascinating to Cialdini was that people explained their donations by saying that they liked the song, they had some spare change, or they felt sorry for the musician. These explanations did not end up in the finished program. "To me, that was the most interesting thing, the fact that people are susceptible to these social cues but don't recognize it," says Cialdini. "I think that's my bone to pick with journalists—they're frequently interested in the phenomenon rather than the cause of the phenomenon."

Others are frustrated by the premium journalists place on appealing to a mass audience. Duncan Watts, a Columbia University sociologist, designed an experiment for *Primetime* to test Milgram's small-world theory—commonly known as "six degrees of separation"—that people divided by great social or geographical distance are actually connected by a relatively small number of links. In the experiment, two white Manhattan residents competed to connect with a black boxer from the Bedford-Stuyvesant neighborhood of Brooklyn using the fewest links, then the boxer had to connect with a Broadway dancer. All three connections were made using at most six links. Watts says that after the segment aired in late 2006, he received an e-mail from its producer, Thomas Berman, saying that its ratings had been poor. (An ABC spokeswoman insists that the network was satisfied with the ratings.) "One of the limitations of this model is that it's crowd-driven, it's about entertainment," says Watts. "It's a bit of a Faustian bargain."

Another quibble that some social psychologists have with these journalistic experiments is the use of the word "experiment" to describe them in the first place. To a dyed-in-the-wool researcher, an experiment involves comparing a control group with an experimental one, in which a single condition has been varied so that any changes in the outcome can be clearly attributed. Practically no journalistic "experiment" meets this standard, but many golden-age experiments didn't either, strictly speaking. In addition, practically every journalistic experiment includes a disclaimer that its results are decidedly unscientific.

Wendell Jamieson, city editor at *The New York Times* who assigned the subway-experiment story, chafes at calling the exercise an "experiment," pointing out that it was conducted in connection with another article about the original experiment. "It's just a fun way to take a different approach to a story," Jamieson says, comparing it to when he was at the New York *Daily News* and sent a reporter to Yankee Stadium during a subway series dressed in Mets regalia. "It's tabloid trick two-hundred and fifty-two." Bill Wasik, the *Harper's* editor who started flash mobs, points out that using the word "experiment" is a way for journalists to appropriate the "alpha position" of science, lending their endeavors a sort of added legitimacy. "The piece is wearing a lab coat," Wasik says of his own article, which repeatedly describes flash mobs as an experiment, "but it's not entirely scientific by any means."

Perhaps no media outlet has tried harder to achieve uniformity in conducting its experiments than *Reader's Digest*. Detailed instructions for how to conduct its "studies" are distributed to researchers in more than thirty cities around the world to ensure that their results will be comparable. For the courtesy tests, researchers were told how long dropped papers were to be left on the ground, how far to walk behind people entering buildings to see whether they would hold the door, and what sort of demeanor to adopt when speaking with clerks who were being tested to see whether they would say "Thank you." Nonetheless, despite all the careful planning, New York City's courtesy title may need to be affixed with an asterisk. Robert Levine, a social psychologist at California State University, Fresno, did a series of helpfulness experiments in the early nineties in which New York City placed dead last out of thirty-six United States cities. While this doesn't necessarily contradict the *Reader's Digest* result, in which New York was the only U.S. city tested among a global selection of cities, Levine points out that all the *Reader's Digest* New York tests were carried out at Starbucks, yielding a potentially skewed sample. What if Starbucks employees and customers are simply more courteous than New Yorkers as a whole? "I'm not saying they screwed up," says Levine, "but that was certainly a flag that was raised for me."

So maybe journalists can and should be more careful in how they design experiments, but that debate, in many ways, is beside the point. The best examples of the genre are undeniably good journalism, and the lesser lights, for the most part, amount to innocuous entertainment. Indeed, my hope is that some enterprising reporter is even now hatching a plan to find out whether Joshua Bell really would draw such a big crowd outdoors on a sunny day in D.C.

DANIEL WEISS is a freelance writer based in New York City.

Reprinted from *Columbia Journalism Review*, January/February 2008, pp. 41–44. Copyright © 2008 by Columbia Journalism Review, Columbia University.

Naming Names: Credibility vs. Deportation

Newsrooms are struggling with the dilemma of whether to use the names of illegal immigrants. Anonymous sources are under fire as threats to credibility. Yet identifying undocumented immigrants could lead to their deportation.

Lucy Hood

Gloria Rubio is an upstanding member of her community in Tulsa, Oklahoma. The mother of three young children, she and her husband are active in parent organizations at their children's schools. They volunteer at church, at a local drug-free program and at other community groups. Rubio, an undocumented immigrant born in Mexico, is also diligent about paying her taxes. She told reporter Ginnie Graham of the Tulsa World that she considered it a demonstration of loyalty and support to her adopted country.

Rubio was the subject of a story Graham wrote in March 2005 about a tax service in Tulsa that caters to both legal and illegal immigrants. Graham hoped to shed light on a segment of the city's burgeoning immigrant population that contributes to both state and national tax rolls. "The intent of the story was not to find an illegal immigrant," she says, "but to showcase this service that helps immigrants to assimilate and pay taxes."

Graham, who covers the social services beat, had written about undocumented immigrants before. At times she'd withheld a name at the request of an immigrant or an agency that had facilitated an interview, but whether to use Rubio's name in this particular story was never an issue. Rubio had spoken to community groups about paying taxes; the tax service had handpicked her to be a spokesperson for the story; and when Graham asked her if she had a problem with her name and photograph appearing in the paper, Rubio said no. "And we asked her again," Graham says.

About a month after the story ran, agents from U.S. Immigration and Customs Enforcement showed up at Rubio's house. They arrested her and began deportation proceedings after ICE's Oklahoma City office received an anonymous letter containing a copy of the story.

A year later, Graham still wonders what she could have done differently. "If this were to come up again, I would make it abundantly clear what the consequences would be," she says. "We tried to do that with this case. We asked her several times, 'Are you sure?' We explained she'd be on the front page and her picture would be there . . .

"I still have a hard time with that case," Graham says. "It obviously didn't turn out the way I wanted."

Rubio's story illustrates a dilemma faced by an increasing number of newsrooms in areas where large immigrant populations are integral parts of the community. These immigrants make news for all the same reasons—good and bad—as anyone else. Some graduate at the top of their class, run large, multinational corporations or, as members of the armed forces, risk their lives in defense of the country. Others engage in gang activity, hold up convenience stores and cause fatal accidents while driving drunk.

They also make news because as immigrants they're effecting change at every layer of society. They're altering everything from the way teachers teach to the way preachers preach. Census data from 2004 put the immigrant population at nearly 34.3 million, almost double what it was in 1990. Immigrants now make up 12 percent of the population and, according to a study by the Pew Hispanic Center, an estimated 30 percent of them are in the country illegally.

Of the undocumented, 78 percent are from Latin America, most of them from Mexico, and in unprecedented numbers they are going to places they've rarely gone before. "The highest growth of Latinos in the country is not happening in the big cities," says Rafael Olmeda, assistant city editor of the South Florida Sun-Sentinel and vice president for print of the National Association of Hispanic Journalists. "The largest percentage increase was in Raleigh, North Carolina. I love saying that, because it just shocks everyone."

In addition to North Carolina, they're going to Georgia, Nevada and Arkansas, as well as Utah, Tennessee and Iowa. And in many of these places, immigration has become a hot-button issue, pitting those who want to help immigrants assimilate against those who want them to go away. In fact, it's become a contentious issue nationwide, the result of both the immigrant influx and the terrorist attacks of September 11, 2001.

Five years ago, "The climate was a lot different," says Daniel Gonzalez, an immigration reporter for the Arizona Republic. President Bush had just been elected, and one of the first things he did was meet with Mexican President Vicente Fox. "It looked like immigration reform was going to happen that year," Gonzalez says. But it didn't, not that year, or the next, or the next.

It still hasn't happened. Meanwhile, antiterrorism legislation has brought immigrants under greater scrutiny, and antiterrorism sentiment has spilled over into anti-immigrant sentiment, making immigrant sources—especially the undocumented—more leery about appearing in the press. "People are much more reluctant to be interviewed," Gonzalez says, "and much more reluctant to let us use their name."

Richard Ruelas, a metro columnist at the Arizona Republic, says Arizona is one arena where immigrants have been thrown into the spotlight by divisive efforts to restrict their rights and/or send them home. "The rhetoric heats up," Ruelas says, "and that's when you see a tendency for the people to want to stay quiet."

In short, the undocumented are retreating, becoming less willing to talk, while interest in immigrant issues is on the rise. That means reporters and editors often must decide if they are willing to conceal the identity of an illegal immigrant if that's what it takes to get the story. And if they do, how do they do it? Do they use the first name, or the last? Which details do they include and which ones do they leave out? Is it ethical to use a name, even with permission, if it could get someone deported?

It's analogous to writing about rape victims, whistle-blowers and people living under repressive regimes. Figuring out if, when and how to do that can be a daunting task, and with the credibility of journalism at a low point, if not an all-time low, it's even more difficult today. A 2005 survey by the Pew Research Center for the People & the Press found that newspapers' credibility with readers had fallen by 30 percentage points since 1985, when 84 percent of those surveyed said they believed most of what they read in their daily newspaper. That figure was 54 percent in 2004.

People are much more reluctant to be interviewed and much more reluctant to let us use their name.

Some journalists believe that in the wake of fabrication scandals at such news organizations as the New York Times and USA Today, anonymous quotes should be used sparingly. "Survey after survey shows that readers think we just make up these quotes," says Owen Ullmann, deputy managing editor for news at USA Today, where a strict sourcing policy was put in place after the lies of former reporter Jack Kelley came to light in early 2004. "We try hard," Ullmann says, "to see if we really need to apply anonymity at the cost of reader skepticism or disbelief."

Editors will confront such balancing acts with increasing frequency as the immigrant issue moves to the forefront of debate, Ullmann predicts. "We'll be writing quite a bit about it in the coming months," he says, and each decision will be made on an individual basis. If another source can provide the same information, then there's no need to rely on an undocumented—and unnamed—immigrant. But "we've read stories before about people who are virtually treated as slaves or who suffocate in a truck," he says. "If one of them survives and tells an eyewitness story of their ordeal, I could see us granting them anonymity in that case."

According to Tom Rosenstiel, the director of the Project for Excellence in Journalism, the decision to use a name or not hinges on a simple test—not an easy test, but a simple test: "Does the information I'm getting by promising confidentiality outweigh what I'm withholding from my audience to get it?"

The Society of Professional Journalists' ethics code says journalism's top priority is to report the truth. Journalists should "identify sources whenever feasible," the code says, yet they should use "special sensitivity" when dealing with inexperienced sources, and they should "show compassion for those who may be adversely affected by news coverage."

Says Kelly McBride, ethics group leader at the Poynter Institute, "You have to assess the risk and make a decision that minimizes the harm to that individual but maximizes the ability to tell the truth."

The Arizona Republic is published in Phoenix, a city of 1.3 million people 150 miles north of the Mexican border. Like most other newsrooms, reporters and editors at the Arizona Republic make sourcing decisions about illegal immigrants on a case-by-case basis. But unlike most other newsrooms, the one at the Arizona Republic has a long tradition of covering immigrant issues and a long history of dealing with undocumented immigrants.

Phoenix is a major stopover for immigrants—legal and illegal—coming into the United States from Mexico. While many simply pass through on their way to destinations farther north, many others stay and settle in the Phoenix area, which is currently home to a foreign-born population of 304,000. Of the 810,000 immigrants statewide, an estimated 500,000 are undocumented. Of those, several have appeared in the paper, but never under a false name and very rarely without any name at all.

"We almost always try to name people," says immigration reporter Gonzalez. In his six years covering either Latino affairs or immigration, Gonzalez says he can't recall using an unnamed source. And the paper has a strict policy against the use of pseudonyms, so he typically works with—or around—the real name. "Mexican people have two last names," he says. "Sometimes we might use the least common of the two names."

Sometimes, he uses just the first name, or the first name and an initial, as he did in an October 2005 story about Javier P. and his wife, Janet, the parents of three children "who jumped a wall in Nogales in 1992," and, despite their illegal status, have become taxpaying members of the American middle class. Part of a four-day series, the story goes into great detail about the family. "They

Article 30. Naming Names: Credibility vs. Deportation

live in a tidy three-bedroom, two-bath house in a quiet northwest Phoenix neighborhood with leather sofas in the living room and a pickup and SUV in the garage," Gonzalez wrote.

But he also chose to omit certain details, particularly ones that might have tipped off the neighbors. He didn't, for example, include the make and year of the truck or the names of the schools attended by the children. "We have all these details," Gonzalez says, "which as a journalist is what you strive for, but you have to strike a balance."

Quite often, however, it doesn't become a balancing act. Both Gonzalez and columnist Ruelas, who also writes extensively about immigration, have used the complete names of undocumented immigrants, and as far as they know, there have never been negative repercussions for sources in their stories or anyone else's at the paper. "There's such a large number of undocumented immigrants," says Gonzalez, "it would be hard to figure out what Juan Martinez we're talking about."

Not only that, but the prevailing wisdom among immigration reporters and some attorneys is that the authorities are not likely to waste their time tracking down undocumented immigrants just because their names appear in the news stories. Ruelas says immigration officials have told him (unofficially) that they're not really interested in individual cases. "They're looking into smuggling operations," he says. "They concentrate on the big stuff. It's almost like the drug war. They're not concerned with the guy with the joint. They're concerned with the guy bringing in the truckload from Mexico."

But that's not always the case, Poynter's McBride says. Law enforcement officials may take action for any number of reasons. They may very simply have a visiting official to impress; or, as was the case in Tulsa, they may receive an anonymous note urging them to take action; or they may perceive a real threat. "Once you point out to law enforcement officials that someone is breaking the law," she says, "you sort of back them into the corner."

A case in point involved Raleigh's News & Observer. In March 1998 it published an in-depth story about an undocumented grocery worker named Julio Granados. The paper's purpose, McBride says, was to write about a growing community that was largely invisible to most of the N&O's readers. But the story attracted the attention of the Immigration and Naturalization Service (ICE's predecessor), and INS agents raided Granados' workplace and arrested him, four coworkers and a customer. (See "Too Much Information?" June 1998.)

At the time, then-Editor Anders Gyllenhaal (now editor of Minneapolis' Star Tribune) wrote an article saying those involved in the story thought they had taken all the appropriate steps, but in retrospect, the paper should have done things differently. "The fact is," he wrote, "we could have painted just as exhaustive a portrait of Granados without providing a road map that seemed to incite agents to make an example of someone who stands out merely because their story was published."

There's such a large number of undocumented immigrants, it would be hard to figure out what Juan Martinez we're talking about.

It's paramount that reporters be aware of the risks involved when they interview undocumented immigrants, McBride says, and they must know that there are no simple answers. "Journalists call us," she says, "and they want the rule." But there is no rule. Instead there's a process, one in which the reporter must evaluate whether the source is likely to be fired, deported or harassed. Is the source capable of assessing the risk? Does he or she understand the legal implications? "You have to ask a lot of questions," McBride says, "including what your own journalistic purpose is."

Gonzalez, who has gone through the process many times, explains to his sources in as much detail as possible what the story is about, and he tells them very clearly what the consequences might be. At times, he says, the undocumented are willing to take the risk because they believe the story addresses an important issue. And some give their consent out of bravado. "It's important in those situations," he says, "to always make it clear that the person understands there could be an implication." And "once you've done that, you've done your job."

Across the country in Charleston, South Carolina—1,500 miles from the nearest border crossing into Mexico—the city's burgeoning immigrant population is a very new phenomenon. Drawn by jobs in construction and landscaping, the immigrant community has rapidly become an integral part of the local economy. It grew in Charleston County by nearly 200 percent, from 5,832 to 15,409, between 1990 and 2004. "If you took away the ones that are illegal," says journalist Dave Munday, "we suspect it would kill the whole economy."

Yet until last spring the immigrant population was "fairly invisible," says Munday, a reporter at Charleston's Post and Courier. While the paper and other local media outlets have reported on the demographic shift in their midst, coverage of the immigrant community was sparse, Munday says, until a local politician brought the issue of illegal immigration to the forefront. Before that, there was rarely a need to ponder the pros and cons of naming undocumented sources. "I happened to be thrust into it," he says, "when the Rotary Club had a golf tournament."

It was a fundraising event the paper originally planned to mention in a blurb, but it morphed into a human-interest story when Munday learned that the proceeds would go toward a life-saving heart operation for a young boy from Mexico. Munday didn't expect that it would become anything more than that, not until he visited the boy's home and learned that the family was in the country illegally. He returned to the newsroom, he recalls, "and said, 'Now what?'"

He checked with immigration officials, who told him they were typically busy chasing criminals and didn't have the time to pursue a single undocumented immigrant in North Charleston. He also checked with the Rotary Club, which did not have a problem with mentioning the boy's illegal status. But the family did, so Munday ultimately identified the boy only by his first name, Oscar, and mentioned that the family was undocumented. The alternative, he says, was that "we don't have a story at all."

That alternative—coupled with a growing inclination of immigrants to shy away from public exposure—concerns some journalists. There's a tendency "for the people to want to stay quiet," says the Arizona Republic's Ruelas. It's the result of heated anti-immigrant rhetoric, he says, and it worries him because it means that important stories will not be told, and other stories will be told in a way that skews perceptions. Take, for example, an undocumented high school student with stellar grades who is trying to get into college, or the college graduate prepared for a professional career. "It can be an education to some readers," Ruelas says, "to see a name and a face and not have it be a stereotype they associate with illegal immigrants."

Olmeda, of the South Florida Sun-Sentinel, agrees. "I would hate to see good stories not told because of these considerations," he says. But there are other considerations.

"I don't advocate running out there," he says, "getting names, addresses and a picture, along with a map about how to get there for the ICE, all of which would be truth but not journalistically necessary."

Then again, he says, "It's not our job to protect the world... If you're here illegally, you're running the risk. As a journalist, I am not your risk. Your risk is what you've done."

It's easy to go back and forth. What's difficult, Olmeda says, is striking the proper balance between the need to tell the truth and an obligation to protect the people who are put in precarious positions because of that need to tell the truth.

"Is there a quick answer to that?" he muses. "Heavens no!"

LUCY HOOD (lahood5@aol.com), a former reporter for the San Antonio *Express-News,* is a Washington, D.C.-based writer.

The Lives of Others
What Does It Mean to 'Tell Someone's Story'?

JULIA DAHL

On March 22, *America's Most Wanted* told my story. I wasn't the fugitive, or the victim, and it shouldn't have been my story. It should have been Tyeisha's. But as the producer from AMW told me, "Girls die in ditches every day. The reason Tyeisha stands out is because she was profiled in *Seventeen* magazine." I met Tyeisha Martin at a Red Cross shelter in Henry County, Georgia, on a sunny September afternoon in 2005. She was barefoot, wearing a tank top and Capri jeans, waiting in line to get a tetanus shot. I was living in a small town nearby called McDonough, south of Atlanta. I'd moved there a year earlier from New York City with my boyfriend. We were both writers, still thinking we might be able to publish the novels we'd written in grad school. I knew I wanted to write for a living, but I'd left my job at a women's magazine certain I'd never go back. I didn't like what I'd been able to write in that world. Every time I put together an article, it felt like I was building a little lie. Whether it was culled from quotes e-mailed through a publicist, like the cover story I did on the movie star; or built upon crude stereotypes, like the "profile" of the three beauty queens who lived together in Trump Place; or the time I followed the rules of a dating book and neatly concluded that it's better to just be yourself if you want to meet a guy. My instincts as a writer were nowhere in these stories. They weren't little windows on the human condition, they didn't wrestle with questions about the world; they passed the time on the StairMaster, at the dentist, by the pool.

I justified it plenty. I told myself that Joan Didion had started at *Vogue*. I told myself it meant something that I could make it in the glossies. That I was successful. The problem was that I didn't feel successful. I decamped to Georgia, in part, to get some perspective on all this. But still, I wanted to write. So when *Seventeen* called and asked me to do a story for its Drama section about a young girl in Tennessee who'd been drugged and raped by her cousin, I said yes. Hell, yes. I did stories like this for two years. I went to Birmingham, Alabama, to learn about twelve-year-old Jasmine Archie, who died, according to police reports, after her mother poured bleach down her throat and sat on her chest until she stopped breathing. I went to Wythe County, Virginia, and knocked on the door of the home where fourteen-year-old Nakisha Waddell had stabbed her mother forty-three times and buried her in the backyard. I wrote about two teenage lesbians who murdered one's grandparents in Fayette County, Georgia. The stories were still formulaic, but instead of chasing publicists and trailing beauty queens, I got to read trial transcripts, track down family members, and hang out in county jails. Each story was an adventure, and, at least initially, the reporting felt like the kind of work I imagined a "journalist" would do.

Tyeisha was an accident. I was in Virginia reporting Nakisha's story when Hurricane Katrina hit, and my editor called to ask if I knew anybody in New Orleans. They wanted to profile a teenage evacuee. I said I might know someone—a girl I knew from the local coffee shop had been headed to Tulane—but I'd have to get back to her.

I promptly forgot about it. There was no easy way to find this girl, since I didn't even know her last name, and I was tired from the reporting trip. Sitting for hours with Nakisha's grandmother had been mentally exhausting. This was the second Drama piece I'd done, and I knew what *Seventeen* wanted was brief and uncomplicated. I wouldn't be able to tell how the old woman's hands shook, or how cigarette smoke was stitched into every fiber in her trailer. Or that hanging in the back hallway where Nakisha stuck a knife in her mother's throat was a plaque that read: "This house shall serve the Lord."

When I got home, I needed to get out of myself, so I went to the Red Cross shelter at the local church where my boyfriend's mom, a nurse, was helping tend to the hundreds of suddenly homeless people from New Orleans. That's when I saw Tyeisha, standing in the middle of a group of boys. Tall, bored, beautiful. I remembered the editor from *Seventeen* and I approached her. She agreed to be profiled. Over the next several days, as she waited for FEMA money in a Days Inn near Atlanta and tried to decide where to go next, Tyeisha told me about her life. She'd dropped out of school in the ninth grade and had a baby at seventeen (she was nineteen when we met). When Katrina hit, she had a GED, a job at a linen factory, and though she and her daughter, Daneisha, were living at her mother's house, Tyeisha dreamed of getting her own place.

On the evening of August 28, 2005, when residents were bracing for the storm, Tyeisha took her daughter to the little girl's father's apartment; he lived on the third floor and she thought two-year-old Daneisha would be safer there. Tyeisha spent the night with her sister, Quiana, and Quiana's boyfriend, Chuck. Before dawn, the water broke down their front door. Tyeisha was terrified as the water rose; she couldn't swim, and thought she was about to die. But Chuck and Quiana helped her, and the three of them climbed out a window and found a wooden door to float on. After several hours of paddling through the filthy water, they found a three-story house that had been abandoned, kicked in a window, and spent the night.

The next morning, the three refugees climbed up to the roof, and at the end of the day were lifted to safety by an Army helicopter. After several sweltering days in the gym at the University of New Orleans, they boarded a bus to Atlanta, where Quiana had friends. Through a series of fortunate coincidences, Tyeisha got in touch with her mother, who had Daneisha and was in Dallas. Her on-again, off-again boyfriend was in Texas, too. Tyeisha decided that's where she should be.

On Friday, September 16, 2005, I dropped Tyeisha off at the Atlanta Greyhound station. She bought a ticket to Dallas and set off for the fifteen-hour ride. Six months later, Tyeisha was dead. She was found in a ditch beside a rural road in Fort Bend County, Texas. She'd been shot in the back of the head.

I learned about Tyeisha's death from Quiana, who called me one night in March 2006 and whispered, "Tyeisha's gone." When she hung up, I went to my computer and found an article in the Texas paper: there was a sketch, and though her features were exaggerated, it was clearly Tyeisha. The article said the body they'd found had tattoos: *Daneisha, RIP Larry.* I remembered those tattoos. I'd asked about them as we sat on a bench outside the church. Larry was Tyeisha's father, who had died, she said, about a year before Katrina hit.

I called the number in the paper and asked to speak to the detective in charge. I explained that I hadn't seen or heard from Tyeisha in months, but I told him what I knew: that she'd survived Katrina, and that she'd apparently gone to Texas to be with her mother, daughter, and boyfriend. He asked me to fax him a copy of the article I wrote for *Seventeen.* He said they didn't have many leads. I gave him Quiana's number, and he promised to call me back. I called *Seventeen,* thinking that if the editors would allow me to write about her death, I could finance a trip to Texas. I could help find her killer. The impulse was a combination of personal outrage (I'd never known anyone who'd been murdered), curiosity, and ambition. I knew the victim and already had the family's trust. I began having visions of writing the *In Cold Blood* of the Katrina diaspora. But there was a new editor on the Drama section, and she didn't sound terribly excited about the idea. She said she'd talk to the editor-in-chief and get back to me.

Days passed. My editor called and said they might want to mention Tyeisha's death in the next issue, but that they didn't want a story about it. "It might be too morbid for the readers," she told me. In my three years covering crimes for *Seventeen,* I had written about four female murderers, about stabbings and suffocation and gunshots to the head. The editors I'd worked with talked a lot about what their readers "wanted." Those readers' attention spans were short, apparently, and their eyeballs had to be hijacked with big, red letters and shocking graphics. When my story about Nakisha ran, "She killed her mom" was splashed in red letters across the first page; pictured below was a hunting knife "similar" to the one she'd used, and opposite was a grainy yearbook snapshot of Nakisha with stab marks Photoshopped all around her. I called to complain. My editor was polite, but said they knew what was needed to grab the readers' attention in this "media-saturated" environment.

Of course, I was as culpable as the editors at *Seventeen.* I did the reporting that revealed nuance and uncertainty, and then did what I was told and turned in simplistic, straightforward stories with immutable lines between cause and effect. So why didn't Tyeisha's unsolved death make the cut? It occurred to me that the story didn't fit the fiction of the magazine. The rigid code that dictated a certain number of pages be given to fashion, celebrities, and make-up also assured that lines didn't get crossed. Tyeisha's story had been one of triumph over tragedy. To have her escape Katrina and six months later be found by a roadside in rural Texas was just too complicated.

But I didn't push. I dashed off pitches to various other publications I thought might be interested in her story: *Texas Monthly,* the *Christian Science Monitor, The New York Times.* No one bit. So I let go. Quiana and I talked every few days, then every couple of weeks. The case went nowhere.

Six weeks later, I got a call from *America's Most Wanted.* Karen Daborowski, a producer, had read about Tyeisha in the *Houston Chronicle* and said they wanted to do a segment on her death. "Maybe we can find her killer," she said. I had not watched *America's Most Wanted* in years. In fact, had you asked me about the show the day before Karen called, I probably would have said it had been pulled by Fox a long time ago. But what I remembered as a mildly creepy combination of *Unsolved Mysteries* and *A Current Affair* had been airing nonstop every Saturday night since 1988. The show was still hosted by a man named John Walsh, who'd been thrust into the spotlight in 1981 when his son, Adam, was kidnapped and murdered. To date, it has helped catch a thousand fugitives.

So I agreed to the interview. But the interview turned into a request to travel with the producers and a crew to Texas. "We want the story to be about you," said Karen. "About your bond with Tyeisha and how you cared enough to find her killer." Calling my fleeting relationship with Tyeisha a bond was a stretch, but in my mind, Karen was asking how much I was willing to do to help Tyeisha. The story of her death deserved to be told, and if I couldn't convince *Seventeen* or any other publication of that, I figured I could get in front of a camera and help someone else tell it. I didn't think about what it meant, journalistically, to become an advocate for someone I'd written about. Having had no formal training in the craft I practiced, I navigated articles and the people involved by my gut, and I felt I owed Tyeisha this much. It also didn't occur to me that I'd become to Karen what Tyeisha had been to me: a subject. Just as I'd asked Tyeisha to relive Katrina beneath a magnolia tree so I could write an article about her for *Seventeen,* Karen was asking me to be a character in her own television report about Tyeisha.

On October 13, 2006, I met Karen and Sedgwick Tourison, another producer, at the American Airlines terminal at Baltimore's BWI. We landed in Dallas around noon and drove to a Whattaburger restaurant near the airport to meet Dave Barsotti and Tom Overstreet, the local camera and audio guys. We all said hello, then Dave dropped a mini-microphone down my blouse, tucked a battery pack into my pants, and told me to get in the driver's seat of the rented Jeep Cherokee. As I drove, Tom aimed his camera at me and Sedg prompted me to talk about what I was doing.

"I'm driving," I said, lamely.

"To . . . " steered Sedg.

"I'm driving to visit Tyeisha's mom, Cabrini, and her daughter Daneisha," I said.

We exited the freeway and made our way into Cabrini's apartment complex. As the crew unloaded the equipment, I wondered how I would greet Cabrini. The woman's daughter had been murdered not six months before, and here I was waltzing in with cameras and lights and four more strangers to poke at her pain. The point, obviously, was to find Tyeisha's killer. I hoped Cabrini knew that. Karen gave the word, and I walked down the outdoor hallway toward Tom, who had his camera positioned on his shoulder, and knocked on the door. Quiana opened it, looking gorgeous, just liked I remembered her. We hugged and I stepped toward Cabrini, who was wearing a T-shirt with a picture of Tyeisha on it. I wasn't sure if I should hug her or shake her hand, but she came toward me with her arms open, and I was glad. The crew flipped on the lights, wired everyone up, and we started talking on-camera, first about Katrina, then about what Cabrini remembered of Tyeisha's arrival in Texas. Tyeisha didn't want to stay in Dallas a day longer than she had to. "She was like, 'Mama, it's all old people around here,'" said Cabrini. So she took Daneisha and left for Houston, where her boyfriend lived. For the first time in her entire life, Tyeisha got her own apartment. Her own furniture. "She was so excited," said Cabrini. "She said, 'Mama, there's no rules. I can wake up when I want.' I said, 'Lord, I wouldn't want to live where there's no rules.'" In February, Tyeisha stopped calling. On March 9, 2006, six months to the day after I met her, her body was found in a grassy ditch at the bend of a county road.

We woke up early the next morning and met downstairs at the hotel for breakfast. Sedg laid out the day's schedule, which began with an hour of them filming me typing on my laptop in my room. Sedg wanted more shots of Quiana and me, so we picked her up and drove to a nearby park. Quiana was six years older than Tyeisha, and more articulate and outgoing. Life hasn't been easy for her. She is twenty-nine, and has four children. She had an emergency hysterectomy just a few months before Katrina hit. The storm washed away her home and separated her from her mother, sister, and children. She settled in Atlanta with her boyfriend, but they broke up. And then her sister was murdered.

When the cameras were ready, we said our lines. I asked her about the last time she talked to her sister, and she said it had been weeks and that she'd begun to worry. We repeated this sequence several times so they could film us from different angles. Quiana didn't seem to mind. I remembered what she said to me months ago, when she called and told me about the murder: "I don't want to see my sister on *Cold Case Files* in five years. I want somebody caught."

After we dropped off Quiana, Sedg and Karen told me they wanted some *Sex and the City* shots of me, so we stopped at an upscale strip mall to do more filming. Trailed by Tom and his camera, I dutifully walked into a boutique and gazed at racks of clothing I couldn't afford. Karen assured me that they needed shots like this to "set me up" as a former New York City magazine writer. They thought it important to play up the "fish out of water" angle: big-city girl gets caught up in a small-town murder. The whole thing was false, and I reminded Karen that I hadn't been on staff at a women's magazine since 2002. But in the language of reality television, three years of my life are boiled down to a shopping trip in order to facilitate a story arc.

That night we flew to Houston, and the next morning we showed up at the Fort Bend County sheriff's station. Inside, Detective Campbell—who Sedg had warned me was "all business"—opened his case file, and pulled out color photographs of the crime scene. There she was: lying in the grass, her skinny legs sticking out from under a yellow tarp. She had on the same blue jeans and belt she was wearing when I met her. The grass around her body was long and lush, green and damp. I wondered if it rained on her while she laid, eyes wide open, in the clover. She was found just a few feet off the road, and according to Campbell, had been shot there. There were minimal wounds other than the fatal bullet wound, which Campbell said suggested that she had been killed by someone she knew. Campbell told us that when he visited her apartment, "it was organized and homey. Like she was focused on raising a child." He showed us birth certificates and FEMA correspondence. She'd kept her papers in a shoebox. "She was doing all the things she should," he said. "She was setting up her future."

The big Texas sky was crowded with clouds in every shade of gray as we drove past fields of cows and ducks, past an old country homestead with a gated family cemetery in the front yard, past Trav's Roadhouse, to the bend in the road where Tyeisha was murdered. A house sat just a few hundred yards away, but Campbell interviewed the people there, and they didn't hear the gunshot. "The TV was probably on," he said. As Tom and Dave set up the shot, I stepped onto the grass, half expecting to feel some sort of ghostly presence. The sun shone through the clouds, but I tried to imagine the road at night. I tried to see her in her last moments. I tried to feel her fear. But I couldn't. All I could do was what I was doing, standing before the cameras to make sure she was not forgotten.

Months went by. And then a year. Occasionally, I would get a phone call from Karen, saying they were planning to air the show soon, but then she'd drop out of contact for a couple of months. At one point, it had apparently been slated to run as part of a special Hurricane Katrina hour in late 2007, but then she told me it was "so strong," they wanted it to anchor another episode. Tyeisha had been dead more than two years when the segment finally aired on March 22, 2008.

I was back in Georgia that weekend, visiting my boyfriend's family. We got take-out BBQ from a local rib shack and gathered in front of the TV. Before each commercial break, they teased my segment: "Coming up: a magazine writer leaves behind the glitzy New York fashion world in a quest for justice." I covered my face as they pasted my voice over clips of Sarah Jessica

Parker adjusting her skirt on the street and cringed at the reenactments. The "Julia" in the segment had a big apartment with leather couches, and the "Tyeisha" was much more conservative than the tattooed girl with messy, maroon-tinted hair extensions I'd met in Georgia. They flashed images of the real Tyeisha on the screen, but my face was the most prominent. The piece even ended with John Walsh giving me a "personal thanks" for being involved.

To me, the compelling story is still Tyeisha's. How, like thousands of her friends and neighbors in New Orleans, she was torn from her support system, separated from the people who looked out for her. She'd tried to rebuild a life for herself and her child in a new state and instead became the victim of a brutal murder. But no one else seemed particularly interested in that story. According to the Centers for Disease Control, homicide is the second leading cause of death for black women between ages fifteen and twenty-four, but even to *America's Most Wanted,* Tyeisha's tale was only worth telling in relation to me.

I suppose I knew that the press tends to illuminate the exceptions, the extremes. The plight of the family with septuplets instead of the more common burden of unexpected twins; the detained immigrant with the amputated penis instead of the thousands with untreated depression. The impulse is understandable, and certainly an oddball story can draw attention to a worthy issue, but what of the issues inside the more common stories? By their very nature, such issues—like mental illness in immigrant communities, or the high murder rate among young black women—are more intransigent, harder to untangle and fit into a facile narrative. I imagine that maybe Jill Leovy, a reporter at the *Los Angeles Times,* was thinking this way when she created The Homicide Report, a blog on the paper's Web site that attempts to report on every single homicide in Los Angeles County; last year, there were 324. As the explanatory page puts it, "only the most unusual and statistically marginal homicide cases receive press coverage, while those cases at the very eye of the storm—those which best expose the true statistical dimensions of the problem of deadly violence—remain hidden."

It remains to be seen whether my appearance on *America's Most Wanted* will lead to the capture of Tyeisha's killer. Two months after the show aired, there are no promising leads, but I believe I did the right thing, as a human being and as a journalist, when I realize that had I walked out of that Georgia church ten minutes later, or turned left instead of going straight out the door, Tyeisha Martin—not yet twenty years old, mother, sister, daughter, hurricane survivor—would have died not only too soon, but in silence.

JULIA DAHL is a writer who lives in Brooklyn.

Reprinted from *Columbia Journalism Review,* July/August 2008, pp. 32–36. Copyright © 2008 by Columbia Journalism Review, Columbia University.

›
The Shame Game
'To Catch a Predator' Gets the Ratings, but at What Cost?

DOUGLAS MCCOLLAM

It was just before 3 P.M. on a Sunday afternoon last November when a contingent of police gathered outside the home of Louis Conradt Jr., a longtime county prosecutor living in the small community of Terrell, Texas, just east of Dallas. Though the fifty-six-year-old Conradt was a colleague of some of the officers, they hadn't come to discuss a case or for a backyard barbeque. Rather, the veteran district attorney, who had prosecuted hundreds of felonies during more than two decades in law enforcement, was himself the target of an unusual criminal probe. For weeks the police in the nearby town of Murphy had been working with the online watchdog group Perverted Justice and producers from *Dateline NBC's* popular "To Catch a Predator" series in an elaborate sting operation targeting adults cruising the Internet to solicit sex from minors. *Dateline* had leased a house in an upscale subdivision, outfitted it with multiple hidden cameras, and hired actors to impersonate minors to help lure suspects into the trap. As with several similar operations previously conducted by *Dateline,* there was no shortage of men looking to score with underage boys and girls. In all, twenty-four men were caught in the Murphy sting, including a retired doctor, a traveling businessman, a school teacher, and a Navy veteran.

Conradt had never shown up at the *Dateline* house, but according to the police, using the screen name "inxs00," he did engage in explicit sexual exchanges in an Internet chat room with someone he believed to be a thirteen-year-old boy (but was actually a volunteer for Perverted Justice). Under a Texas law adopted in 2005 to combat Internet predators, it is a second-degree felony to have such communications with someone under the age of fourteen, even if no actual sexual contact takes place. Armed with a search warrant—and with a *Dateline* camera crew on the scene—the police went to Conradt's home to arrest him. When the prosecutor failed to answer the door or answer phone calls, police forced their way into the house. Inside they encountered the prosecutor in a hallway holding a semiautomatic handgun. "I'm not going to hurt anybody," Conradt reportedly told the police. Then he fired a single bullet into his own head.

Standing outside the house with his crew, the *Dateline* correspondent Chris Hansen said he did not hear the shot that ended Conradt's life, but did see his body wheeled out on a gurney. Discussing Conradt's death over lunch a couple of weeks later, I asked Hansen how it made him feel. Hansen said his first reaction was as a newsman who had to cover the story for his network (Hansen filed a report the next morning for NBC's *Today* show). Hansen said that on a human level Conradt's death was a tragedy that, naturally, he felt bad about. But he understood the true import of my question: "If you're asking do I feel responsible, no," Hansen said. "I sleep well at night."

Others aren't so sanguine. Galen Ray Sumrow, the criminal district attorney of Rockwall County, Texas, who heads the office where Conradt worked as an assistant district attorney, has reviewed evidence surrounding the case and believes it was badly botched. Among the problems he cites are that the search warrant obtained by the Murphy police officers was defective because it had the wrong date and listed the wrong county for service, basic errors that he believes would have gotten any evidence seized from Conradt's home tossed out of court. He is also mystified as to why the police would force their way into Conradt's home when they could have tried to talk him out, or just picked him up at work the next day. "He was here in the office every morning," says Sumrow, who is himself a former police officer and has been prosecuting cases for more than twenty years. "You generally like to do an arrest like that away from the home to avoid things like what happened." A sworn affidavit supporting the warrant also shows that the information about Conradt's online activities was given to the Murphy police by Perverted Justice just hours before they went to arrest him. Why were the police in such a rush to pick up Conradt? Texas Rangers are investigating that question, but Sumrow thinks he knows the answer: "It's reality television," he says. Sumrow says an investigator told him the police pushed things because the *Dateline* people had plane tickets to fly home that afternoon and wanted to get the bust on film for the show. He says investigators also told him that film excerpts show *Dateline* personnel, including Hansen, interacting with police on the scene, supplying them with information, and advising them on tactics. Sergeant Snow Robertson of the Murphy police says accommodating *Dateline's* schedule "wasn't a factor at all."

Rather, he says, the urgency was to keep Conradt from contacting another minor. *Dateline*'s Hansen confirms that he was to fly out that Sunday, but says such plans are always subject to change and that he hadn't even checked out of his hotel. He also denies advising the police during the operation at Conradt's house. "This stuff is not remotely based in fact," Hansen says.

At a town meeting called to discuss the *Dateline* sting operations, several Murphy residents expressed outrage that a parade of suspected sexual predators were lured to their community. Neighbors recounted police takedowns and car chases on their blocks, and some said fleeing suspects tossed drugs and other contraband into their yards. In a statement to the Murphy City Council, Conradt's sister, Patricia, directly implicated *Dateline* in her brother's death. "I will never consider my brother's death a suicide," she said. "It was an act precipitated by the rush to grab headlines where there was no evidence that there was any emergency other than to line the pockets of an out-of-control group and a TV show pressed for ratings and a deadline." She added: "When these people came after him for a news show, it ended his life." In an interview, she was even more direct: "They have blood on their hands," she said, referring to *Dateline,* the police, and Perverted Justice.

In a sense, Conradt's death was a tragedy foretold. In a piece for *Radar* magazine about the show, the writer John Cook quoted an unnamed *Dateline* producer as saying that "one of these guys is going to go home and shoot himself in the head." When I asked Hansen and David Corvo, *Dateline*'s executive producer, if they were reviewing the show's procedures in light of Conradt's death, both said that there was no evidence to suggest that Conradt was aware of *Dateline*'s presence when he shot himself (though a camera crew was apparently on his block for hours before the police arrived), and that there were no plans to alter how the "Predator" series is handled. "I still feel like the show is a public service," said Corvo. "We do investigations that expose people doing things not good for them. You can't predict the unintended consequences of that. You have to let the chips fall where they may."

The reluctance to tinker with the show's formula is no doubt attributable to the fact that since its debut in the fall of 2004, "To Catch a Predator" has been the rarest of rare birds in the television news world: a clear ratings winner. The show regularly outdraws NBC's other primetime fare. It succeeds by tapping into something that has been part of American culture since the Puritans stuck offenders in the stockade: public humiliation. The notion of delighting in another's disgrace drives much of the reality TV phenomenon, and is present in the DNA of everything from *Judge Judy* to *Jackass* to *Borat.* "Predator" couples this with a hyped-up fear of Internet sex fiends, creating a can't-miss formula. The show's ratings success has made it a sweeps-week staple and turned Chris Hansen into something of a pop-culture icon. To date, by the show's own count, it has netted 238 would-be predators, thirty-six of whom have either pleaded guilty or been convicted. Hansen regularly gives talks to schools and parent groups concerned about Internet sex predators, and he was even summoned to Washington to testify before a congressional subcommittee investigating the problem, where he and *Dateline* received effusive praise for their efforts.

When the comedian Conan O'Brien filmed a bit to open this year's Emmy Awards that showed him parading through the sets of hit shows of every network, his last stop was a "Predator" house where Hansen confronted him and O'Brien gave a spot-on rendition of the sweaty, shaky dissembling that most of the show's targets display.

All that is a long way from where "To Catch a Predator" started. The *Dateline* producer Lynn Keller says she first contacted the Perverted Justice group about the possibility of doing a show in January or February of 2004. Perverted Justice had already worked with several local television stations, including one in Detroit, where Chris Hansen knew one of the producers and had talked with him about a sting operation the station had filmed using Perverted Justice's online expertise to lure targets. *Dateline*'s first sting house was set up in Bethpage, Long Island, about an hour outside of New York City. Hansen recalls being nervous that no one would show up and that he might have to explain to the network why he had blown a bunch of money on a flop investigation. "We thought we might get one person," Keller recalls. They needn't have worried. Before he could even reach the house for the first day of filming, Hansen got a frantic call from Keller that the first target was inbound. Hansen beat him there by just fifteen minutes.

The Long Island sting netted eighteen suspects in two and a half days. Eight months later, the show set up a sting house in Fairfax, Virginia (at a home belonging to a friend of Hansen's in the FBI), and snared nineteen more men, including a rabbi, an emergency-room doctor, a special-education teacher, and an unemployed man claiming to be a teacher, who memorably walked into the house naked. The third show, filmed in early 2006 in southern California, drew fifty-one men over three days. But even as the stings expanded and ratings soared, critics inside and outside the network raised serious questions about whether "To Catch a Predator" was erasing lines that even an increasingly tabloid newsmagazine show should respect.

To begin with, the show has an undeniable "ick" factor. The men (and to date they are all men) are mostly losers who show up packing booze and condoms. It is also undeniably compelling television. Each show follows a similar pattern: after asking the mark to come in, the decoy disappears to change clothes or go to the bathroom. Then, in a startling switcheroo, Hansen appears from off-stage and directs the man to take a seat. The men almost always comply, concluding that Hansen is either a cop or a father. The marks then proffer comical denials about what they are doing at the house, which never include their intent to have sex with a minor. Hansen then produces some particularly salacious details from their Internet chat with the decoy ("But you said you couldn't wait to pour chocolate syrup all over her and lick it off with your tongue"). The mark then switches gears to say he has never done anything like this before and was just kidding around or role playing, which in turn cues Hansen to say something like, "Well, you're playing on a big stage, because I'm Chris Hansen from *Dateline NBC,*" at which point cameras enter from off stage like furies summoned from hell. The mark, now fully perceiving his ruin, usually excuses himself, often pausing to shake hands with Hansen—the cult of celebrity apparently transcends even this awful reality—then exits into the waiting arms of police outside who swarm him as if he had just shot the president.

The police busts are the emotional capper to the encounter, one that highlights the show's uncomfortably close affiliation with law enforcement. On the first two "Predator" stings, the show didn't involve arrests, an omission that garnered complaints from viewers and cops alike. Though certain individuals from the initial episodes were subsequently prosecuted, the lack of police involvement from the outset made it hard to make cases that would stick. "The number one complaint from viewers was that we let them walk out," says Keller. Starting with the third show and in the five subsequent stings, police were waiting to take down the suspects. In our interview and in his congressional testimony, Hansen is careful to refer to those arrests as "parallel" police investigations, as if they just happened to be running down the same track as *Dateline*, but the close cooperation is always evident. At a time when reporters are struggling to keep law enforcement from encroaching on news gathering, *Dateline*, which is part of NBC's news division, is inviting them in the front door—literally. Hansen tried to deflect this criticism of the show by saying that the volunteers from Perverted Justice serve as a "Chinese wall" between the news people at *Dateline* and the police.

But as we've learned from recent corporate scandals, such Chinese walls are often made of pretty thin tissue. In the case of "To Catch a Predator," Perverted Justice does most of the groundwork preparing the shows and roping in the men. Initially, *Dateline's* responsibility was to cover the group's expenses, procure the house and outfit it with hidden cameras and, of course, supply Chris Hansen and airtime. However, after the third successful "Predator" show, Perverted Justice hired an agent and auctioned its services to several networks. NBC ended up retaining the group for a fee reported in *The Washington Post* and elsewhere to be between $100,000 and $150,000. Hansen would not confirm an amount but said he saw nothing wrong with compensating the group for its services, likening it to the way the news division will sometimes keep a retired general or FBI agent on retainer. "In the end I get paid, the producers get paid, the camera guy, why shouldn't they?" says Hansen.

O n the surface that certainly seems reasonable, but it ignores a few relevant points. First, Perverted Justice is a participant in the story, the kind of outfit that would traditionally be covered, not be on the news outlet's payroll. "It's an advocacy group intensely involved in this story," says Robert Steele, who teaches journalism ethics at The Poynter Institute. "That's different from hiring a retired general who is no longer involved in a policy-making role." Second, it is clearly a no-no, even at this late date in the devolution of TV news, to directly pay government officials or police officers. Yet in effect that's what *Dateline* did in at least one of its stings. The police in Darke County, Ohio, where *Dateline* set up its fourth sting in April 2006, insisted that personnel from Perverted Justice be deputized for the operation so as not to compromise the criminal cases it wished to bring against the targets. After some discussion, NBC's lawyers agreed to the arrangement, which the network shrugs off as less than ideal but an isolated circumstance.

Further, though Hansen and *Dateline* reject allegations that they are engaging in paycheck journalism by paying Perverted Justice—arguing for a distinction between paying a consultant and paying a source for information—the line looks a little fuzzy. For example, Xavier von Erck, who founded Perverted Justice, says via e-mail that the operation had come to a point where it could "not bear any further costs relating to the shows. Hence, we obtained a consulting fee." In turn, local law enforcement groups have stated that without the resources provided by Perverted Justice they couldn't afford to do the criminal investigations they've mounted in conjunction with the "To Catch a Predator" series. See the problem? But for NBC's deep pockets, no "parallel" police actions would take place. And are they really parallel? One lawyer I spoke with, who asked not be identified because her client's case is still pending, claims the man was entrapped and said she has every intention of subpoenaing members of *Dateline's* staff to testify if the case goes to trial. "They are acting as an arm of law enforcement and are material witnesses," the lawyer said. "They definitely crossed a line."

There is also the question of whether the series is fair to its targets. Let's concede up front that this is an unsympathetic bunch of would-be perverts. But are they really that dangerous? Hansen himself divides those snared in the probes into three groups: dangerous predators, Internet pornography addicts, and sexual opportunists. But by Hansen's own calculation fewer than one in ten of the men who show up at a sting house have a previous criminal record.

But the image projected by the "Predator" series is clearly meant to inflame parental fears about violent Internet sex fiends. The show has invoked the specter of famous child abduction cases like Polly Klaas. The very term "predator" calls to mind the image of the drooling, trench-coated sex fiend hanging out at the local playground with a bag full of candy. Reading through the chat transcripts posted on the Perverted Justice Web site, however, it seems clear that a lot of the men snared aren't hard-core predators. Many express doubts about what they're doing and have to be egged along a bit by the decoys, many of whom come off as anything but innocent children. Consider a few of these exchanges. In the first, the mark (johnchess2000) is talking to someone he believes is an underage girl (AJ's Girl). She has agreed to let him come over to watch a movie:

johnchess2000: anything you want me to wear or bring?

AJ's Girl: hmm

johnchess2000: wow your thinking for a long time

AJ's Girl: lol sowwy

AJ's Girl: u beter bring condoms

johnchess2000: wow. condoms???

johnchess2000: wow. your thinking big huh? ;0

johnchess2000: ;)

AJ's Girl: :">

johnchess2000: wow so you like me that much? :)

AJ's Girl: maybe

johnchess2000: maybe?? why did you say condoms?

AJ's Girl: :"> i duno

johnchess2000: haha. be honest

johnchess2000: you must like me a lot then huh?

AJ's Girl: yea

AJ's Girl: ur cute

Or this exchange between Jason, a twenty-one-year-old fireman and the decoy, a girl he thinks is thirteen:

jteno72960: so what kinda guys u like

katiedidsings: hot fireman 1s

jteno72960: ok what else is sexy to you

katiedidsings: tats

jteno72960: i have 2 inside my arm

jteno72960: will u kiss them for me?

katiedidsings: ya

jteno72960: what about on the lips

katiedidsings: ya

jteno72960: i love to kiss

katiedidsings: me 2

jteno72960: really what else

katiedidsings: i dunno watevr u wantd 2 do

jteno72960: well what have u done

katiedidsings: evry thing

katiedidsings: wel not evrything

katiedidsings: but alot of stuff

jteno72960: well what did u like

katiedidsings: from behind

Or this last exchange between Rob (rkline05) a twenty-year-old from Ohio, and *Dateline's* online decoy "Shia," who poses as an underage girl. After days of chatting, Rob expresses doubts about their age difference and about a sexual encounter, but Shia dismisses his concerns and reassures him:

rkline05: but idk about everything we talked about

shyshiagirl: why not

rkline05: well you sure you wana do all that

shyshiagirl: yeaa why not

rkline05: idk i just wasnt sure you wanted to you are a virgin and all

rkline05: you sure you want it to be me that takes that

shyshiagirl: yea why not. ur cool

rkline05: i just. . ... you really sure i feel weird

about it you being so much younger than me and all

shyshiagirl: ur not old. dont feel weird

Rob came to the *Dateline* sting house and later pleaded guilty for soliciting a minor online.

Entrapment is a legal term best applicable to law enforcement. Perverted Justice says it's careful not to initiate contact with marks, nor steer them into explicit sexual banter. But as these chats and others make clear, they are prepared to flirt, literally, with that line. Under most state statutes passed to combat online predators, the demonstrated intent to solicit sexual acts from a minor is sufficient to land you in jail regardless of whether the minor is a willing participant. So, as a legal matter, the enticements offered by the decoys are of little importance to the police, or to issue advocates like Perverted Justice. But journalistically it looks a lot like crossing the line from reporting the news to creating the news.

Dateline has run afoul of this distinction before. Famously, in 1993, several producers and correspondents were fired for rigging a General Motors truck to explode in a crash test. More recently the program took heat for bringing Muslim-looking men to a NASCAR race to see what might happen (the program never aired). "Predator" seems to fall somewhere between those two examples. Perhaps its most direct counterpart in recent journalistic history is the famous sting operation mounted by the *Chicago Sun Times*. In 1978 the paper set up the Mirage Tavern in Chicago and snared a host of city officials for seeking bribes from the "owners," who were actually undercover reporters. The Mirage was controversial in its day, but it seems tame by comparison to the *Dateline* stings. Al Tompkins, who teaches the ethics of television journalism at the Poynter Institute, draws a clear distinction between the Mirage and "Predator." Mirage, he notes, was targeted at public officials who were known to be abusing the power of their offices for personal enrichment. "It was a legit question whether you could have covered the story any other way," Tompkins says. "You couldn't go through law enforcement because you didn't know if police were involved in the corruption." Tompkins, who has watched the *Dateline* series, says it looks more like a police prostitution sting than a news investigation.

Dateline has argued that "Predator" serves a genuine public good, but it could be argued that, in fact, *Dateline* is doing the public a disservice. When Attorney General Alberto Gonzales gave a speech about a major initiative to combat the "growing problem" of Internet predators, he cited a statistic that 50,000 such would-be pedophiles were prowling the Net at any given moment and attributed it to *Dateline*. Jason McLure, a reporter at *Legal Times* in Washington, D.C., (where I was formerly an editor), asked the show about the number. *Dateline* told him that it had gotten it from a retired FBI agent who consulted with the show. When the agent was contacted he wasn't sure where the number had come from, terming it a "Goldilocks" figure—"Not small and not large." He added that it was the same figure that was used by the media to describe the number of people killed annually by Satanic cults in the 1980s, and before that was cited as the number of children abducted by strangers each year in the 1970s. *Dateline* has now disowned the number, saying solid statistics about Internet predators are hard to find, but that the problem seems to be getting worse, a sentiment echoed by lawmakers in Congress.

But actually there isn't much evidence that it is getting worse. For example, many news reports have cited a Justice Department study as saying that one in five children is approached online by a sexual predator. But as Radford Benjamin of *The Skeptical Inquirer* pointed out, what that 2001 study actually said was that 19 percent had received a "sexual solicitation" online, about half of which came from other teens and none of which led to a sexual assault. According to the study, the number of teens aggressively solicited by adults online was about 3 percent. A more recent study by the Crimes Against Children Research Center at the University of New Hampshire found that the number of kids getting unwanted sexual advances on the Internet was in fact declining. In general, according to data compiled by the National Center for Missing and Exploited Children, more than 70 percent of sexual abuse of children is perpetrated by family members or family friends.

That doesn't mean Internet sex predators don't exist, but *Dateline* heavily skews reality by devoting hour after hour of primetime programming to the phenomenon. As Poynter's Tompkins notes: "Is there any other issue that's received that much airtime? The question is whether the level of coverage is proportional to the actual problem."

The answer, it seems, is no, and the explanation of why *Dateline* has seized on this mythical trend to anchor its venerable news show is that reality TV has so altered the broadcast landscape that traditional newsmagazine fare—no matter how provocative—just doesn't cut it anymore. "Reality programs came in and newsmagazines no longer looked so great," says one former producer for NBC News. While newsmagazines are cheap compared to other primetime shows, they don't have the potential to be gigantic hits like *Survivor* or *American Idol*. For that reason, the producer notes, the entertainment divisions at the networks never really liked newsmagazines, which they had little hand in producing and for which they received no credit. At NBC, the former producer says, Jeff Zucker, formerly the president of the network's news and entertainment group and now the c.e.o. of its television operations, regularly put the squeeze on *Dateline*, maintaining that the network needed its time slots to either develop new programming or schedule hit shows. "About the only thing they really want newsmagazines to do now is crime," says the former producer. "If it's not crime, they don't think they can sell it. The traditional investigative reporting on shows like *Dateline*, or *48 Hours*, or *Primetime Live* is no more." (A notable exception, he says, is *60 Minutes*.)

Dateline's executive producer David Corvo prefers to see the change as a setting aside of older journalistic conventions to focus on new kinds of issues. The "Predator" series, he says, is just another form of enterprise journalism, one suited to the Internet age. But the distinction between enterprise and entertainment can be a difficult one. *Dateline* hasn't so much covered a story as created one. In the process it has further compromised the barrier between reporters and cops that is central to the mission of journalism. If humiliating perverts and needlessly terrifying parents is the best use that newsmagazines can make of hours of primetime television, then perhaps they should be allowed to die and the time given over to the blood sport of reality programming. At least no one would dare to call it news.

DOUGLAS MCCOLLAM is a contributing editor to *CJR*.

Reprinted from *Columbia Journalism Review*, January/February 2007, pp. 28–33. Copyright © 2007 by Columbia Journalism Review, Columbia University.

UNIT 4
A Word from Our Sponsor

Unit Selections

33. **Generation MySpace Is Getting Fed Up,** Spencer E. Ante and Catherine Holahan
34. **The Massless Media,** William Powers
35. **The Hollywood Treatment,** Frank Rose
36. **Girl Power,** Chuck Salter
37. **Online Salvation?,** Paul Farhi
38. **Home Free,** Lori Robertson
39. **A Fading Taboo,** Donna Shaw
40. **Nonprofit News,** Carol Guensburg

Key Points to Consider

- What is your take on how Nielsen Media Research data are collected, and how that data is used?
- What is the difference between media that appeal to older versus younger adults? Males versus females? If an advertiser wanted to sell a product to you, specifically, where should she put her dollars?
- If ratings and sales figures indicate that the public is attracted to lowbrow content, should media owners give media consumers what they want? Why or why not?
- Is it worth it for you to pay more for television, magazines, newspapers, radio, and/or the Internet with fewer or no advertising messages? Why or why not?
- How do you respond to product placement in entertainment media? Do you notice it? Do you have objections to it? To what degree do you think it affects consumer behavior?

Student Web Site
www.mhcls.com

Internet References

Advertising Age
http://adage.com
Citizens Internet Empowerment Coalition (CIEC)
http://www.ciec.org
Educause
http://www.educause.edu

Advertising is the major source of profit for newspapers, magazines, radio, and television, and advertising tie-ins are a common element in motion picture deals. While media writers may have the potential of reflecting their own agendas and social/political viewpoints as they produce media messages, they depend largely upon financial backing from advertisers, who have their own interests to protect. Advertisers use media as a means of presenting goods and services in a positive light. They are willing to pay generously for the opportunity to reach mass audiences, but unwilling to support media that do not deliver the right kind of audience for their advertisements.

Mass advertising developed along with mass media; in fact, commercial media have been described by some as a system existing primarily for the purpose of delivering audiences to advertisers. The price for selling commercial space is determined by statistical data on how many and what kinds of people are reached by the media in which the ad is to appear. In 2007, a 30-second spot on *American Idol* sold for $780,000, and on *Grey's Anatomy* for $400,000. A 30-second spot in the 2007 Super Bowl ran about $2,600,000. In a local market, an ad on a daytime program that reaches about 10,000 viewers might cost as little as $50 or $60, and slots between midnight and 5 AM in some markets sell for even less. The American Association of Advertising Agencies and Association of National Advertisers statistics report 18 minutes of each hour (30%) during prime time television is devoted to commercials, up from 13 minutes in 1992.

As the number of media choices increases and audiences diffuse, advertising agencies have largely adjusted their media-buying focus from quantity to quality of potential consumers who will be exposed to a single ad. According to a recent study by Marian Azzaro, professor of marketing at Roosevelt University in Chicago, advertisers would need to buy 42% more time on the three major networks than they did 10 years ago to reach the same number of consumers. The current focus of many agencies is niche advertising, with particular interest in ratings/circulation data split by age, gender, ethnic background, and income factors that determine how a given consumer might respond to a product pitch. The outgrowth of niching is seen in media products from the Food Network and Home & Garden Television, to magazines targeted to narrowly defined interests (e.g., *Golf*), to ads on the Web, in video games, over cell phones, on "airport TV," and in classrooms on Channel One. Google sold $6.1 billion in ads in 2005, double its 2004 sales, and more than any single newspaper chain, magazine group, or television network.

Sometimes, product pitches creep directly into entertainment media, where they can strike below the level of consumer awareness. Market research finds viewers 25% more likely to shop at Sears after viewing "Extreme Makeover: Home Edition," which features Sears Kenmore appliances and Craftsman tools. Coke is on the judges' desk on "American Idol," Doritos and Mountain Dew presented to challenge winners on "Survivor." BMW donated 32 Mini Coopers to be demolished in the production of *The Italian Job*, and reported a 20% spike in Mini Cooper sales following the movie's 2003 release. Pepsi-Cola financed the 2005 snowboarding documentary "First Descent," about five snowboarding icons, to "build buzz by association" with Mountain Dew. The Mountain Dew logo appears in subtle places, such as on the boarders' helmets. Products or logos may also be inserted into already filmed movies and television programs—not a new practice—but one attracting new attention, as technological advances make it easier to do so, and as VCRs, DVRs, and TiVo allow consumers to bypass traditional commercial messages.

"Generation MySpace Is Getting Fed Up" reports consumer backlash to advertising on social networking sites.

The next set of articles lend insight into contrasting business models. "The Hollywood Treatment" describes the development of the Web video within the Hollywood system, following a traditional media business model. In contrast, "Girl Power" describes evolution of a bottom-up media product, started by a teenager, becoming lucrative via a new-media business model.

The last four articles are about traditional media in a new media landscape. "Online Salvation?" describes the challenges facing newspapers, which competed first with television and now with the Internet for advertiser support. "Home Free" suggests one response: increasing circulation by delivering newspapers for free, getting them into the hands of young adults with good incomes and with families who don't buy traditional newspapers, but who are attractive to advertisers. "A Fading Taboo" is about selling front page space for advertising, a mixing of news space and commercial space that is subject to criticism, though not without historical precedence. Media are expensive. Separating content decisions from commercial pressures increasingly requires alternative sources of support. "Nonprofit News" looks at some exceptions, which are supported by philanthropic foundations and trusts.

Advertisers are subject to federal agency rules that regulate their content. For example, until recently, the Federal Drug Administration tightly restricted advertising of prescription drugs. The Federal Trade Commission monitors deceptive advertising. However, from a media literacy standpoint, analyzing the truth and values communicated by advertisements themselves is only part of the picture. It is important to understand the gatekeeping role financial backers have in overall media content. Most advertising account executives admit their unwillingness to be associated with media that create negative publicity. All recognize that target marketing puts a premium on reaching certain advertiser-desirable groups; media targeted to the interests of those audiences proliferate, while those attractive to other audiences do not. In light of such trends, some critics contend that in the future, true "mass" media may no longer be considered commercially viable.

Generation MySpace Is Getting Fed Up

Annoyed with the ad deluge on social networks, many users are spending less time on the sites.

SPENCER E. ANTE AND CATHERINE HOLAHAN

If you want to socialize with Chris Heritage, you won't find him on Facebook. The 27-year-old Port St. Lucie (Fla.) business analyst joined the social network last year after his buddies bugged him to get an account. But he soon became fed up with the avalanche of ads, especially those detailing what his friends were buying, and he quit the site in November. Now, Heritage expresses himself through a blog, happy to pay $6 a month to publish on a promo-free Web site. "It's worth it to not have to look at the ads," he says.

Uh-oh. Social networking was supposed to be the Next Big Thing on the Internet. MySpace, Facebook, and other sites have been attracting millions of new users, building sprawling sites that companies are banking on to trigger an online advertising boom. Trouble is, the boom isn't booming anymore. Like Heritage, many people are spending less time on social networking sites or signing off altogether.

The MySpace generation may be getting annoyed with ads and a bit bored with profile pages. The average amount of time each user spends on social networking sites has fallen by 14% over the last four months, according to market researcher ComScore. MySpace, the largest social network, has slipped from a peak of 72 million users in October to 68.9 million in December, ComScore says. The total number of people on such sites is still increasing at an 11.5% rate, but that's down sharply from past growth rates. "What you have with social networks is the most overhyped scenario in online advertising," says Tim Vanderhook, CEO of Specific Media, which places ads for customers on a variety of Web sites.

Wishful Thinking?

Advertising on social networking sites is growing fast. Last year global ad spending on these sites shot up 155%, to $1.2 billion, says researcher eMarketer. This year, eMarketer expects it to jump 75%, to $2.1 billion. During its Nov. 4 earnings call, News Corp. gave an upbeat forecast for Fox Interactive Media, which includes MySpace.

But the forecasts for torrid growth may prove unrealistic. Besides the slowing user growth and declining time spent on these sites, users appear to be growing less responsive to ads, according to several advertisers and online placement firms. If advertisers can't figure out how to reverse these trends, social networking could end up as a niche market in the online ad world, smashing hopes and valuations across Silicon Valley.

The current strength in advertising on social networks may be exaggerated by guaranteed ad deals and hopeful experimentation. Google and Microsoft, in hot competition with each other, promised a number of sites a minimum amount of advertising revenue in exchange for the exclusive right to place ads on those sites.

But the early results from those deals are mixed. On Jan. 31, Google said it didn't generate as much revenue from social networking ads as expected. Google, which has a $900 million guaranteed deal with MySpace for placing ads alongside search results, says existing ad approaches aren't working well on social networks so far. "I don't think we have the killer, best way to advertise and monetize social networks yet," said Google co-founder Sergey Brin.

When News Corp. reported its earnings, it said revenues for Fox Interactive Media surged 87%, to $233 million. But $62 million of that came from Google's guaranteed deal with MySpace. It's unclear whether Google, which ad experts believe is losing money on the deal, will sign similar agreements in the future.

Another big slug of ad revenue is coming from companies experimenting with social networks because they are such a popular new medium. But for some, the results have not been encouraging. Many of the people who hang out on MySpace,

Article 33. Generation MySpace Is Getting Fed Up

Facebook, and other sites pay little to no attention to the ads because they're more interested in kibitzing with their friends.

Social networks have some of the lowest response rates on the Web, advertisers and ad placement firms say. Marketers say as few as 4 in 10,000 people who see their ads on social networking sites click on them, compared with 20 in 10,000 across the Web. Mark Seremet, president of video game publisher Green Screen, stopped advertising on MySpace last spring because of a 13-in-10,000 response rate. "It's really hard to make money on that anemic click-through rate," says Seremet.

MySpace and Facebook recognize the issue but say increased targeting and other innovations will spur users to pay more attention. Last fall, both rolled out programs allowing marketers to pitch products to people in hundreds of categories of interest, such as fashion and sports. News Corp. President Peter Chernin said on Feb. 4 that response rates on MySpace improved as much as 300%. Owen Van Natta, chief operating officer at Facebook, says there will be more experimentation in the future. "There's so much innovation that needs to happen," he says.

But there's a catch-22: More aggressive ad programs can lead to more frustrated users. Ryan Lake, 34, just left MySpace because of the ads. "There are so many, and they are getting more and more obtrusive," he says.

Facebook, the second-largest social networking site, which continues to grow rapidly, introduced an ad program in November, called Beacon, that alerted users to the purchases of friends in hopes of spurring sales. More than 75,000 Facebook members signed an online petition against the effort. Carol Kruse, Coca-Cola's vice-president for global interactive marketing, says that while she thinks social networks present a big opportunity, Coke is avoiding Beacon for now.

MySpace has had complaints, too. Nina Pagani, a 20-year-old New York student, grew furious last year when MySpace began automatically posting on users' home pages notifications of friends' favorite products. "Your personal MySpace page became an advertisement," she says. Pagani, a five-year MySpace member, deleted her account in December. "It caused too much drama in my life," she says.

Reprinted by special permission from *BusinessWeek*, February 7, 2008, pp. 54–55. Copyright © 2008 by The McGraw-Hill Companies, Inc.

Article 34

The Massless Media

With the mass media losing their audience to smaller, more targeted outlets, we may be headed for an era of noisy, contentious press reminiscent of the 1800s.

WILLIAM POWERS

One day last June, as a hot political summer was just warming up, a new poll was released. This one wasn't about which candidate voters favored for the White House. It was about which news channels they were choosing with their TV remotes.

"Political polarization is increasingly reflected in the public's news viewing habits," the Pew Research Center for the People and the Press reported.

Since 2000, the Fox News Channel's gains have been greatest among political conservatives and Republicans. More than half of regular Fox viewers describe themselves as politically conservative (52%), up from 40% four years ago. At the same time, CNN, Fox's principal rival, has a more Democrat-leaning audience than in the past.

It's no surprise, of course, that Fox News viewers are more conservative than CNN viewers. But it is rather surprising that even as the network's audience is growing in sheer numbers, it is also growing increasingly conservative. The months following the poll offered further evidence of the ideological sorting of cable-news viewers. During the Democratic National Convention, in July, CNN came in first in the cable ratings, prompting a Fox spokesman to say, "They were playing to their core audience." Weeks later, during the Republican National Convention, Fox News played to its core audience and scored ratings that beat not only CNN and the other cable channels but even the broadcast networks—a historical first. When election day came around and George Bush won, it wasn't hard to predict that Fox News would again be the cable ratings victor: the conservative candidate took the prize, and so, naturally, did the news channel favored by conservatives.

Committed partisans on the left and the right have always had ideological media outlets they could turn to (*The Nation* and *National Review*, for example), but for most Americans political affiliation was not the determining factor in choosing where they got their news. The three national networks, CBS, NBC, and ABC, offered pretty much the same product and the same establishment point of view. That product was something you shared with all Americans—not just friends, neighbors, and others like you but millions of people you would never meet, many of them very unlike you.

For some time now Americans have been leaving those vast media spaces where they used to come together and have instead been clustering in smaller units. The most broad-based media outlets, the networks and metropolitan newspapers, have been losing viewers and readers for years. But lately, thanks to the proliferation of new cable channels and the rise of digital and wireless technology, the disaggregation of the old mass audience has taken on a furious momentum. And the tribalization is not just about political ideology. In the post-mass-media era audiences are sorting themselves by ethnicity, language, religion, profession, socioeconomic status, sexual orientation, and numerous other factors.

"The country has atomized into countless market segments defined not only by demography, but by increasingly nuanced and insistent product preferences," *Business Week* reported last July, in a cover story called "The Vanishing Mass Market." To survive in this environment even old mass-media companies have had to learn the art of "niching down." Though national magazines have produced targeted sub-editions for years, the slicing grows ever thinner. Time, Inc., the granddaddy of print media for the masses, has launched a new women's magazine just for Wal-Mart shoppers. Radio now has satellite and Web variants that let listeners choose their taste pods with exceptional precision. The fast-growing XM Satellite Radio has not just one "urban" music channel but seven, each serving up a different subgenre twenty-four hours a day.

Some niches are so small they're approaching the vanishing point. There are now hundreds of thousands of bloggers, individuals who publish news, commentary, and other content on their own idiosyncratic Web sites. Some boast readerships exceeding those of prestigious print magazines, but most number their faithful in the double and triple digits. Find the one who shares your tastes and leanings, and you'll have attained the ne plus ultra of bespoke media: the ghostly double of yourself.

To sensibilities shaped by the past fifty years, the emerging media landscape seems not just chaotic but baleful. Common sense would suggest that as the vast village green of the broadcast era is chopped up into tiny plots, divisions in the culture will only multiply. If everyone tunes in to a different channel, and discourse happens only among like minds, is there any hope for social and political cohesion? Oh, for a cozy living room with one screen and Walter Cronkite signing off with his authoritative, unifying "That's the way it is."

It's instructive to remember, however, that the centralized, homogeneous mass-media environment of Cronkite's day was really an anomaly, an exception to the historical rule. For two centuries before the arrival of television America had a wild, cacophonous, emphatically decentralized media culture that mirrored society itself. And something like that media culture seems to be returning right now.

When primitive newspapers first appeared in seventeenth-century London, they were just official bulletins about the doings of the monarchy. Royally sanctioned and censored, they had no ideology other than that of the throne. The first real American newspaper, the *Boston News-Letter*, came straight from this mold. It was put out by an imperial official, the postmaster of colonial Boston, and stamped with the same seal of governmental approval worn by its British predecessors: "Published by Authority."

That timid approach didn't last long in America, however. In 1721 a Boston printer named James Franklin, older brother of Benjamin, founded a paper called the *New England Courant*, which brashly questioned the policies of the colony's ruling elite. The very first issue attacked Cotton Mather and other worthies for their support of smallpox inoculations. The paper was on the wrong side of that argument, but the real news was that it made the argument at all. The *Courant* was "America's first fiercely independent newspaper, a bold, antiestablishment journal that helped to create the nation's tradition of an irreverent press," Walter Isaacson writes in his recent biography of Benjamin Franklin (whose first published writings appeared in his brother's paper).

Franklin's paper set the tone for the evolution of the media in this country. Outspoken newspapers played a crucial role in the Revolutionary War, and when it was over the leaders of the young republic consciously used public policy to nurture a free press. As the Princeton sociologist Paul Starr notes in his recent book, *The Creation of the Media: Political Origins of Modern Communications*, the United States dispensed with the European tradition of licensing papers and policing their content. Congress even granted American publishers lower rates for postal delivery, a valuable subsidy that made starting up and running a paper more economical.

Such policies, combined with the freewheeling ethos that had already taken root in the press, set off a wild journalistic flowering in the nineteenth century. By the 1830s newspapers were everywhere, and they spoke in a myriad of voices about all manner of issues. Alexis de Tocqueville, who was accustomed to the reined-in newspapers of France, marveled at all the variety.

> The number of periodical and semi-periodical publications in the United States is almost incredibly large . . . It may readily be imagined that neither discipline nor unity of action can be established among so many combatants, and each one consequently fights under his own standard. All the political journals of the United States are, indeed, arrayed on the side of the administration or against it; but they attack and defend it in a thousand different ways.

In this the media reflected the political scene. The nineteenth century was a time of intense national growth and fervent argument about what direction the country should take. Numerous political parties appeared (Democratic, Whig, Republican, Free Soil, Know-Nothing), and the views and programs they advocated all found expression in sympathetic papers. In fact, the parties themselves financially supported newspapers, as did the White House for a time. Starr notes that according to a U.S. Census estimate, by the middle of the nineteenth century 80 percent of American newspapers were avowedly partisan.

This partisanship was not typically expressed in high-minded appeals to readers' better instincts. As Tocqueville wrote, "The characteristics of the American journalist consist in an open and coarse appeal to the passions of his readers; he abandons principles to assail the characters of individuals, to track them into private life and disclose all their weaknesses and vices." When Martin Chuzzlewit, the central character of the Dickens novel by the same name, arrives in the New York City of the early 1840s, he is greeted by newsboys hawking papers with names like the *New York Slabber* and the *New York Keyhole Reporter*. "Here's the *New York Sewer*!" one newsie shouts. "Here's the *Sewer*'s exposure of the Wall Street Gang, and the *Sewer*'s exposure of the Washington Gang, and the *Sewer*'s exclusive account of a flagrant act of dishonesty committed by the Secretary of State when he was eight years old."

Partisan and scandalously downmarket, the nineteenth-century media nonetheless helped forge a sense of national identity.

Yet even though the media of this period were profuse, partisan, and scandalously downmarket, they were at the same time a powerful amalgamator that encouraged participatory democracy and forged a sense of national identity. Michael Schudson, a professor of communication and sociology at the University of California at San Diego and the author of *The Sociology of News* (2003), says that the rampant partisanship displayed by newspapers "encouraged people to be attentive to their common enterprise of electing representatives or presidents." Commenting that "politics was the best entertainment in town in the middle of the 19th century," Schudson compares its effect to that of sports today. "Professional baseball is an integrative mechanism even though it works by arousing very partisan loyalties," he says. In other words, newspapers helped pull the country together not by playing down differences and pretending everyone agreed but by celebrating and exploiting the fact that people didn't. It's the oldest American paradox: nothing unifies like individualism.

We tend to think of the rise of the modern mass media as primarily a function of technology: the advent of television, for example, enabled broadcasters to reach tens of millions of Americans, but the cost of entry was high enough to sharply limit the number of networks. However, technology was only one of several factors that determined the character of the media establishment that arose in the United States after World War II. Beginning in the nineteenth century the idea of objectivity began to cross over from science into business and popular culture. As the historian Scott Sandage notes in his new book, *Born Losers: A History of Failure in America*, a whole new industry rose up in nineteenth-century New York when a handful of creative entrepreneurs discovered they could gather "objective" information about businesses and people (the precursor of modern-day credit ratings) and sell it to other businesses for a profit. Soon journalists, including the muckrakers of the Progressive Era, were embracing a similar notion of objective, irrefutable fact. When the Washington journalist Walter Lippmann wrote in the 1920s that "good reporting requires the exercise of the highest of scientific virtues," and called for the founding of journalistic research institutes, he was, as Starr notes, codifying a standard of disinterested inquiry that would influence generations of journalists to come.

At the same time, a federal government that had once used policy to encourage the growth of a free press now faced a very different challenge. Unlike newspapers, the public airwaves were a finite resource, and someone had to decide how to dole it out. The solution was a federal regulatory structure that sought to ensure fairness but could never offer the ease of access or the expressive freedom of the press. (Not that the networks necessarily wanted the latter; in order to pull in the large audiences that ad buyers demanded, all strove for a safe neutrality that offended no one.) For these reasons, although the broadcast media reached more people, the range of content they offered was actually more constricted than that of the print media that preceded them.

Finally, the political culture of the 1940s and 1950s discouraged extremism. The two major political parties of that period certainly had their differences, but they shared a basic set of beliefs about the country's priorities. Politics hewed to the center, and the media both reflected and reinforced this tendency. The centrist, "objective" networks and large newspapers didn't just *cover* the political establishment; they were an essential part of it. The anchormen who appeared on television and the columnists of the great papers were effectively spokesmen for the ruling postwar elite. (On occasion literally so: Lippmann, the great proponent of objectivity, worked with his fellow reporter James Reston on a famous speech by Senator Arthur Vandenberg; both journalists then turned around to write about the speech for their respective papers.)

That establishment consensus exploded in the 1960s and 1970s, with Vietnam and Watergate, but the mass media hung on for a few decades, a vestigial reminder of what had been. The Reagan era and the end of the Cold War dealt the old politico-media structure the final blows. In the 1990s partisan politics really took hold in Washington, and again the news media followed suit. The demise of the postwar consensus made the mass media's centrism obsolete. Long-simmering conservative resentment of the mainstream media fueled the rise of Rush Limbaugh and Fox News. Their success, in turn, has lately inspired efforts on the left to create avowedly liberal radio and cable outlets.

Socially, too, our fragmented media are to this era what James Franklin's newspaper was to the 1720s and the CBS evening news was to the 1950s. The cultural sameness and conformity that prevailed after World War II—the era of *Father Knows Best* and Betty Crocker—have been replaced by a popular pursuit of difference and self-expression. In explaining why McDonald's has shifted a significant portion of its advertising into niches, an executive of the company told *BusinessWeek*, "From the consumer point of view, we've had a change from 'I want to be normal' to 'I want to be special.'" In a mass-media world it's hard to be special. But in the land of niches it's easy. What is blogging if not a celebration of the self?

The "Trust us, we know better" ethos that undergirded the broadcast era today seems increasingly antique. If red and blue America agree on anything, it's that they don't believe the media. To traditionalists worried about the future of news, this attitude reflects a corrosive cynicism. But in another way it's much like the skepticism that animates great journalism. As the media have become more transparent, and suffered their own scandals, the public has learned to think about the news the same way a good journalist would—that is, to doubt everything it's told.

Although network ratings continue to plummet, there's still evidence elsewhere of an enduring demand for the sort of connectedness that only broad-based media can offer. For the six months that ended last September 30 many of America's largest newspapers saw the now customary declines in circulation. But among those that saw increases were the only three with a national subscriber base: *The New York Times, The Wall Street Journal*, and *USA Today*. The presidential debates last year drew impressive audiences to the broadcast networks, suggesting that although Americans no longer go to mass outlets out of habit, they will go by choice when there's good reason. In one of those debates Senator John Kerry cracked a Tony Soprano joke, and it was safe to assume that most viewers got the allusion. When we rue the passing of mass togetherness, we often forget that the strongest connective tissue in modern culture is entertainment—a mass medium if ever there was one.

Moreover, for all the pointed criticism and dismissive eye-rolling that niche and mass outlets direct each other's way, the two are becoming more and more symbiotic. Where would the *Drudge Report* and the blogging horde be without *The New York Times*, CBS News, and *The Washington Post*? Were it not for the firsthand reporting offered by those media dinosaurs, the Internet crowd would have nothing to talk about. Conversely, where would the Web versions of mass outlets be without the traffic that is directed their way by the smaller players? If there's a new media establishment taking form, it's shaped like a pyramid, with a handful of mass outlets at the top and innumerable niches supporting them from below, barking upward.

Whenever critics of the new media worry about the public's clustering in niches, there's an unspoken assumption that viewers watch only one outlet, as was common thirty years ago—that is, that there are Fox people and CNN people, and never the twain shall meet. But the same Pew poll that showed the increasingly ideological grouping of cable audiences revealed that most Americans watch the news with remote at the ready, poised to dart away at any moment. Pew also detected an enormous affinity for "inadvertent" news consumption: a large majority of Internet users from almost all demographic groups say that while online they encounter news unexpectedly, when they aren't even looking for it. "Fully 73% of Internet users come across the news this way," Pew reported, "up from 65% two years ago, and 55% as recently as 1999." Thus it appears that one of the great joys of newspaper reading—serendipitous discovery—lives on.

And although much changes in the media over time, there are some eternal truths. Most outlets crave two things, money and impact, and the easiest path to both is the old-fashioned one: grow your audience. Ambitious niches will always seek to become larger, and in so doing to attract a more diverse audience. It's only a matter of time before the first mass blog is identified, celebrated, and showered with minivan ads.

Finally, there's no substantive evidence yet that the rise of the niches is bad for democracy. The fractious, disunited, politically partisan media of the nineteenth century heightened public awareness of politics, and taught the denizens of a new democracy how to be citizens. Fast forward to the present. The United States just held an election that was covered by noisy, divisive, often thoroughly disreputable post-broadcast-era media. And 120 million people, 60 percent of eligible voters, showed up to cast their ballots—-a higher percentage than have voted in any election since 1968. Maybe we're on to something.

WILLIAM POWERS is a columnist for *National Journal* and a former reporter for *The Washington Post*. He writes frequently about the media, politics, and culture.

From *The Atlantic Monthly*, January/February 2005, pp. 122–126. Copyright © 2005 by William Powers. Reprinted by permission of the author.

Article 35

The Hollywood Treatment

FRANK ROSE

A Quintessential Hollywood Moment: a star on a soundstage, the focal point of every person and every piece of equipment in the room. The star on this particular January day is Rosario Dawson, the 29-year-old actress who earned her cred as an Uzi-wielding prostitute in *Sin City*. She's being filmed against a greenscreen in extreme close-up, highlighting her sculpted cheekbones and olive skin. "We've got this joke in vice," she murmurs in a voice that's uncommonly sultry for a police detective. "Love costs 10 bucks. *True* love costs 20."

In her studded black tunic and high-heeled boots, Dawson is apparently Tinseltown's idea of how to clean up the streets. "She looks like she can kick some ass," observes Brent Friedman, the chief screenwriter, who's watching on a nearby monitor. But even though we're in a Hollywood zip code, this is no film or television shoot. The rented space looks more like an oversize garage than a studio soundstage. Instead of the usual army of grips and gaffers, the production is staffed by a skeleton crew. And the parking lot outside? Barely big enough for 20 cars.

All of which can mean only one thing: another Web production. Two years after the success of *Lonelygirl15*—the groundbreaking YouTube serial that turned out to be not the DIY diary of a 16-year-old girl but the work of three wannabe auteurs in Beverly Hills—Web video has finally captured Hollywood's imagination. Last year, former Disney chief Michael Eisner launched *Prom Queen*, a daily 90-second teen drama; Judd Apatow has joined Will Ferrell on Funny or Die, a sort of YouTube for comedy; producers Ed Zwick and Marshall Herskovitz had a modest success with *Quarterlife*, a web show about self-obsessed twentysomethings, only to see it flop on TV. But *Gemini Division*, the sci-fi serial Dawson is shooting today, will be the first Web series to feature a bona fide Hollywood star.

Sure, the YouTube explosion was fueled by amateurs, but it will be showbiz professionals who cash in on Web video. That's because most big corporate advertisers want a safe, predictable environment—not the latest YouTube one-off, no matter how viral. Once the major brands get on board, millions of ad dollars will follow. Which is why when the writers' strike idled most of Hollywood last winter, talent agents fielded calls from clients eager to try their hand. At the same time, the fact that a three-minute clip can be shot for as little as $2,000 means Web video will be more open to ambitious neophytes than television ever was—witness the guys behind *Lonelygirl15*, who now have a second hit Web series called *KateModern* and a deal to develop more for CBS.

So far, however, this is a gold rush without any gold. Nobody knows how the business is supposed to work—what kind of stories to tell, whether to tell them in 90 seconds or 20 minutes, whether to build a destination site or distribute episodes across the Net, how to generate revenue, how to do it all on a shoestring. The *Gemini* team is betting they can figure it out. "People ask, 'What's your business model?'" says the director, Stan Rogow, during a lull in the shoot. "And I say, 'This morning's or this afternoon's?' It's only partly a joke."

A wiry figure who wears his long silver hair brushed straight back, Rogow is dressed in softly faded jeans and an extravagantly collared white shirt open halfway to the waist, a set of aviator glasses tucked neatly into the V. In an earlier life he was "the king of tweens," the producer who made *Lizzie McGuire* for Disney and turned Hilary Duff into a star. *Gemini Division* is the first of eight Web serials he has in the works at Electric Farm Entertainment, the production company he's formed with Friedman, the writer, and Jeff Sagansky, a former copresident of Sony Pictures Entertainment and head of CBS Entertainment before that.

Right now they need a distributor, and they've been talking with everyone from NBC Universal to MySpace about putting *Gemini Division* on their sites. Whoever they partner with would sell advertising and maybe even help fund the production. MySpace isn't offering money up front, but it does sell ads and split the revenue with producers. Eisner partnered with MySpace on *Prom Queen*, as did Herskovitz on *Quarterlife*, but Rogow is hoping for a more lucrative arrangement—which is why he has spent half the afternoon squiring around a pair of suits from NBC. The deal he's discussing would put Electric Farm well on its way to recouping the $1.75 million or so it will cost to make the 50 three-minute episodes Rogow plans to shoot. But the deal's not done yet.

Meanwhile, Rogow has been talking with Cisco and a handful of other companies about another way to make money: product placement. As a *Buck Rogers*–style serial set "five minutes in the future," the show presents many possibilities for tech companies. Dawson's smartphone, for instance, is the aperture through which we see the entire series. She talks urgently into the device throughout each episode, sending the feed to someone—we don't know whom—and occasionally holding it up to capture what's going on around her. It's a prominent branding opportunity for any handset maker willing to plunk down the money.

Like *Prom Queen* and *Lonelygirl15*, *Gemini Division* is essentially a female first-person confessional—in this case, a confessional about biotech run wild. Dawson plays Anna Diaz, a New York City detective having a crazy fling with a guy who's tall, blond, and ripped. By episode 4, the one they're shooting now, he has spirited her off to Paris for a romantic getaway, but she realizes something isn't right. Like, what's with the orange ring he left around the bathtub? "I really do love Nick," Dawson confides to the camera. "But being a cop, you get cynical. And you learn to trust your gut."

For the next scene, two crew members wheel a queen-size bed into place. Justin Hartley, the 6'3" *Smallville* actor who plays Nick, is lolling on the bed in his boxer shorts, sporting six-pack abs and a bright orange belly button. The script calls for Anna to come out in a sexy black negligee and climb into bed with him. The sound man cues up Marvin Gaye's "Let's Get It On." Everybody laughs.

For Anna, romance has given way to suspicion: first the orange tub ring and now, as she settles reluctantly into Nick's arms, his orange navel. If the camera were to pan a little wider, it would also catch two grips crouching behind the headboard to keep the bed from sliding across the set. Rogow smiles ruefully at the amateurishness of it all. "I think we should keep those guys in the background," he quips. "It's a nice touch."

Two years ago, when *Lonelygirl15* first showed that a scripted Web-only serial could attract a sizable audience, most people in show business thought of the Web as a promotional vehicle—if they thought of it at all. Then a couple of major players caught the bug. Michael Eisner was one; another was Jeff Sagansky, who was investing in small production companies like the one that makes *The Tudors* for Showtime. Web video was uncharted territory: no rules, limitless potential. "We're at the vanguard of something that can explode," Sagansky declares a few weeks after the January shoot. A trim 56-year-old, he's seated in his elegantly appointed town house on Manhattan's Upper East Side. "You know TV; it's been around in its present form since *Hill Street Blues*," the '80s ensemble show that's still the template for most drama series. "But this is all new."

Fans of *Mad Men, Weeds,* and *Battlestar Galactica* may think television has entered a new golden age, but many in the business see a medium in decline. TV programs used to be made by independent production companies. Now, with few exceptions, a handful of giant media conglomerates own the networks that air the shows, the film studios that make the shows, and the shows themselves. Network suits tell the producers what to do, and when it doesn't work—which is most of the time—they cancel the show. The Web puts power back in the hands of the creators: Producers own their shows and answer only to themselves. If they develop spinoffs for television, videogames, or the movies, they're well positioned to retain control when a property migrates to other media. That's why everyone took note of the deal NBC made last year to air *Quarterlife* in prime time. For the first time in memory, the producers of a TV show got full ownership and creative control.

There's a downside, of course. Top writer-producers in television live like pampered pets, the kind that get caviar for breakfast. To succeed online, they'll have to be as entrepreneurial as anyone in Silicon Valley. Instead of pulling in millions a year, they'll be scrambling for nickels and dimes. No surprise, then, that some of them think of Web video as a sort of farm club for TV: Why spend $2 million to make a half-hour pilot when you can shoot some high-quality Web episodes at $10,000 to $30,000 a pop, post them online to build buzz, string them together to make a series, and then port the whole thing back to television, where the real money is?

Quarterlife looked like the perfect prototype. Its episodes even happened to be seven to 10 minutes long, the typical interval between commercial breaks on TV. But while it did OK online, garnering some 6 million views after its November launch, its premiere on NBC drew only 3.9 million viewers—an all-time low for the network in that slot. When it was summarily canceled, Herskovitz was stunned. Not Sagansky. "This is a whole new medium," he says. "To think that it's going to fix the old medium is a warped way of looking at things."

Not that anyone yet has a recipe for success online. "We know that the Internet is about short-form entertainment," Sagansky says. "And most of it is personally narrated," as *Lonelygirl15* was. Other people, Eisner among them, will tell you that Web video isn't about Hollywood stars like Dawson, that this medium is for regular people. But the truth is that nobody really knows what form Web video will eventually take. The technology that has made it possible—broadband Internet connections, more-efficient data compression, ever-cheaper storage and servers, hi-res computer and smartphone screens—could seem ludicrously primitive before long. In 1908, movies were 10 minutes long because that's all you could get on a reel of film, and the actors who appeared in them were anonymous. Movies as we know them were still years away.

Sometimes even Rosario Dawson wonders if people want to see a Hollywood star in a Web serial. "The thing that's succeeded on the Web—besides, obviously, porn—is people themselves," she says over lunch. She's on a break from shooting the DreamWorks thriller *Eagle Eye* with Shia LaBeouf; soon she'll start rehearsals for *Seven Pounds,* a Sony film in which she plays a desperately ill heart patient Will Smith falls in love with. "They're putting up their own stuff—really off the cuff, no money involved. So we're taking a huge risk. But it's exciting to be part of something new. Even if we mess it up, we were the first, you know? That's kind of awesome in itself."

But if casting Dawson was a break from the nascent conventions of Web video, the format of *Gemini Division* is not. It isn't just that this is short-attention-span entertainment. It's that, like *Lonelygirl15* and *Prom Queen* and even such TV shows as *Lost* and *Heroes, Gemini Division* is designed to involve the audience in ways that more closely resemble videogames than conventional narrative drama.

That's no coincidence. A seasoned film and television writer, Friedman left Hollywood three years ago for Electronic Arts, where he wrote the best-selling *Command & Conquer 3: Tiberium Wars* and the soon-to-be-released *Tiberium.* At EA, he had to relearn scriptwriting, because the conventions of TV don't work in interactive media. In a one-hour drama, he explains, "you put the characters together over some beers and let them bring out the plot. It's exposition disguised as dialog." But games dispense with the entire first act, the part that sets the plot in motion. "When the story begins, you're in-world—you have a gun, all hell is breaking loose, and your job as a player is to stay alive and figure out where you are." Web video gets subjected to that same compression algorithm. "We're starting every episode with Anna on the run," Friedman says. "She's already in the second act—the part where everything goes wrong."

But Friedman's ambition is to merge television with videogames in a form of storytelling that engages audience members on multiple levels—and not just with the narrative but with each other. So while Anna dodges "sims" (simulated life forms, with their telltale orange stigmata) and agents from the mysterioso outfit known as Gemini Division, fans will be able to log on to the show's Web site and get transmissions from Anna's partner in the police department. Users will be recruited as Gemini agents themselves, at which point they can talk with other agents—er, users—by webcam. "I think this is where entertainment is heading," he says. "It's where *I* want entertainment to head, because that's what I want to experience."

Rogow and Friedman first tried this approach to storytelling in an earlier Web effort, an animated serial called *Afterworld.* Developed just after *Lonelygirl15* made such a splash, *Afterworld* was where they met Rosario Dawson. Dawson is a comics geek, and as a favor to a comics writer she knew who was working on *Afterworld,* she agreed to do a voice-over for one of the characters. Rogow asked her about doing a video series based on *Occult Crimes Taskforce,* a comic she had helped create. That didn't happen because a film deal was already in the works. But a couple of months later, Rogow called to say they were developing *Gemini Division.* It had been written for a male lead, but they were thinking of reworking it for her. They would make her a partner in the production and give her a cut of any profits.

Dawson had already signed on to play a military investigations officer in *Eagle Eye,* and her character in *Occult Crimes Taskforce* is also a detective. "When Stan told me I'd be playing an officer in *Gemini Division,* I was like, you know, this is going to seem weird." Even so, she liked the idea. She'd been acting for a dozen years, ever since she was discovered on the stoop of her parents' squat on Manhattan's Lower

East Side and cast in Larry Clark's *Kids*. "Normally at this point it starts to get stagnant," she says. "You're worrying about looking older, are they going to like you anymore. But I'm more going, what new can I do? I'd rather put myself into the fray than sit back and go, well, I played it safe."

On a sunny afternoon in march, Rogow pulls his black Porsche SUV to the curb, collects a ticket from the valet, and walks briskly into the Creative Artists Agency building on LA's Avenue of the Stars. Perfectly framed in an enormous glass wall is the Hollywood sign, 8 miles away. Rogow is here to meet with Anita Lawhon, the Cisco executive in charge of entertainment partnerships. This is crunch time for *Gemini Division*, the weeks when everything—advertising, distribution, financing, production—must come together. On a table in the vast marble reception zone sits this morning's *Daily Variety*. "CHANGES TO BIZ GIVE TOWN THE JITTERS," reads the front-page headline.

Today, Rogow is focused on how to get that business model working. It's going well—so well that Herskovitz recently met with his CAA agents to learn how Electric Farm is doing it. Cisco is key. Those *Gemini Division* agents are going to wield some pretty cool tech, much of it—thanks to a deal brokered by CAA—actual products from Cisco: a video surveillance system that sends an alert when someone penetrates the wrong sector; digital billboards that can be reprogrammed on the fly; TelePresence, a teleconferencing system with life-size video so hi-def it makes virtual meetings seem almost real. In the past few weeks, similar deals have been cut with Acura, Intel, Microsoft, and UPS. "In a cold business sense," Rogow confides, "this show is a self-financing marketing vehicle."

Settling into an all-white conference room, Rogow tells Lawhon they think it would be cool to show TelePresence on a private jet. "You think Rosario's at a table on the plane talking to people," he explains, "and we pull back and reveal they're not there."

Lawhon isn't sure—after all, TelePresence isn't being marketed for private jets, and the goal here is to show Cisco's products as they're actually used. She'll check. "But if you could look at other insertion opportunities . . ."

"Like putting it in an office? Absolutely."

Rogow is thrilled with Cisco's digital signs, which can be remotely programmed to display anything you want—like a coded message for Anna. "Which is, I think, why you really invented it: for superspies to get secret messages in malls," he quips. "We think that's real cool." He's equally happy with the surveillance system, which can send Anna a digital alert on her smartphone. "But we want to make sure we've got the Cisco logo in a prominent position," Lawhon points out. The days when product placement meant going full frontal on a Coke can are supposed to be over, but the client still has to get something in exchange for its six-figure fee. "That's why I love being able to see the script," she says.

"That's great," Rogow replies. "I'll have script material for you next week."

The next day, Friedman is at Electric Farm, in a Santa Monica office park, reworking the scripts to integrate all the products they've done deals for. There's the Acura TSX, the superspeedy UPS delivery, the search and mapping functions from Microsoft. He's not sure yet what to do with Intel. Maybe slap a POWERED BY INTEL badge on Dawson's smartphone? "It has to pass the creative smell test," he says, "so we feel like we're enhancing the story rather than trying to sell you something." In any case, they'll have to make up a brand for the phone itself: CAA approached several handset manufacturers, but none bit.

There's one other way to bring in money: venture capital. Funny or Die was funded by Sequoia Capital, the Silicon Valley venture firm behind YouTube. VCs like the idea that big Hollywood names can break through the clutter. But VCs also want an exit—a sale or stock offering that will net them the kind of payoff Sequoia got with YouTube. And while many would-be Web producers see venture money as manna from heaven, they haven't yet had to report to a frustrated money guy who doesn't know show business.

"There's an old joke," Rogow says, trying to explain why Electric Farm hasn't tried this route. "A filmmaker dies and goes to heaven. Saint Peter greets him at the pearly gates. 'Good news!' he says. 'You can make any movie you want! You can get Beethoven to do the score. You can get Shakespeare to write the script.' The filmmaker gets all excited. 'And who can I have to play the girl?' he asks." Long pause. "'Well,' comes the reply, 'God's got a girlfriend . . .'"

It's a Saturday afternoon in May. Two weeks earlier, NBC announced the formation of NBC Universal Digital Studio, with *Gemini Division* and *Woke Up Dead*, another Web series Electric Farm has in the works, as its first offerings. Now Rogow is back on a soundstage with Dawson—but this time the soundstage is bigger and the operation is far more professional.

The last shoot, back in January, was almost too bare-bones to work. The camera's shutter speed was set too slow, causing a motion blur so bad that some scenes needed to be reshot. Worse, Dawson's hair wasn't properly styled—it had big, wispy curls that congealed into unsightly blobs once the green backdrop was pulled away. "Hair turds!" cried Duane Loose, the burly EA veteran who's the show's production designer.

Nonetheless, they've put together a couple of episodes. A crew member is playing episode 5 on a computer screen in the corner: Anna Diaz in an abandoned factory in Paris, watching openmouthed as a man in a lab coat inserts a steel rod into Nick's orange navel. Seconds later, a pair of agents bursts in. One gets his arm sliced off by the doc's surgical laser. The other pulls out a weapon of his own and reduces Nick to a boiling puddle of goo. Anna screams: The man she loved is dead—and he wasn't even human!

Today they're shooting episode 12. Dawson is on the greenscreen with a tall, well-muscled actor who's wielding the same kind of weapon that killed Nick. Anna is caught in a war between the sims—creatures like Nick—and the seemingly all-powerful Gemini Division, which is bent on eradicating them. Muscle Man plays a Gemini agent who's just puddled a sim that was gripping Anna's throat. Now he's turning away, leaving her as mystified as ever. "I want in," Dawson cries, reaching for his arm—in on Gemini Division, in on why they destroyed Nick, in on whatever the hell is going on.

On the sidelines, arms folded across his black Che Guevara T-shirt, Friedman nods approvingly. In fits and starts, the world he's imagined is taking shape before him. Not a game world, not a TV world, but something different: a world viewed through the tiny window of Anna's phone. "That's an intimacy you don't get from television," he says. "And our mantra is, we want to do what television doesn't."

Contributing editor **FRANK ROSE** (frank_rose@wired.com) wrote about alternate reality games in issue 16.01.

Originally Published in *Wired*, August 2008, pp. 128–133, 149. Copyright © 2008 by Frank Rose. Reprinted by permission of the author.

Article 36

Girl Power

No rich relatives? no professional mentors? no problem. Ashley qualls, 17, has built a million-dollar Web site. She's lol all the way to the bank.

CHUCK SALTER

Late last year, Ian Moray stumbled across a cotton-candy-pink Web site called Whateverlife.com. As manager of media development at the online marketing company ValueClick Media, he was searching for under-the-radar destinations for notoriously fickle teenagers. Beyond MySpace and Facebook, countless sites come and go in the teen universe, like soon forgotten pop songs. But Whateverlife stood out. It was more authentic somehow. It featured a steady supply of designs for MySpace pages and attracted a few hundred-thousand girls a day. "Clever design, a growing base—that's a no-brainer for us," Moray says.

He approached Ashley Qualls, Whateverlife's founder, about incorporating ads from ValueClick's 450 or so clients and sharing the revenue. At first, she declined. Then a few weeks later she changed her mind. He was in Los Angeles and she was in Detroit, so they arranged everything by phone and email. They still have yet to meet in person.

When did Moray, who's 40, learn that his new business partner was 17 years old?

Pause.

"When our director of marketing told me why FAST COMPANY was calling," says Moray, now ValueClick's director of media development. "I assumed she was a seasoned Internet professional. She knows so much about what her site does, more than people three times her age."

It's like that famous *New Yorker* cartoon. A dog typing away at a computer tells his canine buddy, "On the Internet, nobody knows you're a dog."

At 17 going on 37 (at least), Ashley is very much an Internet professional. In the less than two years since Whateverlife took off, she has dropped out of high school, bought a house, helped launch artists such as Lily Allen, and rejected offers to buy her young company. Although Ashley was flattered to be offered $1.5 million and a car of her choice—as long as the price tag wasn't more than $100,000—she responded, in effect, Whatever:) "I don't even have my license yet," she says.

Ashley is evidence of the meritocracy on the Internet that allows even companies run by neophyte entrepreneurs to compete, regardless of funding, location, size, or experience—and she's a reminder that ingenuity is ageless. She has taken in more than $1 million, thanks to a now-familiar Web-friendly business model. Her MySpace page layouts are available for the bargain price of . . . nothing. They're free for the taking. Her only significant source of revenue so far is advertising.

According to Google Analytics, Whateverlife attracts more than 7 million individuals and 60 million page views a month. That's a larger audience than the circulations of *Seventeen, Teen Vogue,* and *CosmoGirl!* magazines combined. Although Web-site rankings vary with the methodology, Quantcast, a popular source among advertisers, ranked Whateverlife.com a staggering No. 349 in mid-July out of more than 20 million sites. Among the sites in its rearview mirror: Britannica.com, AmericanIdol.com, FDA.gov, and CBS.com.

And one more, which Ashley can't quite believe herself: "I'm ahead of Oprah!" (Oprah.com: No. 469.) Sure, Ashley is a long way from having Oprah's clout, but she is establishing a platform of her own. "I have this audience of so many people, I can say anything I want to," she says. "I can say, 'Check out this movie or this artist.' It's, like, a rush. I never thought I'd be an influencer." (Attention pollsters: 1,500 girls have added the Join Team Hillary '08 desktop button to their MySpace pages since Ashley offered it in March.)

She has come along with the right idea at the right time. Eager to customize their MySpace profiles, girls cut and paste the HTML code for Whateverlife layouts featuring hearts, flowers, celebrities, and so on onto their personal page and—presto—a new look. Think of it as MySpace clothes; some kids change their layouts nearly as frequently. "It's all about giving girls what they want," Ashley says.

These days, she and her young company are experiencing growing pains. She's learning how to be the boss—of her mother, her friends, developers-for-hire in India. And Whateverlife, one of the first sites offering MySpace layouts specifically for girls, needs to mature as well. "MySpace layouts" was among the top 30 search terms on Google in June. Ashley knows that she needs new content—not just more layouts, but more features, to distinguish Whateverlife from the thousands of sites in the expanding MySpace ecosystem. Earlier this year, she created an online magazine. Cell-phone wallpaper, a new source of revenue at 99 cents to $1.99 a download, is in the works.

Running a growing company without an MBA, not to mention a high-school diploma, is hard enough, but Ashley confronts another extraordinary complication. Business associates may forget that she is 17, but Detroit's Wayne County Probate Court has not. She's a minor with considerable assets—"business affairs that may be jeopardized," the law reads—that need protection in light of the rift her sudden success has caused in an already fractious family. In January, a probate judge ruled that neither Ashley nor her parents could adequately manage her finances. Until she turns 18, next June, a court-appointed conservator is controlling Whateverlife's assets; Ashley must request funds for any expense outside the agreed-upon monthly budget.

The arrangement, she says, affects her ability to react in a volatile industry. "It's not like I'm selling lemonade," she says. Besides, it's her company. If she wants to contract developers or employ her mother, Ashley says, why shouldn't she be able to do it without the conservator's approval?

So the teenager has hired a lawyer. She wants to emancipate herself and be declared an adult. Now. At 17. Why not just sit tight until June? The girl trying to grow up fast can't wait that long.

> *I'm doing what everyone says they want to do, "live like there's no tomorrow."*
>
> Ashley in her blog, "The Daily Life of a Simple Kind of Gal," July 1, 2006; 2:43 A.M.

Ashley is different from the recent crop of high-profile teen entrepreneurs. True, her eighth-grade class did vote her "most likely to succeed," but it's safe to say they were predicting 20 or 30 years out, not three years removed from middle school. She created her company almost by accident and without the resources that typically give young novices a leg up. Catherine Cook, 17, started myYearbook.com by teaming up with her older brother, a Harvard grad and Internet entrepreneur. Ben Casnocha, the 19-year-old founder of software company Comcate and author of the new memoir *My Start-Up Life,* is the son of a San Francisco lawyer and has tapped Silicon Valley brains and bank accounts.

But Ashley had no connections. No business professionals in the family. No rich aunt or uncle. In the working-class community of downriver Detroit, south of downtown and the sprawling Ford plant in Dearborn, Michigan, she bounced back and forth between her divorced parents, neither of whom attended college. Her father is a machinist, her mother, until recently, a retail data collector for ACNielsen. "My mom still doesn't understand how I do it," Ashley says. To be fair, she did go to her mother for the initial investment: $8 to register the domain name. Ashley still hasn't spent a dime on advertising.

It all started as a hobby. She began dabbling in Web-site design eight years ago, when she was 9, hogging the family's Gateway computer in the kitchen all day. When she wasn't playing games, she was teaching herself the basics of Web design.

To which her mother, Linda LaBrecque, responded, "Get off that computer. *Now!*" For Ashley's 12th birthday, her mother splurged on an above-ground swimming pool—"just so she'd go outside," LaBrecque says.

Whateverlife just sort of happened, another accidental Web business. Originally, Ashley created the site in late 2004 when she was 14 as a way to show off her design work. "I was the dorky girl who was into HTML," she says. It attracted zero interest beyond her circle of friends until she figured out how to customize MySpace pages. So many classmates asked her to design theirs that she began posting layouts on her site daily, several at first, then dozens.

By 2005, her traffic had exploded; she needed her own dedicated server. Ashley, who had bartered site designs for free Web hosting, couldn't afford the monthly rental, not on her babysitting income. Her Web host suggested Google AdSense, a service that supplies ads to a site and shares the revenue. The greater the traffic, the more money she'd earn.

"She would look up how much she had made," says Jen Carey, 17, one of her closest friends. "It was $50. She thought that was the coolest."

The first check, her first paycheck of any kind, was even cooler: $2,790.

"It was more than I made in a month," her mother says.

"It made me want to do even more designs," Ashley says. But first, she went on a shopping spree at a nearby mall with Bre Newby, her best friend since third grade. Ashley walked out with eight pairs of jeans from J.C. Penney and an armful of other clothes. Without a credit card or a bank account, the 15-year-old paid $600 in cash—the most she'd ever spent.

"Before, I would ask my mom, 'Can I have $10?' and she'd say, 'No, you have to wait a few weeks,'" Ashley recalls.

She hasn't asked since.

In January 2006, a few months after that first payday and six months before her 16th birthday, she withdrew from school. Instead of taking AP English, French, and algebra II, instead of being a straight-A sophomore at Lincoln Park High School, Ashley stayed home to nurture her budding business and take classes through an online high school. "Everybody was shocked," she says. "They asked, 'Are you sure you know what you're doing?' But I had this crazy opportunity to do something different."

That "something different" was Whateverlife. The name came to Ashley in a moment of frustration. After losing a video game to Bre, she dropped the controller and blurted out, "Whatever, life." She liked it instantly. She thought it would be a great name for a Web site, for "whatever life you lead."

Now her life is centered around working in the basement of the two-story, four-bedroom house that she bought last September for $250,000. It's located in a fenced-off subdivision in the community of Southgate, a couple of blocks removed from Dix Highway, a thoroughfare dotted with body shops and convenience stores. She lives with her mother; her 8-year-old sister, Shelby; three cats; two turtles; a rottweiler; a hamster; and a fish.

Ashley's home office is the physical embodiment of her Web site. The business brings in as much as $70,000 a month, but

Article 36. Girl Power

there's not a whiff of corporate convention. It's fun, whimsical, and unabashedly pink. Pink walls. Pink rug. Pink chairs, pillows, and lamp. Even the blue, green, and silver stick-on robots dancing on the wall have tiny pink hearts. It's a teenager's version of the workplace, which earned raves when she posted pictures on MySpace:

"SOO FLIPPING CUTE!"

"OMG I want that office."

"Geez. That's just incredible. I'm what . . . almost ten years your senior and I am inspired by you."

The space reflects Ashley's personality, like everything else about her business. Therein lies one of the main reasons for Whateverlife's success, says Robb Lippitt, whom Ashley considers the only good thing to come out of her legal issues. When her lawyer realized she was running her company alone, he arranged a meeting with Lippitt, the former COO of ePrize, an online promotions outfit that is one of Detroit's fastest-growing companies. Having helped build ePrize to $30 million in annual revenue and 325 employees, he now helps other local entrepreneurs scale the mountain. In April, he became her $200-an-hour consultant and first business mentor.

Since Ashley, his youngest client ever, had never taken a class in accounting or read a business book, she needed a crash course on the basics, such as maintaining two accounts, business and personal. "She was running her business like a piggy bank," says Lippitt, 38.

But he found her to be a quick study and, in many ways, a natural entrepreneur. "She lacks experience, but I was blown away by her instincts," he says. How she makes her layouts compatible with social-networking sites other than MySpace, so her company isn't tied to one site. How she decided to offer her designs as cell-phone wallpaper, creating a new service and revenue stream based on existing inventory. Ashley, he realized, has a vision for Whateverlife that goes beyond a MySpace tools site. It could be a multifaceted community for girls.

Convinced that her fans need help building Web sites, she hired developers in India to create an easy-to-use application and wrote one-teen-to-another tutorials. After the site builder launched in May, though, she told Lippitt she was disappointed by delays and early bugs. Hiccups were common, he assured her; he expected modest results, maybe a few hundred users. But 28,000 signed up in the first week. "There are CEOs across the country who would be dancing in their offices if they got that reaction," he says.

Ashley is the demographic she's serving, which gives her a powerful advantage over far more experienced adults trying to channel their inner teen or glean clues from focus groups. Her site looks and sounds like something made by a teenager, not something manufactured to look that way.

The risk, of course, is that she could lose touch with her audience as she outgrows it. But Lippitt says she already grasps the importance of understanding her customers, not simply assuming they share her taste. She conducts polls about their favorite stores, celebrities, and *American Idol* contestants. She solicits feedback on new features. And she's thinking of the next step: "I may have to hire people younger than me."

Some days I miss school. I miss the laughter, the lunch lines, the jackass of the class, the evil ass teacher, sometimes I even miss the drama.

August 4, 2006; 1:30 A.M.

On a Wednesday in early June, the gang's all here after school. Well, everyone except Bre. Shayna Bone, 17, and Jen—outfitted in matching Whateverlife T-shirts, featuring row after row of multicolored hearts—sit at a table reviewing their W-4 forms. It's official: The staff is doubling for the summer.

Mike Troutt, 16, who's stretched across a white L-shaped couch, won't be joining them. A past contributor to the Whateverlife magazine, he's working as an apprentice at a local tattoo shop for the summer. He's contemplating where he'll get his first tattoo, he announces. Tomorrow's the big day.

As usual, Ashley is working away at her computer, a new desktop with a touch-screen monitor, one of three computers in her basement. Often, she's up at 7 or working into the wee hours on a "designfest" with Bre, fueled with music and Monster energy drinks.

In just 15 minutes, she creates a layout. Blue and pink streaks on a black background with blocks of pink rap lyrics. Her fingers race across the keyboard as she tries different fonts, sizes, compositions, switching out HTML coding as she talks. "Don't worry," she tells a wary Shayna, "I'll teach you."

Ashley the CEO, who has no fewer than 14 hearts on her business card, is both utterly familiar and a complete mystery to her friends. In some ways, she's the same old "Ash"—or "AshBo," a nickname they coined because she didn't have her own room at one point (Ashley + hobo = AshBo). She still plays *The Sims*, still giggles when Jen laughs like Eddie Murphy, and is still up for silliness, like standing by the road holding a sign that says, Honk if you believe in the Loch Ness Monster, or taking breaks on the swing set down the street.

AshBo looks even younger than 17. She has straight brown hair with light streaks down to the middle of her back. She has a French pedicure, like Jen and her mother. Her clothes are nothing fancy. "I don't need $2,000 shirts," Ashley says. "I'm fine with Target." Or a University of Michigan sweatshirt over a summer dress.

In other ways, she's an alien among normal teens. She can go on about hiring freelance developers, studying site-traffic trends, calculating ad rates, maintaining low overhead (her main operating expense is seven servers). "Sometimes when I talk about the site, my friends just stare at me," she says. She carries a BlackBerry and a Coach bag (a recent birthday present to herself). Her friends tease her about her last ring tone, which consisted of The Donald, someone they couldn't care less about, barking, "This is Donald Trump telling you to have an ego!"

Whateverlife has definitely brought out a bolder side. "One minute, she's joking around with us, and then, 'Oh, guys, hold on, I gotta take this call,'" says Mike. "She turns it on like a light switch." She's no longer the shy 15-year-old who would ask her mother or father to make a difficult phone call. Who didn't know

169

how to respond to advertisers' cold calls. Who didn't know how to negotiate. Now, it's "Is that the best you can do for me?"

"Something clicked," says her mother, who can be direct herself. "She's not letting people walk over her."

At one point, Ashley takes a call upstairs in the kitchen, where a fax machine sits on the countertop. The company that's building the application for her cell-phone wallpaper is on the line. The developer walks her through the latest mock-up, answering Ashley's questions. She's one of those teens who has mastered the art of talking to adults as a peer, of making eye contact rather than looking down or away at a moment's blush.

Her mother, whom Ashley hired recently to keep the books, listens in, hand on hip, a cigarette cocked. Afterward, she asks, "What was he talking about?"

Ashley translates. She'll ask her mother for advice, but she doesn't necessarily take it. "I'm stubborn, like her," she says. Ashley has more leverage than the typical teen. She's the breadwinner. And yet for all her newfound independence, she still needs to be driven everywhere. She hasn't taken driver's ed because she wants to take the class with a friend, not alone.

Occasionally, she feels the tug of her old life, traditions like Lincoln Park's Spirit Week, when she'd paint her cheeks orange and blue, the school colors. More than once, she has returned, just for the day, hanging out in her French teacher's classroom. Ashley wonders if she'll be allowed to participate in graduation. By then, she may have already earned an associate's degree in design, at Henry Ford Community College.

She's determined to bring her friends along for this strange and wonderful ride. They rode in the limo to her over-the-top sweet-16 party at the local Masonic Temple, where guests wore pink Whateverlife rubber bracelets and the door prize was an Xbox. She took Bre on a family vacation to Hawaii, Ashley's first flight. And when the friends go out—tonight it's to Chili's—she picks up the tab.

This summer, she's the boss. One of Ashley's friends had pitched in making layouts last year, but things got a tad awkward when Ashley thought her friend's productivity was dipping. Now she insists they've made up—BFF. But after the misunderstanding, she wrote up employee guidelines. She wanted to spell out her expectations. Lippitt is impressed. She's learning from her mistakes, a challenge for any new entrepreneur.

"I told them I need a minimum of 25 layouts a week to get paid," Ashley says. "It's just business."

Do I keep my site? Do I sell and be set for life? God, it's all so overwhelming.

August 4, 2006; 1:30 A.M.

a small desktop application that plays videos and can be easily shared with other sites. It's like "a music poster on a bedroom wall," says Mike More, Nabbr's CEO.

The widget made its Internet debut on Whateverlife. While surfing MySpace for leads, More had noticed how many Jonas Brothers fans used Whateverlife layouts. In less than two months, 60,000 fans transferred the Jonas Brothers' three-part video from Whateverlife to their MySpace pages, in effect becoming 60,000 new distribution points. "This teenage girl in the Midwest got more views for our video than YouTube," says Greenberg, 46. "It wasn't even close." The viral campaign encouraged fans to vote for the band on MTV's *Total Request Live,* and the group's song "Mandy" hit No. 4, unheard of without radio play.

Since then, Whateverlife has become one of the primary vehicles for Nabbr's viral campaigns for artists and movies, breaking acts such as the Red Jumpsuit Apparatus and 30 Seconds to Mars, as well as Lily Allen. More's staff sends Ashley signed CDs and photos to pass on to Whateverlife fans, and artists record personal shout-outs to her and Whateverlife that play on her site. She's light years ahead of traditional media such as *Teen Vogue,* More says. "If I were Condé Nast, I'd figure out a way to buy her," he says. "I would."

As previous suitors can attest, that wouldn't be easy. In March 2006, an associate of MySpace cofounder Brad Greenspan approached Ashley with a bid valued at more than $1.5 million. She passed. Three months later, Greenspan's people came back with a second offer: $700,000, a car, and her own Internet show with a marketing budget of $2 million.

Sorry, fellas. "I created this from nothing, and I want to see how far I can take it," Ashley says. "If I wanted to do an Internet show, I could do it on my own. I have the audience."

Until now, she has maintained a remarkably low profile in the offline world. Her scheduled appearance on the "Totally Wired Teen Superstars" panel at Mashup, a teen-marketing conference in July, was to be her first public-speaking appearance—and her first business trip. An even bigger gig is possible: her own reality-TV show. Rick Sadlowski, a TV production executive in Detroit who worked with Eminem when he was still Marshall Mathers, is eager to pitch the idea to MTV. Ashley is mulling it over.

Move over, Paris Hilton. It's Whateverlife: The Not-So-Simple Life.

Got evaluated by my therapist for emancipation— need to get a few teachers' written letters; should be cool:)

April 7, 2007; 9:53 P.M.

Last year, Steve Greenberg, the former president of Columbia Records and now the head of indie label S-Curve Records, witnessed the power of Whateverlife. Greenberg discovered Joss Stone, produced the Hanson brothers, and helped make Baha Men's "Who Let the Dogs Out" an unofficial sports anthem. Last year, he decided to promote Jonas Brothers, an unknown pop trio, online instead of on radio. He turned to Nabbr, a company that had developed a viral widget,

In February 2006, following a falling-out with her mother, Ashley moved in with her father and older brother. With her business booming, she says, she began supporting them—groceries, bills, rent, renovations. At first, she didn't mind. One of the benefits of Whateverlife was the ability to take care of her family in a way she'd never imagined, certainly not when she was a child overhearing arguments about unpaid bills. Ashley says she bought her brother a used car and paid her grandmother's taxes. The insurance through Whateverlife covered her mother's back surgery. But in August, Ashley moved back in with her mother. She hasn't spoken to her father since. Or to her brother, who later filed (then withdrew) a petition to become her conservator. "I used to trust easily," Ashley says. "I've learned to be careful."

When her brother took his name off a joint bank account with her, Lincoln Park Community Credit Union petitioned the probate court to assign a conservator. After several months, the judge tapped attorney Alan May. He has 40 years' worth of experience with conservatorships, but Ashley's situation makes the case unique in his career. Although May's role is protecting Ashley's interests, it hasn't always felt that way to her, not when she hasn't had complete control over the money she made. But she says, "I don't want this to come across like a war."

Until recently, though, the tension was undeniable. Ashley was unhappy having to get May's approval for expenses such as her mother's nearly $500-a-week pay. May declined to discuss the case, but in papers filed last spring with the court, he characterized LaBrecque as uncooperative and evasive.

"They're making me out to be the bad guy," Ashley's mother says. LaBrecque, 42, had little growing up herself. Her father worked on the assembly line at General Motors until he died of a heart attack at 42, leaving his wife to raise six kids on Social Security. "It was rough but we survived," she says. "I feel so lucky my daughter doesn't have to live the life I lived."

In mid-July, seven months after being assigned a conservator, Ashley finally sat down with everybody for the first time: her mother, her lawyer, her consultant, her guardian ad litem, and her conservator. She says that she feels much better about the situation.

But that doesn't change the fact that she wants to be on her own. The typical conservatorship case involves a minor with an inheritance or an elderly person who has lost his faculties. "It's unusual to be emancipated to run your own business," says Darren Findling, Ashley's lawyer. "But she's the perfect candidate—an Internet superstar who happens to be a minor."

For now, she's trying to block all this out and concentrate on her business.

On Thursday, while her friends are slaving through exams, Ashley meets with Lippitt for two hours. They couldn't appear more different. He's a low-key, analytical sort with a law degree. Lives on the other side of town, in the Tony Bloomfield Hills suburb. Drives a black Lexus, a rarity on her block. As an entrepreneur, though, she relates to him better than anyone else right now.

"I know, I'm always jumping on 10,000 things," Ashley says and then pitches her latest brainstorm, her own social-networking application for girls.

"Hmm," he says. "How do you think the reaction of MySpace would be?"

A teenage CEO, Lippitt is learning, is even more easily distracted and more fearless than an adult entrepreneur. "Failure is an abstract concept to her, and I want it to stay that way," he says. When he was a teenager, his father lost his body shop and had to start over, attending law school in his forties.

Lippitt urges Ashley to prioritize and think about profits as well as design. As clever as her site-building tool is, it doesn't allow a way to run ads on the pages it creates. "You're leaving revenue on the table," he tells her.

At times, Lippitt has to remind himself that she's only 17. "Even if she could go a lot faster, I don't know if that's the best thing for her," he says. "She's already in the adult world doing adult things. I'm reluctant to drive her away from living an important and fun time in her life."

But he's not shy about pushing her when she needs it. Today, he tells her it's time to consider approaching companies to advertise. So far, she has relied largely on Google AdSense, which supplies ads in exchange for what she says is a 40% cut. The direct model is not only potentially more lucrative but also allows her to target brands more suited to teens than, say, Microsoft Office 2007. "I'm not sure that's a good fit," he says of the software ad placed by ValueClick.

Ashley is excited about the idea. And a little nervous. She'll need a sales presentation, a company logo, and ad rates. Eventually, she may want to hire a sales rep, a job she'd never heard of until Lippitt described it. More important, she'll need to sell herself to name-brand companies. "If she can combine 'I'm 17' with a little more about her business, I think she's unstoppable," Lippitt says.

This could be the next growth spurt for Ashley and Whateverlife. It's scary, sure, but she's getting used to the demands and challenges of "this crazy opportunity." She's learning, stretching, getting that much-needed seasoning.

She and Lippitt brainstorm about which brands would resonate with girls like her. This is the fun part. No petitions. No regrets. No family feud. Just a 17-year-old and her big dreams in a pink, pink, pink world full of promise. And if they don't come true? Well, there's always college.

From *Fast Company*, September 2007, pp. 104–112. Copyright © 2007 by Mansueto Ventures LLC. Reprinted by permission via the Copyright Clearance Center.

Online Salvation?

The embattled newspaper business is betting heavily on Web advertising revenue to secure its survival. But that wager is hardly a sure thing.

PAUL FARHI

Even the most committed newspaper industry pessimist might begin to see a little sunshine after talking to Randy Bennett. Yes, the print business is "stagnant," acknowledges the Newspaper Association of America's new-media guru. And yes, he says, newsrooms are under pressure. But—and here comes the sun—newspapers have staked out a solid position on the Internet, he says. Internet revenue is growing smartly: In 2003, Bennett points out, newspapers collected a mere $1.2 billion from their online operations; last year the figure was nearly $2.7 billion. "We're growing at a double-digit rate," he says.

This is the kind of news that soothes beleaguered publishers and journalists. As print circulation and advertising swoon, the newspaper industry, and news providers generally, have looked for a lifeboat online. Newspapers were the first of the mainstream media to extend their traditional news franchises into the world of pixels, giving them an important "first mover" advantage. Web sites run by local newspapers typically remain the most popular sources of news and the largest sources of online advertising in their local communities.

Predictions about where the Internet is headed are, of course, hazardous. A dozen or so years after it began to become a fixture in American life, the Internet is still in a formative stage, subject to periodic earthquakes and lightning strikes. Google didn't exist a decade ago. Five years ago, no one had heard of MySpace. Facebook is just four years old, and YouTube is not quite three. Washington Post Executive Editor Leonard Downie Jr. compares the current state of the Internet to television in the age of "Howdy Doody."

Even so, a few dark clouds are starting to form in the sunny vista. Consider a few distant rumbles of thunder:

- After years of robust increases, the online newspaper audience seems to have all but stopped growing. The number of unique visitors to newspaper Web sites was almost flat—up just 2.3 percent—between August 2006 and August 2007, according to Nielsen/NetRatings. The total number of pages viewed by this audience has plateaued, growing just 1.8 percent last year.
- Newspaper Web sites are attracting lots of visitors, but aren't keeping them around for long. The typical visitor to nytimes.com, which attracts more than 10 percent of the entire newspaper industry's traffic online, spent an average of just 34 minutes and 53 seconds browsing its richly detailed offerings in October. That's 34 minutes and 53 seconds per month, or about 68 seconds per day online. Slim as that is, it's actually about three times longer than the average of the next nine largest newspaper sites. And it's less than half as long as visitors spent on the Web's leading sites, such as those run by Google, Yahoo! and Microsoft.

Many news visitors—call them the "hard-core"—linger longer online, but they're a minority. Greg Harmon, director of Belden Interactive, a San Francisco-based newspaper research firm, estimates that as many as 60 percent of online newspaper visitors are "fly-bys," people who use the site briefly and irregularly. "Everyone has the same problem," says Jim Brady, editor of washingtonpost.com. The news industry's continuing challenge, Brady says, is to turn "visitors into residents."

- As competition for visitors grows, news sites are rapidly segmenting into winners and losers. In a yearlong study of 160 news-based Web sites (everything from usatoday.com to technorati.com), Thomas E. Patterson of Harvard University found a kind of two-tier news system developing: Traffic is still increasing at sites of well-known national brands (the New York Times, CNN, the Washington Post, etc.), but it is falling, sometimes sharply, at mid-size and smaller newspaper sites.

"The internet is redistributing the news audience in ways that [are] threatening some traditional news organizations," concluded Patterson in his study, produced for the Joan Shorenstein Center on the Press, Politics and Public Policy. "Local newspapers have been the outlets that are most at risk, and they are likely to remain so."

Patterson suggests that some of the declines at newspaper sites may be due to increased competition from local broadcast stations, particularly TV. Although they got a late start on the Internet, local TV stations are beginning to catch up, thanks to copious video news clips and strong promotional capabilities.

"A lot of papers are close to maxing out their local audiences," Patterson said in an interview. "It's hard to know where more readers will come from. . . . They have to figure out how to deal with a pretty difficult future."

In other words, for many, that first-mover advantage has vanished.

Most ominous of all is that online ad growth is beginning to slow. Remember those confidence-building double-digit increases in online advertising revenue? They're fading, fast. In the first quarter of this year, the newspaper industry saw a 22 percent gain in online revenue. Not exactly shabby, but still the smallest uptick (in percentage terms) since the NAA started keeping records in 2003. In the second quarter, the industry rate slipped again, to 19 percent. The third quarter promises even less, considering what various companies have been reporting lately. E.W. Scripps Co. saw a 19 percent increase. The Washington Post Co. said its online revenue was up 11 percent in the period, the same as Gannett's. Tribune Co. saw a gain of 9 percent. McClatchy was almost in negative territory, with a weak 1.4 percent increase for the quarter and the year to date.

All of which begins to hint at one of the deeper economic challenges facing online news providers. Even as advertisers move from traditional media to new media, a big question lingers: Can online ad revenue grow fast enough to replace the dollars that are now being lost by the "old" media? And what happens if they don't?

At the moment, the Internet has a long way to go. Newspapers collected $46.6 billion from print advertisers last year; they took in another $11 billion in circulation revenue in 2004, the last time the NAA compiled the total. Even with the double-digit increases online, that's more than 20 times what they're generating from the Internet. Among the industry's most cutting-edge publishers, the Internet still accounts for only a fraction of the overall pie. The leading online newspaper company, the New York Times Co., derives only about 11 percent of its revenue from the Web. This fall, MediaNews Group, which publishes 57 daily newspapers, including the Denver Post and the San Jose Mercury News, touted plans to increase its share of Internet revenue to 20 percent—by 2012.

Philip Meyer, author of "The Vanishing Newspaper" and a former journalist and University of North Carolina journalism professor, believes that it's "in the interest of both newspapers and advertisers to shift content to the Internet." Advertisers get narrower target audiences for their products, he notes, and greater accountability, since they can monitor consumers' behavior. "Newspapers can at last grow their businesses without being held back by the variable costs of newsprint, ink and transportation," he said in an e-mail interview. "In the recent past, newspaper owners have preferred to cut fixed costs, like editorial staff, which gives a quick boost to the bottom line but weakens their hold on the audience. Using technology to cut the variable costs is a better strategy even though the payoff takes longer."

Shedding the big overhead costs of the old media is certainly an attraction of the new one. The problem is, an Internet visitor isn't yet as valuable as a print or broadcast consumer. The cost of reaching a thousand online readers—a metric known in advertising as CPM, or cost per thousand—remains a fraction of the print CPM. The price differential can be as much as 10-to-1, even though many newspaper Web sites now have online audiences that rival or exceed the number of print readers.

Some of this disparity is a result of the witheringly competitive nature of the Web. Unlike the print business, in which newspaper publishers generally enjoy near-monopoly status, the online news world is littered with entrants—from giants like MSNBC.com and AOL.com, to news aggregators like drudgereport.com, to blogs by the millions. This makes it tough for any online ad seller to do what newspaper publishers have done for years—keep raising their ad rates. "Ultimately, it comes down to supply and demand," observes Leon Levitt, vice president of digital media for Cox Newspapers. "And there's an awful lot of supply out there."

Harvard's Patterson offers a more intriguing, and perhaps more unsettling, theory about why it's hard to squeeze more money out of online advertisers: Web ads may not be as effective as the traditional kind. "I'm not sure [advertisers] are convinced yet about how terrific a sales tool [a Web display ad] is," he says. "The evidence isn't strong yet that it can drive people into a store the way a full-page newspaper ad can. They're less confident about what they're getting online." Moreover, unlike their here-and-gone counterparts on the Internet, print subscribers still stay around long enough to see an ad. Some 80 percent of print readers say they spent 16 or more minutes per day with their newspaper, according to Scarborough Research.

These dynamics could change, perhaps as stronger news sources emerge on the Web and weaker ones disappear. But even if the newspaper industry continued to lose about 8 percent of its print ad revenue a year and online revenue continued to grow at 20 percent a year—the pace of the first half of 2007—it would take more than a decade for online revenue to catch up to print.

Journalists, or indeed anyone with an interest in journalism, had better pray that doesn't happen. Because online revenue is still relatively small and will remain so even at its current pace, this scenario implies years of financial decline for the newspaper industry. Even a 5 percent decline in print revenue year after year might look something like Armageddon. Newspapers were already cutting their staffs before this year's advertising downturns. A sustained frost of similar intensity would likely lead to even more devastating slashing. The cuts could take on their own vicious momentum, with each one prompting a few more readers to drop their subscriptions, which would prompt still more cuts. Some daily papers would undoubtedly fold.

Some remain confident that these dire scenarios won't come to pass. "I don't foresee [print dying] in my lifetime," says Denise F. Warren, chief advertising officer for the New York Times Co. and its Web sites. "I'm still bullish on print. It's still an effective way to engage with the audience." On the other hand, she adds, "The business model will keep evolving."

Yes, says Phil Meyer, but it may evolve in ways that render many daily newspapers unrecognizable to today's subscribers: "You want a prediction?" he says. "There will be enough ads for ink on paper to survive, but mainly in niche products for specialized situations."

ANNUAL EDITIONS

Adding It Up

Here is how much print and online ad revenue newspapers have attracted in recent years:

Year	Print Total $Mill	Print Total %change	Online Total $Mill	Online Total %change	Print and Online Total $Mill	Print and Online Total %change
2000	$48,670	5.10%				
2001	$44,305	−9.00%				
2002	$44,102	−0.50%				
2003	$44,939	1.90%	$1,216		$46,156	
2004	$46,703	3.90%	$1,541	26.70%	$48,244	4.50%
2005	$47,408	1.51%	$2,027	31.48%	$49,435	2.47%
2006	$46,611	−1.68%	$2,664	31.46%	$49,275	−0.32%
2007						
Quarter						
First	$9,840.16	−6.40%	$750.04	22.30%	$10,590.20	−4.80%
Second	$10,515.23	−10.20%	$795.68	19.30%	$11,310.90	−8.60%

Source: Newspaper Association of America.

Question: Do you see a smart online business model for traditional media that will permit newspapers and other publications to continue to do deep reporting and attract talented journalists?

Craig Newmark: Not yet. While there are people working on it . . . no one's figured it out yet.

—From an online Q&A with Craigslist founder Newmark, posted on nytimes.com on October 10.

To restore the industry's momentum online, executives like Denise Warren suggest the key may simply be more. More new editorial features that will attract new visitors and keep the old ones engaged on the site for longer.

The Times, for instance, expanded three "vertical" news and feature sections last year (real estate, entertainment and travel) and this year is fleshing out similar sections on business, health and technology. In early December, the paper will launch a Web version of its fashion and luxury goods magazine, called T. The paper has also stopped charging for its op-ed columns, after having determined that it could attract more readers—and hence more advertising dollars—by removing the "pay wall" that blocked unlimited access. (The Wall Street Journal is also considering doing away with online subscriptions and moving to a free, ad-supported model, the Journal's new owner, Rupert Murdoch, said in mid-November.)

Washingtonpost.com has added more blogs, more video and special features, like a religion and ethics discussion called On Faith. In June, it started a hyper-local site-within-the-site called LoudounExtra.com that focuses on exurban Loudoun County in Virginia. Coming next summer: a complete redesign of the site. With so much movement, Brady isn't concerned about traffic slowing down. "I'm not worried that people's interest in the Internet has peaked," he says. "There's a whole generation coming up that uses the Internet a lot more."

Cox Newspapers is focusing on its papers' local markets with freestanding niche offerings that target specific demographic groups underserved by the main newspaper, such as young mothers and pet owners and local sports fans, says Leon Levitt. The idea is to assemble a larger, geographically concentrated online readership bit by bit, with as many as seven to nine specialized publications, he says.

Harvard's Patterson has a simpler idea: Just play the news better online. His study of news sites found "substantial variation" in how local sites display news, with some pushing blogs, ads and "activity lists" over breaking news. "If local news is downplayed, local papers are conceding a comparative advantage in their competition with other community sites for residents' loyalties," the study concluded. "If national and international news is downplayed, local papers may increase the likelihood that local residents will gravitate to national brand-name outlets."

The news may be the primary product, but the way the news is served online needs to be updated, too, says Mark Potts, a Web-news entrepreneur and consultant. He says newspaper-run sites are falling behind the rest of the industry in their use of technology. "For the most part, once you get past the bigger papers, newspapers are not up to date" online, he says. "They've got some video, a podcast, some blogs, yes, but mostly . . . they're just pasting the newspaper up on the screen. That was barely OK five years ago." Potts ticks off the tools that news sites usually lack: social networking applications, database-search functions, mapping, simplified mobile-device delivery technology, services that let readers interact with one another, etc. His one-word description for the state of newspapers online: "Stodgy."

On the ad side, traditional news organizations are starting to join, rather than trying to fight, some of the Internet's giants. In recent months, major newspaper companies have struck alliances with Yahoo! and Google in an attempt to pair newspapers' strength in selling local advertising with the search engines' superior technology and national reach. (See The Online Frontier, page 42.)

Article 37. Online Salvation?

In the first phase of a multipart alliance, some 19 newspaper companies that own 264 daily papers have linked their online help-wanted advertising to Yahoo!'s HotJobs recruitment site. When an advertiser seeking to hire, say, a nurse, in St. Louis buys an ad through the St. Louis Post-Dispatch, the newspaper places the ad on its site, which is co-branded with HotJobs and automatically linked to HotJobs' national listings. As a result, the advertiser gets his message in front of both local job candidates and others across the country. HotJobs, in turn, gets a local sales agent—the Post-Dispatch—to sell more listings. Although the partners have revealed few financial details about the arrangement, revenue from such ads is split between the newspaper and Yahoo!, with the newspapers taking a majority of each dollar generated.

In a second phase of the alliance that is now being tested, publishers such as McClatchy, Lee Enterprises, Media General, Cox and others will attempt to do something similar with display ads. Using Yahoo!'s search capabilities and technology, the companies hope to marry national and local display ads to their visitors' interests. People interested in, say, pickup trucks (as identified by tracking software and registration questionnaires), would likely see national ads for Ford, and perhaps for local Ford dealers, when they logged on to a newspaper's site. Such highly targeted advertising would command much higher CPMs than plain old banner ads, says Cox's Levitt.

While it's still too early to declare victory, the general scheme of the partnership has drawn praise from Wall Street. Deutsche Bank analyst Paul Ginocchio has estimated that some members of the consortium could see online ad growth rates of 40 percent for the next two years, thanks in large part to revenue generated by the Yahoo! tie-in.

However, other publishers have declined to join the Yahoo! consortium, in part out of concern that newspapers may be giving away too much to Yahoo! and leaving readers little reason to visit the newspapers' own sites. For example, Gannett and Tribune Co. are developing a display advertising network of their own.

Another group of publishers, including Hearst, E.W. Scripps and the New York Times Co., have turned to Google. Under an experimental program that was expanded this summer, Google is running auctions that enable thousands of smaller advertisers to bid on ad space—size, section and date of their choosing—on some 225 newspaper Web sites. The newspapers are free to accept the offer, reject it or make a counteroffer (Google says more than half the bids have been accepted). The process is streamlined by Google's technology, which automates billing and payments.

A little less cooperation might help, too. Some argue that news providers made a huge strategic mistake when they decided to make their content available to others online. "Free riders" like Yahoo.com, MSN.com, Google and AOL.com have built massive franchises—far larger than any traditional mainstream news site—in part by posting news stories created and paid for by others. These days, of course, anyone can assemble a series of links and headlines to become a "news" site. The Shorenstein Center put it bluntly in its recent study of news on the Internet: "The largest threat posed by the Internet to traditional news organizations . . . is the ease with which imaginative or well positioned players from outside the news system can use news to attract an audience."

"It's a terribly unfair deal," says Randy Siegel, the publisher of Parade, the weekly newspaper magazine. "Newspapers need to negotiate a more equitable share with search engines that are making billions of dollars by selling ads around newspaper content without the costs of creating that content. . . . The book industry and the movie industry don't give their content away."

Arkansas Publisher Walter Hussman Jr. knows he sounds like a man from another century when he says it, but he thinks newspapers shouldn't be free, online or off. He rues the day that the Associated Press, which is owned by the newspaper industry, agreed to sell stories to the Yahoo!s and AOLs of the world. Free or bargain-priced news, Hussman says, cheapens everyone's news. Free, he says, "is a bad business model."

Hussman has an idea that's so old and abandoned it seems almost new: Make people pay for the news they want, even in the Internet age. Hussman obviously is swimming upstream with this notion. Not long after the New York Times stopped charging for its op-ed columns under the now-jettisoned Times-Select initiative, the Sacramento Bee dropped subscription fees for Capitol Alert, the paper's Web site for political news.

The newspaper Hussman publishes, the Arkansas Democrat-Gazette in Little Rock, is one of the few that charge a fee ($4.95 a month) for full access to its site. The site has a modest base of 3,000 subscribers, but Hussman says walling it off protects a more lucrative franchise: the newspaper. He believes it's no coincidence that the Democrat-Gazette's print circulation is growing—about 2,000 daily in the latest six-month period that ended in September—at a time when so many others are sliding.

But what about the ad revenue that the newspaper is giving up with such a restricted Web site? Hussman says ad rates are so low online that they often don't cover the cost of producing original journalism. Example: An online gallery of photos from a local high school football game might generate 4,000 page views. If an advertiser paid $25 for each thousand views—a premium figure, by the way—the photo feature might generate $100, barely enough to pay the photographer for his work.

"I know what I'm saying is going to sound too simplistic to some people, but it seems to be working," he says. "The reason I advocate this is not some ideological or esoteric reason or because of pride of authorship. I'm basing this on experience."

Hussman sees an industry that generates nearly $60 billion a year in print ad sales and subscription fees, and that supports the expenditure of roughly $7 billion a year on newsgathering operations, and worries about it all slipping away in an era in which news is so abundant—and so free. "It would be wonderful if someone could figure out a way" to do all that online, he says before concluding, "but I just don't see it now."

PAUL FARHI (farhip@washpost.com) is a *Washington Post* reporter who writes frequently about the media for the *Post* and *AJR*. He has written about the San Francisco area's news blues, hyperlocal news Web sites and the business magazine *Portfolio* in recent issues of *AJR*.

From *American Journalism Review*, December 2007/January 2008, pp. 18–23. Copyright © 2008 by the Philip Merrill College of Journalism at the University of Maryland, College Park, MD 20742-7111. Reprinted with permission.

Home Free

Is delivering free newspapers to affluent homes a recipe for success in today's volatile media environment? The fate of Philip F. Anschutz's three Examiner dailies should provide a clue.

LORI ROBERTSON

In 1981, Henry Grunwald, then editor-in-chief of Time Inc., and another company executive paid a visit to newspaper consultant John Morton. Time's Washington Star had recently folded, just three years after the company acquired the daily. But Grunwald still wanted to have a paper in the nation's capital, Morton recalls. The pair asked him to figure out what kind of paper that should be.

Morton, who is also a longtime AJR columnist, conducted an analysis and came back with a verdict: "What it ought to be is free. It ought to have a distinctive but fairly conservative look," he recalls saying. And it ought to be mailed to the 200,000 richest households in the market. For nothing.

"They were appalled," Morton says; they dismissed such a publication as a "throwaway."

But "you can't do it on the same terms as the dominant newspaper," Morton says of his thinking then—and now. "It has to be free. I don't know if it will be successful, but I know every other attempt to establish a newspaper in competition with an existing one has been a failure."

In the end, Time Inc. didn't launch a new D.C. daily. But a variation on Morton's model is being tested. It only took 20-plus years for someone to come along with enough money and conviction to give it a try.

Philip F. Anschutz's Examiner newspapers—in San Francisco, Washington and Baltimore—are the only known free daily newspapers in the U.S. that are home delivered to neighborhoods that exhibit advertiser-enticing characteristics: households inhabited by 25- to 54-year-olds with kids and median incomes around $75,000. The papers have circulations between 190,000 and 250,000, with the majority of those copies dropped off on doorsteps, the rest picked up at street boxes.

But Anschutz's papers, which operate under the aegis of a company called Clarity Media Group, aren't aiming to put the established metro dailies out of business—or even compete with them head to head. Clarity CEO Ryan McKibben sees the Examiner filling both an advertising and content niche exposed by market segmentation and the circulation loss of traditional newspapers. There are readers—would-be newspaper readers—out there, he says. They're just not buying a big, fat daily. With the Examiner, consumers get those things market research says they've been clamoring for—local news, short stories, no jumps—while advertisers get a desirable audience and a good rate.

It's a direct-marketing business plan for a quick-read tabloid. And it's not cheap. The Examiner's distribution approach and its goal of beefing up its journalism make it a more expensive endeavor than your typical free subway-station tab. So far, there's not much, if any, buzz about "great stories in the Examiner." But over the past year, the Washington paper, in addition to employing young reporters, has been assembling a national team of experienced journalists. In January, it lured Stephen G. Smith from his perch as chief of the Houston Chronicle's D.C. bureau—and a long career marked by stints at the three major newsmagazines—to be executive editor. But how much great journalism can you pack into a paper that a reader is supposed to finish during the morning commute? And more important for an industry seeking a way to build readership instead of losing it, will this business model actually work?

Clarity Media Group is a private company, and it won't reveal financial information. But McKibben says he is optimistic about the Examiner's ability to fill a need for a new type of newspaper, coexisting peacefully with the major metros. "Everybody thinks this is a zero-sum game, and it really isn't," he says. "Differentiation is part of our model, and our papers are clearly a different read than the incumbent newspapers."

McKibben, a former publisher of the Denver Post, joined a Gannett paper not long after that company launched the original McPaper, USA Today, in 1982. He remembers people worrying that it would eat into the Wall Street Journal's business. "What everybody found out, it created a whole new marketplace for the reader and didn't hurt the Wall Street Journal at all," he says. "And that's what we are." A local USA Today.

"Free" has been a popular mode of operation for new newspapers in recent years, with media companies launching tabs aimed at the young (see "Hip—*and* Happening," April/May 2005) and Sweden-based Metro International setting up shop in various American cities. Piet Bakker, an associate professor at the University of Amsterdam School of Communications Research, chronicles the free daily phenomenon on his blog, Newspaper Innovation (newspaperinnovation.com). He counts 200 free dailies in 44 countries distributing 35 million copies, a circulation number that has doubled since late 2004. "The last two years, I would call an explosion," he says. "Three (Netherlands, Sweden, Italy, Greece) to four (Spain, Czech Republic, Paris, London) dailies is not an [exception] anymore," he writes of the free papers in an e-mail. "Denmark has 5."

Russel Pergament, the founding publisher of two free dailies, Metro Boston and amNew York, is a firm believer in the need and power of the product. He's launching another one later this year called Boston Now with the backing of the Icelandic company Dagsbrun. He offers kudos for the Examiner's hybrid model but also raises questions. "They're taking a very ambitious approach—high-income delivery as opposed to young commuters, which means they're going head to head with traditional dailies," he says. "The paper is much beefier than the typical commuter daily . . . very ambitious editorial treatment. . . . I think that works for kitchen-table suburban families. Probably not as fitting for the typical commuter" who has 19 minutes to read the whole thing.

Philip Anschutz, a 67-year-old, publicity-averse Denver billionaire who made his money in oil, railroads and entertainment, entered the newspaper business with the February 2004 purchase of the San Francisco Examiner from the Fang family. Later that year, he picked up the Washington-area Journal newspapers, renamed them the Washington Examiner, trademarked the Examiner moniker in 63 U.S. cities and unveiled the home-delivery model for his fledgling newspaper chain. In April 2006, Anschutz started publishing his first Examiner-from-scratch in Baltimore.

"I think he saw that with the decline of market share in advertising and the decline of circulation [at traditional daily newspapers] that there was probably an opportunity," Ryan McKibben says. McKibben, an acquaintance of Anschutz, says he started consulting with the businessman in June 2003. "So that's why I think he called, and we started to dig into this. There's clearly . . . a disconnect between traditional newspapers and the readers and their advertisers." (Anschutz doesn't do interviews, and his spokesman said that would be true for this story as well.)

In the beginning, McKibben says he did not know that Anschutz would buy the San Francisco Examiner, where P. Scott McKibben, Ryan's brother, was publisher. Newspapers pegged the purchase at $20 million, but the Los Angeles Times later reported that, according to a copy of the sale agreement, the price was a better bargain—$10.7 million for the Examiner, the now-defunct Independent newspapers, which were thrice-weekly freebies, and other assets. Florence Fang subsequently sued Anschutz, alleging that the McKibben brothers conspired to give him a favorable deal. The billionaire settled the suit. (Clarity Media won't comment on any of that.)

While Anschutz was becoming a media player, another entrepreneur was in Washington trying to turn around the struggling Journal newspapers. James McDonald, a free-paper believer who had been an executive at Metro International and publisher of the chain's Philadelphia paper, obtained a stake in the Journals in 2004. The three newspapers, distributed in the D.C. suburbs, had begun a less costly version of targeted circulation, home delivering free papers to select neighborhoods based on ZIP codes. In April of that year, McDonald says he went to Denver with a pitch for the Anschutz company: buy the 115,000-circulation Journals, turn them into the Examiner, use that as a common brand and launch newspapers all over the country.

Clarity Media Group spokesman Jim Monaghan says the company was looking for acquisition opportunities. McDonald's pitch found a receptive audience.

In late September 2004, Clarity took over the Journal papers, but it wasn't until the Washington Examiner was about to launch in February 2005 that the unique business approach began to attract attention. "We were into that model when we bought Washington, because we already started in San Francisco," distributing to census block groups, McKibben says.

With an infusion of capital, McDonald says, the distribution system became "a more refined process, because we were able to buy better data and look at census blocks and dig deeper." McDonald stayed on as publisher of the Washington Examiner for just a few months before leaving, because, he says, he "wanted to do my own thing." He's now president of M Six Media, a consulting company in Philadelphia.

A census block group is much smaller than a ZIP code, housing between 600 and 3,000 people, according to the U.S. Census Bureau. The focus in Washington and Baltimore is more on the suburbs than the cities. (Only 37,000 copies are distributed within D.C.)

"We essentially listened and created a product and a model in the eyes of the reader and the advertisers," McKibben says. He touts wide advertiser support from companies such as Macy's, Home Depot, Kohl's, Southwest Airlines, Citibank and Wells Fargo.

But it was the little advertisers—the small retailers who would never dream of buying an ad in the Washington Post—that were a tough sell, at least at first. Charleen Stewart, advertising and marketing director at the Newspaper Association of America, was the vice president of advertising for the Washington Examiner from November 2004 until August 2005. She says mom-and-pops theoretically would be the ideal advertiser. "But the reality was, it was harder to get the smaller guys to sign up, because the distribution model was so sophisticated and different than a daily paper in a metro market, that it took awhile to explain it," she says. "You couldn't buy it on the newsstand, and if they didn't get it at their home or their business, they didn't see it."

The easier pitch was to a larger advertiser who understood targeting and wanted a specific demographic. Stewart, whose career includes a stint as the Washington Post's director of strategic initiatives, says while she was at the Examiner, the paper went through numerous iterations of how to carry out this novel business plan. "We just had to keep tweaking, tweaking, tweaking until we got to a place we wanted to get to," she says.

Controlled circulation is not as attractive to advertisers as paid, says John Morton, but it's more appealing than random distribution in news racks. "At least the advertiser has some confidence that his ad is getting delivered to all these addresses."

The question becomes whether people are actually reading the papers. There have been numerous stories about Examiners littering suburban gutters or piling up on the stoops of vacant houses. Some frustrated residents have told the media their tales of calling to get their homes off the distribution list, to no avail. One man in Baltimore filed a temporary restraining order against the paper to stop delivery. (It eventually did.)

McKibben says that the business plan is based on delivering papers to households in which they are read. But he acknowledges that there are times when a new carrier forgets to stop delivery to a certain home. He says fewer than 3 percent of households selected in Baltimore, San Francisco and Washington have opted out, and Clarity Media Group recently purchased a GPS system to monitor route deliveries. "It's been a significant improvement," McKibben says.

David Gasperetti, who was circulation director at the Washington Examiner at its start, says delivery required constant fine-tuning. "There were some distributors that had to be replaced that couldn't do it well," he says, explaining that the Examiner model calls for teaching people to deliver from an exception list rather than a delivery list. It's like dropping off papers in a hotel but being asked to skip certain rooms.

Outside the U.S., this business model isn't limited to one nascent newspaper chain. In Denmark, there are three free daily home-delivered newspapers with a combined circulation of 1.5 million—and with similar cancellation problems, says Piet Bakker at the University of Amsterdam. Two of Denmark's free dailies were launched by major newspaper companies after the Icelandic company Dagsbrun announced it was going to create such a publication.

One "sensitive" and "very smart" aspect of the Examiner's plan, Bakker says, is to limit the number of papers in each street box. "It creates scarcity: 'Well, you want it now, don't you?'" he says. The community isn't as littered with papers, and "advertisers aren't paying for non-picked-up newspapers."

The Examiner has about 2,000 street boxes in each city, McKibben says. In Washington, 80 percent of the 258,752 daily copies are home-delivered. That means there's an average of 26 copies in each street box. In Baltimore, with 93 percent of the 254,740 circulation home-delivered, there are about nine copies per box. San Francisco's model favors a higher single-copy delivery. The paper puts 36 percent of its 190,000 daily run on news racks. That's 34 papers a box on average.

Fewer papers per box means costlier distribution—more of a marketing model than a circulation one—but a better chance at giving advertisers a good audit. Clarity Media boasts that an audit by Certified Audit of Circulations found eight out of 10 households that get the paper read it, with an average of 2.4 readers per household. A readership study by CAC estimates the Examiner's weekly cumulative readership to be about 700,000 in San Francisco, 590,000 in Washington and 490,000 in Baltimore.

Those sound like great numbers, but they pale in comparison with what the big dailies offer. According to Scarborough Research, the Examiners are reaching a small percentage of the total market. While the San Francisco Chronicle reaches 30 percent of the market weekly with its print edition alone, only 7 percent of San Francisco adults looked at the Examiner during a five-day period. The Washington Post, with one of the highest penetration rates among U.S. newspapers, reaches 48 percent of adults in the market weekly with its print edition (the number jumps to 68 percent with the Web site factored in). The Washington Examiner's print product is seen by 6 percent of the market.

In fact—as Ryan McKibben suggested—the big dailies and even the Baltimore City Paper say they're not feeling any ill effects from the Examiner's launch.

"If anybody puts 250,000 papers in the market, it's going to have some effect. It's just hard to quantify," says Tim Thomas, vice president of marketing at the Baltimore Sun. "Did we lose any big accounts? No."

Anecdotally, he says, there appears to be a lot of overlap between Sun readers and Examiner readers. "If they're print readers," Thomas says, "they tend to be print readers," using the quick Examiner as a complement to the Sun.

If the Examiner is aiming to be meatier than your average free daily, it is succeeding on some fronts but not on others. A report by the Project for Excellence in Journalism released in late 2005 compared three youth-oriented tabloids, the Washington Examiner and the section-front stories in three broadsheets (which the project deemed an apt comparison). It found that the Examiner often fell somewhere between the tabloids and the big dailies.

The majority of the Examiner's stories were 500 words or less, while the majority of the broadsheets' were more than 500 words. But the paper's articles ran longer than those in the youth tabloids. The Examiner, at about 50 pages, was fatter than those tabs, ran about twice as many stories and included more staff-written pieces. Yet stories in both the Examiner and the tabloids were thinner than those in the broadsheets: The Examiner had fewer sources and less diversity of opinion in its articles, with almost half of all stories including one or no source. In stories concerning a conflict, 49 percent of Examiner articles included only one viewpoint; 36 percent of such stories in youth tabloids did so, but a mere 11 percent of pieces in the broadsheets contained only one viewpoint.

The Examiner is trying to take a news-lite model as its foundation and build a decent journalism reputation on it. If the business model was a somewhat risky proposition, this is an even tougher battle.

"In my conversations with people about local news and politics, I have never had a conversation in the last few years, saying, 'Oh did you read that story in the Examiner?' It's always about what was in the [San Francisco] Chronicle," says Michael Stoll, a journalism instructor at San Jose State University who has written critically of the free paper as associate director of Grade the News, a media research organization that examines the quality of Bay Area news outlets. (Stoll worked for the Fang-owned Examiner from 2000 to 2002.)

David M. Cole, editor-publisher of News Inc., a weekly publication about the newspaper business, gets the San Francisco Examiner delivered to him and reads it. "From a down-on-the-street daily journalism perspective, they're covering the board of supervisors as good as the Chronicle covers the board of supervisors," Cole says. "Where you make your bones is investigating BALCO" (the Bay Area laboratory implicated in sports doping charges). "And the Examiner is not going to investigate BALCO. That's not what they're going to do."

But the Examiner would like to do something. Something more than a tabloid, but not something as time-consuming, staff-intensive and, above all, long as what readers find in a broadsheet.

Vivienne Sosnowski, Clarity's vice president and national editorial director, says the company is concentrating on strengthening its journalism, particularly at the Washington paper. In addition to hiring Stephen Smith as executive editor, the paper named Micah Morrison, a former Wall Street Journal writer, as a national investigative reporter. Morrison rounds out a "national team" at the Washington Examiner that includes Bill Myers, from the Chicago Daily Law Bulletin, who covers Capitol Hill, and former Washington Times reporters Bill Sammon and Rowan Scarborough, who cover the White House and national security, respectively. The Times' former Capitol Hill bureau chief, Charles Hurt, is now the Examiner's chief congressional correspondent. All were hired within the past year.

Their stories will be used by the other papers in the budding chain. "Hopefully we'll have more papers down the road, and those people will be more and more valuable to the chain as it grows," says Sosnowski, who first joined the San Francisco Examiner as executive editor in September 2004, then the Washington paper in January 2006, before taking on her current role.

Smith says when he first met Philip Anschutz at the private jet terminal at Washington Dulles International Airport, Anschutz began by saying, " 'All I want to do is put out quality newspapers.' "

That got Smith's attention. And he believes that while the Examiner will never be as great as the dominant daily—"it is silly to say that we're competing head to head with the Washington Post"—it offers something for people who don't want to read the Post or for those who read both papers. "When it comes to our model in a strictly journalistic sense, I think it matches up with a kind of sensibility that is in part shaped by the Internet age and in part shaped by just the hurry-up pace of modern life," Smith says.

He compares the format of the Examiner to old-fashioned newsmagazines, which were neatly divided into easy-to-navigate sections and kept story length to a manageable level. "One of the guiding principles of the traditional newsmagazine was respect for readers' time," Smith says. "And a paper that does respect its readers' time has an opportunity to win its way into their households. So we try to write tight, and we try to write bright, and we try to have a very high story count."

Smith oversees a newsroom of about 60 staffers. Sosnowski won't say how many people are on staff at each paper but says the total newsroom count for the company would be "around the mid one-hundreds."

Such numbers sound low compared with daily newspaper staffs—and mean most reporters are churning out two and three stories a day. But a staff of that size is larger, and more expensive, than that of the typical free paper.

The Examiner, says Smith, will give people quick reads, but occasionally it will offer a somewhat lengthy enterprise piece. As one example, he points to Bill Sammon's five-part series in January on Sen. Barack Obama's memoirs. "Bill read [Obama's writings] carefully and made connections and wrote, I think, the most revealing piece about Obama that's been written yet," Smith says. "If someone wants to claim that we're McPaper, they might want to read that series."

But add too much length, and the Examiner is no longer a paper you can finish with breakfast. "We're very judicious about writing longer, but do we write longer? Yes we do," says Sosnowski. "If we do it all the time, we're not going to be the paper we set out to be."

There has been some questionable journalism. Grade the News, which lost its funding but still maintains its Web site, published stories in late 2005 taking the Examiner and the Palo Alto Daily News to task for blurring the line between news and advertising. In the most egregious case at the Examiner, the paper employed an ad salesman to write a column about area restaurants. He was quite up front in telling Grade the News Director John McManus that the copy was specifically designed to entice restaurants to buy ads. After McManus called Sosnowski, the editor at the time, she said the paper would label the page as "advertising."

Sosnowski says the restaurant column "never looked like news. It looked like advertising." But she adds, "Of course they must be identified as advertising . . . and I was able to make that happen." Ryan McKibben says the practice was a vestige of the old Examiner that the new ownership hadn't had a chance to correct.

McManus is not impressed. "They agreed to be ethical not from their own sense of journalistic integrity but only when threatened with exposure," he says.

The Baltimore paper, too, has taken some hits from the Baltimore City Paper, which has scrutinized sensational stories in the new daily. One report concerned a series of alleged murders of women in the Park Heights neighborhood. Residents told the Examiner that women had been killed and decapitated, though police had no record of such crimes. The Examiner story didn't include names of victims or quotes from friends or relatives. The Baltimore Sun ran a story debunking the rumors of Park Heights murders, and the City Paper challenged the Examiner piece directly in a convincing critique headlined "Habeas Crapus."

Sosnowski, however, is standing by the Examiner's reporting. "I think the story hasn't finished yet, and I think we should maybe look at that again in a few months and see where we are with it." The first Examiner piece was published in October. She adds: "Of course our competitors are going to criticize us where they think they can."

While Clarity Media Group searches for a balance between quality journalism and direct-marketing savvy, it has also embraced the cheap-and-flimsy model of tabloid news. In San Francisco in November, it launched the City Star, a newsletter-like free daily, distributed on news racks in eight ZIP codes in the city. It features local news, mostly wire copy. McKibben calls it beta testing. A similar freebie, the San Francisco Daily, calls it a direct assault on the Daily's existence.

McKibben says the paper isn't an effort to drive the Daily out of business, nor does he see the latest Clarity newspaper as competition for the Examiner. "It's a neighborhood paper," he says of the 6,000-circulation City Star. "The Examiner is a market-wide sort of metropolitan paper in its reach."

Clarity also has made online forays into additional markets. In March 2006, Examiner.com debuted, with fine-tuned sites for its print products and 21 other wire-copy-filled sites for cities, among them Atlanta, Boston, Phoenix and Pittsburgh.

There are no staffers in those venues; instead, the pages are built "through software and a lot of rules and algorithms that we've identified to select the news," says Examiner.com President and CEO David Schafer, MapQuest's former general manager.

Personalization is one of the goals. There are tools to customize news, such as a search function that enables users to type in any word and get an index page filled with related news. The site is soliciting applications for Examiner bloggers.

Spokesman Jim Monaghan says the move doesn't necessarily mean Clarity is preparing to launch newspapers in those cities. "Where opportunities present themselves . . . we'll take a serious look at it, and if it makes sense after some look, we'd move ahead," he says. "And since the electronic footprint is in the major metropolitan areas, it wouldn't be surprising to find new rollouts, if they may occur over the next few years, would be in those areas."

It could be years—many years—before anyone knows whether the Examiner business model is a success. John Morton says it typically takes seven or eight years for a new paper to be profitable. While individual Metro papers were in the black, it took Metro International as a company 11 years to show a profit. As a private company, Clarity isn't likely to reveal financial numbers ever.

"About the only thing we can infer is that, because they've gone on to establish one in Baltimore, and they've kept three of them going, that they must be satisfied with the results so far," Morton says. "That doesn't mean they're a financial success, but they're not such a disaster that they've shut them down."

Miles Groves, a media economist and consultant, says newspaper publishers should be paying attention to how well the Examiner does. "It's a very interesting model that's coming out, and they've put serious talent and serious marketing savvy talent into these things. So I'm hoping they succeed. But I still think it may be too early to make that claim," he says. If it works, major newspapers may have to assess their own circulation models. "Will that mean that people like the Post and the Baltimore Sun and the Chronicle will suddenly have to rethink being a paid product? How important is that for advertisers?"

Primarily, the prognosis for the Examiner depends on the commitment of the billionaire backing it. When he's in an Examiner city, Philip Anschutz, after his morning jog, frequently takes to the streets to hawk the paper.

Sounds like the owner with deep pockets also has deep conviction.

Senior contributing writer **LORI ROBERTSON** (robertson.lori@gmail.com) wrote about the *Richmond Times-Dispatch in AJR's* February/March issue. Editorial assistant Emily Groves contributed research to this report.

A Fading Taboo

Paper by paper, advertising is making its way onto the nation's front pages and section fronts.

DONNA SHAW

Sometimes they snake across the bottom of the page as relatively unobtrusive six-column strips. Sometimes they catch the eye more forcefully as right-corner boxes. And sometimes they scream for attention as in-your-face fluorescent stickers plastered across a newspaper's masthead.

Whatever the shape, size or hue, the long-unfashionable page-one advertisement is gaining grudging acceptance from many editors, page designers and even reporters. As the industry struggles to identify innovative sources of revenue, newspapers not only are launching audacious online ventures (see "Rolling the Dice", page 40, and "*Really* Local," April/May) but also are dangling fresh enticements for advertisers in their old-fashioned print editions.

Page-one ads may net premium prices, but they're distasteful to many journalists who believe they violate the purity of page one and the sacred wall between news and business. From a design standpoint, they can detract from the flow and order of a page. They also eat up space that otherwise could be devoted to stories, particularly in an era of dwindling newsholes.

Among newspapers that recently have published page-one ads are the Wall Street Journal, San Francisco Chronicle, Philadelphia Inquirer and Hartford Courant. Others, such as USA Today and many other Gannett papers, have published them for years (see "Out Front," July/August 1999). Still others—the New York Times, Los Angeles Times, Boston Globe and Minneapolis' Star Tribune, for example—are experimenting with ads on section fronts but so far have kept page one off-limits.

"I don't think anyone in journalism is happy about them, but personally, and here at the paper, we felt we should do it," says Robert J. Rosenthal, managing editor and vice president of the San Francisco Chronicle, which debuted front-page ads on April 18. He sees them as part of the evolution toward the multimedia newsroom, adding, "If the business model supports good journalism, then I'm in favor of it."

As ads creep onto front pages and section fronts, designers are working to minimize how distracting—and sometimes garish—they may appear. "I think that most people in the newsroom realize the [financial] environment we're working in," says Chris Clonts, assistant design director for news at the Star Tribune, which began running section-front ads early this year (so far none on page one). He thinks the ad department also realizes that changing ad placement "will require some hand-holding" for journalists.

Gene Patterson, former chairman of the Poynter Institute and former editor of the St. Petersburg Times, sees the page-one ad as a sign of painful economic times for newspapers. "I find the section-front ads to be acceptable; I find the page-one ads repugnant," he says. "But if they are done tastefully and held down in size, I think perhaps we have to accept them. . . . We have to police it and monitor it and be guided by taste, but I don't think the advertisers want to ruin us. We are their vehicle, after all, and I think we can work with them to achieve compromises."

Others want to hold the line. Gene Roberts, a former managing editor of the New York Times and executive editor of the Philadelphia Inquirer, says front-page ads are just another in a series of industry mistakes triggered by short-term thinking. "It's one more in this kind of death by a thousand cuts that the newspaper business seems to be administering to itself," says Roberts, a journalism professor at the University of Maryland, which houses AJR. "In the long run, the big necessity is to get and maintain readers, and I think without question that front-page ads work against readership."

Roberts says newspapers didn't move away from front-page ads years ago because page one was a holy shrine. They did it because "the front page is what you have to lure readers into the rest of the paper."

What editors hear from their publishers, he says, is, "If you don't do this and you don't do that to keep the profit level up, we're going to have to cut you again." The editors translate that as, " 'Well, if I fight front-page ads I might in effect be inviting a buyout or a layoff of my staff.' "

Page-one placement can spark visceral reactions not only from journalists but also from readers. Take the case in March of the fluorescent advertising stickers (for a motor oil company and a carpet-and-flooring company) pasted atop the front page of the Hartford Courant. Reader Representative Karen Hunter received several indignant comments on her blog. "That is disgusting to have advertising on the front page of my newspaper," wrote one woman. Said another: "This has got to stop." One reader took it further, accusing the Tribune Co., the Courant's parent, of "absolutely whoring for advertising. . . . It screams, 'We're desperate!' It screams, 'Ethics be damned!' "

Hunter says the newsroom isn't crazy about the trend. She's heard complaints, but says her colleagues believe there isn't anything they can do to halt it. "I think they understand it . . . we're struggling like lots of other papers."

ANNUAL EDITIONS

Not that front-page ads are all that new. But at most papers, they've been out of vogue for a while. Among the reasons the ads began to disappear: the advent of professional standards among journalists and heightened competition among publishers.

Kevin G. Barnhurst, a professor and head of the department of communication at the University of Illinois at Chicago, says that in 18th century newspapers "there was not a sharp distinction between ads and editorial matter." What's more, the blurring of news and ads didn't really disturb readers of that era. "People didn't say, 'Oh, here's advertising, here's editorial matter,' because it was all the stuff of news," Barnhurst says.

Nor did early American newspapers offer much in the way of page design. As ads and stories trickled in, they simply were dropped onto the page, starting with the first column. The newspapers generally were four pages; front and back were filled first. So the newest material went inside. "You didn't want the latest stuff on the back page or the front page—you wanted it on the inside where it wouldn't smear on people's clothes," Barnhurst says.

Michael Schudson, a professor of communication at the University of California, San Diego, says that during that era, "page one and page four were almost entirely ads, and a lot of page three was ads." News started to appear on page one in the first half of the 19th century, "but it was still common at that point for there to be a lot of advertising on the front page."

That approach began to change later in the 19th century as newspapers became more competitive, according to Schudson and Mitchell Stephens, a journalism professor and news historian at New York University. When major cities such as New York, Chicago, Philadelphia and Boston each had several newspapers, and publishers relied heavily on street sales, they began splashing more news out front as a way to lure readers.

Then, around 1914, a confluence of events portended the fading popularity of the front-page ad. "The American newspaper was at its absolute height in penetration," and journalists "were feeling their most muscular and able to define themselves as a profession," Stephens says. It was 1914 when Walter Williams—who six years earlier had founded the world's first journalism school at the University of Missouri—wrote "The Journalist's Creed." The American Society of Newspaper Editors was founded in 1922 and adopted a canon of ethics a year later; the Society of Professional Journalists approved its first ethics code in 1926.

"In the 1920s, there's a growing self-consciousness of journalists being in a profession and wanting to distinguish themselves as a profession," Schudson says. Journalists' efforts to codify their increasingly lofty ethical goals—about unbiased truth and "freedom from all obligations except fidelity to the public interest," as the ASNE canon states—distanced newspapers from their commercial origins.

None of this might have mattered so much to publishers, but it happened to coincide with another important development: Prospering financially, the publishers were shedding their partisan affiliations. They gambled that a less biased approach would elevate their standing in the community—and create an opportunity to profit from that standing. "So the commercial interest of publishers and owners converged with the professional aspirations of news workers," Barnhurst says, "and that's the moment, by the 1920s and 1930s, when what you would call the modern newspaper emerged, and that's when the model of page one emerged"—a model that did not include so many ads out front.

But today, with fewer newspapers to choose from, increasing competition from the Internet and decreasing reliance on street sales, the model is changing again. "Newspapers are in big, big trouble," Stephens says, "and I think if I were in a newsroom right now, I'd be more worried about whether I'm putting together an interesting read, a read that justifies the expense . . . and I'd worry less about the particular arrangement of the advertisers."

Barnhurst has a similar view. "There is a notion out there that somehow commerce is dirty—the sacred is what the journalist does and the profane is what the advertiser does," he says. "In fact, this is a profound confusion." What gives a town life, he suggests, is its Main Street businesses, which need to be "rubbing shoulders" with the commercial activity of the local newspaper.

ASNE Executive Director Scott Bosley says that while his organization has no official position on front-page ads, "it's not earth-shattering new ground in my view . . . it's a change, obviously, for people in this era." He recalls that when he was editor of the Journal of Commerce from 1991 to 1995, "we had a quarter-page ad on page one forever." (The Journal is available now in electronic format only.) The ad, Bosley notes, "was not the favorite thing of layout people or even of me, because sometimes it seemed intrusive."

Bosley believes most editors have arrived at the decision to accept page-one ads in consultation with their publishers, as opposed to being ordered to run them. He also thinks editors understand there's a bottom line that must be reached, and they have to help figure out how to get there. "I think we've come to the point where a lot of newspapers have realized that there's not just revenue but enhanced revenue from selling those positions, and in the market we're in, we need revenue," Bosley says.

John Kimball, senior vice president and chief marketing officer for the Newspaper Association of America, believes the challenging economic climate for newsrooms necessitates more flexibility, but he strongly rejects the notion that the page-one ad is compelled by a sense of desperation. "That just really, really drives me nuts, because that is far from reality. . . . To think that we are somehow in this death spiral, I just don't understand that," he says. He can see why that view prevails in newsrooms that have endured repeated cuts and reduced circulation, "but that's not an industry that's fighting for its life—that's one that's going through transition."

The primary impetus for the page-one ad, Kimball says, is that advertisers are increasingly demanding "new and unique and different ways to creatively use the newspaper. I think not necessarily coincidental to that is the fact that newspapers are looking for options for new revenue streams."

Advertisers want "creative shapes, things you might not have seen 10 to 15 years ago, but are exciting and fresh," Kimball says. "What's that somebody said, 'Pain helps make you focus?' When business is great, it's easy to do things the way you've always done them; when it's not so great, you look for new opportunities."

Those options include the six-column strip across the bottom of a page; the "jewel box," a rectangular, two- or three-column ad; and the "stair steps" or "cascading stairs," an ad that steps up from the left to the right of a page. More controversial are the "watermark" or "shadow" ads that appear behind sports agate or stock tables, because such ads are not separated from news content.

Will page-one ads net more business for advertisers than those inside the paper, making it worth the additional cost for them? It's too soon to tell. "We do have clients who are interested in them," says Bob Shamberg, chairman and chief executive of Newspaper Services of America, a Chicago-based firm that places newspaper ads for more than 50 clients, including Sears Holdings, Home Depot and Rite Aid. "Over time, once an advertiser gets experience with it, then they'll decide what it's worth." But if they get the same response as an interior ad, "then obviously it doesn't merit a premium."

Newspaper executives are tight-lipped about how much they're charging for page-one ads, but it's clear they cost significantly more than those inside the paper. Page one is "a premium location, so probably it's as much as the traffic would bear," says Miles Groves, a media economist and consultant in Washington, D.C.

"It is an expensive ad," says Anne Gordon, former managing editor of the Philadelphia Inquirer, which started running page-one ads on April 15. (Gordon left the Inquirer in early May to become a partner at Dubilier & Co., a private investment firm for which she oversees media, technology and entertainment companies.) She agrees that advertisers are waiting to gauge their effectiveness, and says editors wrestled with surrendering that special page-one space. "The reality of it is we spent a long time talking about it and considering it—18 months," she says.

Ultimately, Gordon adds, the Inquirer decided "we needed to be supportive of our advertisers" while maintaining enough control to make the ads palatable: "It needed to be a more dignified advertiser than, say, a mattress company." So the paper has a one-year contract with the University of Pennsylvania Health System for a page-one ad every Sunday, and is expanding that to Monday as well. The Inquirer also has been using those fluorescent stickers atop the front page. Editors assigned an Inquirer reporter to write a story explaining the economic necessity of violating the "sacred province of news."

The paper has received a handful of complaints from readers, Gordon says, but in most cases, "I think people read past this."

It's another manifestation of the Inquirer's more aggressive approach to attracting advertising dollars under its new ownership. When a local group led by former PR and ad executive Brian Tierney bought the paper last year (see "Life with Brian," August/September 2006), Tierney trumpeted his belief that former owner Knight Ridder hadn't done enough to court advertisers. In announcing that it would sell page-one ads, the Inquirer also said it would publish a new business column sponsored by Citizens Bank. The column is boxed in green, the bank's color, and the bank also has been running ads elsewhere on the business section front.

At the San Francisco Chronicle, Rosenthal says only a few readers have called to complain about his paper's page-one, lime-green boxes for utility Pacific Gas and Electric Co. "We created a couple of info boxes next to it to deal with it, so I don't think it looks that bad, personally," he says. His opinion was reinforced when he asked some friends for their views. "They didn't see it," Rosenthal says. "Journalists are very much aware of it, but I think the general public doesn't think of it as a bad thing."

He does point out one possible pitfall: There may come a day when a newspaper has to publish a negative story about a page-one advertiser, so "there's a potential for embarrassment if an advertiser . . . does something inappropriate."

At the Star Tribune, Clonts says reader reaction to section-front advertising has been minimal. One exception is a design known as the spadea, an advertising flap that wraps halfway around the front of a section, obscuring the editorial content. Clonts says it provokes "heavy and aggressively negative reader reaction. When a spadea runs, we know the following day we will get reader calls. Sometimes a few, sometimes dozens." (A 2006 study sponsored by the NAA notes that while few readers like them, 75 percent notice them, and about four in 10 usually notice what's being advertised.)

Designers tasked with making page-one ads blend with the overall look and feel of the page generally aren't thrilled about them, but they're learning to adjust. At the Star Tribune, the deputy managing editor for visuals and presentation, Cory Powell, works with the advertising department "to ensure section-front ads are as clean, simple and attractive as possible," Clonts says. The designers also have discovered that as pages get narrower, the page-one ad does have some benefits, because it works with both horizontal and vertical layouts.

"Drawing pages for the 52-inch web was easyish," Clonts says. "It got harder for the 50 and gets [harder] still for the 48. To put an ad on the front . . . to some extent simplifies things because you have to pare the elements of your fronts down to the essentials." And as the web narrowed, "the page got a lot more vertical, and things that worked best on that page tended to be vertical." He says the six-column strip ad helps square off a page, giving a design team more flexibility.

Occasionally, though, Powell will suggest that an ad be redrawn to make a page look better, Clonts says, and he'll be told it's not possible—like the time the ad department came up with a six-column strip filled with distracting automobile logos. This is what the client wants, the ad department replied. So it ran.

Denise Covert, a copy editor and page designer at the Daytona Beach News-Journal, works on regional publications that are inserted into the mainsheet. In an e-mail interview, she wrote that on some of the regional section fronts and also on the mainsheet's local front, "there are occasional front-page ads, usually 2 by 4. It works if you have a columnist or something that can easily square off with it on the bottom, but it can be a pain for some centerpiece treatments."

She adds: "In all, my personal opinion is that they're OK as long as they're not too distracting. Distracting means they are a) oddly shaped, b) garishly colored, c) black and white on a color front—we get that fairly often—or d) inconsistent, appearing some weeks and not others, so they're impossible to plan around."

Ultimately, though, newspapers may be worrying too much about ad placement. "For me, the bottom line is: Put some better stories on the top of that front page. Don't give me the same story I saw 20 hours ago" online, says NYU's Stephens. "Give me good stories, and I don't care what you put in that little ad on the bottom of the front page."

The Courant's Hunter is pragmatic, too. "I'd rather see ads inside the paper," she says. "But reality has changed."

AJR contributing writer **Donna Shaw** (shaw@tcnj.edu) wrote about hyperlocal Web sites in the magazine's April/May issue.

Article 40

Nonprofit News

As news organizations continue to cut back, investigative and enterprise journalism funded by foundations and the like is coming to the fore.

CAROL GUENSBURG

Since 1993, the Henry J. Kaiser Family Foundation has funded journalism training on health issues, including funneling up to $50,000 to a handful of fellows each year to support reporting projects. But, dismayed by cuts in newsroom staffing, newsholes and airtime—and the sketchy reporting that can result—foundation officials began kicking around other ways to ensure solid coverage of topics they consider crucial.

One possibility: a nonprofit health news service of their own. Matt James, senior vice president for the California-based foundation, remembers running the idea past longtime editor Bill Kovach, founding director of the Committee of Concerned Journalists and an adviser to Kaiser's media fellows program. James chuckles, a little uncomfortably, recalling the start of Kovach's generally encouraging response during a meeting last May. "He basically said, 'Five years ago . . . I would have told you to go to hell and shown you the door.'"

These days, foundations and philanthropists are finding a warmer reception.

Beleaguered journalists who once clung solely to the business model of paid advertising and circulation now recognize the urgency of developing new revenue sources for labor-intensive newsgathering. For some, foundations hold increasing promise as allies in meeting the public's information needs—beyond superficial headlines and celebrity sexploits—so long as there are safeguards for editorial independence.

"The fact of the matter is philanthropic institutions have provided millions of dollars over the years to help journalists do their work. Journalists have an unfortunate habit of not acknowledging that," says Charles Lewis, head of the nonprofit Fund for Independence in Journalism. From 1989 through 2004, he served as founding executive director of the Center for Public Integrity, which "raised and spent $30 million [on journalism projects] in the years I was there."

New forms of nonprofit, grant-funded news operations are proliferating. The lineup includes the Pulitzer Center on Crisis Reporting (see "Funding for Foreign Forays," page 32), Brandeis University's Schuster Institute for Investigative Journalism, MinnPost.com (see Drop Cap, page 14) and at least two state-level health news sites (see "Healthy Initiatives," page 31). The Washington Independent, freshly minted in January, joined the Center for Independent Media's network of four related sites in Colorado, Iowa, Michigan and Minnesota. And there are many more in the mix.

The highest-profile newcomer is ProPublica (propublica.org), an investigative news operation that opened shop in Manhattan in January (see "Big Bucks for Investigative Reporting"). California philanthropists Herbert M. and Marion O. Sandler dreamed up the project—which they're bankrolling at $10 million annually for at least three years—and hired former Wall Street Journal Managing Editor Paul E. Steiger as editor in chief. He and Managing Editor Stephen Engelberg, a former investigative editor at the New York Times, eventually will oversee a staff of about 25 reporters, editors and researchers charged with producing public interest stories of "moral force," as the Web site proclaims. These will be offered free to select news outlets, whose own staffs may join in the newsgathering, as well as being showcased on ProPublica's site.

The Sandlers, who made $2.4 billion when they sold the Golden West Financial Corp. savings and loan in 2006, have given millions to Democratic Party causes over the years, according to news accounts. That—and donors' often heightened emotional investment in money they've earned—prompted Slate media critic Jack Shafer to question Herbert Sandler's role as Propublica chairman (slate.com/id/2175942/). Even though the couple pledged not to interfere with editorial content, Shafer recommended that Sandler guarantee at least 10 years' funding and then resign his position, "so he'll never be tempted to bollix up what might turn out to be a good thing."

Some prominent media leaders and innovators have called for even more philanthropic support to ensure journalism's vital watchdog role.

Geneva Overholser, writing in "On Behalf of Journalism: A Manifesto for Change" (annenbergpublicpolicycenter.org/Overholser/20061011_JournStudy.pdf), urged a greater role for nonprofits in assisting news media. Her 2006 treatise advanced journalist Lewis' suggestion that foundations and philanthropists create a "Marshall Plan" to create more public-minded forms of news coverage. Grantmakers could "increase support for nonprofit media organizations" and "foster new nonprofit media models," wrote Overholser, a Missouri School of Journalism professor. She also recommended steps for corporations, journalists, government and the public.

Jan Schaffer, executive director of the interactive journalism incubator J-Lab, introduced a "Citizen Media" report (kcnn.org/research/citmedia_introduction/) last February by writing that community foundations should "be alert to real possibilities for building community capacity" by supporting citizen media. "Journalism alone will not suffice," she elaborated in a phone interview. "I think foundations and philanthropies will play a role in supplementing that information landscape."

Dan Gillmor, in a September 17 op-ed published in the San Francisco Chronicle (sfgate.com/cgi-bin/article.cgi?file=/c/a/2007/09/17/ED1OS4OIU.DTL) and timed for a Council on Foundations' conference there, urged community foundations to "put the survival of quality local journalism squarely on their own agendas." Gillmor—who in January launched the Knight Center for Digital Media Entrepreneurship at Arizona State University's Walter Cronkite School of Journalism—suggested measures such as paying the salary of a local investigative journalist or providing seed funding for a network of local blogs and media sites, adding journalism training for participants.

And Alberto Ibargüen, president and CEO of the John S. and James L. Knight Foundation, publicly addressed those San Francisco conferees with a like-minded appeal, warning: "If the citizens are unaware, then the democracy is in peril." Knight and the council will cohost a seminar February 20 and 21 on communities' information needs in a democracy. Up to 200 community-foundation representatives will meet in Coral Gables, Florida, to consider media trends, the digital revolution, gaps in coverage and how these might be filled.

Foundations see their growing involvement as compensating for newsrooms' diminished coverage of civic issues. They're stepping in because "the traditional news business is not investing as much as it needs to . . . in getting reporters out to cover stories," Kaiser's James pointedly notes. "We as nonprofits have a duty to figure out: Is there a role for us, in increased training, in direct partnerships with news organizations or even [in] creating a new news service to fill that void?

"What we're talking about is supporting real journalism, not advocacy," adds James, whose foundation already partners with National Public Radio, USA Today, the Washington Post and other news media on public opinion research projects. "We're big believers in the role of journalism in democracy. We believe it's important for nonprofits to find ways to support it."

With newspaper revenue tanking as classified and retail advertisers migrate to the Web and Wall Street tightens its grip, journalists are casting about for financial lifelines. Foundations have the wherewithal to throw some: By law, they must spend a minimum 5 percent of their net assets each year on charitable causes. In 2005, U.S. foundations granted $158 million for media and communications, the Foundation Center reports, though it doesn't break down whether the payouts went for journalism per se or marketing or research dissemination. Nor does that figure necessarily reflect spending on journalism-related education.

Journalism's funders include those affiliated with legacy news media—such as Annenberg, Scripps, Tribune, Reynolds, Gannett—plus longtime supporters like Carnegie, Ford and the Pew Charitable Trusts. (AJR has received support from the Freedom Forum, Ford, Knight, Pew and Carnegie.)

Knight, the leading journalism funder overall, announced more than $21 million in journalism grants in 2006 and more than $50 million in 2007, though some of these are multiyear grants and won't be paid out all at once. "There are years when we are not the largest [journalism] grantmaker," Eric Newton, its vice president for journalism initiatives, said in an e-mail interview. Since the foundation's start in 1950, it has invested nearly $300 million in U.S. and global journalism—emphasizing mid-career training in the 1980s, journalism education in the 1990s and digital media innovation in the current decade.

Knight has contributed to journalism philanthropy in another fundamental way. Shortly after joining the foundation in 2001, Newton—former managing editor of the Newseum and, before that, the Oakland Tribune—helped pull together an informal group of program officers from legacy media foundations and others interested in journalism. Participants included the Bill & Melinda Gates Foundation, which in November announced a three-year, $1.7 million grant to the International Center for Journalists to support Knight health fellowships in sub-Saharan Africa.

"We think all foundations should care about the information needs of communities in a democracy," Newton says.

Done right, the journalism-funder relationship benefits both parties as well as the public they aim to serve. It supplies important news resources, and it satisfies a grantmaker's mission—maybe even bringing a touch of prestige. Done wrong, the association raises concerns about editorial objectivity and whether it has been compromised by a funder's agenda.

It's instructive to look at, or listen to, NPR, perhaps the most successful model of nonprofit journalism. The privately supported membership organization derived a third of its revenue from grants, contributions and sponsorships in 2005. Its biggest revenue share (39 percent) came from programming fees paid by member stations, which conduct their own fundraising.

"We're always engaged in very constructive discussions with the world of philanthropy," says NPR President Kevin Klose, who describes himself as an active participant. The conversations emphasize editorial control, "the starting point for us. . . . One of the reasons why we are attractive to foundations and to corporate sponsorship is because of the integrity and independence of what we do. They wish to align themselves with that set of values."

They probably don't mind that their names, and information they care about, reach 26 million pairs of ears.

Klose says he engages with the foundation world not just to gain financial support. "It's also important to us," he explains, to learn "what people are thinking about. These are often very socially aware organizations that track issues naturally of interest to news organizations."

A sturdy firewall separates NPR's news and business operations. Barbara Hall spent more than 14 years on its fund-raising side, serving as vice president of development through late August 2006. (Near the end of her run her group generated more than $50 million a year, excluding a $230 million bequest from Joan B. Kroc in 2004.)

Over that time, Hall saw a shift in funders' strategies. "The best gift any nonprofit can get is unrestricted support. But the trend we've seen with foundations, and increasingly with individuals, is wanting to designate their support for specific issues and topics," says Hall, who left to head development for the Phillips Collection, an art museum in Washington, D.C. While "most foundations understand that news organizations are not advocacy groups," she adds, "now they're being very focused on what they're supporting and its impact."

"Funders may have their own interests—they often do," Klose says, but they can't dictate story focus. "We're very interested in philanthropic support of a whole range of activities: coverage of foreign news, coverage of children, family and education. We have a foreign desk, a national desk, a political desk. That's what people fund."

By designating funding, a grantmaker aims to raise the visibility of an issue or area and expand public knowledge.

Big Bucks for Investigative Reporting

When its imminent launch was announced last fall, ProPublica brought a double-barreled blast of attention to nonprofit news media. It wasn't just the premise of an independent newsroom devoted to investigative reporting, an endangered species in an era of down-sizing; it was the promise of $10 million-a-year backing to ensure hard-hitting stories that would be given away to other news outlets.

Founders Herbert M. and Marion O. Sandler committed that chunk of their personal fortune—burnished by the 2006 sale of their Golden West Financial Corp. savings and loan to the Wachovia Corp.—to support the stated mission of "producing journalism that shines a light on exploitation of the weak by the strong and on the failures of those with power to vindicate the trust placed in them."

Additional one-time grants are coming from the John D. and Catherine T. MacArthur Foundation ($250,000) and the Atlantic Philanthropies and JEHT Foundation ($25,000 each).

ProPublica's editor in chief is Paul E. Steiger, who led the Wall Street Journal to 16 Pulitzer Prizes while serving as managing editor from 1991 until last May. As his managing editor, Steiger tapped Stephen Engelberg, a managing editor at Portland's Oregonian who'd earlier been an investigative editor for the New York Times. They'll direct a staff of about 25 reporters, editors and researchers based in a Manhattan newsroom and doing stories of national import.

By mid-November, ProPublica had received roughly 400 résumés "from essentially every major news organization in the country," says General Manager Richard Tofel, who worked with Steiger at the Wall Street Journal and most recently was a vice president of the Rockefeller Foundation.

The organization, which launched in January, will gear up during early 2008, regularly spotlighting others' investigative reports on its Web site (propublica.org) while developing its own projects.

Steiger says he has spoken with representatives of leading newspapers, magazines and television news outlets about carrying ProPublica projects. With those that are "90 percent done, we'll be looking for a collaborator who can give the most impact and visibility," Steiger says. "For collaborations that we might start at an early stage, we'll be looking at where there would be mutual advantage" for another news outlet to join in the reporting and editing. ProPublica will publish the work on its own site, in some cases simultaneously with the news organization.

As Michael Miner observed in the Chicago Reader, this approach probably cuts out news organizations—especially those far from population centers—with the fewest resources to keep the powerful in check.

Editorial independence will be crucial not just to ProPublica but to the news organizations disseminating or partnering on its stories. And it may be a challenge to overcome newsrooms' preference for stories they've produced internally.

For example, Philadelphia Inquirer Editor William K. Marimow says he's "agonized a lot about ProPublica." Though he's confident that, "with Paul at the helm, they'll do great work," Marimow expressed concern about a news organization ceding any editorial control. "When it comes to investigative reporting, it's my belief that top editors need to take responsibility from the get-go," he says. "A hybrid project creates diffuse responsibility."

—C.G.

The Carnegie Corp. of New York, for instance, gave NPR $200,000 last year to support education coverage. It began subsidizing that around the 2000 election, says Susan Robinson King, vice president of external affairs and director of the journalism initiative at Carnegie. Back then, NPR "had one reporter who sometimes covered education.... They were able with our money to hire a producer and really increase the level of reporting."

Dynamic social forces affect nonprofit journalism as readily as commercial news operations. Shifts in the economy boost or deflate endowments. Developments in research, demographics or regional politics, changes in leadership or board structure—all can affect attitudes and funding priorities. No wonder only a quarter of all grants get renewed.

I absorbed these lessons as founding director of Journalism Fellowships in Child and Family Policy from early 2000 through mid-2005. The professional development program, based at the Philip Merrill College of Journalism at the University of Maryland, awarded competitive fellowships for all-expense-paid conferences featuring expert briefings and skills training. Select fellows also received project support of up to $25,000 for six months. They contributed to scores of outlets, including NPR, the Chicago Tribune, the Austin American-Statesman, Reuters, Salon, Mother Jones, Reader's Digest, Portland's Oregonian, the Milwaukee Journal Sentinel, the Village Voice, WBUR-FM in Boston and Pacific News Service.

Ruby Takanishi, president of the Foundation for Child Development, a private philanthropy in New York, helped conceive the program and make sure it was funded generously. Her goal was to invest in journalists, particularly young ones who might have a more lasting impact in shaping the news, and "really improve the depth of reporting" on child and family policy, she says. Initially there was no limit to what fellows might explore in conference briefings or their own research: the impact of welfare reform on families, harsh "zero-tolerance" policies that criminalized youth, brain research on toddlers, the growing reliance on grandparents for foster care.

The expansive approach began to narrow after four years. The foundation had been concentrating its other funding on three subjects—children of immigrants, education from pre-kindergarten through third grade and an index of child well-being—and "some very strong voices on our board" wondered why these weren't getting more coverage from the news media, Takanishi recalls. The board decided the fellowship program's training and projects should be more clearly aligned with those issues for any future grants. At the time, we had a multiyear grant good through mid-2005.

I'd come out of newspapers, editing and reporting mostly on the features side. I tried to equate the tightening scope as something

Healthy Initiatives

Carol Gentry doesn't think "it's any mystery why health care is bubbling up so early" as the focus of at least two nonprofit, state-level news services. "People don't understand how it works," says Gentry, founding editor of the year-old FloridaHealthNews.org. "It's hard to get good coverage, particularly at the local and state level."

There's another basic reason. "It's where the money is," explains Carol DeVita, a researcher at the Urban Institute's Center on Nonprofits and Philanthropy. The news services largely are supported by so-called "conversion" foundations, created when nonprofit hospitals were sold to for-profit providers. Dozens of states have required that proceeds from charitable assets be redirected to support community health—through efforts such as clinics, immunization programs and research.

The Kansas Health Institute, an independent, nonprofit policy and research organization in Topeka, in January 2007 introduced the online KHI News Service to cover state health policy. It has four staff journalists with newspaper backgrounds. It features daily spot news stories and a weekly centerpiece. A recent one examined whether a proposed tobacco tax increase could provide reliable funding for health reform.

Vice President for Public Affairs Jim McLean says the free service primarily reaches legislators, government staffers and lobbyists, though it's also intended for consumers. KHI stories have been picked up by the Topeka Capital-Journal (where McLean was a managing editor) and assorted small papers. McLean hopes to increase distribution this year by introducing story budgets to help editors plan.

The institute gets its funding mostly from philanthropy, with some project-based funding from state and federal agencies. The editorial staff works independently, McLean emphasizes, and "there's no advocacy mission at all."

Florida's independent online news service covers a wide range of state and local health issues. Launched in March 2007 primarily as a news aggregator, the St. Petersburg-based FloridaHealthNews.org tracked health care bills when the Legislature was in session and posted original stories. Until mid-December, it had one paid staffer, part-time Managing Editor Pat Curtis, as well as a paid intern. Gentry has signed up a Tallahassee correspondent and is recruiting stringers around the state. She herself didn't start drawing a paycheck until mid-December, instead logging volunteer hours while reporting on health full time for the Tampa Tribune. She resigned from the paper in late November, after the Florida Health Policy Center—a partnership of eight foundations—approved $183,000 in new grants. The center had provided seed money of $59,200 for the news service's first year.

Gentry says she'll "outsource the fundraising, the marketing, the advertising. We want, as much as we can, to have a firewall between the newsroom and the business side.... That's the most important thing, that people can trust us as journalists."

A decade ago, the Oakland-based nonprofit California HealthCare Foundation introduced a health news aggregation site, California Healthline. Now, it may add experienced journalists to produce "in-depth health care reporting in partnership with media organizations," says David Olmos, a former Los Angeles Times reporter and editor who in the fall stepped down as the foundation's communications director. He's researching the project, which might entail partnering with newspapers, public radio and television stations or other news organizations. Like ProPublica, the new nonprofit news outlet for investigative reporting, its services "almost certainly would be free," Olmos says.

Its mission would be "tackling some larger issues that are not sufficiently covered in California," which Olmos describes as "a proving ground or laboratory for some of the health efforts" relevant nationwide.

Both he and Gentry say these niche news services may serve as templates for other areas of coverage, such as education or the environment. Says Olmos: "It's going to be really important that these start-up ventures are thoughtful."

—C.G.

---

akin to the challenge of producing stories for the ad-driven annual dining guide or cruise travel section or the fall prep sports guide. With some effort, you could come up with fresh, worthwhile stories for the dedicated space. But there was a crucial difference: While it was relatively easy to develop briefings and story ideas for covering immigrants and early education, there was no guarantee of real estate or airtime in others' newsrooms.

Our program's compressed focus, combined with industry-wide newsroom cuts in staffing and newsholes, made the fellowships a tougher sell. In the end, my advisory board, my boss at the college of journalism and I decided to seek a final, yearlong grant—which we got—and then put the program to rest.

Most of the former fellows who'd gotten project support said their work wouldn't have proceeded as quickly—or at all—without financial assistance and guidance. Their comments dovetail with those of other journalists who've received fellowships elsewhere—from the Alicia Patterson Foundation, Kaiser and the New America Foundation, to name a few. Funding enabled them to report on issues they cared about passionately. And it's important work, judging from some stories' impact and honors.

Out of my program alone, for instance, reporting by Barbara White Stack of the Pittsburgh Post-Gazette ultimately led the Pennsylvania Superior Court to rule that child-welfare dependency courts should be open to the public. Eric Eyre of the Charleston Gazette, reporting with then-colleague Scott Finn, exposed the high social costs of school consolidation in rural West Virginia. That project, which documented schoolchildren's hours-long bus rides, slowed the consolidation movement and won the Education Writers Association's grand prize in 2003.

Over the years, newsroom leaders and staff repeatedly told me that outside funding from various nonprofit programs validated their journalistic ambitions for projects while delivering vital budget relief.

"It's made a huge difference here. The majority of the long-term investigative projects that we do here would not have been possible" otherwise, says Eyre, a nine-year veteran of the Gazette. The privately owned paper circulates 48,000 copies daily and 74,000 on Sunday. Eyre also won a 2006 Kaiser Media Fellowship in health, which equipped him to do a project on poor oral health in his state.

ANNUAL EDITIONS

Funding for Foreign Forays

With backing from one of journalism's pedigreed families, the Pulitzer Center on Crisis Reporting opened in early 2006 to promote foreign affairs coverage in U.S. media.

The center provides travel grants to journalists—mostly freelancers but also news organization staffers—to do in-depth stories about war-torn, exploited or overlooked lands and people. For instance, it helped send a reporter and photographer from North Carolina's Fayetteville Observer to Afghanistan to chronicle U.S. soldiers' rebuilding efforts there at "Fort Bragg East." It has subsidized stories exploring government corruption in Colombia, Maoist activity in India and an American-led effort to save a Mozambique national park devastated by civil war. It has awarded at least 40 grants to date, with most ranging from $3,000 to $10,000.

"I knew from my own experience that if you got a small grant that got you somewhere, you could turn it into something important," says Jon Sawyer, the center's director. He'd reported from five dozen countries while working in the St. Louis Post-Dispatch's Washington bureau from 1980 through 2005. In that last year, as his paper and other Pulitzer holdings were being sold to Lee Enterprises (see "Lee Who?" June/July 2005), Sawyer proposed the center.

He found a backer in Emily Rauh Pulitzer, once his former chain's principal shareholder. "There's [been] a terrible diminution of quality and a strong cutting back of information about what's going on in the rest of the world," says Pulitzer, a center trustee. "That's incomprehensible, because as the world gets smaller, we need to understand more about it."

She put up $250,000 annually for four years to launch the center and another $250,000 to support educational outreach. Other initial donors include David Moore—a grandson of the first Joseph Pulitzer and a longtime Pulitzer Inc. director—and his wife, Katherine.

The initiative started out as "a modest idea," Sawyer says, but it has quickly grown in scope and reach. The Pulitzer Center is an independent division of the World Security Institute—itself a sponsor of journalism and scholarship—which provides office space in Washington, D.C., staff resources and plenty of synergy. The institute produces "Foreign Exchange," a weekly global affairs program for public television. Pulitzer is the primary supplier of its "In Focus" slice-of-life video segment. Pulitzercenter.org features grantees' blogs from the field. The center also set up a channel on YouTube, whose editors in December featured Pulitzercenter.org at the top of their "News and Politics" page and praised its videos as "some of the most moving journalism you'll find on this site."

Sawyer speaks enviously of the financing of ProPublica, a lavishly funded new investigative reporting enterprise (see "Big Bucks for Investigative Reporting," page 29), even though it's clear he's mastering the art of the deal. He assembled multiple supporters for a Palm Beach Post series last November on "Heroes of HIV" in the Caribbean. First, Pulitzer sponsored reporter Antigone Barton's fellowship with the International Center for Journalists to spend three weeks reporting in Haiti and the Dominican Republic. Then Sawyer arranged for Barton to get a National Press Foundation fellowship to the International AIDS Society conference in Sydney, Australia, which included a week's training on HIV. With part of a $102,000 grant from New York's MAC AIDS Fund, the center hired a videographer and Web producer to accompany Barton to the Caribbean. Three of their videos appeared on "Foreign Exchange"; all are on the Pulitzer Web site, along with interviews and other materials. "He is extremely resourceful," Barton says of Sawyer. "He had a vision of what this could be."

Pulitzer grantees' work has been carried by the Post-Dispatch, Smithsonian magazine, NPR, the New York Times, the Washington Times, the Christian Science Monitor and other outlets. But if Sawyer and Associate Director Nathalie Applewhite believe in an idea, they'll approve funding even without a news organization's prior commitment.

They invested $13,000 to help Utah-based freelance reporter Loretta Tofani travel several times to China for a project on how the lack of safety precautions led to sometimes fatal injuries and illnesses in almost every Chinese industry that exports to the United States. Tofani—who won a Pulitzer Prize reporting for the Washington Post before joining the Philadelphia Inquirer and spending years as its China correspondent—had lined up a news outlet, but that fell through with a change in management. She offered the nearly complete project to the Salt Lake Tribune, which accepted it overnight with the proviso that Tofani localize the story. Tofani says she gladly spent the next month "running all over the state and talking with people about work conditions in the factories they were using."

In October, the Tribune published a four-part series, "American Imports, Chinese Deaths." Editor Nancy Conway says she's "glad that we had the opportunity to work with Loretta and to publish the stories," for which she paid $5,000. The only drawback, says Conway: "It would have been better if we had been in on the story from the beginning."

Sawyer agrees. He wants newsrooms "to be as closely involved as they can be. We're not competing with anybody. We're trying to partner with everybody."

—Carol Guensburg

Colleague Ken Ward received an Alicia Patterson fellowship to examine the coal industry—in December 2005, a month before the deadly Sago mine collapse. He delayed starting the fellowship while contributing breaking stories, then used it to produce a Gazette series on U.S. mine safety and a Washington Monthly article on the Bush administration's mine safety policies. Investigative Reporters and Editors honored Ward's series with a medal—its highest award—and the PBS documentary series "Exposé" focused on Ward's work in a program originally broadcast in November.

"We were pretty happy for them to do this," Ward says. "It certainly made us look good."

Editors in some other places endorse training but decline grant support for newsroom projects. If a story is important enough, they say, they'll find money for it in the budget. They don't want the merest hint of outside influence. Nor do they want to be constrained by a donor's funding scope.

In 2006, as editor of the Lexington Herald-Leader in Kentucky, Marilyn W. Thompson wanted her paper to undertake a major project examining Republican Sen. Mitch McConnell's political fundraising practices and suggestions of influence peddling. When she realized her lean newsroom budget alone wouldn't cover it, Thompson got her Knight Ridder bosses' enthusiastic approval to seek a grant from the nonprofit Center for Investigative Reporting. The California-based center provided $37,500 to underwrite the salary of reporter John Cheves, who took an unpaid six-month leave of absence to do the project, as well as to cover expenses.

Just before the October publication of Cheves' four-part series, "Price Tag Politics," McConnell staff members complained of liberal bias—at the center. They cited center board and staff members' donations to Democratic candidates or causes. They called it "a known liberal entity, but what they seized on was the underlying funding," Thompson remembers. In particular, the McConnell camp objected to involvement by the Deer Creek Foundation of St. Louis, which had funded groups seeking campaign finance reform. McConnell had led the fight against the bipartisan measure in Congress and in court. He was the lead plaintiff in McConnell v. Federal Election Commission, an unsuccessful U.S. Supreme Court challenge to the 2002 law.

By the time the McConnell complaints surfaced, both the newsroom's ownership and leadership had changed. In June, the paper had been acquired by McClatchy; in July, Thompson had gone to the Los Angeles Times as national investigations editor. McClatchy officials "brought me in on several conference calls" before deciding to reimburse the funder, Thompson says. Now an investigative reporter for the New York Times, Thompson says she was disappointed by the decision. Cheves' work—published that October—was excellent and error-free, she says, and "no one likes the suggestion that their reporting was in any way biased."

That was precisely why McClatchy's vice president for news, Howard Weaver, returned the center's grant. "I'm not uncomfortable with the journalism, and I'm certainly not uncomfortable with the journalist," the Herald-Leader quoted Weaver as saying at the time. "I just think that the relationship [with the outside groups] was sufficiently unorthodox that we don't need to do it."

The incident made a lasting impression at the center. While there always has been "a complete firewall" between editorial and fundraising, since then "we have made the case more strenuously to funders that we would prefer general operating support as opposed to project-specific support," says Christa Scharfenberg, the center's associate director. (Funding for the McConnell project had come from money Deer Creek had designated for campaign finance coverage.)

And in mid-December, the center's board voted to offer the executive director job to Robert J. Rosenthal, former managing editor of the San Francisco Chronicle. He accepted. "We decided the organization was ready to grow and evolve," Scharfenberg says. "We wanted an experienced, highly regarded journalist at the helm, which we think also will deflect concerns about the journalistic integrity of the organization."

Takanishi of the Foundation for Child Development believes foundations and journalists have "a shared future" because of the public's right to know. She also encourages "more critical coverage of philanthropy.... It exists in the public trust, so it should be open for examination." But "how do foundations, by making grants, [best] support journalism?" she muses. "How does journalism cover philanthropy? It's sort of biting the hand that feeds you."

Edward Wasserman, the Knight Professor of Journalism Ethics at Washington and Lee University in Lexington, Virginia, agrees that foundation handouts can put recipients at a disadvantage. "Who's going to do the story on the Knight Foundation?" he asks rhetorically, noting his own endowed teaching position. The funder does "a good but not infallible job. The news organizations that should be reporting on them can't," at least not impartially. "Most of the people in media have one eye out for where the money might be coming from."

The plight is a familiar one in many newsrooms, though with different players. Is there "any real difference between advertiser influence and donor influence on editorial sanctity? There shouldn't be," says Lewis, of the Fund for Independence in Journalism. A journalist in residence at American University, he maintains that nonprofit journalism ventures can "basically ensure transparency and credibility, sometimes more so than a commercial outlet does."

To preserve newsgathering integrity, nonprofits "must disclose their donors," Lewis says. "I happen to think it's important to have some discretion about whose money you accept. There are some other schools of thought about that," he acknowledges. "Make sure, to the extent possible, that the journalist inside the nonprofit newsroom doesn't have substantial interaction with the donors"—a condition he couldn't follow as both editor and publisher at the Center for Public Integrity, he admits.

Wasserman says he's especially uneasy with "an almost direct line between funder and news organization," a structure emerging in health news services. "I could very readily see that this opens the door for various trade coalitions to bankroll reporting that could in itself be perfectly OK, but, in terms of subject matter, would have a tilt toward topics of greatest interest to the funders: biofuels coverage funded by Archer Daniels Midland. You get into a murky area pretty quickly."

But Missouri's Overholser is less wary of foundations developing their own news media outlets. "There are a lot of ways to do journalism in the public interest," says Overholser, who also chairs the Center for Public Integrity's board and serves on a handful of other nonprofit journalism boards. "The only key here is transparency.... An educated consumer should be able to see who put [a report] together, who funded it, what are the underlying goals.... I welcome partisan information, as long as it's labeled. What worries me is deceit, when we get people playing on the public stage who don't acknowledge their money is coming from the left wing or the right wing.... We need to have some reliable sources whose goal is to be nonpartisan, to report whatever they find—no matter how unsettling to their funders."

Overholser, like others interviewed for this story, expresses confidence that nonprofit news operations will flourish. She believes these may even bolster their for-profit counterparts.

"I never for a moment think nonprofits are going to supplant commercial media," she says. "The existence of nonprofits can strengthen the journalism done by commercial media. Nonprofits can be more fearless, in some ways, because they don't have to worry" about offending the powerful or risking popularity.

CAROL GUENSBURG (carol.guensburg@verizon.net) is senior editor for the *Journalism Center on Children & Families*, a University of Maryland professional program—and a nonprofit. It receives primary support from the Annie E. Casey Foundation. Guensburg spent 14 years as an editor and reporter for the *Milwaukee Journal Sentinel* after working for three other papers.

From *American Journalism Review*, February/March 2008, pp. 26–33. Copyright © 2008 by the Philip Merrill College of Journalism at the University of Maryland, College Park, MD 20742-7111. Reprinted with permission.

Test-Your-Knowledge Form

We encourage you to photocopy and use this page as a tool to assess how the articles in *Annual Editions* expand on the information in your textbook. By reflecting on the articles you will gain enhanced text information. You can also access this useful form on a product's book support Web site at *http://www.mhcls.com*.

NAME: DATE:

TITLE AND NUMBER OF ARTICLE:

BRIEFLY STATE THE MAIN IDEA OF THIS ARTICLE:

LIST THREE IMPORTANT FACTS THAT THE AUTHOR USES TO SUPPORT THE MAIN IDEA:

WHAT INFORMATION OR IDEAS DISCUSSED IN THIS ARTICLE ARE ALSO DISCUSSED IN YOUR TEXTBOOK OR OTHER READINGS THAT YOU HAVE DONE? LIST THE TEXTBOOK CHAPTERS AND PAGE NUMBERS:

LIST ANY EXAMPLES OF BIAS OR FAULTY REASONING THAT YOU FOUND IN THE ARTICLE:

LIST ANY NEW TERMS/CONCEPTS THAT WERE DISCUSSED IN THE ARTICLE, AND WRITE A SHORT DEFINITION:

We Want Your Advice

ANNUAL EDITIONS revisions depend on two major opinion sources: one is our Advisory Board, listed in the front of this volume, which works with us in scanning the thousands of articles published in the public press each year; the other is you—the person actually using the book. Please help us and the users of the next edition by completing the prepaid article rating form on this page and returning it to us. Thank you for your help!

ANNUAL EDITIONS: Mass Media 09/10

ARTICLE RATING FORM

Here is an opportunity for you to have direct input into the next revision of this volume. We would like you to rate each of the articles listed below, using the following scale:

1. **Excellent: should definitely be retained**
2. **Above average: should probably be retained**
3. **Below average: should probably be deleted**
4. **Poor: should definitely be deleted**

Your ratings will play a vital part in the next revision.
Please mail this prepaid form to us as soon as possible.
Thanks for your help!

RATING	ARTICLE	RATING	ARTICLE
	1. Almost Famous		20. Wonderful Weeklies
	2. Discovering What Democracy Means		21. Beyond News
	3. Off Course		22. Rocketboom!
	4. Reel to Real: Psychology Goes to the Movies		23. Epidemic
	5. Are Newspapers Doomed?		24. Break Up This Band!
	6. Research on the Effects of Media Violence		25. Into the Great Wide Open
	7. Japan, Ink		26. Why Journalists Are Not Above the Law
	8. Chica Lit: Multicultural Literature Blurs Borders		27. Copyright Jungle
	9. Cheap Thrills		28. Distorted Picture
	10. The Diana/Whore Complex		29. What Would You Do?
	11. The Beauty of Simplicity		30. Naming Names: Credibility vs. Deportation
	12. Whatever Happened to Iraq?: How the Media Lost Interest in a Long-running War with No End in Sight		31. The Lives of Others
			32. The Shame Game
	13. "You Don't Understand Our Audience": What I Learned about Network Television at Dateline NBC		33. Generation MySpace Is Getting Fed Up
			34. The Massless Media
	14. What the Mainstream Media Can Learn from Jon Stewart		35. The Hollywood Treatment
			36. Girl Power
	15. Other Voices		37. Online Salvation?
	16. Return of the Sob Sisters		38. Home Free
	17. Climate Change: Now What?		39. A Fading Taboo
	18. Myth-Making in New Orleans		40. Nonprofit News
	19. Double Whammy		

ANNUAL EDITIONS: MASS MEDIA 09/10

BUSINESS REPLY MAIL
FIRST CLASS MAIL PERMIT NO. 551 DUBUQUE IA

POSTAGE WILL BE PAID BY ADDRESSEE

McGraw-Hill Contemporary Learning Series
501 BELL STREET
DUBUQUE, IA 52001

NO POSTAGE
NECESSARY
IF MAILED
IN THE
UNITED STATES

ABOUT YOU

Name   Date

Are you a teacher? ☐ A student? ☐
Your school's name

Department

Address   City   State   Zip

School telephone #

YOUR COMMENTS ARE IMPORTANT TO US!

Please fill in the following information:
For which course did you use this book?

Did you use a text with this ANNUAL EDITION? ☐ yes ☐ no
What was the title of the text?

What are your general reactions to the Annual Editions concept?

Have you read any pertinent articles recently that you think should be included in the next edition? Explain.

Are there any articles that you feel should be replaced in the next edition? Why?

Are there any World Wide Web sites that you feel should be included in the next edition? Please annotate.

May we contact you for editorial input? ☐ yes ☐ no
May we quote your comments? ☐ yes ☐ no